1948 to 1970 DOMINATOR TWINS

Models 7, 77, 88, 99, 650, Sports Specials, Manxman & Mercury

WORKSHOP MANUALS AND ILLUSTRATED PARTS LISTS

A Floyd Clymer Publication by www.VelocePress.com 2023

INTRODUCTION

Welcome to the world of digital publishing ~ the book you now hold in your hand was printed using the latest state of the art digital technology. The advent of print-on-demand has forever changed the publishing process, never has information been so accessible and it is our hope that this book serves your informational needs for years to come. If this is your first exposure to digital publishing, we hope that you are pleased with the results. Many more titles of interest to the classic automobile and motorcycle enthusiast, collector and restorer are available via our website at www.VelocePress.com. We hope that you find this title as interesting as we do.

NOTE FROM THE PUBLISHER

The information presented is true and complete to the best of our knowledge. All recommendations are made without any guarantees on the part of the author or the publisher, who also disclaim all liability incurred with the use of this information.

TRADEMARKS

We recognize that some words, model names and designations, for example, mentioned herein are the property of the trademark holder. We use them for identification purposes only. This is not an official publication.

INFORMATION ON THE USE OF THIS PUBLICATION

This manual is an invaluable resource for those interested in performing their own maintenance. However, in today's information age we are constantly subject to changes in common practice, new technology, availability of improved materials and increased awareness of chemical toxicity. As such, it is advised that the user consult with an experienced professional prior to undertaking any procedure described herein. While every care has been taken to ensure correctness of information, it is obviously not possible to guarantee complete freedom from errors or omissions or to accept liability arising from such errors or omissions. Therefore, any individual that uses the information contained within, or elects to perform or participate in do-it-yourself repairs or modifications acknowledges that there is a risk factor involved and that the publisher or its associates cannot be held responsible for personal injury or property damage resulting from the use of the information or the outcome of such procedures.

WARNING!

One final word of advice, this publication is intended to be used as a reference guide, and when in doubt the reader should consult with a qualified technician.

IMPORTANT NOTE ON PAGE NUMBERING IN THIS MANUAL

Each of the five factory publications reproduced in this manual have their own index and the page numbers that correspond to that index are printed to the bottom center of the pages within each publication.

The page numbers to the right and left hand upper corner of each page are the cumulative page numbers in the book. These are the page numbers used in the 'contents' list below.

CONTENTS

1949-1955 Workshop Manual Model 7	page	1
1956-1970 Workshop Manual 77, 88, 99, 650, Sports Specials, Manxman & Mercury	page	41
1949-1950 Illustrated Parts List Model 7	page	115
1957 Illustrated Parts List 77, 88 & 99	page	143
1964 Illustrated Parts List 88SS, 650SS & 650/99	page	175

Maintenance Manual and Instruction Book

FOR

THE UNAPPROACHABLE

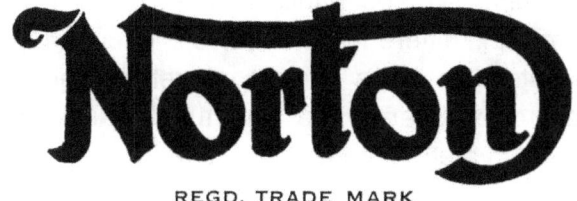

REGD. TRADE MARK

MOTOR CYCLE

Model No. 7

NORTON MOTORS LIMITED

BRACEBRIDGE STREET, BIRMINGHAM, 6, ENGLAND

Telephone:　　　　　　　　　　　　　　　Telegrams:
ASTon Cross 3711 (P.B.X.)　　　　　　　"Nortomo, Birmingham."

IMPORTANT INFORMATION RELATING TO THE CONTENTS OF THIS MANUAL

The first section of this manual includes a copy of the P80 manual (dated 1958) for the 1949-1955 Model 7 that covers both the spring frame (plunger) and swing arm models.

The pages in the second section of this manual were extracted from the P106/P Norton factory publication 'Maintenance Manual and Instruction Book' dated 1970 for the Model 50, ES2, 88, 99, 650, Sports Specials, 750 Atlas & 750 Scrambler. The publication of these combination manuals began in 1960 with the P101 manual followed by the P106 and finally the P106/P manual of 1970. While these 'combination' manuals made publication less expensive than those for individual models the information for multiple different motorcycles is often merged together. Consequently, separating out the appropriate data for a specific model, or series of motorcycles, is a time wasting and confusing exercise. Even more unfortunately, the P106/P manual makes no reference to the model years that are covered.

The earliest dates referenced in the 1970 - P106/P manual are piston sizes for the 1955-1958 Model 88 and a wiring diagram for the 1956-1957 Dominator 88 and 99 models. Therefore, we can assume that the P106/P manual was intended to cover the 1956 to 1970 Dominator models. Unfortunately, as there never was a '1949-1970 Dominator only' manual issued by the factory, we have extracted the information that is exclusive to the 1956-1970 Dominator series from the P106/P manual. However, this means that the paragraphs and illustrations in the P106/P section may no longer be sequentially numbered and we request you overlook this minor issue as it does not affect the correctness of the data in any way.

When the P80 and P106/P manuals are used in conjunction with the three illustrated parts lists included in this publication, they provide a comprehensive maintenance and repair manual exclusive to the 1949-1970 Norton Dominator series.

INDEX

	Paragraph No.
Air Control Lever	78
Ammeter	103
Automatic Timing Control	94
Battery	104
Big End Bearings, renewal	34
Big End Feed Oil Seal	40
Brake Lever	79
Brakes	68, 69
Cables, electrical	107
Camshaft Bushes, removal and fitting	37
Carbon, removal	10
Carburetter, dismantling	82
Carburetter, maintenance	88
Carburetter, reassembly	83
Clutch	43, 44, 45
Clutch Lever	79
Clutch Worm Lever, adjustment	48
Contact Breaker, cleaning	9
Contact Breaker, adjustment	9
Crankpin Bearings, renewal	34
Crankshaft, dismantling and assembly	35
Crankshaft, removal and fitting	33
Cylinder Block, removal	19
Cylinder Block, fitting	24
Cylinder Head, removal	9
Cylinder Head, fitting	15
Dynamo	100
Dynamo lubrication	101
Electrical Cables	107
Electrical System maintenance	92
Engine, removal from frame	32
Float Chamber	86
Footchange mechanism	50, 51
Fork Leg, dismantling	74
Fork Leg, assembly	75
Front Forks, maintenance	70
Front Forks, removal	72
Front Forks, fitting	73
Front Wheel	60, 61
Gearbox, complete removal	57
Gearbox, complete fitting	58
Gearbox, removal	46
Gearbox, fitting	47
Gearbox, outer cover	49
Gearbox, inner cover	53, 54, 55
Gears, removal	56
Gears, fitting	59
Handlebar Controls	78, 79, 80
Headlamps	105
High Tension Cables	99
High Tension Pickup	98
Horn	109
Hub, front, dismantling	66
Hub, front, assembling	67

	Paragraph No.
Hub, rear, dismantling	64
Hub, rear, assembling	65
Ignition Timing	31
Intermediate Gear	39
Lighting Switch	108
Lubrication System	1
Magneto	93
Magneto, lubrication	95
Magneto, timing	31
Main Bearings	38
Mixture Adjustments	87
Oil Bath Chaincase	41, 42
Oil Lubrication	5
Oil Filters	2
Oil Level	4
Oil Pressure Gauge	6
Oil Pump	3, 27, 28
Oil Seal, big end	40
Petrol Tank, removal	7
Petrol Tank, fitting	8
Pistons, removal	20
Pistons, fitting	22
Piston Ring, removal and fitting	21
Pressure Gauge	6
Pressure Release Valve	26
Rear Springing	76, 77
Rear Wheel	62, 63
Rocker Adjustment	16
Rocker, removal and fitting, inlet	17
Rocker, removal and fitting, exhaust	18
Slow Running Adjustment	84
Small End Bush	36
Sparking Plug	110
Spring Frame	76, 77
Steering Head Adjustment	71
Tail Lamp	106
Tappets, removal and fitting	23
Throttle Stop	85
Timing Cover, removal and fitting	25
Timing Sprockets and Chains, removal	29
Timing Sprockets and Chains, fitting	30
Twist Grip	80
Tyres, maintenance	89
Tyres, removal	90
Tyres, fitting	91
Valves, removal	11
Valve grinding	12
Valve fitting	13
Valve Guides, removal and fitting	14
Valve clearance	16
Voltage Control Regulator	102
Wheel, front	60, 61
Wheel, rear	62, 63

DATA

Bore, 66 mm.   Stroke. 72.6 mm.   Capacity, 497 cc.
Compression ratio, 6.7 : 1

IGNITION.
Timing, 31° = ¼in. before top dead centre fully advanced.
Magneto points gap, .012in.
Plug points gap, .015in.
Sparking Plug, KLG.F.70.

VALVE TIMING.
Inlet opens 22° = ⅛in. before top dead centre.
Inlet closes 57.5° = 17/32in. after bottom dead centre.
Exhaust opens 57.5° = 17/32in. before bottom dead centre.
Exhaust closes 22° = ⅛in. after top dead centre.

With .010in. clearance

TAPPET CLEARANCE (cold).
Inlet ... .002in.   Exhaust ... .005in.

AMAL CARBURETTER.
Type, 76 AK/IAT.   Choke diameter, 1in.
Main jet, 170.   Needle jet, 107.
Throttle valve, 3½.   Needle position, 2.

PISTON CLEARANCES.
Top of skirt, .0059in.   Bottom of skirt, .0039in.
  .0054in.   .0034in.

SPROCKETS.

	Engine	Gearbox	Clutch	Rear Wheel
Solo ...	19T	19T	42T	43T
Sidecar ...	18T	17T	42T	43T

GEARBOX RATIOS.
1, 1.21, 1.77, 2.97.

OVERALL RATIOS.
Solo ...	5	6.05	8.85	14.88
Sidecar ...	5.9	7.14	10.43	17.75

TYRE PRESSURES.
Front ... 20 lbs.   Rear ... 23 lbs.

CHAIN SIZES.
Primary Chain ... ½in. pitch × .305in. wide × 76 pitches
Rear Chain ... ⅝in. pitch × ⅜in. wide × 90 pitches
Magneto Chain ... ⅜in. pitch × 3/16in. wide × 42 pitches
Camshaft Chain ... ⅜in. pitch × .225in. wide × 38 pitches
Petrol Tank capacity ... 3¾ gallons
Oil Tank capacity ... 5 pints
Gearbox capacity ... ½ pint approximately
Chaincase capacity ... ½ pint approximately

INTRODUCTION

In preparing these instructions the elementary details and preliminary information that may be necessary to the absolute novice has been omitted, on the assumption that the majority of NORTON owners are already acquainted with the elementary details of starting, driving and maintenance. In connection with the latter we would stress the advisability of cultivating the habit of routine cleaning, lubrication, examination and adjustment of your machine. By this means many minor annoyances will be avoided and major breakdowns averted, and you will acquire the pride of ownership which marks the true enthusiast.

Below is a plan view of the machine with all controls clearly indicated. A short study of this will familiarise you with the position and function of each control. It will be noticed that there is no ignition lever on the handlebar. This is not necessary, since the magneto is fitted with an automatic advance and retard mechanism which adjusts the spark setting to suit the particular engine revolutions, i.e., as the engine speed is increased, so the amount of ignition advance is also increased and vice versa. To obtain an easy start from cold, it is only necessary to turn on the petrol, very slightly flood the carburetter, close or partly close the air lever and with the throttle very slightly open, give a long swinging kick on the starter, opening the air lever to its normal running position as soon as the engine is capable of taking full air. When starting with a warm engine or even in warm weather, it is not necessary to use the air control lever.

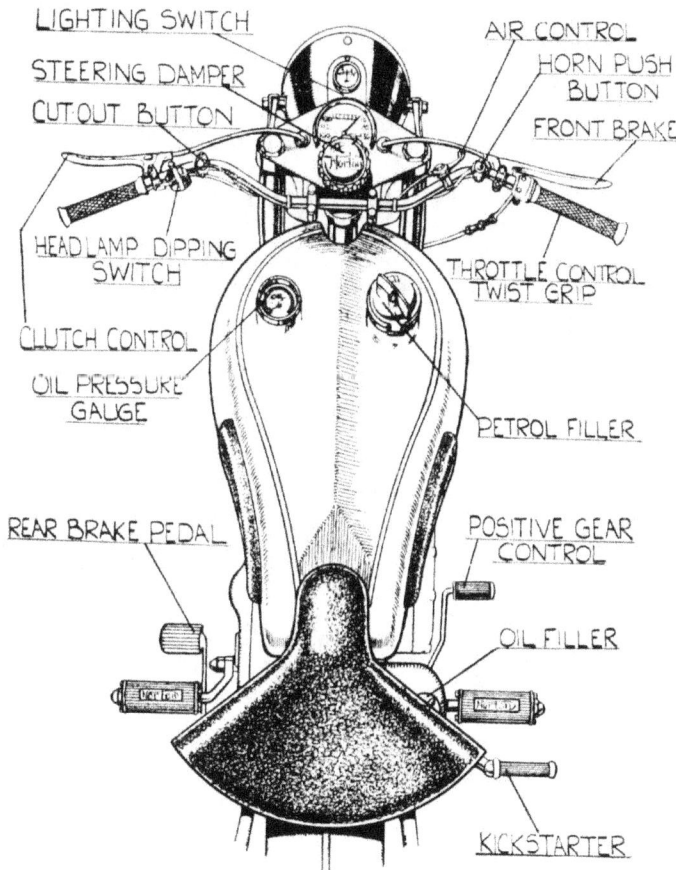

Fig. 1.

Although the machine will have been greased up and all points requiring oil will have been dealt with at the works prior to the road test, it is always a safe policy to ensure that there is adequate oil in the oil tank, gearbox and oil bath chaincase. Remember to remove the level plug from the chaincase before topping up.

New machines should not be driven at more than 30-35 m.p.h. for the first 500 miles in top gear or a correspondingly slower speed in the lower gears afterwards, gradually increasing the speed until the 1,000 mile mark is reached, when it should be perfectly safe to use the machine's full capabilities. It is advisable during the initial running-in period not to open the throttle more than one quarter or one third and to avoid " over revving " and slogging or labouring of the engine in too high a gear. The use of a running-in compound during the initial stages of the engine's life is strongly recommended. The compound, several brands of which are available and may be obtained from all Norton dealers, contains " colloidal graphite " which forms a graphoid surface on all working faces and greatly assists in preserving their high quality finish. The compound should be mixed with the lubricating oil in the proportion of one pint to one gallon of oil during running-in, but if its use is continued after this period, only half the quantity should be used. Remember that these are high efficiency engines which give of their best when running at relatively high revolutions and a change should be made to a lower gear immediately there are any signs of labouring. To obtain the best possible performance from your machine, full use should be made of the gearbox, which is quite capable of withstanding all the loads likely to be imposed upon it by normal usage.

At the end of this book will be found a trouble tracing chart, reference to which will greatly facilitate the location and rectifying of any but the most unusual troubles which may be likely to cause an involuntary stop.

CLEANING

Before attempting to polish the enamel on any part of the machine, all traces of grit adhering to the various components should be washed off, preferably with a reasonably high pressure hose. Polish the enamel periodically with a good quality wax polish. Note that chromium plating is not impervious to rust and should be wiped down when possible, after being in the rain. Wash off any road grit and clean with one of the chromium polishes available from any garage. Do NOT use ordinary metal polish.

LUBRICATION

At the Works, Wakefield Castrol Oils have been used for many years exclusively with highly successful results; the correct grades for the models dealt with in this handbook being:—
 WAKEFIELD CASTROL XXL, for Summer use.
 WAKEFIELD CASTROL XL, for Winter use.
Other very suitable oils for NORTON machines are:—
 SHELL—X-100—40 or PRICE'S ENERGOL S.A.E. 40 for Summer use.
 SHELL—X-100—30 or PRICE'S ENERGOL S.A.E. 30 for Winter use.
 MOBILOIL " BB," for Summer use.
 MOBILOIL "A" for Winter use.
These oils should be used in the engine and gearbox.

For oilbath chaincase use Wakefield's " Castrolite " Single Shell, Price's Motorine E, or Mobiloil Arctic.

All bearings not automatically lubricated are fitted with nipples for grease gun lubrication, and a good quality grease, such as Wakefield Castrolease Medium, Price's Belmoline, Shell Retinax or Mobiloil Hub Grease should be used at these points.

Below is a lubrication chart indicating the approximate periods at which the various lubrication points should receive attention. If this chart is adhered to, excessive wear will not occur on any of the moving parts, the life of the machine will be prolonged and its performance considerably enhanced.

NOTE.—On a new machine, drain and flush out oil tank after 500 miles. Remove crankcase drain plug and allow to drain. Remove level indicator plug from oilbath chaincase and fill to this level.

LUBRICATION CHART.

Period.	Location.	Lubricant.	Period.	Location.	Lubricant.
Every 200 miles.	Oil tank, top up	Oil.	Every 2,000 miles.	Brake pedal	Grease.
Every 1,000 miles.	Spring Frame Fork Ends	Grease		Brake shoe cams (sparingly)	Grease.
				Brake rod jaw joints	Oil.
	Control cables	Oil.		Speedometer driving box	Grease.
	Control levers	Oil.		Drain and refill oil tank	Oil.
	Brake cable " U " clip	Oil.		Steering head races	Grease.
	Wheel bearings	Grease.		Saddle front pivot	Oil.
	Rear chain	Grease.	Every 5,000 miles.	Gearbox, drain and refill	Oil.
	Gearbox, top up	Oil.		Commutator end bracket	Oil.
	Oil bath, top up	Oil.		Telescopic forks	See para. 70
			Every 10,000 miles.	Oil bath, drain and refill	Oil.

THE ENGINE

1. ENGINE. LUBRICATION SYSTEM.

This is of the dry sump type. The oil flows from the oil tank to the pump by gravity, assisted by suction from the feed side of the oil pump, through the gears, and is forced under pressure to various parts of the engine, drains to the lowest part of the crankcase and by suction from the return side of the pump is lifted back to the oil tank.

2. OIL FILTERS.

There are two gauze filters in the lubrication system, the main one being attached to the adaptor screwed into the oil tank to which the oil feed pipe is connected. Clean filter when the tank is drained every two

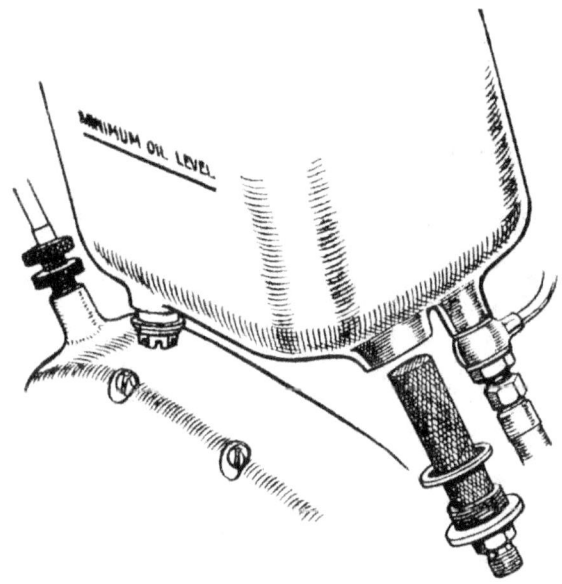

Fig. 2.

thousand miles. A small slightly dished gauze disc is incorporated in the pressure release valve clearly shown in Fig. 3. It is unlikely that this will become even partially clogged unless the main filter is damaged or the oil allowed to become heavily contaminated.

3. ENGINE OIL PUMP.

This is of the gear type. The pump contains two pairs of gears, one on the feed side and the other on the return side.

The gears on the return side are twice the width of those on the feed, having twice the pumping capacity. This ensures that the crankcase is free from oil when the engine is running.

To check the return of the oil to the tank, remove the oil filler cap. The oil return pipe can then be seen. After the engine has been running for a few minutes, the oil return flow will be spasmodic, due to the greater capacity of the return gears.

4. OIL LEVEL.

The oil level in the oil tank should not be above three-quarters and not below half.

If the level is above the three-quarter mark, when the engine is running, the pressure built up in the oil tank by the oil return side of the pump may force the surplus oil through the air release pipe on to the road.

Always run engine for a few minutes before checking oil level. It is possible when an engine has been idle for any length of time for the oil to syphon through the return gears to the sump.

When this happens, all the oil is returned to the tank in the first few minutes that the engine is running.

When the oil level is below the half full mark there is such a small quantity of oil that it tends to over-heat.

5. CIRCULATION OF THE OIL.

The oil pump makes an oil tight joint with the timing cover by means of a synthetic rubber washer under compression.

Oil passes from the pump through drilled oil ways in the timing cover to the hollow timing side mainshaft, an extension of which rotates in an oil seal located in the cover. The built up crankshaft (Fig. 3) is suitably drilled to convey oil under pressure to the plain big ends. Surplus oil escaping from the pressure release valve into the timing cover builds up to a pre-determined level to lubricate the gears and timing chains, afterwards draining into the sump via a drilled hole. A lead from the oil return pipe (external) conveys oil to the hollow o.h.v. rocker spindles, push rod ends and valve guides, surplus oil returning to the sump via a drilled hole in the rear of the timing side cylinder.

Pressure release valve depicted in Fig. 3 is pre-set and incapable of adjustment. A timed breather working at the inner end of the camshaft (Fig. 3) controls the crankcase pressure. Any oil escaping from this source being conducted to the rear chain.

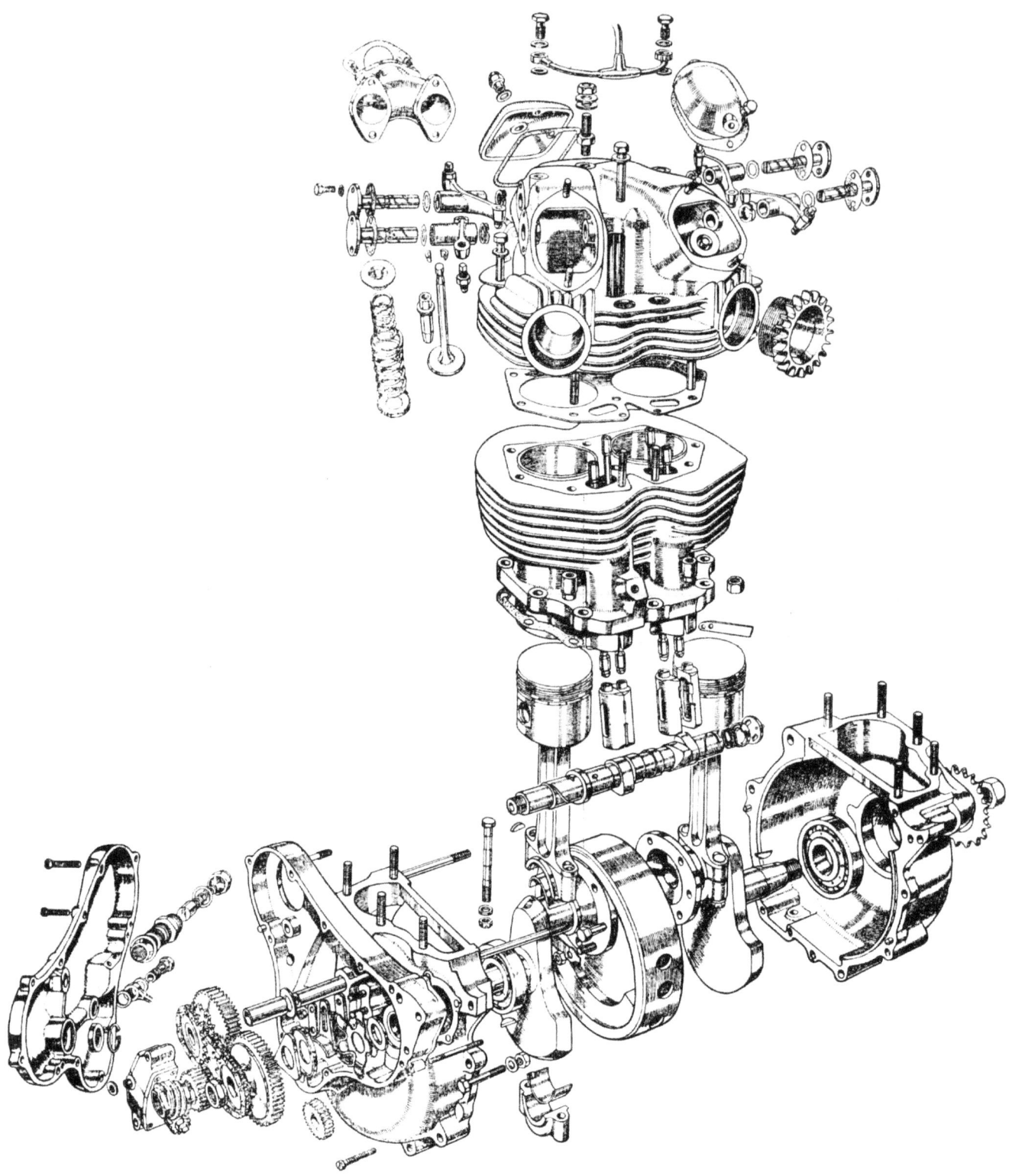

Fig. 3

A drain plug in the bottom of the sump on the driving side of the crankcase enables the case to be drained and flushed out when the occasion arises.

6. PRESSURE GAUGE.

A tapping is made in the pressure side of the lubrication system just below the pressure release valve and a small bore pipe led to the pressure gauge in the tank top. Should the gauge at any time show a sudden drop in pressure or register a fluctuating pressure, an immediate investigation should be carried out. Suspect insufficient oil in tank, seal between timing cover and oil pump broken down or oil seal at timing end of mainshaft failed. It is just possible that the pressure release valve plunger (Fig. 3) may have become stuck or its return spring broken. Under normal running conditions a steady pressure should be registered, an absolute minimum being some 20 lbs., although on a new machine, pressures considerably in excess of this will be indicated and when starting from cold, figures up to 120 lbs. may be obtained.

MAINTENANCE OF ENGINE

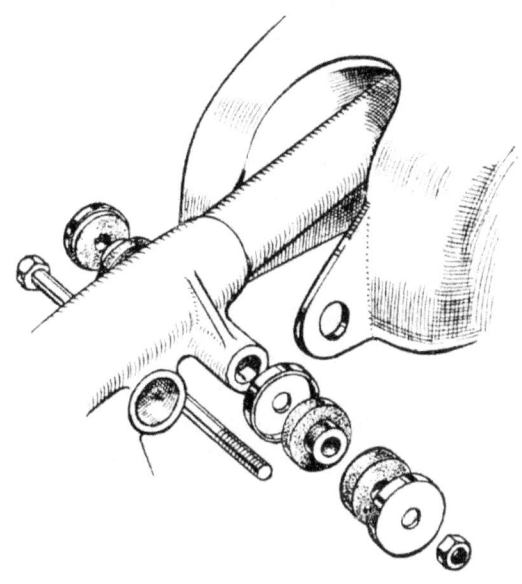 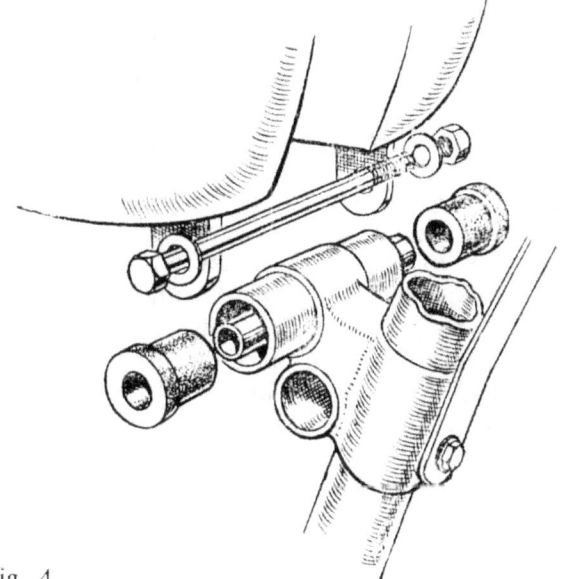

Fig. 4.

7. REMOVAL OF PETROL TANK.

It is not necessary to drain the tank, but make sure that the petrol tap levers are in the "off" position, i.e., with the round end of the lever pressed inwards.

Disconnect petrol pipes from taps, using two spanners, holding the tap with one whilst slackening the union nut. Disconnect the pressure gauge pipe below the tank bottom, again using two spanners to avoid straining the pipe. The tank is secured front and rear by a single cross bolt, removal of which will enable the tank to be lifted off. Ensure that none of the steel or rubber washers are lost whilst removal of the tank is in progress.

8. FITTING PETROL TANK.

First study Fig. 4 and ensure that all the necessary steel and rubber washers are available. Note that the larger rubbers are used in the front mounting and that steel cups are pressed into the frame tube. After fitting the large shouldered rubbers into the front mounting tube, push the loose distance tube into position if these fittings have been removed from the frame. Insert the two remaining shouldered rubbers into the rear tank ears so that the shoulders are on the inside and insert the front bolt (the plain one). Now raise the rear of the tank so that a steel cup can be placed on each of the rear rubbers. Note that three of the steel cups have a larger hole than the fourth, this latter, together with a plain rubber washer, being fitted to the screwed end of the rear bolt. Place a steel cup and plain rubber washer on the rear bolt, insert in position, fit the remaining washers and nuts and tighten. Fit petrol pipes and pressure gauge pipe using two spanners as when removing.

9. CYLINDER HEAD REMOVAL.

Remove petrol tank (para. 7). Remove carburetter, leaving it attached to the machine by the throttle cable only. Remove exhaust pipes and silencers complete as a unit from each side of the machine. Remove high tension leads from sparking plugs and engine steady stay, also the steady stay stud from the top of the rocker box. Disconnect oil feed pipe to rocker mechanism by unscrewing the two banjo connection bolts on the extreme top of the rocker box.

There are five bolt heads visible above the cylinder head finning and two nuts between the exhaust ports. In addition there are three nuts accessible through the cylinder finning, one beneath the inlet port and one under each exhaust port.

Removal of these bolts and nuts should enable the head to be lifted off. If the joint is tight a light blow beneath the exhaust port with a mallet or block of wood should effectively release it. Lift the head and ensure that the gasket is either coming away clean with the head or is remaining in position on top of the cylinder block. Lift the head as far as possible and obtain assistance to feed the four push rods into the head until they are clear of the cylinder block when the head may be tilted backwards and completely withdrawn.

10. REMOVAL OF CARBON.

The piston crowns will now be exposed and the engine should be rotated till the pistons are on top dead centre. Carefully scrape the carbon from the piston crown, using a blunt knife or similar tool, taking care to avoid scratching or cutting the piston material. Deal similarly with the combustion chambers and valve ports although these cannot be thoroughly cleaned without removing the valves.

11. VALVE REMOVAL.

With the cylinder head removed, the rocker inspection covers taken off, and the stud securing the inlet rocker inspection cover also removed, the o.h.v. rockers may be rotated sufficiently clear of the valve stem to enable a normal Universal type valve spring compressor to be used for compressing the springs and removing the cotters. Each valve, together with its springs, should be carefully placed on one side so that it may be refitted in its original position.

Note that although the inlet and exhaust valves have the same head and stem diameters, they are not identical, the inlet head being curved on the underside. It is important that they should not be interchanged.

12. VALVE GRINDING.

Remove all carbon from the valve heads and stems. Lightly smear the seat portion with medium grinding compound, place the valve in the guide and grind lightly, holding the end of the valve stem in a hand vice or chuck. Do not revolve the valve a complete turn, but oscillate rapidly, frequently raising the valve from the seat and placing in a different position.

As soon as the grinding marks make a complete ring on valve and head, cease operations and remove all traces of grinding compound from valve, seat and port. If valves or seats are badly pitted it may be impossible to obtain a perfect seat by grinding. The seats will then have to be re-cut and the valves replaced or renewed.

13. VALVES FITTING.

Thoroughly clean valves, seats and valve pockets. Fit bottom collar over valve guide (if the collar has been removed) and place the spring and top collar in position. Lubricate valve stems and insert through valve guide. Compress valve spring and fit cotters.

A little thick grease smeared on the inside of the cotters will hold them in position until the spring is released.

14. VALVE GUIDES—REMOVAL AND FITTING.

The valve guides are a driving fit in the cylinder head and may be tapped out of position by means of a double diameter brass punch which may also be used for fitting replacements.

The valve seats must be trued up with a cutter after fitting to ensure that guide and seat are in correct alignment.

15. CYLINDER HEAD—FITTING.

If the cylinder head gasket has been removed, refit with the same face uppermost or renew. Rotate engine till pistons are on top dead centre. Place cylinder head on top of cylinder block and tilt it backwards whilst the pushrods are inserted into the two tunnels cast in the cylinder head. Note that

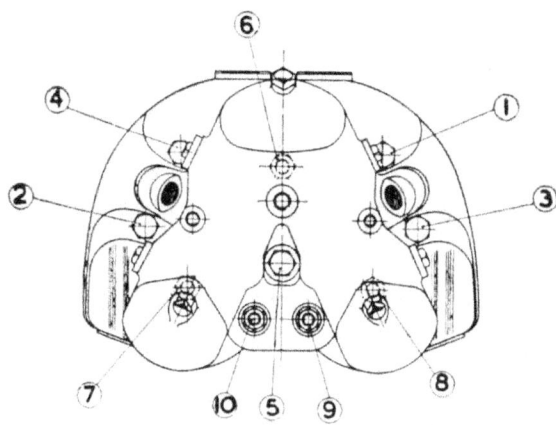

ORDER OF TIGHTENING DOWN CYLINDER HEAD NUTS & BOLTS.

Fig 5.

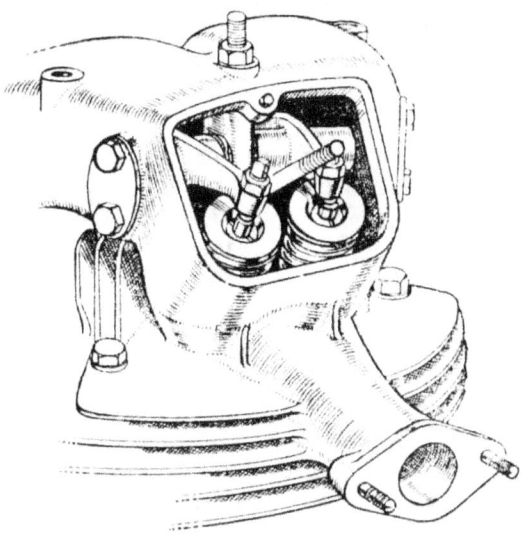

Fig. 6.

the inlet push rods are longer than the exhaust, and one of each, i.e., inlet and exhaust should be inserted into the head, the long rods being nearer the centre, see Fig. 3.

Lower the head into position and allow the push rods to fall on to the tappets as the head approaches its normal location.

When the head is within about ¼in. of the cylinder joint face, it should be supported in this position by using the two short sleeve nuts taken from beneath the exhaust ports as packing between the top fin of the cylinder block and the bottom cylinder head fin, placing them in a horizontal position between the fins whilst the rocker ball ends are entered into the upper ends of the push rods. A piece of bent wire may be found useful for drawing the inlet push rod into position, access being obtained through the exhaust rocker inspection apertures.

Remove temporary distance pieces and lower head on to joint face.

Ensure that rockers and push rods are in correct contact. Attach all nuts and bolts and pinch down lightly, finally tightening in the order shown in Fig. 5.

16. ROCKER ADJUSTMENT.

Removal of the single nut securing the inlet rocker inspection cover will provide access to both inlet rockers and enable the necessary feelers to be inserted between the rocker adjuster and valve stem end (Fig. 6).

Rotate the engine till the particular inlet valve being dealt with is closed.

To adjust the clearance, hold the squared end of the adjuster by means of a special spanner provided and slacken the locknut. Insert a .002in. feeler and rotate the adjuster in a clockwise direction until the feeler is just pinched, but may be still moved about fairly easily. Hold the adjuster whilst tightening the locknut and re-check with the feeler.

Rotate the engine till the other inlet valve is closed, repeat the operations and fit the inspection cover, ensuring that the paper washer is in good condition. and correctly positioned.

To adjust the exhaust rockers remove the inspection cover and proceed as already described, using a .005in. feeler. Always re-check with the feeler after tightening the locknut and readjust if there is any doubt about the accuracy of the original setting.

17. ROCKER REMOVAL & FITTING—INLET.

Remove inspection cover and cover securing stud. This latter may be withdrawn by locking two nuts on the outer end and rotating the lower of the nuts which should bring away the stud. Remove the two pins holding the oval plate to the side of the rocker box. This plate is integral with the rocker spindle and the holes through which the securing pins pass are threaded $\frac{5}{16}$in. diameter × 26 threads per inch so that two bolts suitably threaded and not less than 1¼in. long may be inserted and used as extractors by giving each one about a half turn at a time and so withdrawing the spindle until it is sufficiently free to be removed by hand.

Note that the rocker hub has a spring washer at one end and a plain thrust washer at the other. These may be either carefully removed before the rocker is extracted or allowed to fall when the rocker is removed. Having withdrawn the rocker until the hub is clear of the spindle hole bosses, it is necessary to turn it upside down in order to withdraw it completely. When refitting, the operations should be reversed, placing the rocker in position, adding the plain thrust washer to the outer end of the hub and maintaining an end load on the rocker whilst the spring washer is inserted. The end load put on by the washer will hold the assembly in position whilst inserting the spindle, but before doing so, ensure that the oil hole is in the correct position to mate with the feed hole in the rocker box and that the paper washer is undamaged and in position on the flanged end of the spindle. Remember that the securing pins are fitted with fibre washers.

18. ROCKER REMOVAL & FITTING—EXHAUST.

Remove inspection cover and proceed as for inlet rocker. In the case of the exhaust rocker, its removal is quite straightforward and does not involve any inverting of the rocker. For replacement, proceed as already described.

19. CYLINDER BLOCK—REMOVAL.

Remove petrol tank, para. 7.
Remove cylinder head, para. 9.
Remove dynamo by removing the three end screws, slackening the securing strap and drawing the dynamo out of position, having previously disconnected the electrical leads.

Remove the nine cylinder base nuts (seven large, two small). It is necessary to lift the block slightly before certain of these nuts can be removed completely. When lifting the block, avoid tearing the paper washer fitted to the crankcase joint.

20. PISTONS—REMOVAL.

With the cylinder block removed and the pistons exposed, it will be apparent from the angular position of the valve head recesses in the piston crowns that the two pistons are not interchangeable, and if a new one is required for any reason, it will be necessary to specify whether a nearside (lefthand) or offside (righthand) is wanted.

A new piston may be fitted either way round, but having once been used, should always be replaced in the same position.

To remove a piston, first extract the gudgeon pin retaining circlips by means of a pair of sharp nosed pliers and push out the gudgeon pin. If the engine is badly carboned up it may be desirable to scrape the carbon from the narrow land outside the circlip before attempting to remove the gudgeon pin. Be sure to mark the piston so that it may be replaced in its original position.

21. PISTON RING REMOVAL AND FITTING.

Unless new rings are being fitted it is not advisable to remove the carbon from the bottom of the ring groove or the back of the ring. When fitting new rings, remove all carbon from the piston by means of an old hacksaw blade or similar tool. When the grooves have been cleaned, check the new ring in the groove. There should be a side clearance of .004in. Check also the ring end gap by inserting the ring in the cylinder bore and pushing it down with a piston to ensure that it is lying square. The gap should be:
  Compression rings, .008in.—.010in.
  Scraper rings, .008in.—.010in
Check gap with feeler gauge.

22. PISTONS—FITTING.

Fit rings to piston, spacing the ring gaps equally around the piston circumference. Fit one gudgeon pin circlip if both have been removed for dismantling. Unless great care has been taken in the removal of the circlips it will be advisable to fit new ones. Fit piston to connecting rod, ensuring that it is the correct way round and that the valve head recesses are lying in the right direction. When both pistons are fitted, the forward recesses should be further apart than those at the rear of the engine. When fitting the circlips, make certain that they are properly bedded in the groove.

23. TAPPETS—REMOVAL AND FITTING.

It is most unlikely that the tappets will require any attention until a very large mileage has been covered. They are fitted into the cylinder block and are readily accessible when the block has been removed.

Invert the cylinder block, remove the wire securing the tappet division plate screws and remove the screw nearest to the tappets. This will enable the division plate to be swung out of position on the other screw. If tight, a light blow on the opposite end of the tappets will effectively release the plate.

Note that the tappets must not be interchanged either singly or in pairs, nor should they be fitted the opposite way round.

The refitting is quite straight forward. Remember to rewire the division plate screws.

24. CYLINDER BLOCK FITTING.

Clean both joint faces and ensure that the cylinder base paper washer is in good condition and is fitted so that the oil return hole is quite clear.

Fit piston ring compressors (obtainable from service department) to pistons, ensuring that the ring gaps are approximately equally spaced and that all are covered by the compressor. About ⅛in. of piston should stand above the compressor. Smear the cylinder bores with oil and feed the cylinder block over the pistons, forcing the piston ring compressors down the piston till they fall from the bottom of the piston skirt. Remove the compressors and lower the block to within about ¼in. of the joint, and replace the cylinder base nuts.

Completely lower the cylinder block and just pinch down the two nuts on either side of the block, tightening these in diagonal order. Tighten the three remaining large nuts, and finally the two 5/16in. nuts at the front of the block.

Replace dynamo, tightening the end screws before tightening the securing strap.

25. TIMING COVER—REMOVAL AND FITTING.

Disconnect the pressure gauge feed pipe from the rear of the timing cover by unscrewing the banjo connection bolt. Remove the ten cheese headed screws securing the cover which may then be withdrawn. If tight, lever gently behind the pressure release valve boss, and tap lightly with a wooden block on the opposite end of the cover. Take care not to lose the small rubber washer which forms the oil seal between the pump and the cover.

When refitting, ensure that both faces are quite clean and lightly smeared with jointing compound, preferably "Wellseal," which is non-hardening. Ensure also that the oil pump rubber sealing washer is in position. Take care not to damage the oil seal when entering the mainshaft into the cover, and do not press right home if there appears to be any obstruction. Refit all screws, checking that there is a fibre washer under each head, and just pinch each one down before finally tightening each pair of opposite screws. Re-connect the pressure gauge pipe.

26. PRESSURE RELEASE VALVE— REMOVAL AND FITTING.

When it becomes necessary to examine the pressure release valve or clean the small filter disc with which it is fitted, it is only necessary to remove the large domed-hexagon nut above the pressure gauge banjo connection to expose the spring and pressure release valve plunger, which may be withdrawn. To remove the filter, it is necessary to remove the pressure release valve body which holds the filter in position. Thoroughly clean all components and re-assemble as follows:—Insert the gauze filter with its domed side inwards, and screw home the pressure release valve body to which the larger of the two copper washers has been fitted. Fit the plunger and spring, and finally the nut, remembering to place the remaining copper washer over the threaded end of the body. The nut should be screwed right home.

27. OIL PUMP—REMOVAL AND FITTING.

Whilst the timing cover is removed, no difficulty should be experienced in removing the oil pump, which is held only by the two nuts, situated one on either side of the body.

When these are removed, the pump should be readily withdrawn from its studs. If tight, a gentle leverage may be applied behind the driving spindle.

To replace the pump, clean both faces and apply jointing compound very sparingly, particularly in the vicinity of the oil holes. Fit the pump and nuts, and tighten each nut a turn at a time to ensure even tightening.

28. OIL PUMP.

The oil pump is of the gear type. It is not advisable to dismantle it.

When pump is removed from timing chest, test for play in the spindle by pulling and pushing the worm wheel.

Revolve spindle and place fingers on the oil holes and the action of the gears should be felt if the pump is in good condition.

When revolving pump, any foreign matter obstructing the gears will be felt. Wash out with paraffin.

A marked drop in oil pressure, or oil draining from tank to crankcase may indicate that the pump requires re-conditioning; for which operation it should be returned to the service department who make only a small charge for this work.

29. TIMING SPROCKETS AND CHAINS—REMOVAL.

When removing the chains, it is necessary to withdraw the whole sprocket assembly with the chains in position. This may be accomplished without disturbing the timing chain tensioner secured to a boss in the timing chest by two nuts. Remove the nut securing the camshaft sprocket, and the pin securing the automatic advance mechanism to the magneto spindle. This latter is automatically withdrawn as the pin is removed, but the camshaft sprocket may require the use of a standard type of sprocket extractor. The intermediate gear and sprocket will, of course, readily leave the spindle. Unscrew the oil pump worm, which has a **lefthand** thread, and withdraw the half-time pinion by means of a special extractor available from the spares department.

30. TIMING SPROCKET AND CHAINS—FITTING.

Fit oil retaining disc and triangular washer to mainshaft and fit half time pinion key. Fit half time pinion with the chamfered edge outside and tap home with a tubular drift. Fit steel washer to intermediate shaft and camshaft (the latter is the thicker of the two). Place the spider clutch spring on the camshaft and fit the camshaft key. Rotate engine till the marked tooth on the half time pinion is in the top dead centre position. Smear both faces of the fibre gear which drives the dynamo, with grease, place the gear in position on the flange of the sprocket and to the other face of the gear, fit the steel friction washer locating it on the peg, protruding from the sprocket flange. The grease will hold it in position.

Rotate the camshaft till the keyway is in top dead centre position. Place the magneto chain (the narrower of the two chains) on the inner of the two sprockets on the intermediate gear and the camshaft chain on the other. Rotate the gear until the marked gear tooth is in the bottom dead centre position. This will give a marked sprocket tooth in the topmost position. The camshaft sprocket also has a marked tooth which should also be in the top position when the sprocket is meshed with the chain. The chain and sprocket assembly may now be placed loosely in position, the magneto sprocket and auto advance mechanism meshed with its driving chain and the whole assembly pushed home. Check by using the dynamo shaft hole as a window that the spider spring is located with one leg either side of the peg in the inner side of the cam sprocket flange. Check also that all marked teeth are correctly positioned, i.e., when the marked pinion and gear teeth are in mesh, both marked sprocket teeth are in the top dead centre position, the intermediate sprocket tooth having just entered the chain whilst the camshaft sprocket tooth should be just about to leave the chain. Fit and tighten the oil pump worm and camshaft sprocket nut but do not fit the timing cover until the magneto has been timed (para. 31).

The chain tensioner can be fitted either before or after the chain is in position. It should be adjusted so that there is about ⅛in. whip in the top run of the chain.

31. MAGNETO TIMING.

For purposes of magneto timing, the offside or right-hand cylinder is used. Set the pistons on T.D.C., and attach a degree plate set at zero to the mainshaft.

Rotate the engine in the opposite direction to that in which it normally travels, until the degree plate registers 31° or ¼in. down the cylinder bore if a degree plate is not available. Hold the automatic advance mechanism in the fully advanced position by rotating the moving portion in an anti-clockwise direction until it is against the stop where it may be convenient to wedge it whilst dealing with the contact breaker on the opposite side of the machine. Rotate the contact breaker until the points are just about to open in approximately the nine o'clock position. Insert a very thin feeler gauge or piece of paper between the contact breaker points to obtain the position accurately at which they commence to separate. Tighten the centre pin securing the automatic advance mechanism, and check that the timing has been correctly set. Fit timing cover (para. 25).

32. REMOVAL OF ENGINE FROM FRAME.

Remove petrol tank (para. 7), exhaust pipes and silencers, rocker box oil feed, engine steady stay and carburetter (para. 9), disconnect pressure gauge pipe (para. 25).

Remove main oil feed and return pipes by disconnecting them from the tank unions using two spanners, one to hold the union, and the other to rotate the nut. The crankcase end of the pipes is removed by unscrewing the bolt securing the junction block into which the pipes are sweated. Avoid damaging the sealing washer when removing the pipe assembly.

Remove oil bath chaincase, engine sprocket and clutch (para. 41).

Completely remove the front engine plates secured to the frame by two bolts, and to the crankcase by two bolts. Remove also the nearside rear engine plate by removing the gearbox top bolt, the single nut slightly below and forward of the gearbox bolt, and the remaining bolts or nuts securing the plate to the crankcase.

Remove the two cradle bolts, and the engine may be lifted out through the nearside of the frame.

33. CRANKSHAFT—REMOVAL AND FITTING.

Remove engine sprocket key, remove timing cover, chains, sprockets, etc. (paras. 25 and 29). Remove breather pipe from rear of driving side crankcase, and the nuts from the two top crankcase studs. Remove half time pinion key, and camshaft sprocket key. Remove the short bolt between the top front engine plate bosses, and the two cheese-headed screws, one between the bottom bosses and the other in the corner of the sump. The timing side crankcase may now be removed by levering gently between the crank cheek and the crankcase inner wall with a tyre lever or similar tool. There may be packing shims fitted between the crank cheek and the timing side bearing, ensure that none of these is lost.

Withdraw the camshaft, and from the bottom of the driving side camshaft bush, remove the automatic breather valve and spring. Rest the driving side half face uppermost on two wooden blocks high enough for the manshaft to clear the bench, and rotate the crankshaft till the crankpins are in the B.D.C. position. Withdraw the crankshaft as far as possible, and tilt over till the connecting rod small end clears the tie bar cast across the driving side crankcase, when the crankshaft assembly may be lifted clear. It will bring with it the inner race of the mainshaft roller bearing.

If any new parts have been fitted, or the location of the packing shims forgotten, it will be necessary to re-centralise the crankshaft when refitting. It is almost certain that some shims will be required between the driving side bearing and the crank cheek, so two shims should be placed on the mainshaft before fitting it into the driving side crankcase. Having ensured that the crankshaft is right home against the bearing, take a measurement from the crankcase joint face at a point where there is no upstanding spigot to the upper side of the flywheel. This should measure $\frac{1}{2}$in., and whilst it is reasonably important, a rule measurement is sufficiently accurate. Shim up until this figure is obtained, and fit the timing side case. Pinch the two halves together with three bolts about equally spaced and check the crankshaft for end float. There should be .005in.—.008in. Add the necessary shims to the timing side mainshaft. Dismantle, lubricate bearings, apply jointing compound to crankcase faces and assemble fully.

34. BIG END BEARINGS—RENEWAL.

The normal oil pressure will be an indication whether the bearings require renewing. An absolute minimum safe pressure is in the region of 20lbs., and in the event of such a low pressure being recorded, immediate action should be taken to renew the steel backed thin walled bearings with which the connecting rod big ends are fitted. Check that the end cap and big end of the rod are marked for correct re-assembly and mark the rod and crankshaft to ensure that the rods are fitted the same way round as originally.

Remove the split pins from the big end bolts with a ring or box spanner and noting the pressure required, release castle nuts. Remove the nuts and washers, when a straight pull on the rod should remove the end cap. If the cap becomes wedged due to malalignment, tap carefully home and try another pull. The steel backed bearings may be readily picked out and replaced.

Over an extremely long period, there will be no measurable wear on the crankpins and standard size bearings will be suitable replacements. No difficulty should be experienced in fitting the replacements but care should be taken to ensure that both rod and bearings are perfectly clean when assembled.

Lightly smear the crankpin with oil and re-assemble the end caps on the rod in the same position as originally fitted. With a box or ring spanner, pull down the end cap nuts evenly and quite tightly but without sufficient pressure to cause distortion of the cap. Insert the split pins after checking that the rods revolve freely on the crankpins.

35. CRANKSHAFT—DISMANTLING AND RE-ASSEMBLY.

After a considerable mileage has been covered, the large oil well formed in the centre of the crankshaft assembly, will tend to become partially filled with sludge and carbon deposited centrifugally as the oil passes through. It is impossible to state at what mileage this should be cleaned out as it is entirely dependent on the frequency with which the oil is changed and the general cleanliness of the engine, but obviously it will not be dealt with until the unit is due for a major overhaul.

The flywheel is held between the two crank throws by four bolts and two studs, the nuts of the latter being secured by tab washers.

Before commencing to dismantle, mark the flywheel and one crank cheek to ensure re-assembly in the original position.

Bend back the tab washers on the same side of the flywheel as the bolt nuts, remove all nuts and withdraw the four bolts. This will enable the crank throw and flywheel to be removed.

Thoroughly clean out the centre holes and the feed holes to the bearings, ensure all faces are perfectly clean and re-assemble in the reverse order, lightly pinching down each nut before finally tightening in diagonal order. Remember to re-assemble the flywheel the same way round that it was originally fitted. Lock the bolt nuts with a punch mark and reset the tab washers.

36. SMALL END BUSH— REMOVAL AND FITTING.

Whilst the connecting rod is removed it may be found desirable to renew the small end bush, although removal of the old bush and fitting of a new one can be carried out with only the cylinder barrel and pistons removed. Obtain a bolt at least twice the length of the bush, place a washer at the head of the bolt with an outside diameter slightly less than the bush. Place the bolt in the bush and over the screwed end of the bolt, place a piece of tubing longer than the bush with an inside diameter slightly larger than the outside of the bush. Fit nut to bolt and tighten. As the nut is tightened the bush will be drawn from the connecting rod. Fit new bush in the reverse manner. Before fitting the bush to the rod, the inside diameter should be reamed to the size of the pin as, when fitted in the rod, the bush will compress slightly leaving sufficient material for true-ing with the reamer. Drill oil holes in the bush before reaming to size. The gudgeon pin should finally be a nice push fit in the bush.

37. CAMSHAFT BUSHES— REMOVAL AND REPLACEMENT.

Considerable difficulty will be experienced in removing the camshaft bush from the driving side half-case, if sufficient wear ever occurs for renewal of these bushes to be necessary. It is most strongly recommended to return the crankcase to our service department to have this operation carried out.

38. MAIN BEARINGS— REMOVAL AND REPLACEMENT.

To remove the main bearings, gently heat the case around the main bearing housing, avoiding overheating or a concentration of heat on one spot. Drop the half-case open side downwards square and true on to the bench or wooden block and the bearings (or outer race in the case of the driving side) will fall out. Replacements are more readily fitted whilst the case is still hot and should be pressed or carefully drifted home in the housing. Before fitting, it is wise to check that the replacements are a nice push fit on the mainshafts.

39. INTERMEDIATE GEAR SPINDLE AND BUSH—REMOVAL AND FITTING.

To remove and re-fit the bronze bush in the intermediate gear, adopt exactly the same procedure as for the small end bush (para. 36) although the same tackle will not be suitable.

In the unlikely event of the intermediate gear spindle requiring renewal, it should be drifted out of position whilst the case is still hot from removal of the main bearings. The replacement should be set perfectly square before pressing or drifting home. This operation should again be carried out whilst the case is sufficiently warm for the spindle to be partly inserted by hand. There is no necessity to remove the circlip from the hole into which the spindle fits either for removal or re-fitting.

40. BIG END FEED OIL SEAL—REMOVAL AND FITTING.

This oil seal which is fitted in the timing cover cannot be removed without damaging it beyond all further use and a replacement should be obtained before attempting its removal. Remove the original seal by first removing the retaining circlip and inserting a screwdriver or similar tool into the centre hole, under the seal and levering on the opposite side of the boss. Repeat this procedure a few times on opposite sides of the seal. Take care not to damage the recess into which the seal fits or the face on which it seats. Carefully press or drift the replacement seal into position, the metal covered face being outwards (visible).

THE TRANSMISSION

41. REMOVAL OF OIL BATH.

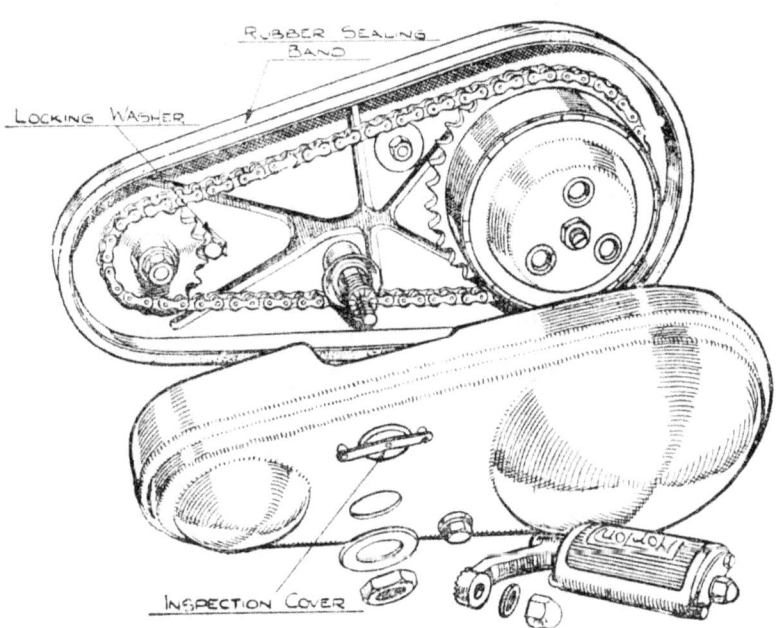

Fig. 7.

Remove the footrests, footrest rod, and brake pedal.

Remove the large nut holding the outer portion of the oil bath, and remove the outer portion.

Remove clutch spring screws, springs and cups (three of each), clutch outer plate, clutch thrust pin, and clutch retaining nut.

Engage low gear and obtain assistance to hold the rear wheel while the nut is being removed.

Remove clutch body.

A special tool may be obtained for this purpose if necessary.

Remove engine sprocket (a claw-type extractor will remove this), and engine sprocket, clutch and chain can be removed together.

Remove rear portion of oil bath, held to the crankcase by bolt, to the engine plate by a nut, to the rear chain guard by a bolt, and by a nut on the gear box pivot bolt.

42. FITTING OF OIL BATH.

Assemble in the reverse order.

Examine rubber washer fitted round the flange of the inner portion. This must be in a good condition to retain the oil in the case.

Fill oil bath with oil to the level of the plug near the bottom of the outer portion of the oil bath.

43. CLUTCH—TO DISMANTLE.

Remove outer portion of the oil bath, and clutch. (Para. 41.)

A steel band is pressed round the clutch sprocket to prevent an excess of oil entering the clutch plates.

The plates can be removed with the band

in position, but it must be removed to examine the driving slots in the sprocket.

Remove circlip holding clutch plates on to the body.

Remove plates.

There are six plain steel plates and five steel plates with ferodo inserts.

Remove clutch sprocket.

Place an old gearbox main axle (if available) in a vice with the splined end above the jaws, and fit body to axle.

Remove the three screws holding the front cover plate.

Remove the cover plate, and the clutch shock absorber rubbers. (Fig. 12)

A large "C" spanner is needed to remove the rubbers. This is placed over the body and engaged in the splines, and the large rubbers compressed while the small ones are removed.

The handle of the spanner should be of such a length that the load can be taken by the user's thigh, allowing both hands to be free to remove the rubbers.

A substitute for a "C" spanner can be made by fixing a handle to an old plain steel clutch plate.

Compress large rubbers and remove the small.

A small, sharp-pointed tool is necessary to remove the rubbers, as after use they adhere to the body.

Large rubbers are easily removed, after the small have been withdrawn.

Remove body from axle and replace in the reverse position.

Remove the three stud nuts on the back cover plate.

Back plate, roller race, back cover and body can be separated.

44. EXAMINATION OF CLUTCH PARTS.

Examine clutch inserts. They should be "proud" of the plate.

Fitting of separate inserts to a plate is not advisable, as the new insert would be "proud" of the remainder and take all the drive on the plate in which it had been fitted.

It is advisable, if possible, to replace plates with either new or reconditioned ones.

If all the new inserts are fitted to a plate, ensure that the inserts are level and flat and all contact the steel plates, taking their share of the drive.

Examine the drive on the plates for wear.

The plates with the inserts, drive on the outside diameter, and the plain steel, on the inside.

The splines on the body and the plain steel plates driven by the body rarely show any sign of wear.

The tongues on the plates with inserts, driving the sprocket, may show signs of wear and they may have "cut" in to the driven part of the sprocket.

This wear obstructs the free movement of the plates when the clutch is operated.

This can be rectified by filing or grinding the tongues on the plates square. Also the edge of the driven part of the sprocket.

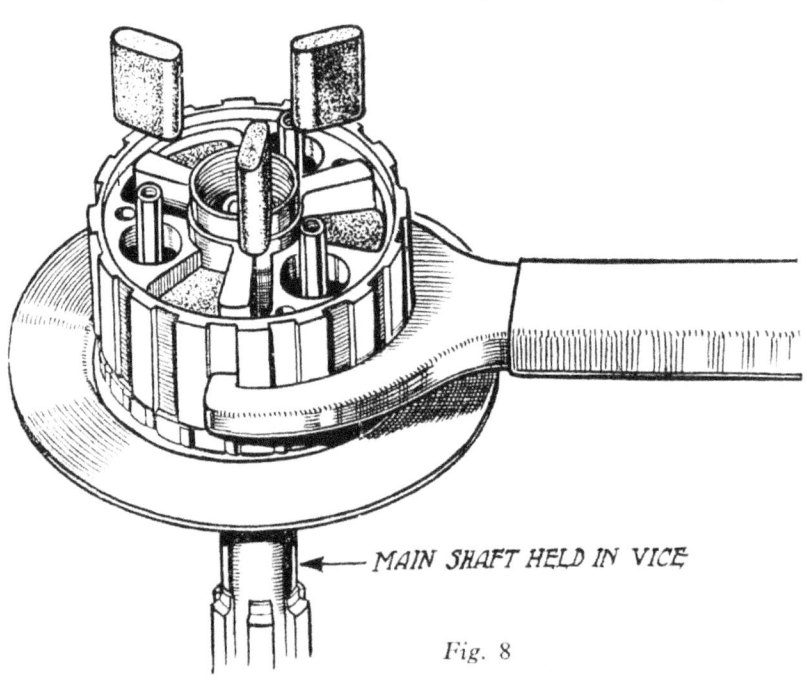

← MAIN SHAFT HELD IN VICE

Fig. 8

The only effect this will have on the clutch is a slight amount of "back-lash" when the clutch is engaged or disengaged.

Examine plain steel plates for any roughness. The back plate sometimes develops this fault.

Examine the roller race, rollers and the cage.

Examine the back cover plate face for wear by the clutch body centre.

Examine clutch shock absorber rubbers. They may have become soft or cracked.

45. ASSEMBLY OF CLUTCH.

Fit clutch body back cover plate to body, ensuring that the holes in the cover plate are in line with the holes in the body, and the spring studs an easy fit.

Fit clutch body centre and fit clutch large shock absorber rubbers in the position to take the drive.

Compress the rubbers in position and fit the small ones.

Fit body front cover and tighten screws.

Fit roller race on to the back cover plate, fit clutch back plate, and spring studs, fit stud nuts and tighten. Lock nuts with a centre punch.

Test roller race for freeness on its track.

Fit steel band on to the sprocket. This should not be tight enough to distort the sprocket.

Check all the clutch plates in the sprocket and on body for freeness.

Fit sprocket to body. Revolve sprocket on race to check free movement.

Fit plates to sprocket and body. Order of fitting is—plain steel, inserts, plain, etc.

It will be noticed on examination that the plates are slightly bevelled on the one edge. Fit the bevelled edge towards the sprocket.

Revolve sprocket, ensuring that the plates are free.

Fit circlip, retaining the plates, and fit clutch to gearbox axle.

Fit clutch thrust pin, clutch outer plate, spring cups, springs, and spring pins. Tighten right home.

Fit oil bath outer portion. (Para. 42.)

THE GEARBOX

46. REMOVAL FROM FRAME.

Remove kick starter crank, gear indicator and gear lever.

Remove outer cover held by seven cheese head screws and release the clutch cable from the operating arm by rotating the worm with a large screwdriver.

Remove cable adjuster from inner cover.

Remove oil bath, clutch and engine sprocket. (Para. 41.)

Remove rear portion of oil bath (para. 41), rear chain guard and rear chain.

Remove nut and adjuster bolt from the offside of the gearbox top bolt and extract the bolt from the nearside.

Remove prop stand spring and nut from the offside of the gearbox bottom bolt, remove the nut and tap out the bolt.

The whole box may now be swung round in an anti-clockwise direction and lifted out of the frame on the offside.

47. FITTING TO FRAME.

Reverse the order of removal operations, leaving the top and bottom bolts slack until the primary chain has been correctly tensioned ($\frac{1}{4}/\frac{3}{8}$ in. up and down movement) by means of the adjuster on the offside of the machine. Remember that any adjustment of the primary chain will affect the rear chain.

48. CLUTCH WORM LEVER, ADJUSTMENT.

When further adjustment of the clutch cable is impossible or brings the clutch worm lever into an unsuitable position, further adjustment may be obtained at the clutch worm lever accessible through the oval cover attached to the gearbox outer cover by two screws. This oval cover also forms an outrigger bearing for the clutch worm and is a good fit in the outer cover. Should it be difficult to remove after the screws have been withdrawn, it should be tapped round until the ends stand away from the outer cover and thus provide two lips beneath which suitable levers may be inserted, but care should be taken to avoid overstraining the small cover. After slackening the cable adjuster right down, the lever may be rotated on the shank of the worm by releasing the pinch bolt and holding the shank by means of the slot machined across its end, whilst rotating the lever in an anti-clockwise direction until it is about 45° below the horizontal. Readjust the cable as necessary and check that when the clutch is withdrawn the angle between the cable and the worm lever is approximately a right angle.

49. OUTER COVER, REMOVAL AND FITTING.

Remove the kick starter crank by releasing its pinch bolt and pulling off the crank.

Remove gear indicator by unscrewing the centre bolt from the positive spindle.

Remove the gear change lever by unscrewing the pinch bolt and pulling off the lever.

Remove the seven cheese headed screws holding the cover in position and withdraw the cover carefully in order to avoid tearing the paper washer fitted to this joint. If the joint is difficult to break, there is a point at either end which overhangs the inner cover to which careful punching may be applied.

No difficulty should be experienced when refitting, the coverscrews should all be just pinched down and finally tightened in opposite pairs.

Some oil will have been lost due to the cover removal and should be replenished through the clutch worm inspection hole until oil begins to drip from the level plug hole normally plugged by the square headed level plug situated to the rear of and on the same level as the kick starter crank.

50. POSITIVE FOOT CHANGE, DISMANTLING.

With the outer cover removed the positive foot change mechanism becomes accessible. To dismantle, remove the two nuts securing the U section outer plate and withdraw the plate followed by the lever return spring, pawl carrier and ratchet plate. Note that there is a spacing shim fitted behind the latter. It is unlikely that the cam plate secured behind the shoulders of the two studs which carry the assembly will ever need removal, but the procedure is obvious.

51. POSITIVE FOOTCHANGE, ASSEMBLY.

Examine all parts for wear likely to result in lost movement, particularly the spindle bushes in both covers, the ends of the pawls and the pawl pin; obtain any replacements necessary and reassemble, checking first that the two studs are quite secure and placing the spacing shim on the short shaft of the ratchet plate. Remember to insert the knuckle pin visible through the aperture in the inner cover into the hole in the ratchet plate arm whilst the ratchet plate is being fitted. Spread the pawls to enter the ratchet teeth whilst pushing home the pawl carrier.

52. INNER COVER, REMOVAL.

Screw the clutch cable adjuster as far down as possible, and with a large screwdriver and moveable spanner, rotate the clutch worm lever in a clockwise direction till the cable nipple is clear of the lever and withdraw the cable from its slot in the lever. Unscrew the adjuster and the cable is completely disconnected from the gearbox.

Remove the eight nuts securing the cover and withdraw it from the studs, being careful not to tear the paper washer fitted to the joint. The cover will bring with it the kick starter crank, clutch worm and fittings and the mainshaft bearing.

53. INNER COVER, FITTING.

Thoroughly clean the joint faces and apply a little jointing compound to each face, place the paper washer in position over the studs and against the gearbox face. Fit the cover into position. It will probably be necessary to press the kick starter pawl into its recess in the kick starter crank before the cover can be pushed right home. Fit the eight securing nuts and washers and just pinch each one, finally tightening the nuts in opposite pairs. Refit the clutch cable and adjust as described in para. 48.

54. INNER COVER, DISMANTLING.

The dismantling of the footchange mechanism having already been dealt with, only the clutch operating mechanism and kick starter remain. The clutch worm may be completely unscrewed from its nut and with the nut removed from the cover, the mainshaft bearing may be drifted out. The hardened roller in the end of the clutch worm which rubs on the clutch thrust rod may also be drifted out and a replacement fitted if necessary. Lever off the cupped pressing which covers the kick starter return spring and remove the spring, when the kick starter axle complete may be withdrawn from its bush. This will enable the pawl pin, pawl, plunger and spring to be removed. If the nose of the pawl is badly worn or chipped, it should be renewed.

It is unlikely that the kick starter bush will ever require renewal, but it may be drifted out if necessary.

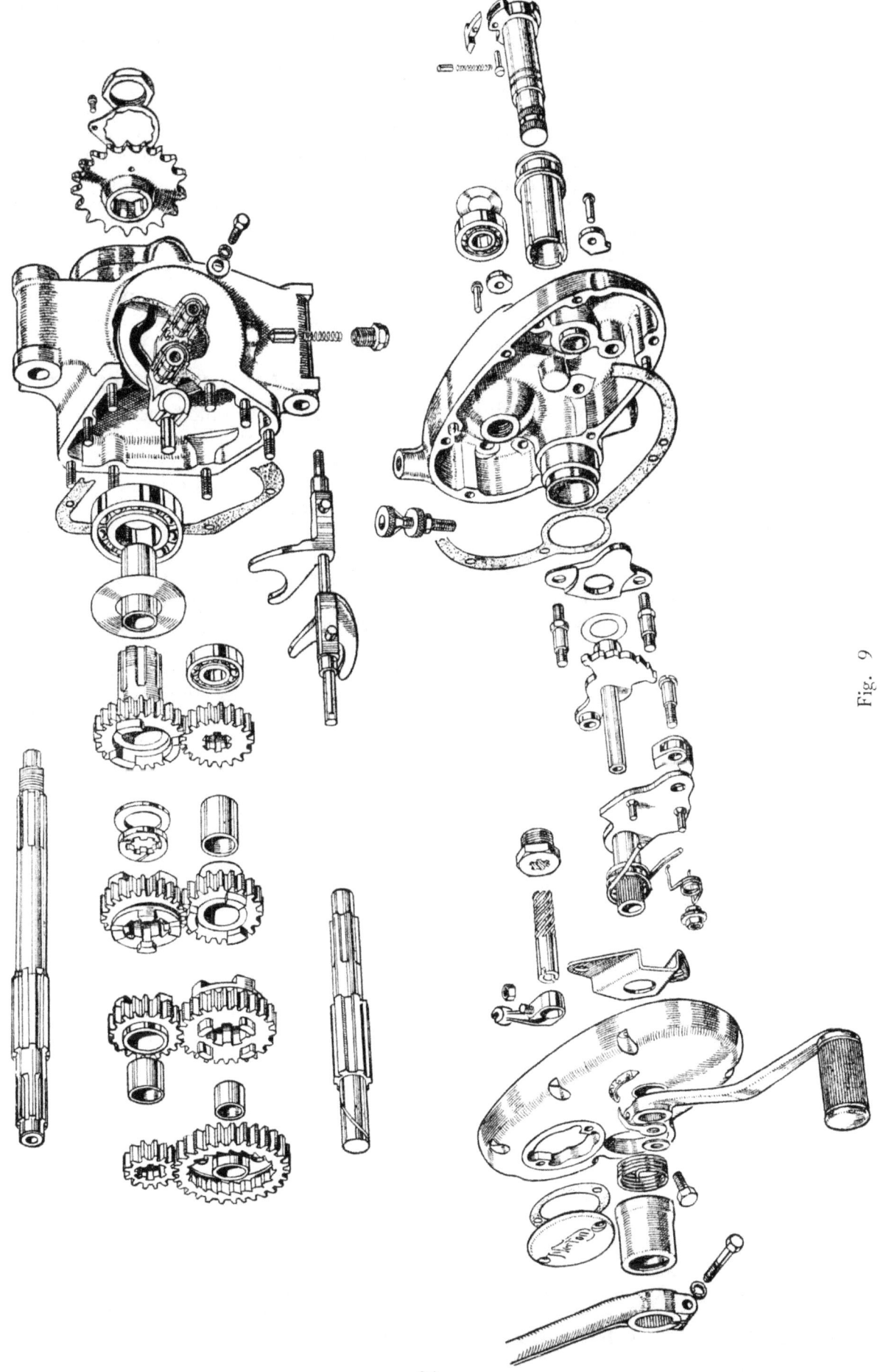

Fig. 9

55. INNER COVER, ASSEMBLING.

Examine the kick starter cam and stop pieces riveted into the cover. They should never need renewing, but may have worked loose and require re-riveting.

Press the kick starter axle bush and mainshaft bush into the cover and screw home the clutch worm nut. Fit kick starter pawl, plunger and spring to kick starter axle. Remaining parts may be fitted now or after the cover is fitted to the gearbox.

When fitting the kick starter return spring, its free end which locates in one of the slots in the bush should be forced round into the second or third slot beyond its free position.

56. REMOVAL OF GEARS.

If the clutch has been removed, it will be necessary to fit a short length of tubing over the end of the main axle and hold it in place with a clutch nut to retain the axle in position whilst the gears are being removed.

Remove end cover (paras. 49 and 52).

Remove the low gear and kick starter wheel—the large gear on the layshaft which has a bronze bush pressed into its centre.

Remove the small wheel from the end of the main axle.

Remove the mainshaft second gear; this is fitted with a fully floating bush. Unscrew the striker fork shaft by means of the two flats machined on its outer end and remove it together with the layshaft second gear and the striker fork.

Remove the tubular distance piece or clutch and withdraw the main axle together with the third gear and striker fork.

The bore of the main gear wheel, which still remains in position, carries 13 rollers which should be retained in position by inserting a roll of stiff paper in place of the main axle now removed. The axle will bring with it the bronze clutch thrust washer which should be examined, and if there are no grooves visible across the face which rubs on the main gear wheel, it should be renewed. Withdraw the layshaft and the two remaining gears, which will expose the outer race of the layshaft roller bearing in the far end of the box. The inner race with rollers and cage will most probably come away with the layshaft. The outer race may be removed by gently heating the case and dropping it—joint face downwards on the bench or a wooden block.

Remove axle sprocket nut which has a left hand thread and is held with a locking washer and screw, and withdraw the main gear wheel. If the gearbox is in the frame and the rear chain in position, obtain assistance to hold the rear wheel whilst the nut is being removed.

If the gearbox is removed from the frame, the sprocket may be held by passing a length of old chain around it and holding the ends in a vice.

Examine the steel roller retaining washer and if it is badly scored or worn down, it should be renewed. The main gear wheel bearing may be drifted from the shell. Remember that there is a pen steel washer fitted either side of this bearing.

57. REMOVAL OF CAM PLATE.

Remove the domed hexagon nut from beneath the forward side of the gearbox. This contains the cam plate indexing plunger which will drop out when the nut is removed.

Remove the two bolts fitted with spring and plain washers visible on the forward side of the gearbox shell. These secure the cam plate and cam plate quadrant, both of which may be pushed through into the box when the bolts are removed. Both cam plate and quadrant are carried in a bronze bush. It is unlikely that these bushes will ever require renewing, but they may be readily pressed or drifted out should the necessity arise.

58. FITTING CAM PLATE.

Place the quadrant in position and secure it with its bolt and washers. Place the cam plate in position so that one of the end grooves in its circumference is across the centre of the indexing plunger hole in the gearbox shell and meshing its gear with the last tooth but one on the quadrant, ensuring that the correct end of the quadrant rack is being used. Assemble the positive mechanism on to the inner cover (para. 51). Place cover in position and connect quadrant lever to ratchet by means of knuckle pin (para. 53).

Set positive footchange to top gear and check that the indexing plunger groove lies in the correct position to mesh with the indexing plunger when fitted. Withdraw cam plate and re-mesh as necessary until the correct position is obtained when the cam plate bolts and washers should be fitted and tightened. Fit indexing plunger, spring and plunger bush.

59. FITTING GEARS INTO GEARBOX.

Drop pen steel washer (the smaller of the two) into the bottom of the bearing housing before pressing in the bearing. Fit main gear wheel bearing and layshaft bearing outer race.

Fit rollers (13) to main gear wheel, smearing the assembly with grease, and insert the paper tube to retain the rollers.

Fit large pen steel washer over the shank of the main gear wheel, press the wheel home in its bearing, fit gearbox axle sprocket, tighten the nut, fit locking washer and pin.

Fit bronze clutch thrust washer to main axle so that the face having the three oil grooves will be against the main gear wheel. Carefully remove the paper tube from the main gear and insert main axle into position.

Fit distance tube in place of clutch and add clutch nut.

Fit third gear wheel (20 teeth) and top gear wheel (18 teeth) to layshaft and fit inner race with rollers and cage to end of the shaft. Grease the rollers and fit shaft into box.

Set the cam plate into the second gear position, i.e., with indexing plunger in the groove next to the shallow neutral groove.

Fit striking fork to mainshaft third gear (22 teeth) and fit gear to main axle, meshing it with the layshaft gear already in position.

Fit the second fork to the layshaft second gear (24 teeth) and fit the second gear with the fork to the layshaft. The pegs on the striking forks fit into the cam plate slots.

With the gearbox in the frame, little trouble will be experienced in holding the first fork in position. Fit the first fork in position and hold with a screw driver or similar tool whilst the second is placed in position.

Fit striking fork shaft and screw into the case.

Fit the remaining gears.

Fit end cover (paras. 55 and 53).

Remove tubular distance piece from clutch end of mainshaft. Remember to finally refill with oil to the level plug level (para. 49).

WHEELS AND HUBS

60. FRONT WHEEL, REMOVAL.

Place machine on both stands. Detach brake cable from cam lever and cable adjuster from brake plate. Remove spindle nut from off-side of spindle. Slacken pinch bolt in near side fork end. Take the weight of the wheel in the left hand and withdraw the spindle by means of a Tommy Bar placed through the hole in the head of the spindle.

61. FRONT WHEEL, FITTING.

Re-assemble in the reverse order. Insert spindle from near side. Lock pinch bolt in near side fork end after tightening the spindle nut.

62. REAR WHEEL, REMOVAL.

With machine on rear stand, remove rear chain and mudguard tail piece. Disconnect tail lamp lead at the brass connection.

Remove brake rod adjusting nut. Disconnect speedometer drive. Slacken rear wheel spindle nuts and withdraw the wheel from the fork ends.

63. REAR WHEEL, REFITTING.

See that fork ends are lying reasonably parallel. Place wheel in position, ensuring that the ears of the adjusting stirrup are lying flat against the sides of the fork end and that the cupped adjuster washer is located on the small shoulder at the open end of the fork end slot.

Make sure that the anchor pad on the brake plate is entering the slot on the inside of the near-side fork end.

Fit rear chain with the closed end of the spring connecting clip facing the direction of travel of the chain.

Track up the wheel and adjust until there is $\frac{3}{8}$in. to $\frac{1}{2}$in. up and down movement midway between the sprocket.

NOTE.—It is important that this condition is obtained with the weight of the machine on the rear wheel.

Adjust brake rod as necessary. Reconnect speedometer drive.

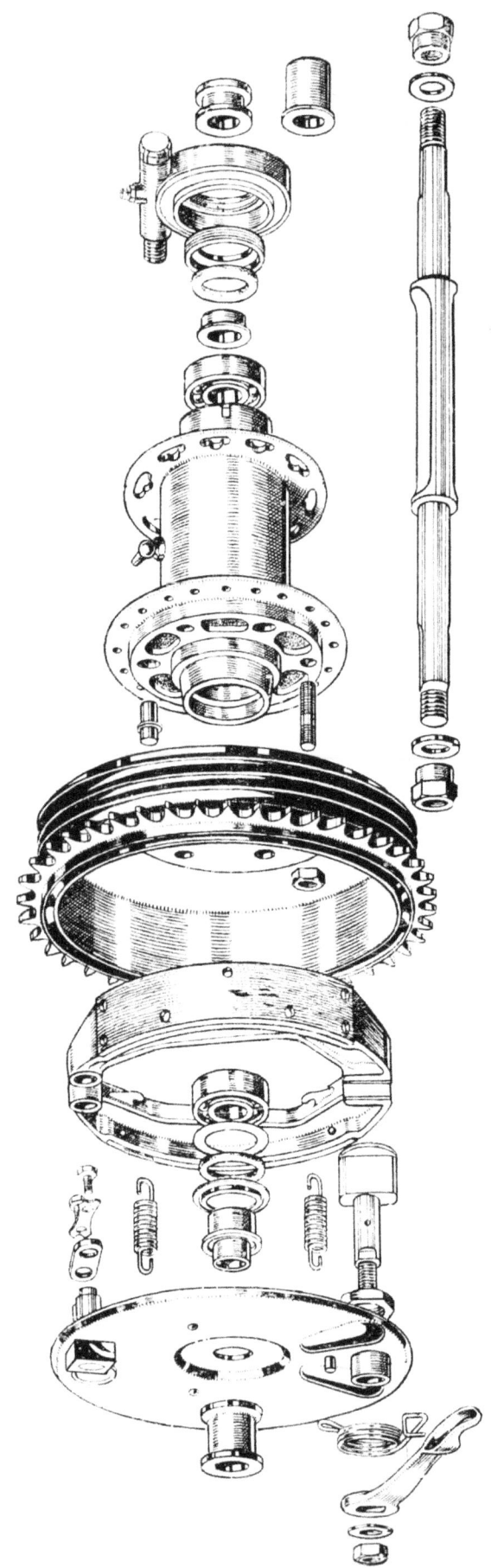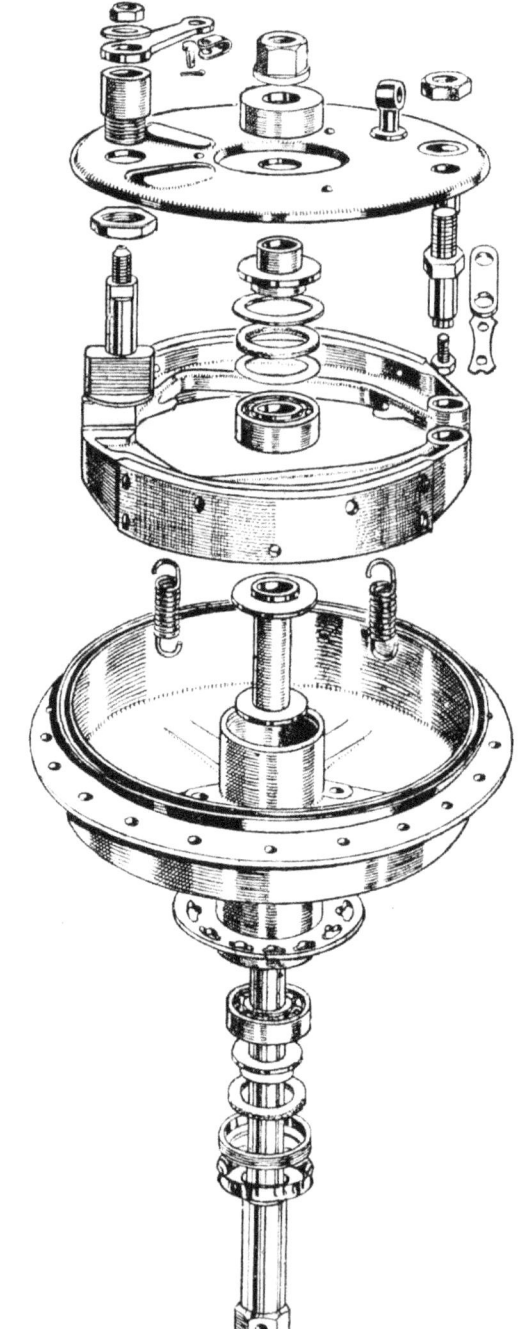

Fig. 10

64. DISMANTLING REAR HUB.

Remove rear wheel complete. (Para. 62.) Remove spindle nuts, adjusting stirrups, brake plate, speedometer driving box and distance pieces.

Remove ball-race locking ring from plain side of hubshell.

Remove distance piece and felt washer. Knock out the spindle and it will bring with it the single row bearing fitted to the plain side of the hub.

Drift out the remaining bearing together with the peened in washer, the felt and pen steel washers fitted into the brake drum side of the hubshell. Separate brake drum and hubshell if necessary.

65. REAR HUB, RE-ASSEMBLING.

Re-assemble in reverse order.

Pack bearings with grease before assembly. Ensure that long end of spindle protrudes through the brake side of the hub.

66. FRONT HUB, DISMANTLING.

With machine on both stands remove front wheel. (Para. 60.)

Remove brake plate together with its inner and outer distance piece.

Remove locking ring, felt washer and distance piece from opposite side of hub.

With suitable punch knock the bearing in the brake side further into the hub until the single row bearing drops clear.

Remove distance tube.

From this side of the hub, drift out the remaining bearing, together with the peened in washer, felt washer and pen steel washer.

67. FRONT HUB, RE-ASSEMBLING.

Pack bearings with grease.

Press single row bearing into position followed by the distance piece (with collar against the bearing) felt washer and locking ring which can be tightened up.

Insert distance tube through brake side of hub, ensuring that it is right home against the bearing just fitted.

Press double row bearing into position.

Fit pen steel washer and felt washer.

Lightly rivet remaining washer into its recess.

BRAKES

68. DISMANTLING OF THE BRAKES.

Remove brake plate from the drum.

Remove brake lever return spring from the lever.

Remove nut and washer from the cam spindle.

Remove brake lever.

Remove cam spindle from bush in the brake plate.

Tap the end of the spindle lightly until the cam is clear of the shoes.

Remove brake shoe return springs.

Remove the small pin from the end of each pivot pin and lift off the pivot pin tie plate.

Remove the brake shoes.

Cam spindle bush can be removed from the plate after removing the nut holding bush to plate.

69. ASSEMBLY OF BRAKES.

Fit cam spindle bush to plate.

Fit brake shoes. Smear a little oil on the pivot pins.

Fit ONE shoe to pivot pin.

Fit spring to the shoe fitted to the pin, near pin.

Hold second shoe near to the one fitted and fit the spring, stretch the spring and fit second shoe to pivot pin.

Fit second spring to both shoes.

Fit cam spindle to plate. Hold shoes apart with screwdriver or similar tool and allow cam to pass the ends of the shoes.

Fit tie plate over shoulders on pivot pins. Fit and tighten both pins.

FRONT FORKS

70. MAINTENANCE.

Replenish damping oil at approximately 5,000 mile intervals.

Remove hexagon headed filler plug from top of each fork leg. Remove drain plug from each fork end. Allow oil to drain out and operate the forks a time or two to eject the last drops.

Replace drain plugs.

Refill each leg with a measured $\frac{1}{4}$ pint of Wakefield's Castrolite, Single Shell, Price's Motorine E, Mobiloil Arctic, or Energol S.A.E. 20. Work the forks a few times to remove any air-locks.

Replace filler plugs.

71. STEERING HEAD ADJUSTMENT.

Place a wooden block or box under the engine cradle of sufficient height to raise the front wheel clear of the ground. Place thumb of left hand on the joint between the steering head of the frame and the fork head clip.

Attempt to lift the forks with the right hand. Any movement at the head races will be readily felt.

To adjust slacken the steering column locking nut and the pinch bolt clamping each leg into the fork crown.

Adjust by means of the nut situated on the steering column below the head clip, until all play is removed, but the forks are still free to rotate on the head races.

Re-tighten the steering column locking nut and the pinch bolts.

72. REMOVAL OF FRONT FORKS FROM FRAME.

This may be carried out either with or without the front wheel and mudguard in position.

Remove switch panel from headlamp.

Detach steering damper arm from frame.

Detach speedometer driving and lighting cables from speedometer head.

Remove all cables from the handlebar levers, remove handlebars.

Slacken off steering damper completely, remove steering column locking nut complete with damper knob and rod.

Remove oil filler plugs and speedometer panel.

Remove head clip and head race adjusting nut.

Withdraw forks carefully to avoid losing any head race balls.

Take care to avoid spilling any damping oil from the fork legs. If any oil is lost it will be necessary to replenish as instructed. (Para. 70.)

73. FITTING OF FORKS TO THE FRAME.

Examine head races and balls (17 per race).

Races are pressed into their housings and may readily be knocked out for renewal.

Note that the races fitted in the frame embody a small hole to allow the entry of grease.

Liberally grease the track in the race fitted to the bottom of the steering column and the top frame race. Place 17 balls in position in each and carefully insert the column through the frame.

Place the top race and dust cover in position and screw the adjusting nut down the column till the hexagon is finger tight against the top race.

Refit the head clip and speedometer panel, the column locking nut loosely and the filler plugs which should be tightened up.

Adjust the head races. (Para. 71.)

Refit all remaining parts and check that all bolts and nuts have been tightened.

74. FORK LEG, DISMANTLING.

This may be carried out with the forks in position, but before commencing the work it is advisable to obtain from our Service Department a "pull through" to facilitate removal and replacement of the main tube.

Remove front wheel. (Para. 60.)

Remove front mudguard.

Remove oil filler and drain plugs from top and bottom of fork leg and allow oil to drain off.

Slacken the pinch bolt in the crown lug.

Fork end, complete with bottom cover, springs and main tube may be withdrawn.

If difficulty is encountered the "pull-through" already mentioned should be screwed into the top of the main tube which can then be tapped out with a mallet.

Remove from the main tube the top leather washer (this may have stuck to the inside of the upper cover), the short buffer spring and main spring.

Remove the bottom cover, held to the fork end by two screws.

Remove leather washer.

Remove locking ring from top of fork end.

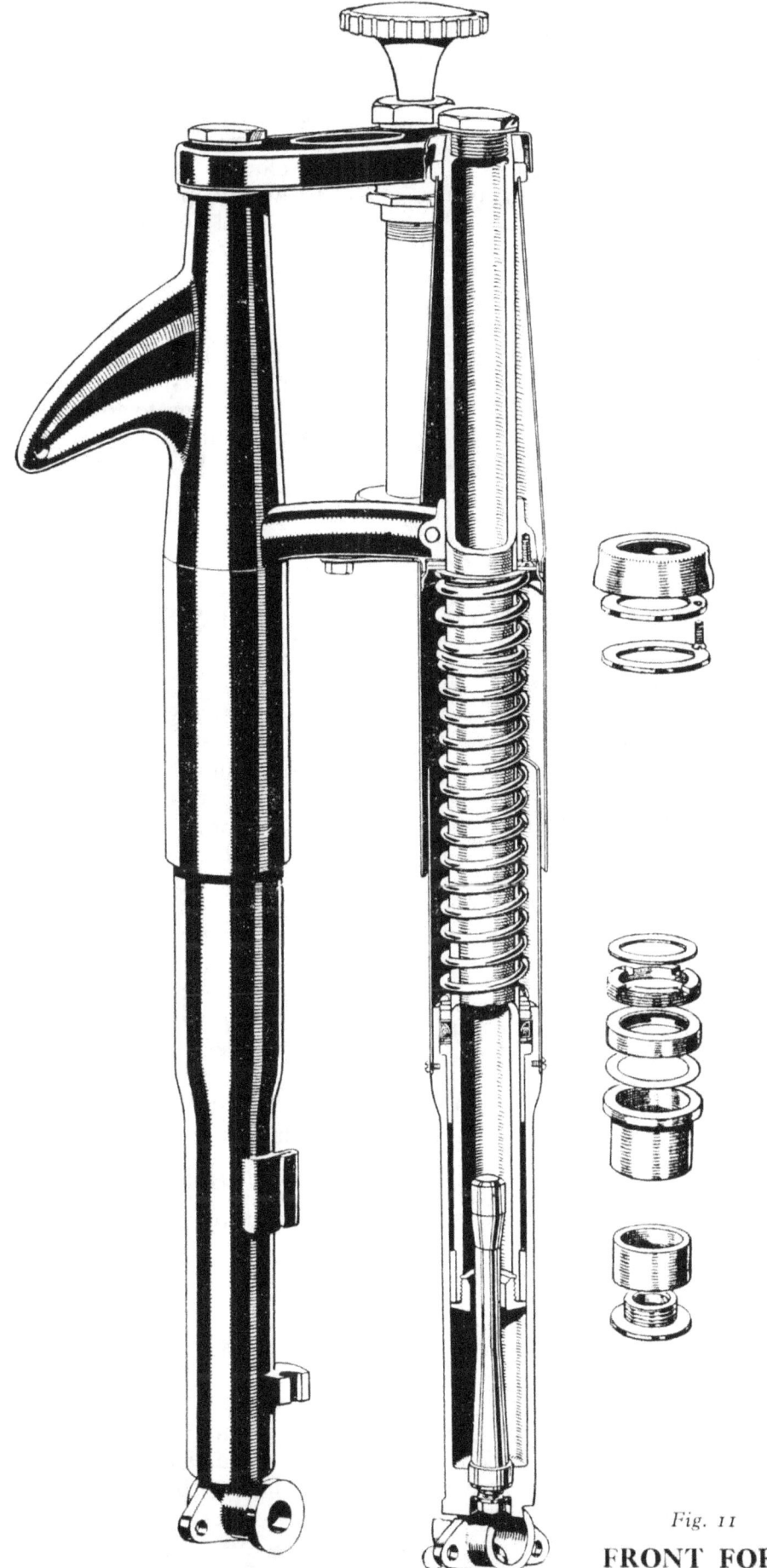

Fig. 11
FRONT FORKS

Withdraw fork end from main tube.

The remaining components may now be removed from the main tube.

75. FORK LEG, ASSEMBLY.

Thoroughly clean all components and obtain any renewals necessary.

Attach the bottom bush to the main tube by means of the securing nut.

Place fork end in position on the main tube.

Fit shouldered bush into fork end followed by the super oil seal, being very careful that the leather has its radiused side uppermost.

Screw home the locking ring and tighten sufficiently to be secure without distorting the case of the super oil seal.

Fit the smaller of the two leather washers over the locking ring followed by the main spring, the buffer spring and the remaining leather washer.

Fit bottom cover and securing screws.

Screw " pull-through " into top end of main tube and pass through crown lug and head clip.

Draw into position by means of Tommy bar inserted across the " pull-through," and temporarily tighten the pinch bolt in the crown lug.

Remove " pull-through."

Fit filler plug to main tube and slacken pinch bolt. Lock main tube in position with filler plug. Re-tighten pinch bolt.

Fit drain plug to fork end.

Remove filler plug.

Replenish with oil. (Para. 70.)

PLUNGER TYPE REAR SUSPENSION

76. DISMANTLING AND RE-ASSEMBLY OF REAR SPRINGING.

Remove rear wheel. (Para. 64).

Slacken the pinch bolt across the top of the rear frame member.

Unscrew the locking bolt at bottom of stationary bearer rod a few turns and tap the bolt head with a hammer to release the bearer rod from its taper.

Remove bottom bolt.

Withdraw bearer rod upwards.

Insert a tyre lever or large screw driver between the frame member and the side of the top and bottom spring covers.

Lever sideways until sufficient of the central hole is exposed beyond the edge of the rear member to insert a $\frac{1}{4}''$ or $5/16''$ diameter rod fitted with suitable washers and wing nuts into the hole to prevent the assembly flying apart when completely removed from the frame.

Thoroughly clean all components and smear the bearing surfaces with oil or grease.

Fit the springs and covers to the fork ends and compress the assembly by means of the rod used during dismantling, until it is sufficiently compressed to enter the jaw of the rear member.

Place the assembly as far as possible into the jaw, remove the rod and tap the assembly into an approximately central position.

Smear the bearer rod with oil and insert taper end first into the upper end of the rear frame member.

Push or tap the bearer rod right home.

Fit and tighten bottom bolt.

Tighten top pinch bolt.

SWINGING ARM REAR SUSPENSION

77. SWINGING ARM REMOVAL AND ASSEMBLY.

With the rear wheel withdrawn, remove the rear suspension units secured only by a single bolt and nut at either end. Remove the nut and washer from one end of the swinging arm bolt, withdraw the bolt, and remove the swinging arm. To renew the silent block bushes, drift out one end, remove the tubular distance piece and drift out the remaining bush. Press in replacement till the outer steel sleeve is flush with the end of the tube. Remember to replace the distance piece before inserting the second bush.

When securing the swinging arm in position in the frame, a dimension of 11⅜in. should be taken from the hole forming the top absorber anchorage to the shock absorber anchorage hole in the swinging arm, the arm being held in this position whilst tightening the swinging arm pivot bolt.

Rear Suspension Units.

These fittings embody quite complicated oil damping arrangements which are carefully set to provide the correct suspension characteristics for your machine. They are sealed and are virtually leak proof and should NOT BE INTERFERED WITH. In the unlikely event of any attention being necessary, their removal is quite simple and straightforward and they should be taken to your usual Norton dealer or the nearest Norton distributor.

No attempt whatever should be made by the normal rider to dismantle, drain or refill these units.

HANDELBAR FITTINGS

78. AIR CONTROL LEVER.

The air control lever is shown in Fig. 13 in the position in which it should be assembled, having first greased both sides of the lever.

After fitting the adjusting nut it should be tightened to give the required tension.

To remove the control cables from the lever, open the lever as far as possible, hold the outer cable, and as the lever is closed, pull the outer cable from the lever body.

Remove nipple from the lever.

To fit the cables, fit nipple into the lever, close the lever, pull the outer cable away from the lever and fit the cable to the lever body.

79. CLUTCH AND FRONT BRAKE CONTROL LEVERS.

The clutch and front brake controls are so simple as to require no instructions for their dismantling or assembly.

The pivot bolts have shoulders machined on them, allowing the nuts on the bolts to be tightened while allowing clearance for easy movement of the lever.

To remove the clutch cable from the lever, turn the clutch operating arm on the clutch worm by other means than the cable, and

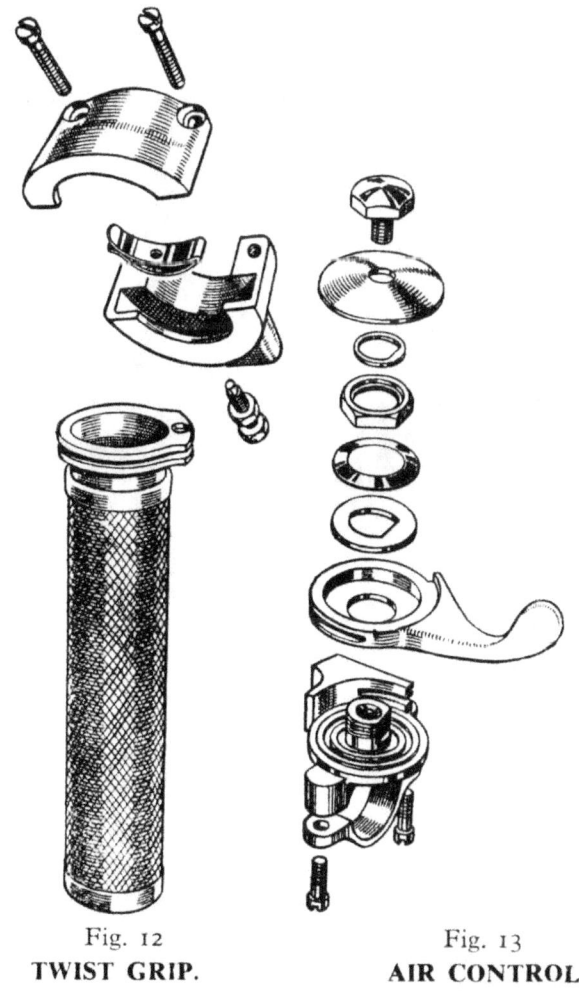

Fig. 12
TWIST GRIP.

Fig. 13
AIR CONTROL LEVER.

the nipple can be removed from the arm, and inner and outer cables can be removed from the lever.

To remove the brake cable from the lever, remove the split cotter and pin holding the "U" clip to the brake arm, and the inner and outer cables can be removed from the lever.

Re-assemble in the reverse order.

80. TWIST GRIP.

The twist grip assembly is shown in Fig. 12.

To assemble the twist grip, grease the portion of the handlebar where the grip works.

Fit the sleeve to the bar.
Grease the drum on the sleeve.
Fit spring and adjuster bolt and nut to the bottom half clip.
Thread the cable through the hole in the half clip.
Fit the nipple to the drum on the sleeve.
(Sufficient length of cable can be obtained by lifting the throttle slide and holding in position by piece of soft wood placed in the air intake.)
Fit the top half clip.
Adjust the tightness of the grip with the adjusting screw and lock in the desired position.
Dismantle in the reverse order.

AMAL CARBURETTER

82. DISMANTLING OF THE CARBURETTER.

A. Mixing Chamber.
B. Throttle Valve.
C. Jet Needle and Clip.
D. Air Valve.
E. Mixing Chamber Union Nut.
F. Jet Block.
G. Cable Adjuster (Throttle).
G1. Cable Adjuster (Air).
H. Jet Block Barrel.
J. Pilot Orifice.
K. Passage to Pilot.
M. Pilot Outlet.
N. Pilot By-Pass.
O. Needle Jet.
P. Main Jet.
Q. Float Chamber Holding Bolt.
R. Float Chamber.
S. Needle Valve Seating.
T. Float.
U. Float Needle.
V. Float Needle Clip.
W. Float Chamber Cover.
X. Float Chamber Lock Screw Tickler (to left of W).
Y. Mixing Chamber Top Cap.
Z. Mixing Chamber Lock Ring.
Z1. Spring for above.

Remove the carburetter.

Remove the slides and needle. The slides and needle can be examined without removing the cables.

The throttle slide is the one that is drum-shaped and has the jet needle attached to it.

To remove the throttle slide from the cable, compress the spring, allowing the nipple on the end of the cable to leave the hole in which it is fitted, and on releasing the spring allow the nipple to pass through the larger hole, and the slide is free from the cable.

To remove the air slide, compress spring as before and release nipple from the end of the slide, and the slide is free.

To remove the needle from the throttle slide, remove the spring clip at the top of the slide. The needle is normally fitted into the middle notch.

The lower the needle the weaker the mixture.

Remove the float chamber. It is held by

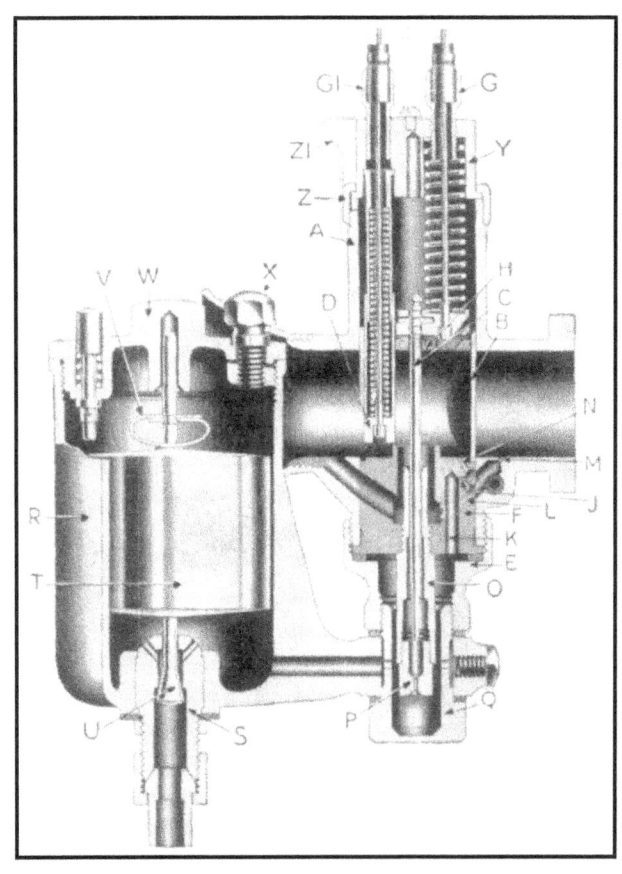

Fig. 14.

a bolt at the base of the mixing chamber. There are two fibre washers on this bolt, one under the head and one between the float and mixing chambers.

To remove the float needle, release the float chamber cap locking screw and remove the cap.

Compress the spring clip on the top of the float and lift float from the chamber.

Remove the bolt at the base of the float chamber, and the needle will fall out.

On the bolt at the base of the float chamber two fibre washers are fitted in the same order as on the bolt at the base of the mixing chamber.

Remove the jet. The main jet is now exposed and can be removed from the needle jet.

Remove the needle jet from the jet block.

Remove the jet block by removing the union nut at the base of the mixing chamber.

83. RE-ASSEMBLY OF THE CARBURETTER.

Fit needle jet to the jet block.

Fit main jet to needle jet.

Fit jet block to mixing chamber, located by groove and pin.

Fit mixing chamber union nut and fibre washer.

Fit float to the float chamber.

Fit float needle through the base of the chamber and the centre of the float, compress the spring clip on the top of the float and allow the needle to enter the clip.

Release the clip and the clip will drop into the groove in the needle.

Fit the chamber top and lock with the locking bolt.

Fit the chamber to the mixing chamber. (Two fibre washers.)

Fit the bolt holding the union to the base of the float chamber. (Two fibre washers.)

Fit needle to throttle slide in middle position.

Thread cables through the mixing chamber, the throttle cable to be nearer to the cylinder barrel. The throttle cable has the shorter length of inner cable protruding from the outer cable.

Fit return springs to cables, the larger to the throttle.

Fit slides to cables.

Fit air slide to throttle slide.

Fit slides to the mixing chamber, carefully entering the needle into the needle jet. DO NOT FORCE.

Fit mixing chamber top.

Fit carburetter upright on induction stub.

84. SLOW RUNNING ADJUSTMENT.

Start engine and screw pilot air adjuster right home whilst carefully closing the throttle. The engine should now eight stroke and run heavily.

Gradually unscrew the pilot air screw; the engine speed will increase and the throttle will need further closing.

Repeat the process until by a combination of throttle and pilot air adjustment a regular even slow running is obtained.

85. THROTTLE STOP AND STARTING SETTING.

It is desirable to be able to close the twist grip completely without the engine stopping, for this purpose an adjustable throttle stop is provided.

Slacken the small screwdriver headed locking pin and holding the shaped stop piece against the mixing chamber body with the left thumb, rotate the adjuster until a slight increase in engine revolutions is heard.

Turn the adjuster back until the engine resumes its original speed and re-tighten the screw.

For easy starting rotate the adjustment as far as possible in a clockwise direction. This will raise the throttle slide to the best starting position. Return the adjuster to its normal position after starting.

86. FLOAT CHAMBER.

The function of the float chamber is to control the petrol in the carburetter at the correct level and anything which upsets its correct working will cause constant flooding, heavy engine running and high petrol consumption.

Dirt on the needle seating, a bent needle, a punctured float, a badly worn needle, or a carburetter not fitted upright will all give the above symptoms.

87. MIXTURE ADJUSTMENT.

The pilot air adjuster controls the mixture of air and petrol up to $\frac{1}{8}$ throttle opening, from $\frac{1}{8}$ to $\frac{3}{4}$ throttle in mixture is controlled by the needle in the throttle valve. From $\frac{3}{4}$ to full throttle the main jet is the control. Weak mixture is indicated by spitting and blue flames from the carburetter, pinking, running hot and plug points showing indications of intense heat.

To cure, raise needle in throttle valve one notch.

Rich mixture is indicated by thumpy running, black exhaust and the engine does not respond readily to throttle opening. To remedy, lower the needle.

88. CARBURETTER MAINTENANCE.

Clean regularly by dismantling and washing in clean petrol.

Clean all holes with a fine bristle.

Renew any worn or damaged parts.

TYRES

89. MAINTENANCE.

Keep tyres at correct pressures. Front 20 lbs. Rear 23 lbs.

Examine regularly and remove any flints, etc., which may have become embedded in the tread.

Replace valve cap as soon as possible should one become lost.

90. REMOVAL.

Deflate tube by removing valve inner.

Remove valve nut and security bolt nut, and push the bead of the cover into the well of the rim at a point remote from either valve or security bolt, and proceed to remove cover commencing at the opposite side. Remove one side completely, remove tube and other side of cover.

Remove security bolt if desired.
Remove one side completely.
Remove tube and other side of cover.

91. FITTING.

Lubricate with french chalk the cover beads, inner tube and inside of rim, and ensure that the well-filler tape is in position. Fit one side of cover, insert security bolt in position, fit inner tube and inflate very slightly. Ensure that valve is protruding squarely through the rim. Fit remaining side of cover, commencing at a point remote from both valve and security bolt, and ensuring that the security bolt head is not preventing the cover bead from going home. Force the cover into the well of the rim, and inflate to recommended pressure.

ELECTRICAL SECTION

92. ESSENTIAL MAINTENANCE.

Battery. Inspect the battery regularly and keep acid level to the top of the separators by adding distilled water.

UNLESS YOU DO THIS YOUR BATTERY WILL QUICKLY DETERIORATE.

Wiring. Keep all connections and terminals tight. See that the cables are clear of moving parts.

Dynamo. Keep brushes and commutator clean. (Para. 100).

Magneto. Keep contact breaker clean. If necessary, polish the contacts with fine carborundum stone or emery cloth, and afterwards wipe with cloth moistened with petrol. (Para. 97.) Occasionally check contact breaker opening (using gauge on ignition spanner). (Para. 96.)

Replace high-tension cables if they become worn or perished.

Head Lamp. Focus head lamp after fitting new bulb. (Para. 104.)

IGNITION

93. MAGNETO.

The magneto is of the rotating armature pattern, and also incorporates an automatic timing control. The automatic timing control employs a driving gear carrying a plate fitted with two pins. A weight is pivoted on each pin, and the movement of the weight is controlled by a spring connected between the pivot end of the weight and a toggle lever pivoted at approximately the centre of

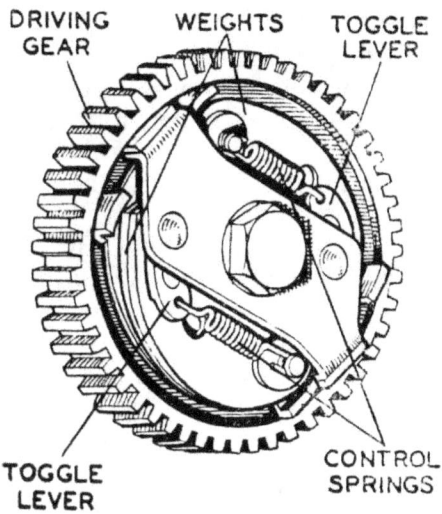

Fig. 15.

the weight. Holes are provided in each toggle lever in which are located pegs on the underside of a driving plate secured to the magneto spindle. This plate is also provided with stops which limit the range of the control. When the magneto is stationary, the weights are in the closed position and the magneto retarded for starting purposes. As the speed is increased, centrifugal force acting on the weights overcomes the restraining influence of the springs and the weights move outwards causing relative movement to take place between the driving gear and the magneto spindle so advancing timing. By careful design of the springs, the characteristics of the control can be arranged to conform more closely with the engine requirements than is the case with other types of control.

94. AUTOMATIC TIMING CONTROL.

Since this operates in the timing chest it is automatically lubricated and should run indefinitely without attention. A tight magneto chain tends to upset the normal working of the parts and there should always be at least $\frac{3}{16}$ in. whip in the chain. Failure of the timing control mechanism will usually result in overheating and loss of performance.

95. LUBRICATION.

Every 3,000 miles.

The cam is supplied with lubricant from a felt pad contained in a pocket in the contact breaker housing. A small hole in the cam fitted with a wick enables the oil to find its way on to the surface of the cam. Remove the contact breaker cover and turn until the hole in the cam can be clearly seen, and then carefully add a few drops of thin machine oil. Do not allow any oil to get on to the contacts.

The contact breaker rocker arm pivot also requires lubrication, and the complete contact breaker must be removed first. Take out the hexagon-headed screw from the centre of the contact breaker and pull the contact breaker off the tapered shaft on which it fits. Push aside the rocker arm retaining spring, prise the rocker arm off its bearing and lightly smear the bearing with Mobilgrease No. 2, or if this is not available, clean engine oil may be used. At the same time, lightly smear the contact breaker spring with clean engine oil. When replacing the contact breaker, take care to ensure that the projecting T on the tapered portion of the contact breaker face engages with the key way cut in the magneto spindle. Tighten the hexagon-headed screw with care. It must not be too slack, nor must undue force be used.

96. CONTACT BREAKER— ADJUSTMENT.

Remove the contact breaker cover and rotate the engine until the contact points are fully opened, check the gap with the gauge having a thickness of .012in. The gauge should be a sliding fit between the points, and if the gap varies appreciably on the gauge, it should be adjusted. Slacken the locknut and turn the contact screw by its hexagon head until the gap is correct, finally tighten the locknut and recheck the setting.

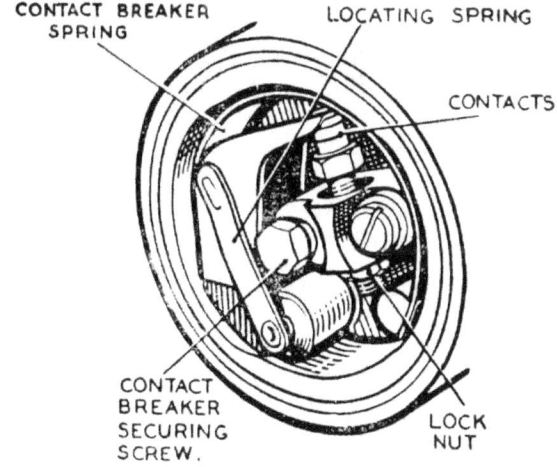

Fig. 16

97. CONTACT BREAKER, CLEANING.

Every 6,000 miles take off the contact breaker cover and examine the contact breaker. If the points are burned or blackened, clean them with a fine carborundum stone, or with very fine emery cloth, afterwards removing any dust or dirt with a petrol-moistened cloth. Cleaning of the contacts is made easier if the contact breaker is removed as described in the lubrication instructions. (Para. 95.)

98. HIGH TENSION PICK-UP.

Remove the high tension pick-ups, wipe clean with a fine, dry cloth. The pick-up carbon brush must move freely in its holder; if it is dirty, clean with a petrol-moistened lint-free cloth.

99. HIGH TENSION CABLES—REPLACEMENT.

Inspect the high tension cables and replace at any signs of perishing or cracking by suitable lengths of 7mm. rubber-covered ignition cable. To fit a new cable to a pick-up terminal, bare the end of the cable for about ¼in., thread the knurled moulded nut over the cable, thread the bare wire through the washer, removed from the end of the old cable and bend back the strands. Finally, screw the nut into the pick-up.

LIGHTING AND ACCESSORIES

100. DYNAMO—INSPECTION OF COMMUTATOR & BRUSHGEAR.

About once every six months remove the dynamo cover for inspection of commutator and brushes.

The brushes must make firm contact with the commutator. The brushes are held in boxes by means of springs; move the brush to see that it is free to slide in its holder. If it sticks remove it and clean with a cloth moistened with petrol. Care must be taken to replace the brushes in their original position, otherwise they will not bed properly on the commutator. If, after long service, the brushes have become worn to such an extent that they will not bear properly on the commutator, they must be replaced. Always use genuine Lucas brushes. Brushes should be fitted by a Service Agent.

Now examine the commutator. It should be free from any trace of oil or dirt and should have a highly polished appearance. Clean a dirty or blackened commutator by pressing a fine dry cloth against it while the engine is slowly turned over by hand. If the commutator is very dirty, moisten the cloth with petrol.

101. LUBRICATION.

The bearings in the dynamo are packed with grease during assembly and will last until it is necessary for the dynamo to undergo a complete overhaul.

102. CUT-OUT AND REGULATOR UNIT.

This unit (Fig. 18) which is housed in the toolbox, consists of the cut-out which is an automatic switch to prevent discharge of the battery when the dynamo is not charging, and the voltage regulator which

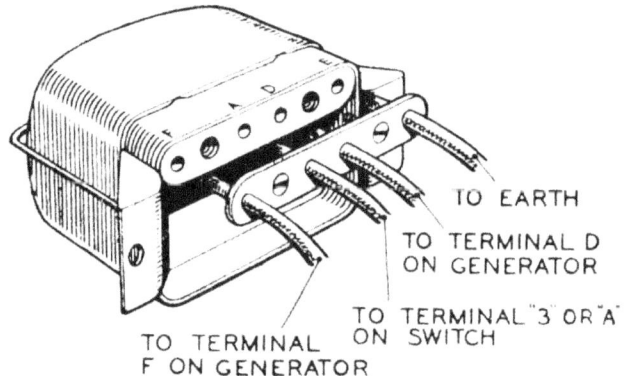

Fig. 17.

controls the output of the dynamo. With a fully charged battery the dynamo is only permitted to pass a small charge to the battery, whilst with a fully discharged battery a heavy charge is passed in order to boost up the battery rapidly. Both components are accurately set and should not be tampered with or adjusted.

103. AMMETER.

Fitted in the switch panel of the headlamp, this instrument indicates when current is being taken from the battery in a greater quantity than is being fed to the battery (discharge).

It also shows when the dynamo is charging and hence by means of the regulator the state of charge of the battery.

104. BATTERY.

When examining a battery, do not hold naked lights near the vents as there is a danger of igniting the gas coming from the plates.

Remove the vent plugs and see that the ventilating holes in each are quite clear.

Remove any dirt by means of a bent wire.

A clogged vent plug will cause the pressure in the cell to increase, due to gases given off during charging, and this may cause damage.

Make sure that the rubber washer is fitted under each vent plug, otherwise the electrolyte may leak.

Battery—Topping-up.

About once a month, remove the battery lid, unscrew the filler caps and pour a small quantity of **distilled** water into each of the cells to bring the acid level with tops of the separators.

Acid must not be added to the battery unless some is accidentally spilled.

Should this happen, the loss must be made good with acid diluted to the same specific gravity as the acid in the cells.

This should be measured by means of a hydrometer.

Checking Battery condition.

The state of charge of the battery should be examined by taking hydrometer readings of the specific gravity of the acid in the cells.

The specific gravity readings and their indications are as follows:—

1.280—1.300. Battery fully charged.
About—1.210. Battery about half discharged.
Below—1.150. Battery fully discharged.

These figures are given assuming the temperature of the acid is about 60° F.

Each reading should be approximately the same.

If one cell gives a reading very different from the rest, it may be that the acid has been spilled or has leaked from this particular cell, or there may be a short circuit between the plates.

This will necessitate its return to a Repair Depot for rectification.

Wipe the top of the battery to remove all dirt or water.

Note.

Do not leave the battery in a discharged condition for any length of time.

If a motor cycle is to be out of use, the battery must first be fully charged, and afterwards given a refreshing charge about every two weeks.

Earthing Connections.

Before disconnecting the battery, note which terminal is connected to the machine and re-connect accordingly.

Charging.

If the previous tests indicate that the battery is merely discharged, and if the acid level is correct, the battery must be recharged from an external supply.

105. HEADLAMP.

The headlamp incorporates a Lucas Light Unit which embodies a "pre-focus" bulb ensuring a correct beam without any necessity for focusing.

Setting.

Check the setting of the lamp. Stand the machine about 25ft. from a light coloured wall and adjust the headlamp position until the main driving beam is projected straight ahead and parallel to the ground, the centre of the beam being the same height as the headlamp centre.

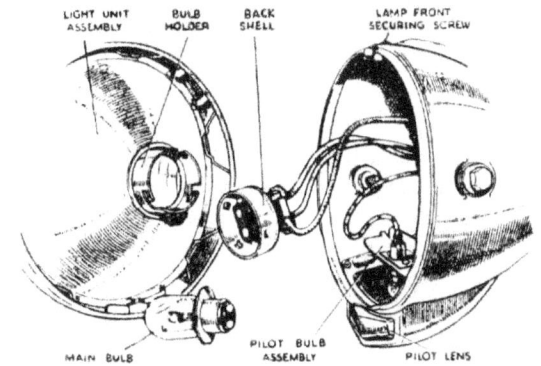

Fig. 18

Bulb Replacement.

To remove the headlamp front, slacken the screw at the top of the lamp and lift off the front rim complete with light unit assembly. The pilot bulb is carried in a small metal plate in the base of the lamp body. The plate must be slid out in order to replace the bulb. To replace "pre-focus" bulbs, twist the back shell in the centre of the reflector back in an anti-clockwise direction and pull off. The bulb may now be removed from the rear of the reflector. Place the correct bulb in the holder, engage the projectors on the inside of the back shell with the slots in the bulb holder, press home and twist in a clockwise direction. To replace headlamp front, locate the bottom of the light unit assembly in the lamp body, press into position and tighten locking screw.

Note.

It is important that only genuine Lucas bulbs should be used as replacements, in order to ensure accurate and correct focusing.

Main bulb Lucas No. 312 6 volt
30/24 watt.
Pilot bulb Lucas No. 988 6 volt 3 watt.

106. TAIL LAMP.

The tail lamp is fitted with a 6 volt 3 watt single contact bulb (Lucas No. 200). The portion of the lamp carrying the red glass can be removed by pushing in and turning to the left. When refitting, engage the bayonet fixing, push in and turn to the right to secure the body in position.

The correct bulb is a 6 volt, 3 watt S.B.C. Lucas No. 200.

107. CABLES.

Before making any alterations to the wiring or removing the switch from the headlamp, disconnect the positive lead at the battery to avoid the danger of short circuits.

The lead, about 1 foot long, from the positive battery terminal, is connected to the lead from the switch by means of a brass connector.

The connector is insulated by a rubber sleeve, which must be pushed back to allow the connector to be unscrewed.

Do not allow the brass connector to touch any metal part of the engine as this will short circuit the battery.

When connecting up again, pull the rubber sleeve over the connector.

108. LIGHTING SWITCH.

All leads to the headlamp are taken direct to the switch, which, together with the ammeter, is incorporated in a small panel.

The panel can be removed when the three fixing screws are withdrawn.

The ends of all the cables are identified by means of coloured sleevings.

The colour scheme and the diagram of connections are shown in the wiring diagram.

109. HORN.

Electric horns are adjusted to give their best performance before leaving the works and will give a long period of service without any attention.

If the horn becomes uncertain in action, or does not vibrate, it has not necessarily broken down.

The trouble may be due to a discharged battery or a loose connection, or short circuit in the wiring of the horn.

The performance of the horn may be upset by the fixing bolt working loose, or by the vibration of some part adjacent to the horn.

To check this, remove the horn from its mounting, hold it firmly in the hand by its bracket, and press the push.

If the note is still unsatisfactory, the horn may require adjustment and should be taken to a Lucas Service Station.

110. SPARKING PLUG.

Clean periodically by dismantling and removing all carbon from the electrodes. Scrape inside of plug body clean of carbon, reassemble and set gap at .015in.-.020in.

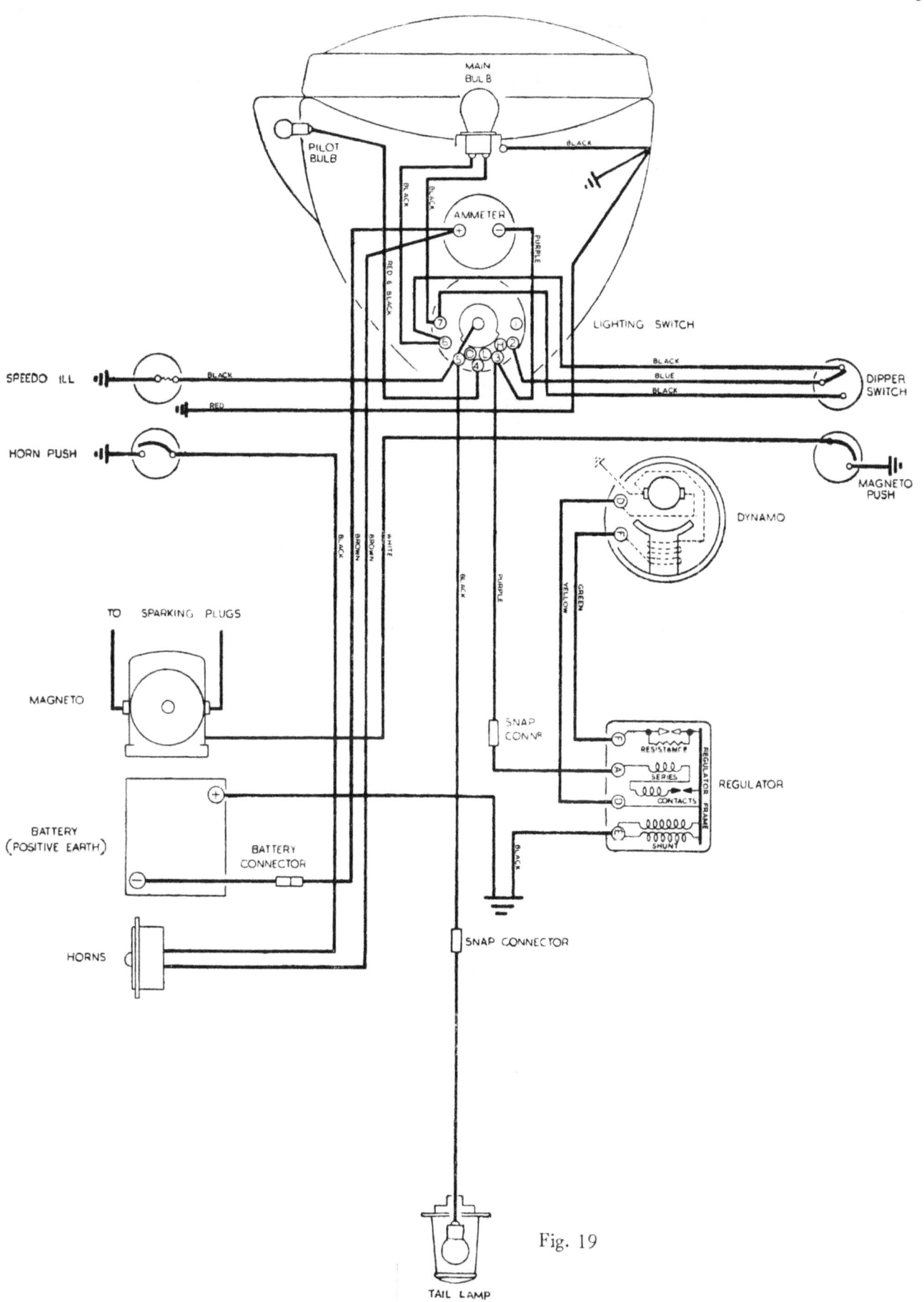

Fig. 19

WIRING DIAGRAM FOR LUCAS ELECTRICAL EQUIPMENT.

LOCATING AND RECTIFYING POSSIBLE TROUBLES.

TROUBLE.	POSSIBLE CAUSE.	REMEDY.
Failure to start.	Over flooding.	Open twist grip and kick vigorously a few times.
	Weak mixture due to failure to close air lever (if cold).	Ensure that air slide falls as lever is shut.
	Broken throttle cable.	Ensure that throttle slide rises as twist grip is rotated.
	Lack of fuel.	Check that there is petrol in tank.
	Failure of fuel to reach mixing chamber.	Check that petrol taps, or tap, is in the "on" position and that petrol is flowing through. Clean carburetter.
	Contact breaker points dirty or out of adjustment. Pick up brush work. Slip ring oily. Moisture in magneto.	Remove high tension lead from one plug and hold end about ⅛in. from cylinder whilst revolving engine. If no spark, examine contact breaker points, clean, check gap. Examine pick up and clean slip ring.
Firing on one cylinder.	Faulty plug. Faulty high tension lead. Water on plug.	Change plug. Examine high tension lead, renew if necessary.
Erratic slow running.	Pilot air screw requires resetting.	Adjust as para. 84.
	Air leaks from carburetter joint or sparking plug.	Check joint washer and nuts for tightness. Check plug for tightness.
	Faulty valve seats.	Examine and re-grind as necessary.
	Worn inlet valve or guides.	Dismantle, check and renew as necessary.
Loss of power.	No tappet clearance.	Check and reset as necessary.
	Broken piston rings.	Examine and replace.
	Loose carbon on valve seat.	Can often be removed by kicking engine over a few times.
	Tight front chain.	Examine and adjust.
Excessive oil consumption.	Broken piston rings. Worn cylinder block.	Examine and make necessary replacements.
	Oil not returning to tank, due to:— Stoppage in oil way; pump drive failed; pump gears fouled by foreign matter.	Trace through and clean out or take any other action necessary.
Engine runs harshly.	Tight chains.	Check and adjust.
Engine cuts out at large throttle openings.	Dirt in carburetter.	Dismantle and clean.
	Dirt in petrol tap.	Remove petrol taps and clean.
	Dirt in filters.	Have magneto examined by experts.
	Condenser in magneto broken down.	
Loss of oil pressure.	Oil overheated or unsuitable.	Drain and refill with fresh oil of correct grade.
	Oil pump nipple washer failed.	Examine and renew.
	Timing side oil seal worn or collapsed.	Examine and renew.
	Pressure release valve plunger stuck.	Examine, clean and free off.

LOCATING AND RECTIFYING POSSIBLE TROUBLES.

TROUBLE.	POSSIBLE CAUSES.	REMEDY.
Inefficient Brakes. (Front or Rear).	Grease on lining.	Examine and wash in petrol. Do not wash in paraffin.
	Tightness in mechanism.	Make sure that cam is free in its bearing and pedal not binding on spindle due to mud.
Slipping Clutch.	Cable adjusted too tightly.	Re-adjust cable until there is some movement on handle-bar lever before clutch operates.
	Inner cable too long. Clutch worm lever fouling gear box casing.	Shorten and re-adjust.
	Oil on plates (usually caused by overfilling oil bath).	Dismantle clutch plates and wash in petrol.
	Tightness in operating mechanism.	Examine, clean and free off as necessary.
Clutch Hard to Free.	Clutch cable adjuster screwed right out, clutch worm lever not at correct angle and therefore not having a straight pull.	Re-set clutch worm lever to give straight pull. Shorten inner cable and re-adjust.
Gear-Changing Accompanied by Excessive Noise.	Slack rear chain.	Adjust as necessary.
Footchange Lever hard to Operate.	Footchange requires greasing.	Nipple on indicator retaining screw.
Failure of Footchange Lever to Return to Normal Position.	Broken hairpin return spring.	Remove positive mechanism cover and front plate. Examine spring, renew as required.
Steering Rolls or Wanders.	Loose head adjustment.	
Steering Poor on Corners with tendency for Machine to Lie over too much.	Loose fork adjustment.	
Twist Grip Closes if Released.	Tension requires adjusting.	Screw in adjuster one or two turns.
Steering appears Tight on Corners.	Steering damper binding, caused by bent frame anchor bracket.	Remove anchor bracket and re-set to correct angle.

NOTES

Maintenance Manual and Instruction Book

FOR

The Unapproachable

REGD. TRADE MARK

MOTOR CYCLE

Models No. 88, 99, 650, Sports Specials, Manxman & Mercury

(Pages Extracted From Factory Publication P106/P)

NORTON VILLIERS LIMITED

NORTON MATCHLESS DIVISION

PLUMSTEAD ROAD, WOOLWICH
LONDON, S.E.18, ENGLAND

Telephone: WOOlwich 1223

IMPORTANT INFORMATION RELATING TO THE CONTENTS OF THIS MANUAL

The first section of this manual includes a copy of the P80 manual (dated 1958) for the 1949-1955 Model 7 that covers both the spring frame (plunger) and swing arm models.

The pages in the second section of this manual were extracted from the P106/P Norton factory publication 'Maintenance Manual and Instruction Book' dated 1970 for the Model 50, ES2, 88, 99, 650, Sports Specials, 750 Atlas & 750 Scrambler. The publication of these combination manuals began in 1960 with the P101 manual followed by the P106 and finally the P106/P manual of 1970. While these 'combination' manuals made publication less expensive than those for individual models the information for multiple different motorcycles is often merged together. Consequently, separating out the appropriate data for a specific model, or series of motorcycles, is a time wasting and confusing exercise. Even more unfortunately, the P106/P manual makes no reference to the model years that are covered.

The earliest dates referenced in the 1970 - P106/P manual are piston sizes for the 1955-1958 Model 88 and a wiring diagram for the 1956-1957 Dominator 88 and 99 models. Therefore, we can assume that the P106/P manual was intended to cover the 1956 to 1970 Dominator models. Unfortunately, as there never was a '1949-1970 Dominator only' manual issued by the factory, we have extracted the information that is exclusive to the 1956-1970 Dominator series from the P106/P manual. However, this means that the paragraphs and illustrations in the P106/P section may no longer be sequentially numbered and we request you overlook this minor issue as it does not affect the correctness of the data in any way.

When the P80 and P106/P manuals are used in conjunction with the three illustrated parts lists included in this publication, they provide a comprehensive maintenance and repair manual exclusive to the 1949-1970 Norton Dominator series.

Index

	Page
Amal Monoblock Carburetter	40
Amal Concentric Carburetter	70
Capacitor - Ignition System	63
Cleaning	8
Controls	9
Data	4, 5, 6
Electrical Section	43
Engine	11
Front Forks	35
Gearbox	28
Handlebar Fittings	39

	Page
Introduction	7
Locating and Rectifying possible troubles	72, 73
Lubrication	8
Notes	52, 53, 54
Rear Springing	38
Running-in	8
Transmission	23
Tyres	42
Wheels, Hubs and Brakes	32
1967 Models	60

	Paragraph
Alternator	122
Battery	129
Brakes	98, 99
Big End Bearings—renewal	33
Camshaft Bushes, removal and replacement	36
Carbon removal	10
Carburetter, dismantling	111
Carburetter, assembly	112
Carburetter, maintenance	114
Carburetter, rich mixture	115
Carburetter, tuning	113
Carburetter, weak mixture	116
Chain adjustment	71
Clutch, adjustment	72
Clutch, assembly	76
Clutch, dismantling	74
Clutch, examination of parts	75
Crankshaft, dismantling and re-assembly	34
Crankshaft, removal and fitting	32
Cylinder Block, removal	18
Cylinder Block, fitting	23
Cylinder Head, removal	9
Cylinder Head, fitting	15
Electrical Section	120 to 137
Electrical Wiring Diagrams	Pages 55 to 59, 62, 66
Engine, removal from frame	31
Foot Change, dismantling and assembly	80, 81
Forks, Front, maintenance	100
Forks, Front, removal	102
Forks, Front, refitting	103
Forks, Front, dismantling	104
Forks, Front, assembly	105
Forks, Rear, pivoted removal and assembly	106
Gearbox	77 to 89
Gear Intermediate Spindle and Bush	38
Handlebar fittings	108, 109, 110
Headlamp	130
Hubs, dismantling	94, 96
Hubs, assembly	95, 97

	Paragraph
Ignition	121
Ignition Timing, coil ignition models	30a
Ignition Timing, magneto models	30b
Lubrication System	1
Magneto	136
Main Bearings, removal and replacement	37
Oil Bath, removal and fitting	73
Oil Circulation	5
Oil Filters	2
Oil Level	4
Oil Pressure	6
Oil Pump	3, 27
Oil Pump, removal and fitting	26
Oil Seal, Big End	39
Petrol Tank, removal and fitting	7, 8
Pistons, fitting	21
Pistons, removal	19
Piston Rings, removal	20
Plug, Sparking	135
Rocker (Tappet), adjustment	16
Rocker, removal and fitting	17
Small End Bush, removal and fitting	35
Steering Head, adjustment	101
Suspension, rear	107
Tappets, removal and fitting	22
Timing Cover, removal and fitting	24
Timing Sprockets and Chains	28, 29
Tyres, maintenance	117
Tyres, removal	118
Tyres, fitting	119
Valves, grinding	12
Valves, removal	11
Valve Guides, removal and fitting	14
Valve Pressure Relief, removal and fitting	25
Wheels, removal	90, 92
Wheels, fitting	91, 93

Data

IDENTIFICATION MARKS. Engine No. and Prefix numbers stamped on driving side of crankcase below cylinder base flange. Frame No. stamped on left hand frame gusset below battery box. Should be the same as the Engine No. Quote fully when writing or ordering spares.

	Model 88	Model 99
Bore	66 mm. (2.598″)	68 mm. (2.677″)
Stroke	72.6 mm. (2.859″)	82 mm. (3.228″)
Capacity	497 cc. (30.384 cu. in.)	597 cc. (36.485 cu. in.)
Compression Ratio ...	8.5 to 1	8.2 to 1
Sparking Plug	KLG. FE75 or FE80 Lodge 2HLN. Champion N5.	KLG. FE75 or FE80 Lodge 2HLN. Champion N5.
IGNITION TIMING		
B.T.D.C. fully advanced	30° ¼″ 6.35 mm.	32° .307″ 7.8 mm.
VALVE TIMING	Marked on all engines. Mesh gears and sprockets as instructed. Push rods to be free to rotate without up and down movement with piston on compression stroke.	
Tappet clearance cold		
Inlet	.003″	.003″
Exhaust	.005″	.005″
AMAL CARBURETTER		
Type	Monobloc 376	Monobloc 376
Main Jet	**240**	250
Throttle Valves	3½	3
Needle Jet	106	106
Needle position	2	3
Pilot Jet	30	25
Choke Size	1″	1 1/16″
ENGINE SPROCKET		
Solo	19T	20T
Sidecar	17T	18T
GEAR RATIOS		
Solo	5.00, 6.1, 8.5 and 12.75, to 1	4.75, 5.8, 8.08 and 12.16, to 1
Sidecar	5.59, 6.8, 9.5 and 14.28, to 1	5.28, 6.45, 8.97 and 13.45, to 1
CHAINS		
Primary	½″ × .305″ × 75 rollers	½″ × .305″ × 75 rollers
Rear	⅝″ × ¼″ × 98 rollers	⅝″ × ¼″ × 97 rollers
Distributor/Magneto ...	⅜″ × 6/32″ × 42 rollers	⅜″ × 5/32″ × 42 rollers
Camshaft	⅜″ × .225″ × 38 rollers	⅜″ × .225″ × 38 rollers
Petrol Tank Capacity		
Oil Tank Working Capacity		
Tyre size front	3.00″ × 19″	3.00″ × 19″
Tyre size rear	3.50″ × 19″	3.50″ × 19″
Tyre pressure front solo...	25 lbs. p.s.i.	25 lbs. p.s.i.
Tyre pressure rear solo ...	22 lbs. p.s.i.	22 lbs. p.s.i.
Weight dry	390 lbs. approx.	395 lbs. approx.

Data

IDENTIFICATION MARKS. Engine No. and Prefix numbers stamped on driving side of crankcase below cylinder base flange. Frame No. stamped on left hand frame gusset below battery box. Should be the same as the Engine No. Quote fully when writing or ordering spares.

	Model 650	Remarks
Bore	68 mm. (2.677″)	
Stroke	89 mm. (3.503″)	
Capacity	646 cc. (39.446 cu. in.)	
Compression Ratio	9 to 1	1962 Model 88 S.S., 9.45 to 1.
Sparking Plug	KLG. FE75 or FE80	S.S. Models KLG. FE80 or FE100.
	Lodge 2HLN.	Lodge 2HLN or 3HLN.
	Champion N5.	Champion N4.

IGNITION TIMING
B.T.D.C. fully advanced — 32° .343″ 8.69 mm.

VALVE TIMING — Marked on all engines. Mesh gears and sprockets as instructed. Push rods to be free to rotate without up and down movement with piston on compression stroke.

Tappet clearance cold
- Inlet .006″
- Exhaust .008″

88 and 99 S.S. Model .006″ inlet .008″ exhaust. When setting tappet adjustment on all twin cylinder models, opposite similar valve to one being adjusted to be exactly wide open.

AMAL CARBURETTER

Type	Monobloc 376 (twin carbs.) 389 (single).	
Main Jet	250 (twin carbs.) 320 (single)	Regard these sizes as min., use one or two sizes larger for prolonged full throttle work.
Throttle Valves	3½ ,, ,, 3 ,,	
Needle Jet	106 ,, ,, 105 ,,	
Needle position	3 ,, ,, 2 ,,	
Pilot Jet	25 ,, ,, 25 ,,	
Choke Size	1 1/16″ ,, ,, 1 1/8″ ,,	Model 88 S.S. 1 1/16″.

ENGINE SPROCKET
Solo	21T	Sidecar sprocket sizes are approx. and may vary one tooth up or down.
Sidecar	19T	

GEAR RATIOS
- Solo — 4.53, 5.52, 7.57, and 11.6, to 1
- Sidecar — 5.00, 6.1, 8.5 and 12.75, to 1

CHAINS
- Primary — ½″ × .305″ × 76 rollers
- Rear — ⅝″ × ¼″ × 97 rollers
- Distributor/Magneto — ⅜″ × 5/32″ × 42 rollers
- Camshaft — ⅜″ × .225″ × 38 rollers

Petrol Tank Capacity		650 American Model 2½ gallons approx.
Oil Tank Working Capacity		
Tyre size front	3.00″ × 19″	650 American 3.25″ × 19″
Tyre size rear	3.50″ × 19″	650 American 4.00″ × 18″
Tyre pressure front solo	25 lbs. p.s.i	
Tyre pressure rear solo	22 lbs. p.s.i	650 American 24 lbs. p.s.i ⎫ S.S. Models see note
Weight dry	408 lbs. approx.	650 American 20 lbs. p.s.i ⎭ after Para. 119.

Data

IDENTIFICATION MARKS. Engine No. and Prefix numbers stamped on driving side of crankcase below cylinder base flange. Frame No. stamped on left hand frame gusset below battery box. Should be the same as the Engine No. Quote fully when writing or ordering spares.

	650 MANXMAN
CYLINDER BARREL	
Finished bore size	2.6786"/2.6780"
Tappet bore size	1.1875"/1.1865"
Tappet guide bore	Guides not used
INLET VALVE	
Head diameter	1.406"
Stem diameter	.310"/.309"
EXHAUST VALVE	
Head diameter	1.312"
Stem diameter	.310"/.309"
VALVE GUIDES	
(In. & Ex.) bore size	.3145"/.3135"
GUDGEON PIN	
O/dia.	.6868"/.6866"
SMALL END	
Bore of Con. Rod eye (no bush fitted)	.6878"/.6873"
PISTON RING GAP	
Compression	.014"/.009"
Oil scraper	.014"/.009"
ROCKER SPINDLES	
O/Dia.	.499"/.4985"
ROCKERS	
Bore Dia.	.5003"/.4998"
PUSH RODS	
Overall length Inlet	8.194"
Overall length Exhaust	7.351"
VALVE SPRINGS	
Free length—Inner	1.531"
Free length—Outer	1.700"
CRANKSHAFT	
Journal dia. D.S.	1.1815"/1.1812"
Journal dia. T.S.	1.1812"/1.1807"
Journal dia. Big End	1.7505"/1.7500"
CAMSHAFT	
Bearing Dia.	.874"/.8735"
	.8735"/.873"
Bore of Bushes	.875"/.8745"
MAIN BEARINGS	
Driving side	R330L- (3 DOT) 30 × 72 × 19
Timing side	MJ30- 30 × 72 × 19
PRESSURE RELIEF VALVE SPRING	
Free length	1.171"
O/Dia.	.435"/.430"
INTERMEDIATE GEAR	
Shaft Dia.	.5615"/.5610"
Bore of Bush	.5625"/.5620"
TORQUE SPANNER LOADINGS	
Big End Cap Nuts	15 lb. ft.
Cylinder head nuts	25 lb. ft.

Introduction

In preparing these instructions the elementary details and preliminary information that may be necessary to the absolute novice have been omitted, on the assumption that the majority of NORTON owners are already acquainted with the elementary details of starting, driving and maintenance. In connection with the latter we would stress the advisability of cultivating the habit of routine cleaning, lubrication, examination and adjustment of your machine. By this means many minor annoyances will be avoided and major breakdowns averted, and you will acquire the pride of ownership which marks the true enthusiast.

Below is a plan view of the machine with all controls clearly indicated. A short study of this will familiarise you with the position and function of each control.

To start the engine from cold, turn on the petrol and very slightly flood the carburetter, until petrol seeps from the top of the float chamber.

On coil ignition models, turn the ignition key in the top of the headlamp switch in a clockwise direction to 'IGN'. In cold conditions, close or partly close the air lever, this should however, be fully opened as soon as possible after the engine has started.

Machines with magneto ignition have a cut-out button for stopping the engine, this is similar to a horn button and is fitted on the handlebar.

With coil ignition machines, always remember to TURN OFF THE IGNITION AND REMOVE THE KEY when leaving the machine.

Should the battery become run down the engine can be started, either by turning the key to 'EMG' position, when a far more 'hefty' kick is required than when starting normally, or by push starting in say 2nd gear with the switch in the normal ignition position.

When an engine with Lucas equipment has been started in 'EMG' switch position, it must be immediately switched over to normal 'IGN', otherwise damage to contact points and condenser will result.

A flat battery can be recharged at an increased rate by the procedure outlined under the heading of Increased Charging in the electrical section.

All models provide for a reserve fuel supply. The single petrol tap is of the two positional type, the knurled circular knob being pulled out for normal running and turned and pulled a further amount when the reserve is required. The reserve should supply fuel for about 5 to 8 miles dependant upon how the machine is driven.

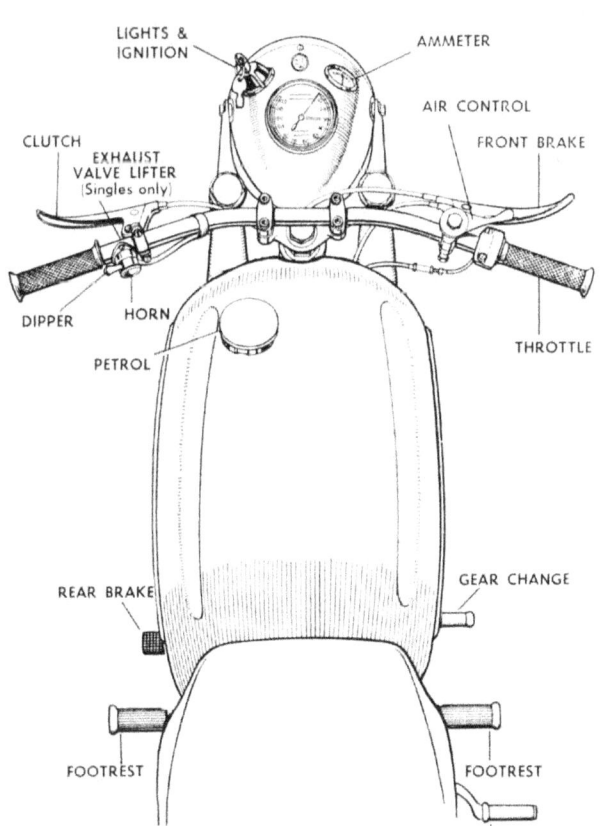

Fig 1

Running-In

Although the machine will have been greased up and all points requiring oil will have been dealt with at the works, prior to the road test, it is always a safe policy to ensure that there is adequate oil in the oil tank, gearbox and oilbath chaincase. Remember to remove the level plug from the chaincase before topping up.

Immediately the engine has been started, remove the oil tank filler cap and check that the oil is circulating. If the machine has been standing, oil should be returning in a constant stream and should be visible on looking in the filler orifice. After a few moments, when the return pump has scavenged the sump clear of oil having collected there during standing, the stream will become intermittent.

The first 1000 miles in the life of a new machine are of the utmost importance and the advisability of careful running-in cannot be overstressed. At no time during the first 500 miles, should the throttle be more than $\frac{1}{4}$ to $\frac{1}{3}$ open and care should be taken to avoid labouring of the engine by 'hanging on' to too high a gear when conditions warrant a change down.

This does not mean that road speeds should be strictly limited to 30 m.p.h. as a twin cylinder machine would achieve about 50 m.p.h. on little over $\frac{1}{8}$ throttle.

A high road speed is not detrimental if it is obtained without opening the throttle wide: for example, when going down hill. Speed can be varied quite appreciably, but the engine must always run lightly loaded.

When the 500 mile figure has been reached, short bursts of higher speed may be indulged in but allow the engine to reach these easily and progressively. When 1200 to 1500 miles have been covered, it should be possible to use the the machines full capabilities with safety.

Over-revving in the lower gears and violent acceleration should be avoided even when the machine is fully run-in—it merely reflects bad riding causing excessive noise and overloading of chains, clutch, gearbox, etc.

The use of running-in compound during the initial stages of the engine's life is strongly recommended. The compound, several brands of which are available and may be obtained from all Norton dealers, contains "colloidal graphite" which forms a graphoid surface on all working faces and greatly assists in preserving their high quality finish. The compound should be mixed with the lubricating oil in the proportion of one pint to one gallon of oil during running-in, but if its use is continued after this period, only half the quantity should be used. Remember that these are high efficiency engines which give of their best when running at relatively high revolutions and a change should be made to a lower gear immediately there are any signs of labouring. To obtain the best possible performance from your machine, full use should be made of the gearbox, which is quite capable of withstanding all the loads likely to be imposed upon it by normal use.

At the end of this book will be found a trouble tracing chart, reference to which will greatly facilitate the location and rectifying of any but the most unusual troubles which may be likely to cause an involuntary stop.

Cleaning

Before attempting to polish the enamel on any part of the machine, all traces of grit adhering to the various components should be washed off, preferably with a reasonably high pressure hose. Polish the enamel periodically with a good quality wax polish. Note that chromium plating is not impervious to rust and should be wiped down when possible, after being in the rain. Wash off any road grit and clean with one of the chromium polishes available from any garage. Do NOT use ordinary metal polish.

Lubrication

LUBRICANTS TO USE. Efficient lubrication is of vital importance and it is false economy to use cheap oils and grease. We recommend the following lubricants to use in machines of our make.

RECOMMENDED LUBRICANTS

Efficient lubrication is of vital importance and it is false economy to use cheap grades of oil. When buying oils or grease, it is advisable to specify the brand as well as the grade and, as an additional precaution, to buy from sealed containers.

ENGINE

Ambient temperature above 32° F use S.A.E. 20/50 or straight S.A.E. 30 oil.

Ambient temperature below 32° F use S.A.E. 10/30 or S.A.E. 20 oil.

The following brands are recommended:

Mobiloil, Castrol, Energol, Essolube, Shell, Regent Advanced Havoline.

GEARBOX

Ambient temperature above 32° F: S.A.E. 50 or GX90

Ambient temperature below 32° F: S.A.E. 30

HUB AND FRAME PARTS

Mobilgrease MP, Castrolease Heavy, Energrease C3, Regent Marfax, Shell Retinax A. or C.D.

TELEDRAULIC FRONT FORKS

Mobiloil Arctic (S.A.E. 20), Castrolite (S.A.E. 10W-30), Energol (S.A.E. 20), Essolube 20 (S.A.E. 20) Shell X-100 Motor Oil 20/20 W (S.A.E. 20)

REAR CHAINS

Mobilgrease MP, Esso Fluid Grease, Energrease A.O., Castrolease Grease Graphited

LUBRICATION CHART

Period	Location	Lubricant	Period	Location	Lubricant
Every 200 miles.	Oil tank, top up	Oil	Every 2000 miles.	Contact break spindle ES2 and 50	Oil
Every 1000 miles.	Control cables	Oil	Every 3000 miles.	Magneto C.B. rocker arm and cam ring	Oil
	Control levers	Oil	Every 5000 miles.	Gearbox, drain and refill	Oil
	Brake cable 'U' clip	Oil		Brake cams, cam spindles and shoe pivot pins	Grease
	Gearbox, top up	Oil			
	Oilbath, top up	Oil	Every 10,000 miles.		
Every 2000 miles.	Brake pedal	Grease		Front forks	See para. 100
	Brake rod jaw joints	Oil		Oilbath, drain and refill	Oil
	Speedo gearbox	Grease		Hub bearings, repack	Grease
	Drain and refill oil tank	Oil			

Controls

Throttle Twist Grip. On right handlebar. When shut, warm engine should continue to tick over by adjustment of cable and throttle stop on carburetter. Twist grip may be adjusted to close or remain open when released, as preferred.

Air Lever. On right handlebar. Close or partly close when starting from cold. Open as soon as engine will run properly with full air. Should remain open for normal running.

Gear Change Lever. Adjacent to right footrest. Engages the various gears (4) and neutral or free engine position between bottom and second gear. Move upward for first or bottom gear and downwards for all other gears. Use deliberate pressure—do not jab.

Kickstarter. Lever behind right footrest. Depress to rotate engine.

Steering Damper (when fitted). Knob or wing nut behind handlebar centre. Rotate clockwise to stiffen handlebar movement.

Front Brake Lever. On right handlebar. This is, perhaps, the most important control on the machine and its proper use should be mastered at the earliest opportunity. Because, when the brakes are applied, weight of rider and machine is transferred forward, more braking power can be applied to the front wheel before it will lock than to the rear. On a firm, dry surface, therefore, it will be found that the brake can be applied very hard without risk of locking the wheel. The rear brake should, of course, be applied at the same time, but in the case of an emergency stop you should not withdraw the clutch until the last moment before coming to rest, as otherwise the rear wheel may be locked causing the machine to skid.

The front brake should be adjusted so that the lever comes almost parallel with the handlebar when the brake is hard on and in this way with practice, it will be found that with the brake applied with the fingers, the twist grip can be operated with the inside of the thumb to make downward gear changes.

Different road conditions of course, call for modified braking technique and on a road away from the traffic, the rider should find out for himself how hard the brakes can be applied without locking either wheel. On a very wet road when grease and mud films have been washed away, it will be found that the front brake can be used hard without risk of a skid provided the machine is kept in a straight line. In damp greasy conditions, the brakes should only be 'caressed' and the machine slowed by use of the gearbox. On ice and snow the brakes should not be used at all and the machine should be allowed to roll to rest in a low gear.

When riding in traffic queues with many pedestrians about, you should ride with the front brake lever 'in your hand', you can then apply it as you think instead of having to 'find it' and consequently grab it.

Always remember that you cannot match the stopping power of a modern four wheeled vehicle if you do not use both brakes properly.

Clutch Lever. On left handlebar. Allows engine to run with gear engaged without forward movement of machine. Release gently to obtain forward motion.

Rear Brake Pedal. Adjacent to left footrest. It is important that this control should be properly adjusted so that when the brake is quickly applied the wheel is not suddenly locked. The pedal stop should be set so that with the rider normally seated with insteps on the footrests and left foot in a 'normal rotational' position on its rest, the pad is just below the ball of the foot. To apply the brake, it is then merely necessary to 'rotate' the foot to make contact with the pad. If the pedal pad is set too high, it becomes necessary to step on it which is dangerous apart from the rider having to ride 'splayed footed' since his boot must then be alongside the pedal pad instead of above it.

Lighting and Ignition Switch. Left hand top of headlamp body. Three positional rotating light switch—off, low and high. Central removable ignition key—OFF straight in line. Ignition ON, turn clockwise. Emergency starting, turn anti-clockwise.

Sports Special Models and others with Magneto Ignition have a lighting switch giving similar positions but without the ignition switch in the centre.

Headlamp Dipping Switch and Horn Push. Combined fitting on inside of left handlebar. It is desirable that when the dipper switch lever is in the 'UP' position, the main filament should be on, then when the switch lever is 'flipped down' the dipped beam is obtained. Remember that this is a very important control when riding at night and a light 'flicked' the wrong way at a critical moment of dazzle may cause an accident.

If the dip switch becomes non-positive in action, dismantle it and apply a spot of oil to the lever pivot and change over toggle.

THE ENGINE Twin Cylinder

1. ENGINE. LUBRICATION SYSTEM

This is of the dry sump type, the oil flows from the tank to the pump by gravity, assisted by suction from the feed side of the oil pump round the gears and is forced under pressure to various parts of the engine. It then drains to the lowest part of the crankcase and by suction from the return side of the pump, is lifted and pumped back to the oil tank. A connection is taken from the return pipe between pump and oil tank which feeds the overhead rocker gear.

2. OIL FILTERS

There are three filters in the lubrication system.

(1) A course mesh filter in the tank itself.

(2) A small 'cigarette' type filter is incorporated in the pressure release valve on standard models. Removal of the hexagon plug from the rear edge of the timing cover exposes the filter and its attached spring. This filter is not to be found on S.S. models which have the earlier timing cover suitable for rev-meter drive. These have a larger pressure relief valve which can be unscrewed complete from the timing cover and which has a fine mesh gauze over its inner end to prevent foreign matter from causing the valve to stick.

(3) A large 'corrugated gauze' filter in a bronze plug in the crankcase sump.

The purpose of the tank filter is to ensure that the feed to the engine is never blocked by a large foreign body. It is of coarse mesh and large dimensions so as not to restrict the flow of cold oil. It need not be removed when the oil is changed, it is better on all models to remove the tank complete from the machine and wash it out thoroughly with paraffin or petrol at say every 2nd or 3rd oil change. The filter is then automatically cleaned without removal and does not have its joint disturbed. The relief valve filters need not normally be disturbed except when the engine undergoes a major overhaul.

The sump filter is the most important and should be removed and cleaned when the oil is changed except when a quick oil change is done at a roadside garage.

The filter body has a $\frac{7}{8}$" Whit. hexagon and a right hand thread and the gauze is secured in it by an aluminium washer and steel wire circlip. Dismantle and wash in petrol and examine for metal particles. Take care on re-assembly that the circlip is properly home in its recess.

Note that when the sump filter is removed for cleaning, about $\frac{1}{2}$ pint of oil will come out and a suitable receptacle should be placed underneath beforehand.

3. ENGINE OIL PUMP

This is of the gear type. The pump contains two pairs of gears, one on the feed side and the other on the return side.

The gears on the return side are twice the width of those on the feed, having twice the pumping capacity. This ensures that the crankcase is free from oil when the engine is running.

To check the return of the oil to the tank, remove the oil filler cap. The oil return pipe can then be seen. After the engine has been running for a few minutes, the oil return flow will be spasmodic, due to the greater capacity of the return gears.

4. OIL LEVEL

Maintain at or near the 'Recommended Oil Level' usually indicated by a transfer on the outside of the tank.

If the level is maintained higher than this, the excess may be discharged via the oil tank breather pipe, especially at high speeds and cause over oiling of the rear chain and oil to be deposited on the rear tyre.

Conversely, if the machine is used mainly about town without much high speed work, then the rear chain may not receive sufficient oil. Under these conditions, a higher level should be maintained. See also under 'Chain Maintenance'.

Always run the engine for a few minutes before checking oil level. It is possible when an engine has been idle for any length of time for the oil to drain through the pump into the sump.

When this happens, all the oil is returned to the tank in the first few minutes that the engine is running. In some cases after very long standing, there may be so much oil in the sump, that some will be discharged via the crankcase breather before the return pump has fully scavenged the sump.

If the oil level in the tank is allowed to become too low, then there is risk of over-

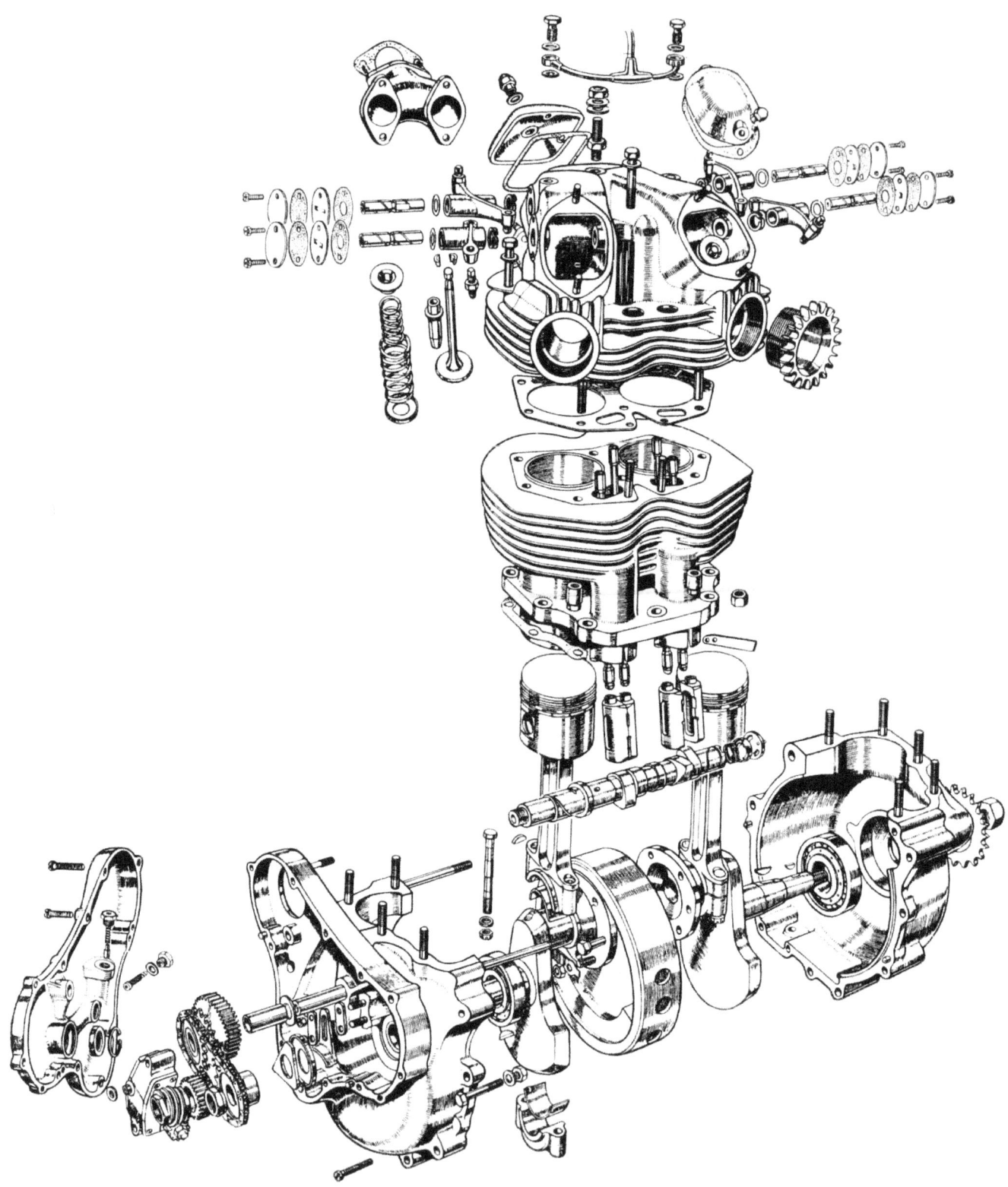

Fig. 2

heating due to the relatively small quantity which is in circulation.

5. CIRCULATION OF THE OIL

The pump makes an oil tight joint with the timing cover by means of a synthetic rubber washer under compression.

Oil passes from the pump through drilled oil ways in the timing cover to the hollow timing side mainshaft, an extension of which rotates in an oil seal located in the cover. The built up crankshaft (Fig. 2) is suitably drilled to convey oil under pressure to the plain big ends. Surplus oil escaping from the pressure release valve into the timing cover builds up to a pre-determined level to lubricate the gears and timing chains, afterwards draining into the sump via a drilled hole. A lead from the oil return pipe (external) conveys oil to the hollow o.h.v. rocker spindles, push rod ends and valve guides, surplus oil returning to the sump via a drilled hole in the rear of the timing side cylinder.

Pressure release valve depicted in Fig. 5 is pre-set and is non-adjustable. A timed breather working at the inner end of the camshaft (Fig. 2) controls the crankcase pressure. Any oil escaping from this source being conducted to the ground.

6. OIL PRESSURE

Since no pressure gauge or indicator is fitted, the only check that oil is circulating is an inspection through the oil tank filler orifice. With the engine running an intermittent stream of oil will be seen returning into the tank, the surface of the oil being covered with bubbles.

On S.S. models with the old type timing cover, there is a $\frac{1}{16}$" B.S.F. set screw below the relief valve and a pressure check can be made from here using a rocker box banjo bolt which has the same thread, and a suitable banjo with which to connect the gauge. On standard and de Luxe models it is not possible to do this without drilling and tapping the filter holder. A pressure check should be made with the oil hot as there is almost certain to be adequate pressure with cold oil.

With oil at normal working temperature and engine ticking over, there should be a minimum pressure of some 5 lbs. which should increase progressively with rising r.p.m. The ultimate pressure being dependant on engine condition and state and/or grade of oil.

Periodically, when the engine is ticking over, place a finger over the hole in the return pipe in the oil tank. This will send more oil to the rocker mechanism and serve to flush out the small holes that feed oil to the rocker ball ends.

7. PETROL TANK—REMOVAL

Ensure that the petrol tap is in the off position. Disconnect the petrol pipe using two spanners if necessary, holding the tap with one whilst releasing the union nut with the other.

Remove the dualseat by releasing the single Dzus fastener at the back, then lift the seat and withdraw rearwards from the two pegs on the frame at the front. These carry the seat by means of rubber bushes secured to its underside.

Release the single rubber band which secures the tank at the rear and unscrew the two inverted bolts at the front.

These have rubber washers above and below the lugs on the frame, the lower ones being in steel cups and the upper ones having a plain steel washer between them and the tank itself.

The bolts are shouldered so that when fully tightened the rubber washers are not over compressed.

The tank can now be lifted clear.

8. PETROL TANK—REFITTING

Check that the two rubber pads on which the tank rests at the rear and which are taped to the frame tubes, are so positioned that the tank does not make metallic contact with the frame. Refit the two bolts with their cups, rubbers and washers at the front and pull the rubber band over the hook at the rear.

Refit the petrol pipe and do not overtighten the union nut as otherwise the tap may unscrew when the pipe is next disconnected. Refit dualseat.

9. CYLINDER HEAD REMOVAL

Remove petrol tank (para. 7). Remove carburetter, leaving it attached to the machine by the throttle cable only. Remove exhaust pipes and silencers complete as a unit from each side of the machine. Remove high tension leads from sparking plugs and engine steady stay from the top of the rocker box. Disconnect oil feed pipe to rocker mechanism by unscrewing the two banjo connection bolts on the extreme top of the rocker box.

There are five bolt heads visible above the cylinder head finning and two nuts between the exhaust ports. In addition there are three nuts accessible through the cylinder finning, one beneath the inlet ports and one under each exhaust port.

Removal of these nuts and bolts should enable the head to be lifted off. If the joint is tight a light blow beneath the exhaust port with a mallet or a block of wood should effectively release it. Lift the head and ensure that the gasket is either coming away clean with the head or remaining in position on top of the cylinder block. Lift the head as far as possible and obtain assistance to feed the four push rods into the head until they are clear of the cylinder block when the head may be tilted backwards and completely withdrawn.

10. REMOVAL OF CARBON

The piston crowns will now be exposed and the engine should be rotated until the pistons are on top dead centre. Carefully scrape the carbon from the piston crown, using a blunt knife or similar tool, taking care to avoid scratching or cutting the piston material. Deal similarly with the combustion chambers and valve ports although these cannot be thoroughly cleaned without removing the valves.

11. VALVE REMOVAL

With the cylinder head removed, the rocker box caps taken off and the stud securing the inlet rocker cover also removed, the rockers may be rotated sufficiently clear of the valve stem to enable a normal Universal type valve spring compressor to be used for compressing the springs and removing the cotters. Each valve together with its springs, top and bottom collars, collets and heat insulating washers should be carefully placed on one side so that it may be refitted in the original position.

Note that the inlet valves have appreciably larger heads than the exhausts.

12. VALVE GRINDING

Remove all the carbon from the valve heads and stems, polish with emery tape in a drilling machine if available.

Lightly smear the seat portion with medium grinding compound, place the valve in the guide and grind lightly, using a rubber sucker on the valve head or valve grinding tool on the stem. Rotate to and fro frequently lifting the valve to redistribute the compound.

Do not over grind, as soon as the grinding marks make a complete ring on valve and head cease operations and remove all traces of compound. If the seats are not badly pitted, the use of fine paste only may be sufficient, but if the reverse is the case it may be impossible to obtain a perfect seat by grinding.

The seats will then have to be recut and the valves refaced or renewed.

13. VALVES—FITTING

Thoroughly clean valves, seats and ports. Lubricate valve stem and fit valve, fit heat resisting washer, bottom spring collar, springs, and top collar over valve guide. Compress springs and fit cotters. A little thick grease smeared on the inside of the cotters will hold them in position until the spring is released.

14. VALVE GUIDES—REMOVAL AND FITTING

Valve guides are removed and fitted with a double diameter drift. This should be of mild steel, 6 to 8 inches long, its smaller diameter should be an accurate fit in the bore of the guide and its outer diameter should be fractionally less than the O/D of the valve guide. The shoulder should of course, be turned square and the pilot or small diameter part should be almost as long as the valve guide itself.

The head must be heated to at least the temperature of boiling water and the old guides can be knocked out. If any work is to be done on the ports, it should be done before the new guides are fitted. In any case re-heat the head before they are fitted. The valve stem diameter new is .309"-.310" and the valve guide bore fitted is .3145"-.3135".

Valve seats must be re-cut when new guides are fitted.

15. CYLINDER HEAD—FITTING

If the cylinder head gasket has been removed, refit with the same face uppermost or renew. Rotate engine until pistons are on top dead centre. Place cylinder head on top of cylinder block and tilt it backwards whilst the pushrods are inserted into the two tunnels cast in the cylinder head. Note that the inlet pushrods are longer than the exhaust, and one of each, i.e., inlet and exhaust should be inserted into each tunnel, the long rods being nearer the centre, see Fig. 2.

Lower the head into position and allow the pushrods to fall on to the tappets as the head approaches its normal location.

When the head is within about ¼ in. of the cylinder joint face it should be supported in this position by using the two short sleeve nuts taken from beneath the exhaust ports as packing between the top fin of the cylinder block and the bottom cylinder head fin, placing them in a horizontal position between the fins whilst the rocker ball ends are entered

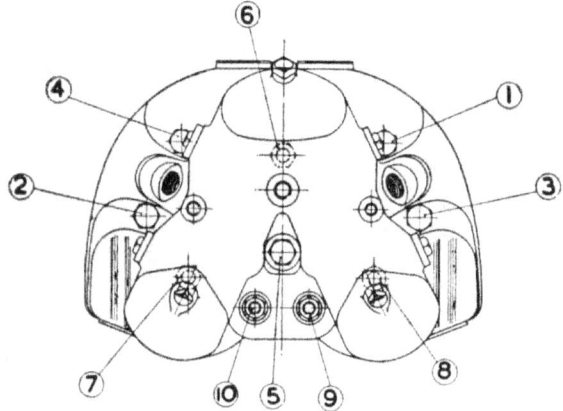

ORDER OF TIGHTENING DOWN CYLINDER HEAD NUTS & BOLTS.
Fig. 3

into the upper ends of the push rods. A piece of bent wire may be found useful for drawing the inlet push rod into position, access being obtained through the exhaust inspection apertures.

Remove temporary distance pieces and lower head on to joint face.

Ensure that rockers and push rods are in correct contact. Attach all nuts and bolts and pinch down lightly, finally tightening in the order shown in Fig 3.

16. ROCKER ADJUSTMENT
(Tappet adjustment)

Removal of the single nut securing the inlet rocker cover will provide access to both inlet rockers and enable the necessary feeler to be inserted between the rocker adjuster and valve stem end. Rotate the engine until the opposite inlet valve to the one about to be adjusted is exactly wide open. This is necessary because the cams on these engines have quietening ramps and in order to adjust with the tappet clear of the ramp it must be on the centre of the base circle.

To adjust the clearance, hold the squared end of the adjuster by means of the special spanner provided and slacken the locknut. Insert a .003″ feeler (.006″ S.S. models) and rotate the adjuster in a clockwise direction until the feeler is just pinched, but may still be moved about fairly easily. Hold the adjuster whilst tightening the locknut and re-check with the feeler. Now rotate the engine until this inlet valve is just fully open and adjust the opposite one.

Refit the rocker cover, ensuring that the joint washer is in good condition and correctly positioned. To adjust the exhaust tappets, remove both exhaust covers, and proceed as described above, setting one adjuster whilst the opposite valve is exactly wide open. Set to .005″ except on S.S. models when the clearance should be .008″.

Always re-check with the feeler after tightening the locknut and re-adjust if there is any doubt about the accuracy of the original setting.

For prolonged full throttle work with standard models, it is advisable to set tappets to S.S. clearances, i.e. In. .006″, Ex. .008″.

17. ROCKER REMOVAL and FITTING

Before removing or fitting rocker spindles, the cylinder head should be heated as for valve guide removal and fitting.

Remove inlet rocker inspection cover and cover securing stud. This latter may be with-

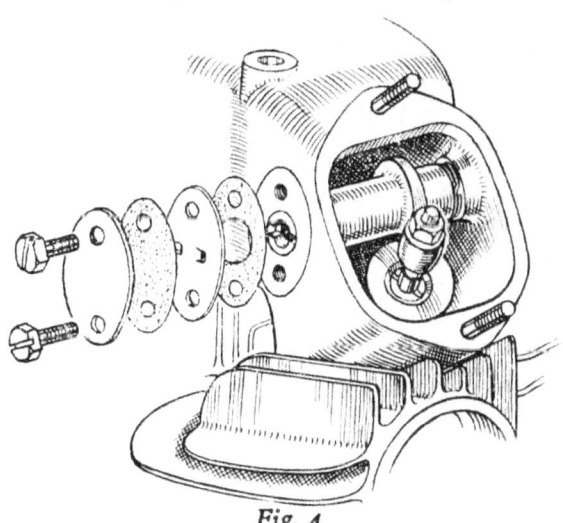

Fig. 4

drawn by locking two nuts on the outer end and rotating the lower of the nuts which should bring away the stud.

Remove the two screws securing the oval cover plates over the ends of the rocker spindle holes (Fig. 4). Note that the inner of these has two projections for locating the radial position of the spindle and that the spindle has a threaded hole at its outer end. A ⅕ in. × 26 thread bolt taken from some part of the machine may be used as an extractor bolt having first interposed a piece of tube or large nut between the cylinder head and the bolt.

Note that the rocker hub has a spring washer at one end and a plain thrust washer at the other. These may be either carefully removed before the rocker is extracted or allowed to fall when the rocker is removed. Having withdrawn the rocker until the hub is clear of the spindle hole bosses, it is necessary to turn upside down in order to withdraw it completely.

Removal of the exhaust rockers is carried out in an identical manner but is rather more simple since it is not necessary to invert the rocker in order to extract it.

It will be noticed that the rocker spindles have a "flat" on one side. The spindles should be fitted with all "flats" facing inwards to the centre of the engine and with the slot across the spindle end lying horizontal. The spindle should be a reasonable push fit in the head or tighter.

The end load put on by the spring washer will hold the assemby in position whilst inserting the spindle.

Fit paper washer to oval face by means of a smear of oil. Fit oval washer with tags engaged in spindle slot, fit another paper washer, followed by the plain oval washer and secure with two screws (Fig. 4).

18. CYLINDER BLOCK—REMOVAL

Remove petrol tank, para. 7.

Remove cylinder head, para. 9.

Remove the nine cylinder base nuts (seven large, two small). It is necessary to lift the block slightly before certain of these nuts can be removed completely. When lifting the block, avoid tearing the paper washer fitted to the crankcase joint.

19. PISTONS—REMOVAL

With the cylinder block removed and the pistons exposed, it will be apparent from the angular position of the valve head recesses in the piston crowns that the two pistons are not interchangeable, and if a new one is required for any reason, it will be necessary to specify whether a nearside (lefthand) or offside (righthand) is wanted.

To remove a piston, first extract the gudgeon pin retaining circlips by means of a pair of sharp nosed pliers and push out the gudgeon pin. If the engine is badly carboned up it may be desirable to scrape the carbon from the narrow land outside the circlip before attempting to remove the gudgeon pin. Be sure to mark the piston so that it may be replaced in its original position.

Gudgeon pins can best be removed or fitted by first heating the piston with a 'soft' flame or rag soaked in hot water.

20. PISTON RING REMOVAL AND FITTING

Unless new rings are being fitted it is not advisable to remove the carbon from the bottom of the ring groove or the back of the ring. When fitting new rings, remove all carbon from the piston by means of an old hacksaw blade or similar tool. When the grooves have been cleaned, check the new ring in the groove. There should be a side clearance of from .0015" to .0035". Check also the ring end gap by inserting the ring in the cylinder bore and pushing it down with a piston to ensure that it is lying square. The gap should be:

Compression rings, .008 in.—.010 in.
Scraper rings, .008 in—.010 in.

Check gap with feeler gauge.

Fitting instructions for special "Twiflex" oil control ring. 650 c.c. models only.

1. Make sure the grooves and oil drain holes are quite clean and then wind a rail on to the piston skirt just below the scraper ring groove.
2. Place expander in the groove with its ends butted and in line with pin hole. Great care must be taken to ensure the ends of the expander do not overlap. THEY MUST BUTT.
3. Slip the ends of the rail on the skirt into the groove beside the expander. The gap of rail should be 1" to left of butted ends of expander.
4. Do not, at this stage, push the back of the expander into the piston groove. Wind the other rail down over the lands into the scraper groove on the upper side of the expander with the gap 1" to the right of the butted ends of expander.
5. Now work the back of the expander down into the groove between the rails with the thumb nail. Centralise the ring on the piston, but do not move the assembly more than necessary.
6. The ring will now be complete in the groove with the rails supported on the lugs of the expander, and although it may feel somewhat stiff to move in the groove, this can be ignored.
7. Use an ordinary ring clamp to enter piston with rings into cylinder.

8. There is no need to check groove depths.

21. PISTONS—FITTING

Fit rings to piston, chromium plated top compression rings are now reversible unless marked 'top'. The 2nd compression ring is taper faced when new and is therefore marked 'top'. The scraper rings are reversible. Rings which have already been run, should always be re-fitted the same way up and on the same piston.

Space the ring gaps equally round the piston circumference. Fit one gudgeon pin circlip if both have been removed for dismantling. Unless great care has been taken in the removal of the circlips, it will be advisable to fit new ones.

Fit piston to connecting rod having first heated it as described for removal, ensuring that it is the correct way round and that the valve head recesses are lying in the right direction.

When both pistons are fitted, the forward recesses should be further apart than those at the rear of the engine. When fitting circlips, make certain that they are properly seated in the grooves.

22. TAPPETS—REMOVAL AND FITTING

It is most unlikely that the tappets will require any attention until a very large mileage has been covered. They are fitted into the cylinder block and are readily accessible when the block has been removed.

Invert the cylinder block, remove the wire securing the tappet division plate screws and remove the screws. This will enable the tappets and plate to be pushed out. If tight, a light blow on the opposite end of the tappets will effectively release the plate.

Note that the tappets must not be interchanged either singly or in pairs, nor should they be fitted the opposite way round.

The refitting is quite straightforward, remember to wire the division plate screws.

When tappets are correctly fitted their bevelled edges are together and to the front of the engine.

23. CYLINDER BLOCK FITTING

Clean both joint faces and ensure that the cylinder base paper washer is in good condition and is fitted so that the oil return hole is quite clear.

Fit piston ring compressors (obtainable from service department) to pistons, ensuring that the ring gaps are approximately equally spaced and that all are covered by the compressor. About $\frac{1}{8}$ in. of piston should stand above the compressor. Smear the cylinder bores with oil and feed the cylinder block over the pistons forcing the piston ring compressors down the piston until they fall from the bottom of the piston skirt. Remove the compressors and lower the block to within about $\frac{1}{4}$ in. of the joint, and replace the cylinder base nuts.

Completely lower the cylinder block and just pinch down the two nuts on either side of the block, tightening these in diagonal order. Tighten the three remaining large nuts, and finally the two $\frac{5}{16}$ in. nuts at the front of the block.

24. TIMING COVER REMOVAL AND FITTING

Remove the ten cheese-headed screws securing the cover which may then be withdrawn. If tight, lever gently behind the pressure release valve boss, and tap lightly with a wooden block on the opposite end of the cover. Take care not to lose the small rubber washer which forms the oil seal between the pump and the cover.

When refitting, ensure that both faces are quite clean and lightly smeared with jointing compound, preferably "Wellseal", which is non-hardening. Ensure also that the oil pump rubber sealing washer is in position. Take care not to damage the oil seal when entering the mainshaft into the cover, and do not press right home if there appears to be any obstruction. Refit all screws, just pinch each one down before finally tightening each pair of opposite screws.

25. PRESSURE RELIEF VALVE— REMOVAL AND FITTING

On standard models the pressure relief valve can only be completely dismantled when the timing cover is removed from the engine, although the filter can be withdrawn for cleaning by removing the external plug on the rear edge of the cover, without disturbing the cover itself. A glance at Fig. 5 makes the order and location of the various parts quite clear.

On S.S. models, the earlier type relief valve is used and this can be removed as a complete unit without disturbing the cover.

26. OIL PUMP—REMOVAL AND FITTING

Whilst the timing cover is removed, no

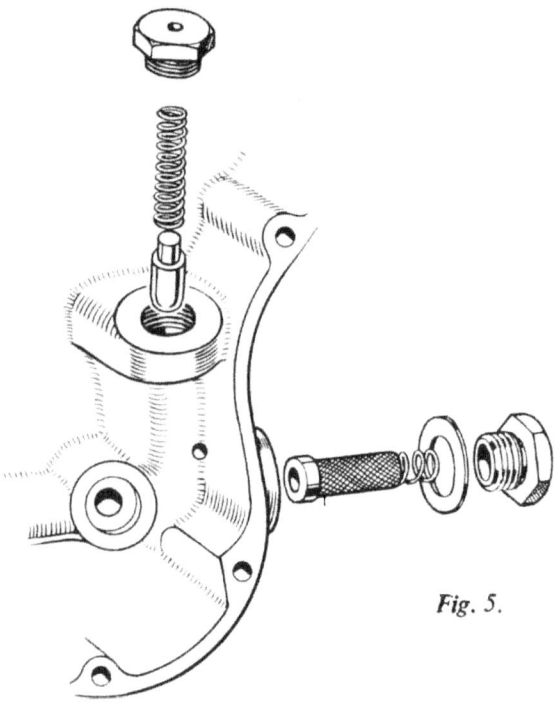

Fig. 5.

difficulty should be experienced in removing the oil pump, which is held only by the two nuts, situated one on either side of the pump body. When these are removed, the pump should be readily withdrawn from its studs, if tight, a gentle leverage may be applied behind the driving spindle.

Before replacing the pump, clean both faces, fit the pump and nuts (no washers) tightening each nut a turn at a time to ensure that the pump is held down evenly.

27. OIL PUMP

The oil pump should not be dismantled unless the oiling system is deranged. With the pump removed, pull and push on the worm nut, to test for end play, which should be nil. End play will cause a loss of oil pressure. The pump body face, where it abuts against the crankcase, must be perfectly flat, a slight bow here will let the pump suck air, affecting the oil return from the sump. Wear in the oil pump will allow oil to seep into the engine when left standing for any length of time. The pump should be returned for service if found to be unsatisfactory.

28. TIMING SPROCKETS AND CHAINS—REMOVAL

Before this work is undertaken it is most useful to have the use of a cut away dummy timing cover to support the intermediat gear spindle whilst the camshaft nut is slackened for dismantling and for tightening it on re-assembly (R.H. thread).

Also the special Norton timing pinion puller is required if it is intended to split the crankcase and remove the chankshaft assembly.

When removing the chains, it is necessary to withdraw the whole sprocket assembly with the chains in position as both are endless.

This cannot be done until the camshaft chain tension slipper and its clamping plates have been removed, the camshaft nut unscrewed, the oil pump driving worm unscrewed—L.H. thread, and the driving pin removed from the distributor spindle.

Care must be taken in removing and fitting the latter, a $\frac{1}{8}$ in. parallel pin punch is most suitable and as the pin is driven out the sprocket boss should be supported by a suitable weight from the opposite side. The pin can be used again but it should be replaced with a new one if there is any doubt about the way it fits when it is replaced and re-rivetted. Again, when rivetting, a weight such as a second hammer head should be held against one end of the pin whilst the other is being turned over.

Removal of the camshaft sprocket may require the use of a standard type sprocket puller, both this sprocket and the crankshaft pinion are on parallel shafts and not on tapers.

There is a hardened steel washer on the intermediate gear spindle between the gear and the crankcase.

29. TIMING SPROCKET AND CHAINS FITTING AND ADJUSTMENT

Fit oil retaining disc, flange to outside, and triangular washer to mainshaft, and fit half-time pinion key. Fit half-time pinion with the chamfered edge outside and tap home with a tubular drift. Fit hardened steel washer to intermediate shaft and fit the camshaft key. Rotate engine until the marked tooth on the half-time pinion is at T.D.C. Rotate the camshaft until the keyway is also at approximately T.D.C.

Place the distributor chain (the narrower of the two) on the inner of the two sprockets on the intermediate gear and the camshaft chain on the other. Rotate the gear until the marked space between teeth is at B.D.C.

(because the chains when fitted obscure this mark, mark the tooth on either side of it with crayon or pencil which will facilitate checking that it is correctly meshed with the crankshaft pinion).

This will give a marked sprocket tooth in the 11 o'clock position. The camshaft sprocket also has a marked tooth which should be at 11 o'clock when the chain is fitted to both sprockets.

Six outer plates inclusively on the camshaft chain should separate these marked teeth. See Fig. 6.

When the chains sprockets and gears are properly meshed, push them home on their shafts, fit camshaft nut, oil pump driving worm and chain tension slipper parts. The thinner of the two clamping plates goes on first with long end down, followed by the tensioner and the thicker plate with long end up. Fit fan disc washers and nuts and tighten lightly. Set camshaft chain tension so that there is ⅜ in. minimum up and down movement in the centre of the chain run at the tightest point. Tighten tensioner nuts and re-check. Do not set this chain too tight. Whilst this is being done the distributor sprocket should be pushed over the driving spindle making certain that the copper washer and tubular steel spacer are already on the spindle. Remove the distributor cap and place a finger on the rotor whilst the sprocket is pushed home.

Unlike the camshaft sprocket, it is possible to get the distributor sprocket clear of its spindle and re-mesh it with the chain if necessary without disturbing the intermediate gear.

Fit dummy timing cover and tighten cam-

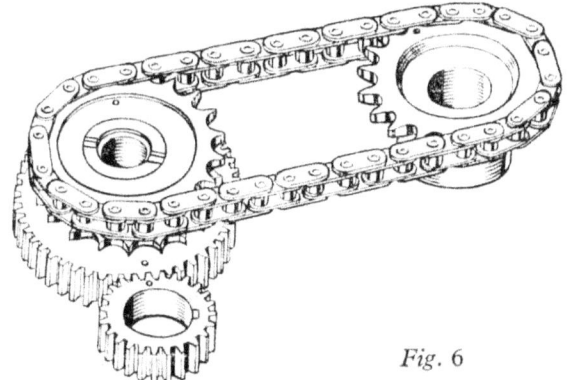

Fig. 6

shaft nut, tighten oil pump driving worm— L.H. thread.

On magneto ignition models, the automatic advance unit and driving sprocket should be meshed with its driving chain at the same time as the camshaft chain and sprocket assembly is pushed on to its shafts. It should be entered on the magneto armature spindle and the securing nut started a few threads prior to timing as described in next paragraph.

30a. IGNITION TIMING— COIL IGNITION MODELS (see also para. 121)

Before timing the ignition ensure that the distributor driving chain has ⅜ in. up and down movement in one run at its tightest point. A slack chain will upset the timing. Adjust as necessary by slackening the two Allen nuts near the upper edge of the distributor adaptor. A tap with a mallet or gentle leverage will pivot the assembly about the bottom stud sufficiently to allow for normal chain adjustment. Set the C.B. points gap to .015" when wide open. To set the timing remove the sparking plugs and rotate engine until the marked tooth on the camshaft sprocket is on top centre position. This will bring the pistons also to T.D.C. with the driving side on the firing stroke. The distributor should now be turned until the brass contact of its rotor is pointing directly downwards. Now note if the driving pin holes in sprocket and spindle line up. If they do not, ease sprocket off spindle and remesh it with the chain to the nearest tooth, push back on spindle and fit driving pin as described in para. 28.

Rotate the engine backwards until the piston is the required amount down the stroke before T.D.C. (see data page). Slacken the pinch bolt on the distributor clamp (this has a captive nut) and turning the rotor clockwise to the advanced position, slowly rotate the distributor body until the contact breaker points just separate. Tighten the clamping bolt and recheck. A thin strip of cigarette paper is useful for determining the exact position at which the points separate or it can be done electrically as follows—

Prepare a bulb and battery in circuit with short leads. Disconnect the coil lead from the distributor and attach one end of the circuit to this terminal; earthing the other end on the distributor body, or other part of engine or machine.

If the contact breaker points are closed, the light will come on and will go out when the precise breaking point is reached.

It is generally better and more accurate to use a timing disc on the crankshaft and time in degrees B.T.D.C. rather than measure piston travel back from T.D.C. With either method it is equally important that T.D.C. should be accurately determined to start from.

30b. IGNITION TIMING—MAGNETO MODELS

Before timing the magneto, check the contact breaker points gap. It should be .012" plus or minus .001" when wide open. Check on both cams.

Screw up the nut securing the automatic timing device to the armature shaft and check the chain tension. The magneto is flange mounted on three waisted studs which permit of chain adjustment when slackened. The chain should have about ⅛ in. whip midway between the sprockets at its tightest point.

Now slacken the nut and continue to unscrew it until it just pulls the A.T.D. off the taper.

Set the piston position as for the coil ignition models that is with the L.H. cylinder on compression stroke, the rearward H.T. lead from the magneto goes to this cylinder. The magneto feeds this lead when the contact breaker rocker heel strikes the bottom cam.

Using a small nut or small wooden wedge, prop the automatic advance unit fully advanced. Rotate the contact breaker with the fingers until a thin strip of cigarette paper can be just withdrawn from between the points. Hold the C.B. still and with other hand screw up the centre nut on the A.T.D. Remove the wedge holding it advanced and tighten the nut preferably with a ring spanner. Replace wedge and check timing on both cylinders. Be particular to remove wedge before fitting timing cover.

31. REMOVAL OF ENGINE FROM FRAME

The engine and gearbox assembly is intended to be removed from the frame as a unit, and for this purpose it is advisable to support the frame on a block or box to provide rather more stability than is available from a central stand. Remove the petrol tank, oil bath chaincase, the oil tank and battery, together with their platform. Remove also the engine steady stay and disconnect all cables and electric wiring likely to prevent the engine/gearbox assembly being removed when all attachments are released.

Remove the remaining bolts holding the engine/gearbox assembly to the frame and lift the assembly clear of the frame. It will probably be necessary to obtain assistance to hold the cycle steady whilst removing the unit. No difficulty should be experienced in disconnecting the engine from the gearbox or vice versa.

32. CRANKSHAFT—REMOVAL AND FITTING

Remove engine sprocket key, remove timing cover, chains tensioner, sprockets, etc., and oil pump, paras. 24, 26 and 28.

Remove breather pipe from rear of driving side crankcase, and the nuts from the top two crankcase studs. Remove half-time pinion key and camshaft sprocket key. Remove the short bolt between the top front engine plate bosses, and the two cheese headed screws. One between the bottom bosses and the other in the corner of the sump.

The drive side crankcase may now be removed by levering gently between the crank cheek and the crankcase inner wall with a flat tyre lever or similar tool. It will take with it the outer race of the roller bearing, leaving the inner race with cage and rollers on the shaft.

Withdraw the camshaft from the timing side case and remove from the bottom of the drive side camshaft bush, the rotary breather valve and spring.

Turn the crankshaft in the timing side bearing to approx. bottom centre and with the lever used for the drive side, attempt to lever the crankshaft out of the timing side ball bearing. If it does not move without undue force, the crankcase will have to be heated so that the ballrace complete will withdraw from the crankcase when the bearing can be levered off the crankshaft.

Shims are no longer used between main bearings and crank cheeks.

The timing side ballrace should be a light driving fit on the crankshaft and if it is found to be very tight, the shaft should be carefully eased down with emery tape. This bearing does not require to be so tight on the shaft as does the roller race on the opposite side because it is finally held endwise when the oil pump driving worm is tightened up. If it is desired to replace the roller race, the drive side crankcase should be heated up over a soft flame, taking care that excessive heat does not reach the oil seal. If the case is then dropped squarely on flat wooden surface, the outer race of the bearing should drop out. If the case is quickly cleaned the new race may drop into position without reheating.

Reheat the timing side case keeping the intermediate gear spindle as cool as possible and refit the timing side ballrace or fit a new one as required.

With the flywheel assembly thoroughly cleaned, mount drive side crankcase inside up on wooden blocks sufficiently high to give clearance between mainshaft and bench when the crankshaft is in position. Smear joint faces of both halves of case with good quality jointing compound such as 'Wellseal', pour a little clean engine oil over rollers and cage of drive side bearing. Fit crankshaft into drive side case. Fit rotary breather valve, spring and camshaft into bush in drive side case, making certain that the dogs on the valve are engaged with the slots in the camshaft end. Do not turn camshaft until the timing side case is fitted and pushed home.

Timing side crankcase can now be fitted engaging two top studs in drive side case and camshaft in timing side bush.

Dependant upon how tight the timing side mainshaft is in the ballrace, this side of the case may require to be tapped home with a hide or wooden mallet.

Pinch the two halves of the case together with nuts on two top studs and use two other studs as near opposite as possible. Check that the camshaft is free to rotate which will prove that the rotary valve is properly positioned.

It will not be possible to check crankshaft end float if the timing side shaft is very tight in the ballrace but with the bolts tight and the crankcase cold there should be about .005" to .008" end float.

To check, mount crankcase on wooden blocks drive side uppermost. Fit nut to drive side mainshaft and with hide or copper hammer drive crankshaft assembly hard down towards timing side.

Set up a dial test indicator with its spindle on the end of the shaft. Set it to read zero. Now with levers under the mainshaft nut or under an old alternator rotor secured by the nut, lever on suitable packing pieces to 'pull' the crankshaft towards the dial indicator. Note reading.

End float is not critical but connecting rods should be fairly accurately centralised in cylinder bores. If for any reason, they are not, shims are available from the spares department.

To complete, fit remaining crankcase bolts and screws and tighten fully.

33. BIG END BEARINGS—RENEWAL

The necessity for big end bearings renewal will be apparent by a thumping noise from the region of the crankcase, when the engine is pulling, and by a very low oil pressure—if checked. Check that the end cap and big end of the rod are marked for correct re-assembly and mark the rod and crankshaft to ensure that the rods are fitted the same way round as originally.

With a ring or box spanner and noting the pressure required, release the shakeproof nuts from the big end bolts.

Remove the nuts and washers, when a straight pull on the rod should remove the end cap. If the cap becomes wedged due to misalignment, tap carefully home and try another pull. The steel backed bearings may be readily picked out and replaced.

Over an extremely long period, there will be no measurable wear on the crankpins, and standard size bearing will be suitable replacements. No difficulty should be experienced in fitting the replacements but care should be taken to ensure that both rod and bearings are perfectly clean when assembled.

Lightly smear the crankpin with oil and re-assemble the end caps on the rod in the same position, as originally fitted. With a box or ring spanner, pull down the end cap nuts evenly and quite tightly but without sufficient pressure to cause distortion of the cap. If a torque wrench is being used tighten to 170/180 in./lbs.

Although the 650 cc. models have larger big end bearing bolts, the same torque setting is used and has been found satisfactory.

NOTE—Big end nuts should not be used again if they are not tight on threads.

34. CRANKSHAFT—DISMANTLING AND RE-ASSEMBLY

After a considerable mileage has been covered, the large oil well formed in the centre of the crankshaft assembly, will tend to become partially filled with sludge and carbon deposited centrifugally as the oil passes through. It is impossible to state at what mileage this should be cleaned out as it is entirely dependent on the frequency with which the oil is changed and the general cleanliness of the engine, but obviously it will not be dealt with until the unit is due for a major overhaul.

The flywheel is held between the two crank

throws by four bolts and two studs, the nuts of the latter being secured by tab washers.

Before commencing to dismantle, mark the flywheel and one crank cheek to ensure re-assembly in the original position.

Bend back the tab washers on the same side of the flywheel as the bolt nuts, remove all nuts and withdraw the four bolts. This will enable the crank throw and flywheel to be removed.

Thoroughly clean out the centre holes and the feed holes to the bearings, ensure all faces are perfectly clean and re-assemble in the reverse order, lightly pinching down each nut before finally tightening in diagonal order. Remember to re-assemble the flywheel the same way round that it was originally fitted. Lock the bolt nuts with a punch mark and reset the tab washers.

35. SMALL END BUSH—REMOVAL AND FITTING

Whilst the connecting rods are removed it may be found desirable to renew the small end bushes. Should this be the case, the rods should be returned to the Service Department for the work to be carried out. In this way they will be reamed square with the big end eyes. (Note—on 650 cc. models the gudgeon pins bear direct in the small ends of the dural connecting rods).

36. CAMSHAFT BUSHES—REMOVAL AND REPLACEMENT

Considerable difficulty will be experienced in removing the camshaft bush from the driving side half-case, if sufficient wear ever occurs for renewal of these bushes to be necessary. It is most strongly recommended to return the crankcase to our Service Department to have this operation carried out.

37. MAIN BEARINGS—REMOVAL AND REPLACEMENT

To remove the main bearings, gently heat the case around the main bearing housing, avoiding overheating or a concentration of heat on one spot. Drop the half-case open side downwards square and true on to the bench or wooden block and the bearings (or outer race in the case of the driving side) will fall out. Replacements are more readily fitted whilst the case is still hot and should be pressed or carefully drifted home in the housing. Before fitting bearings in crankcase, it is wise to check their fits on the respective mainshafts. The timing side ball bearing should be a good push fit, its inner race is finally held endwise by the assembly on the shaft secured by the oil pump worm. The inner race of the roller bearing on the driving side mainshaft requires to be a light driving fit.

If the bearings are too tight, ease the shafts down carefully with emery tape.

38. INTERMEDIATE GEAR SPINDLE AND BUSH—REMOVAL AND FITTING

To remove the bush from the gear, obtain a bolt at least twice the length of the bush, place a washer at the head of the bolt with an outside diameter slightly less than the bush.

Place the bolt in the bush and over the threaded end of the bolt, place a piece of tubing longer than the bush with an inside diameter slightly larger than the outside of the bush. Fit nut and large washer to the bolt and tighten. As the nut is tightened the bush will be withdrawn.

Fit new bush in reverse manner or press home carefully in a plain jaw vice. Ream to .5620"/.5625" after fitting.

In the unlikely event of the intermediate gear spindle requiring renewal, it should be drifted out of position whilst the crankcase is still hot from removal of the main bearings.

The replacement should be set perfectly square before pressing or drifting home. This operation should again be carried out whilst the case is sufficiently warm for the spindle to be partially inserted by hand.
There is no necessity to remove the circlip from the hole into which the spindle fits either for removal or refitting.

39. BIG END FEED OIL SEAL—REMOVAL AND REFITTING

This oil seal which is fitted in the timing cover cannot be removed without damaging it beyond all further use and a replacement should be obtained before attempting its removal. Remove the original seal by first removing the retaining circlip and inserting a screwdriver or similar tool into the centre hole, under the seal and levering on the opposite side of the boss. Repeat this procedure a few times on opposite sides of the seal. Take care not to damage the recess into which the seal fits or the face on which it seats. Carefully press or drift the replacement seal into position, the metal covered face being outwards (visible).

THE TRANSMISSION

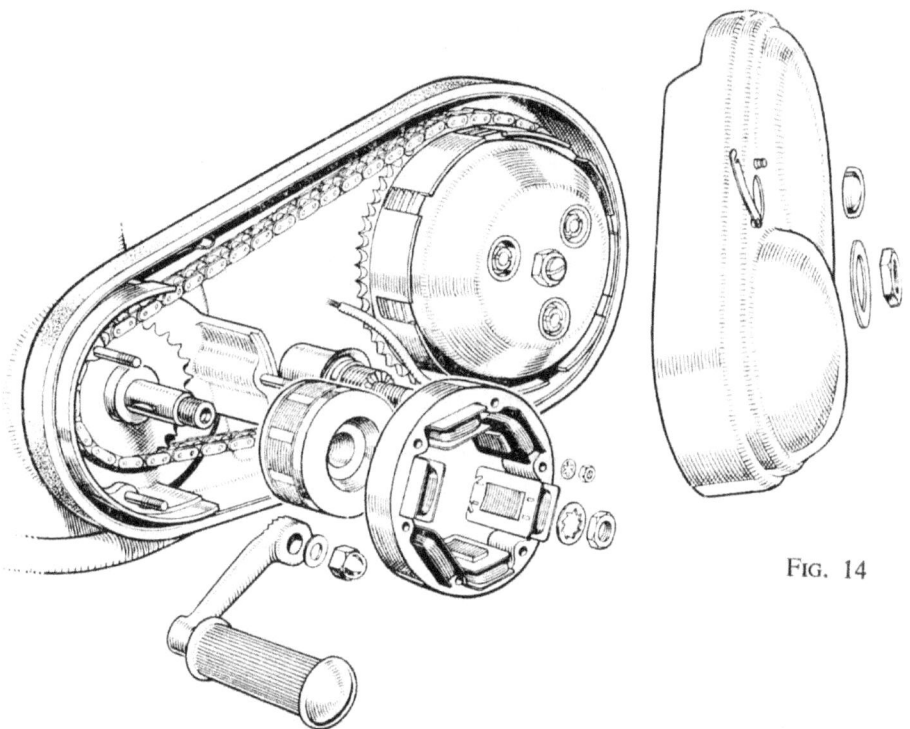

Fig. 14

71. CHAIN ADJUSTMENT

If maximum chain life and minimum power loss is to be obtained, chains must be run in correct adjustment and be properly lubricated.

The gearbox pivots on its lower mounting bolt and there are elongated holes in the mounting plates for the top bolt so that the box can be moved back and forward to adjust primary chain tension.

A drawbolt fitted to the gearbox top bolt has a $\frac{3}{16}''$ Whit. hexagon nut on either side of a stop rivetted to the offside mounting plate.

Primary Chain. To tighten the primary chain therefore, remove the chaincase inspection cap, slacken forward drawbolt nut and run it back with the fingers one or two threads. Slacken top gearbox bolt ($\frac{7}{8}''$ Whit. hex.) and slacken only slightly, bottom bolt ($\frac{3}{8}''$ Whit. hex.). With a spanner on rearward drawbolt nut, pull gearbox back until the chain is tight. Now slacken rearward nut a few turns and tighten the forward nut so that it pushes the gearbox forward until there is $\frac{1}{2}''$ to $\frac{3}{4}''$ up and down movement in the run of the chain midway between the sprockets. Tighten top and bottom gearbox bolts and operate kickstarter to check for tightest point of chain tension. There should be $\frac{1}{2}''$ up and down movement minimum. Set on the slack rather than the tight side with the primary chain. Tighten the forward drawbolt

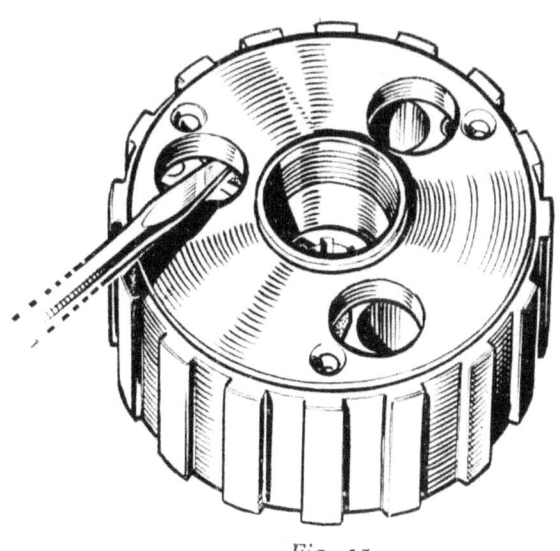

Fig. 15

nut against the stop so that it tends to push the gearbox forward all the time and tighten the rearward nut just sufficiently to prevent it becoming lost. In this way backlash in the

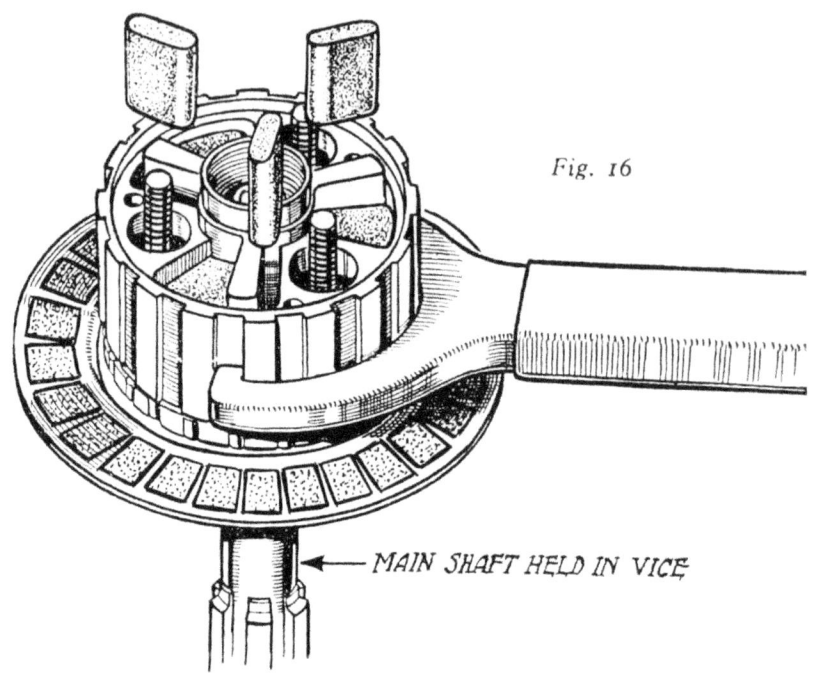

Fig. 16

MAIN SHAFT HELD IN VICE

adjusting mechanism will be all taken up so as to hold the gearbox forward against the greater pull of the rear chain.

The pull of the rear chain, always greater than that of the primary, can move the gearbox back after say, a jerky start, or a very quick gearchange up or down, or when rider and passenger sit on the machine, if the rear chain tension has been set too tight with the weight of the machine only on the wheels.

The important point to remember in view of this is that any final adjusting movement should always be in a forward direction.

Rear Chain. Before adjusting the rear chain make certain that the front is adjusted as described above.

Check that the ends of the rear wheel adjuster screws are hard up against the collars on the rear wheel spindle nuts and then slacken the spindle nuts ($\frac{1}{2}$" Whit. hex). Do not slacken fully but about half a turn so that the spindle will not move about too easily in the fork ends.

Slacken the adjuster screw locknuts ($\frac{3}{16}$" Whit. hex.) and count the number of flats you unscrew each adjuster ($\frac{1}{8}$" Whit. hex) so that you move the spindle back the same amount each side, and thus maintain wheel alignment.

WITH THE REAR SHOCK ABSORBERS COMPRESSED TO MID-STROKE there should be $\frac{3}{4}$" to 1" up and down movement in the run of the chain mid-way between the sprockets. At this point the chain is at its tightest.

Obtain assistance if necessary to hold the shock absorbers down—it will help if it is done single handed—to set the shock absorbers to the softest position and sit astride the rear number plate cuff (taking care not to break the tail lamp), with the machine off the stand, of course. The tension of the chain can now be checked with the left hand. Check for the tightest point as described for primary. Tighten wheel spindle nuts and adjuster locknuts, holding the adjusters themselves with a second spanner if necessary to prevent them screwing in and thus away from the wheel spindle, as the locknuts are tightened.

After adjustment of rear chain, check rear brake adjustment as, of course, this is altered by movement of rear wheel spindle.

Check wheel alignment, preferably with a straight edge, and note that because the rear tyre has a greater cross section than has the front, when the wheels are in line, a straight edge placed squarely on the side of the rear tyre at two points, should pass the front tyre leaving a small gap (usually about $\frac{1}{8}$" to $\frac{3}{16}$") at two points, and when the straight edge is transferred to the opposite side of the machine, these gaps should be the same.

Should this not be so, note whether chain requires to be tightened or slackened, slacken wheel spindle nut on appropriate side and by means of adjuster, move wheel in required direction.

Tighten all nuts and check again.

If the chain has been slackened off, and to ensure that the rear spindle is hard up against the adjusters, place a hammer shaft, or piece of wood between rear tyre and offside pivoted fork tube (swinging arm). 'Lever' wheel over towards nearside and tighten offside nut.

Pull wheel forward on nearside by 'squeezing' lower run of chain against pivoted fork tube with left hand whilst tightening spindle nut with right. (If the machine has a full chaincase, it is possible to apply some weight to the top run of the chain through the inspection orifice and obtain the same effect).

Rear Chain Lubrication. This is by oil vapour fed to it by the oil tank vent pipe which is connected to the forward end of the chainguard or chaincase. The amount of oil the chain receives will vary according to the way the machine itself is used. For example, with a normal oil level in the tank, and using the machine for a ride to work or short trips about town, the chain may not receive much oil, but if long fast runs are undertaken, it will certainly receive more which may become too much if a long full-bore run is made on say, a motorway. It will help to use a higher oil level in the tank for short journeys and a lower one for very fast ones, remembering that with a very low level there may be overheating at very high speeds due to the smaller amount in circulation.

On twin cylinder models, the crankcase breather pipe is normally diverted to the ground with a rubber extension of 8" to 10" long leading to a point near the centre stand pivot. This can be removed by taking out the single screw which secures it to the back of the crankcase, the copper part can be straightened out somewhat (but not fully) and the rubber part shortened so that it discharges on to the rear chain at a point where it passes over the gearbox axle sprocket, and the pipe re-fitted. This, of course, will feed more oil vapour to the chain.

Chain Hints. CHAINS SHOULD NEVER BE RUN OVERTIGHT. It is better to run them on the slack side provided they are not so slack that they make contact with the inside of their cases or guards.

If the primary chain is run too slack an intermittent metallic tap will be heard as the lower run 'flips' upwards and strikes the underside of the tube in the chaincase which surrounds the footrest hanger. When this happens, of course, the chain should be adjusted up.

There should always be sufficient oil in the front chaincase for the lower run of the chain to 'dip' as if the chain is run for only a short distance with insufficient oil, it will overheat and wear rapidly and oleate of rust formed in its bearings will give the remaining oil a 'cocoa like' appearance.

Most riders are aware that when the springclip is fitted to the connecting link, its blind end should be fitted pointing in the direction in which the chain travels. Many do not seem to know however, that the spring is not flat, but has a concave and convex side. It should be fitted blind end forward and

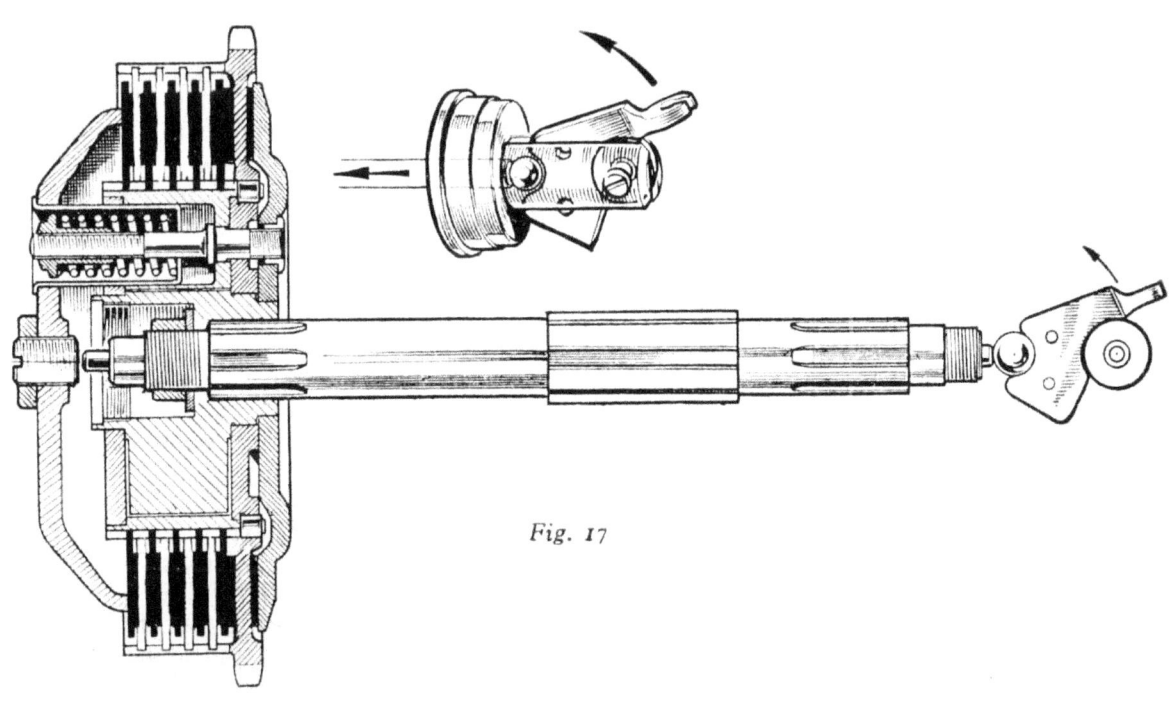

Fig. 17

convex side out so that it holds the side plate snugly up against the bushes of the inner links.

Rear chain life can be increased by removing the chain, say every 1000 miles (for this purpose keep an old chain to join on to the present one and run it round the sprockets whilst the chain is removed). This will greatly facilitate removal and refitting.

Wash the chain thoroughly in paraffin and after allowing the paraffin to dry off, immerse the chain in lubricant which has been heated in a container until liquid. After about 10 minutes immersion during which the chain is moved about with a stick to 'work' the joints and ensure penetration of the lubricant, the latter is allowed to cool with the chain still in it. After cooling the chain is removed and the surplus grease wiped off. The chain can then be refitted to the machine after cleaning the chain wheels.

It should be noted that not all greases are suitable for heating to thinness without deterioration, and when purchasing the purpose for which the lubricant is required should be stated, as special ones are marketed for the job.

It is useful to know the extent of chain wear, and wear up to $\frac{1}{4}''$ per foot of chain length is accommodated by the depth of hardening of the bearing surfaces, and when this limit is reached, the chain should be replaced.

The test should be made carefully to ensure an accurate result. The chain is first washed in paraffin to ensure all joints are free and laid unlubricated on a flat board. If it is anchored at one end by a nail, the necessary tension to pull it out to its fullest extent can be applied with one hand, whilst measuring between the centres of the bearing pins.

72. CLUTCH ADJUSTMENT

The clutches of all these machines have bonded on friction material and it is bonded to the driven plates instead of inserts in the driving plates and chainwheel as on earlier models.

In order to obtain quick clean gear changing and freedom from clutch drag, correct adjustment is vital.

With the control cable adjuster slackened off, there should be about $\frac{1}{8}''$ free movement in the small operating lever in the kickstarter case. This is illustrated on the extreme right of Fig. 17. If there is more or less than this, the primary chaincase outer half should be removed (para. 73).

Now release the locknut ($\frac{7}{16}''$ Whit. hex.) on the adjuster screw in the centre of the aluminium pressure plate and set the screw as necessary. If it is first screwed in until it is hard on the pushrod and then slackened back half a turn this should give about the right amount of free movement in the lever as described.

Tighten the locknut and adjust the cable so that there is about $\frac{1}{8}''$ free movement at the handlebar lever. The clutch pressure plate should now come off squarely and rotate true laterally when the kickstarter is operated with the clutch withdrawn. If it does not do so, adjust individual springs to obtain this result.

If the clutch is dismantled for any reason such as cleaning of the plates, check that the nut securing the clutch centre to the gearbox mainshaft is tight before refitting the pressure plate and springs, etc.

If a replacement handlebar lever is fitted at any time, make certain that it has the correct centres for cable nipple and fulcrum pin these should be $\frac{7}{8}''$.

73. REMOVAL AND REFITTING OF OIL BATH

Remove the brake pedal by withdrawing the jaw joint pin and unscrewing the grease nipple from the pedal boss. Take care whilst doing so not to push the pedal down farther than it normally travels as otherwise the pedal return spring housed in the pedal boss will be strained and require to be replaced.

Remove the left hand footrest and the large nut screwed on to the footrest tube ($1\frac{1}{16}''$ Whit. hex.). This will enable the outer cover to be withdrawn exposing the driving chain clutch and generator. Remove the three nuts holding the stator and withdraw it from its studs drawing the cable carefully through the grommet in the inner chaincase until the stator can safely be rested on the rear engine plates. Remove mainshaft nut and rotor from mainshaft.

Remove primary chain and withdraw engine sprocket using sprocket puller. Remove the three clutch spring nuts, springs and cups and clutch pressure plate.

Engage top gear and obtain assistance to hold the rear wheel while the clutch retaining nut is being slackened. The rear brake can be held on with a ring spanner on the cam spindle nut.

With the clutch centre nut removed, the clutch itself can be withdrawn, it is on a parallel spline but if tight, a special withdrawal tool can be obtained from the Service Department.

Remove the three countersunk 'Allen' screws securing the stator housing to the crankcase. The inner chaincase is now held by three screws at the front end, by the nut on the nearside gearbox bottom bolt and by the nut on a hexagon spacer stud on the nearside engine/gearbox plate.

Note the paper washer fitted between crankcase and chaincase.

Re-assemble in the reverse order watching that the slots in the stator housing are correctly positioned to pass the chain and fitting the spring on the chain connecting link with its closed end pointing in the direction of travel of the chain and with its convex side out. Do not fit outer portion until clutch has been adjusted (para. 72). Note that the rubber sealing band has a thin lip on one edge only. This should be on the outer diameter of the band and towards the outer cover. If the band has stretched it is permissible to cut a piece out and join with wire provided the joint is positioned on the top side of the case.

Fit stator with the edge from which the leads are taken innermost and drawing surplus cable through to behind the inner portion. Fit outer cover, giving the rim a few blows with the ball of the hand or a rubber mallet whilst tightening the nut. Do not overtighten or the case may be distorted. Usually one or two threads only should protrude through the nut.

74. CLUTCH—TO DISMANTLE

Remove the outer portion of the oil bath (para. 72). Remove clutch spring adjuster nuts with divided screwdriver, or use a small screwdriver on one side only. There is a locking 'pip' under the head of these screws and considerable torque may be necessary to get over it during the first one or two revolutions.

Pressure plate will now come away, remove clutch plates, and note that the first driven plate has bonded friction material on one side only and must therefore always be the end plate.

Disconnect primary chain and remove clutch chainwheel. Engage top gear and unscrew clutch centre nut. R.H. thread, $\frac{7}{8}''$ Whit. hexagon box spanner required. Remove nut and single spring washer. Clutch centre can now be withdrawn from splined gearbox mainshaft.

To dismantle the clutch centre and examine the shock absorber rubbers, remove the three screws holding the front cover plate and tap the plate round until a screwdriver can be used to prise it off (Fig. 15).

At the works, the rubbers are removed by mounting the clutch centre on an old mainshaft held in a vice and with a special 'C' spanner on the splines of the centre the large rubbers are compressed whilst the small ones are removed first.

A small sharp pointed tool is necessary to remove the rubbers, as after use they adhere to the body. Large rubbers are easily removed after the small ones have been withdrawn.

The body is then removed from the mainshaft, the 'spider' or shock absorber centre is taken out and the body turned upside down on the bench.

The three nuts on the spring studs should then be removed when the backplate, roller race, race plate and body can be separated.

If a spare mainshaft and special 'C' spanner are not available, the rubbers can be removed from the shock absorber with the clutch centre on the mainshaft of the machine.

A spare 'driven' clutch plate is necessary on which should be welded a piece of steel tube for a handle about 24" long. (This is a useful tool to have in the workshop in any case as it provides a good means of holding the clutch centre whilst the centre nut is tightened or slackened).

Top gear should be engaged and the rear wheel stopped with the brake, or a rod passed through the spokes of the wheel which must be held on a spoke nipple hard up against the rim and then allowed to come up against the tubes of the pivotted fork (swinging arm) —remove rear chaincase or guard as necessary.

Now using the tool as described turn the clutch centre to compress the large rubbers and 'pick' out the small ones. The large ones will now come out easily and the body dismantled as described above.

75. EXAMINATION OF CLUTCH PARTS

Examine the driven plates with their bonded on strips of friction material and ensure that none are missing. Clean them thoroughly with petrol and a stiff brush. Place the plain driving plates together and check that they are flat. These should be of the 'pin point planished' type—that is they should have small 'pop' marks all over. Plates so treated will stand high temperatures without buckling.

The splines on the body and the bonded plates which drive the body rarely show any signs of wear, but the tongues on the plain driving plates may be worn and may have cut slots in the chainwheel. This wear obstructs the free movement of the plates when the clutch is operated, this can be rectified by carefully filing or grinding the tongues on the plates square also the driving edge of the slots in the chainwheel.

The only effect this will have on the clutch is a slight amount of backlash, when the clutch is engaged or disengaged.

Examine roller race, rollers and cage, examine the race plate, face and bore for wear by the clutch body centre or 'spider'. Examine the shock absorber rubbers, they may have become soft or cracked. Examine the 'spider' itself for wear on race plate and cover plate diameters also the internal splines for any fractures.

76. ASSEMBLY OF CLUTCH

Fit race plate to clutch body, ensuring that the holes in the plate are in line with the holes in the body, and the spring studs an easy fit. Fit roller cage, rollers and back plate. Fit shock absorber centre or 'spider' in body and lock up nuts on studs. Fit large rubbers followed by small ones. Fit cover plate and three screws (these may be countersunk or have cheese heads). See illustration for correct position of large and small rubbers. Test roller race for freeness on its track, and apply a little medium grease or anti-centrifuge grease.

Check all the clutch plates on the body and in the sprocket (clutch case) for freeness.

Fit sprocket to body, revolve sprocket on race to check free movement, fit plates as follows:

First a double sided bonded driven plate followed by a plain driving plate and so on in alternate order until the last bonded plate which is single sided is fitted. This, of course, should present its plain steel side to the pressure plate.

Fit clutch to gearbox mainshaft, fit spring washer and nut, engage top gear and tighten nut.

Fit clutch push rod, clutch pressure plate, spring cups, springs and spring adjuster nuts. Screw up nuts until studs come up just flush with end of nuts, and adjust as necessary to ensure square withdrawal of pressure plate.

Gearbox

77. REMOVAL FROM FRAME

With this frame it is not possible to remove the gearbox as a separate unit and if, therefore, it becomes necessary to remove the gearbox shell, then it is essential to lift the engine/gearbox assembly from the frame as described in para. 31 and to remove the gearbox as a subsequent operation.

78. OUTER COVER, REMOVAL

Remove the kickstarter crank by unscrewing the pinch bolt taking it right out and pulling off the crank. Remove gear indicator by unscrewing the centre bolt from the positive spindle. Remove oil filler and inspection plate and disconnect clutch inner wire from operating lever.

Do not remove foot change pedal.

Remove five screws holding cover in position and carefully pull the cover away by means of the footchange pedal. Take care not to tear paper washer.

79. OUTER COVER, FITTING

Ensure paper washer is undamaged or carefully scrape off old washer and fit new.

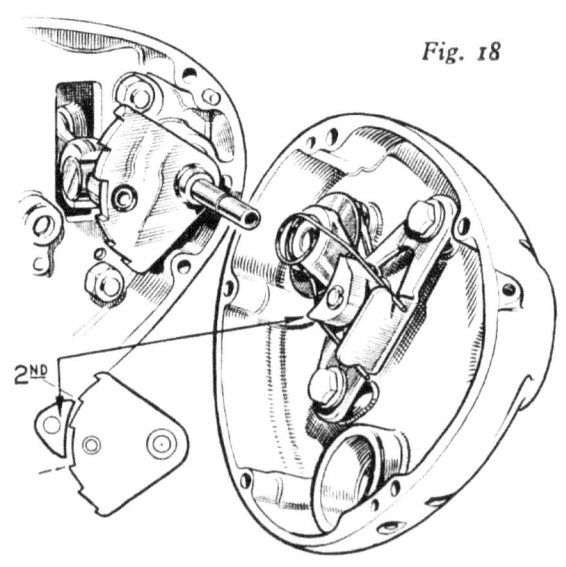

Fig. 18

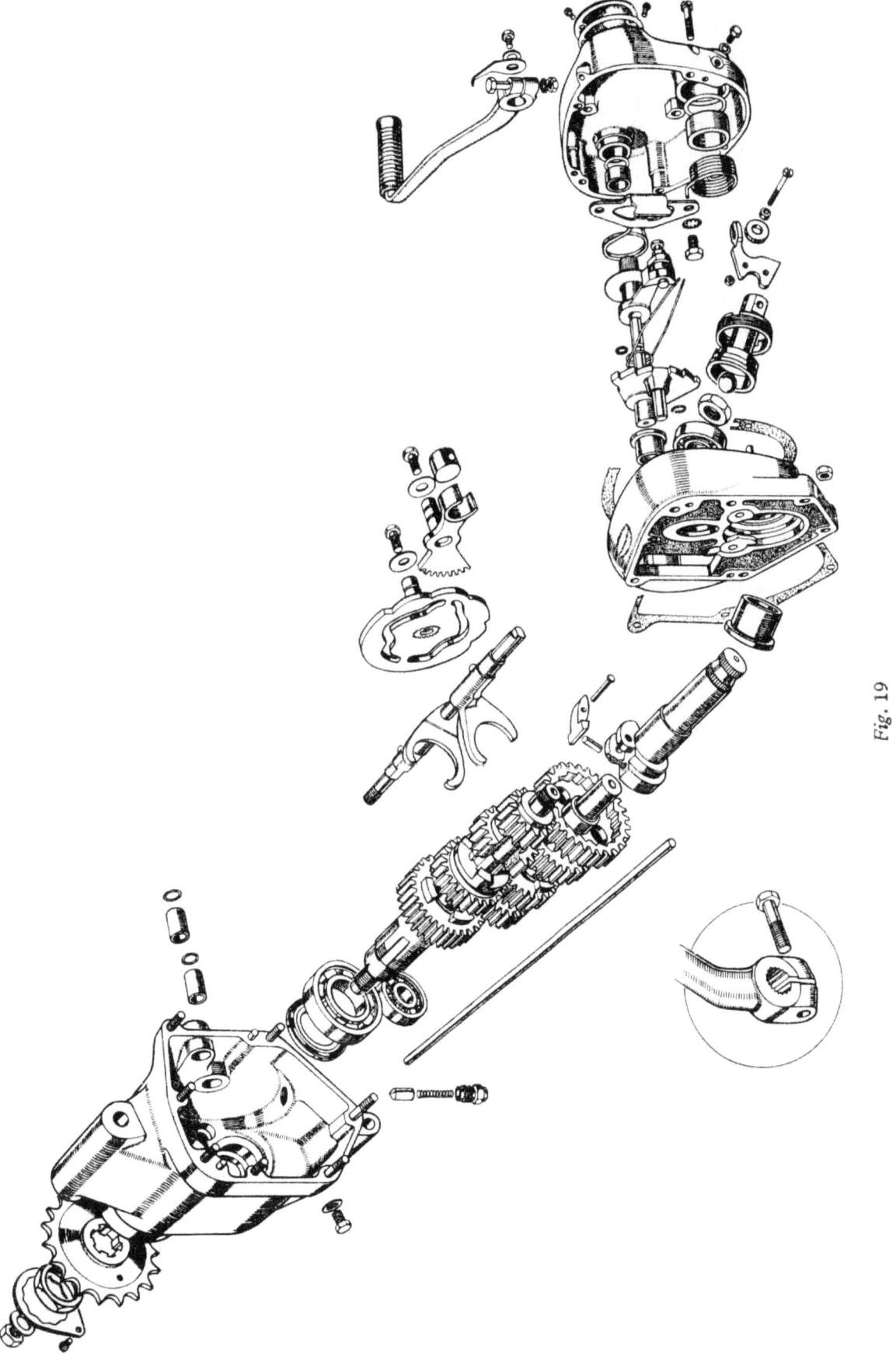

Fig. 19

Ensure also foot change pawl spring not dislodged and lying correctly with its straight leg uppermost, each leg resting on the rocking pawl (Fig. 18) before fitting cover. Replace remaining parts.

Some oil will have been lost due to cover removal and should be replenished through the filler hole after the level plug: i.e. the small hexagon headed pin to the rear of the kickstarter axle, has been removed. Engine oil should be **slowly** poured in until it commences to drip through this screw hole.

80. POSITIVE FOOT CHANGE DISMANTLING

Removal of the outer cover will bring with it the positive footchange mechanism.

To dismantle, remove gear indicator and withdraw ratchet plate and spindle.

Remove pawl spring.

Remove operating lever, disengage return spring legs from pawl pin and withdraw pawl carrier.

New return spring cannot be fitted without removing spring stop plate.

81. POSITIVE FOOT CHANGE ASSEMBLY

Obtain any necessary replacements and ensure all parts clean.

Smear oil on all moving parts.

Place return spring in position and fit plate.

Place washer on pawl carrier spindle, insert into bush and push home whilst manoeuvring springlegs into position in groove in pawl pin.

Refit pawl spring with straight leg uppermost.

Fit ratchet and spindle.

Refit operating lever and gear indicator before fitting cover.

Use indicator to move ratchet plate into position to pilot operating pin into selector fork roller whilst fitting cover. Probably necessary to remove indicator, finally, to adjust lever to individual requirements.

82. INNER COVER, REMOVAL

With outer cover already removed, remove ratchet plate with spindle. Before unscrewing locking ring securing clutch withdrawal device, mark rotational position of lever slot on end cover just outside lock ring. Otherwise it is unlikely that operating lever will be at correct angle for cable entry when outer cover is fitted.

Unscrew lock ring (R.H. thread) and remove operating lever body ensuring that $\frac{1}{2}$" steel ball does not become lost. Unscrew mainshaft nut now exposed (R.H. thread).

Remove the seven nuts holding the cover to the shell and withdraw the cover from the studs, tapping behind the front end to loosen if necessary. Avoid damaging the paper washer.

83. INNER COVER, FITTING

Ensure paper washer undamaged and faces clean.

Fit cover and its seven securing nuts, just pinching all down and finally tightening opposite nuts in pairs.

Fit and tighten mainshaft nut.

Fit clutch operating body with ball but before tightening the locking ring ensure that the operating lever is lying in alignment with clutch cable adjuster hole, in order to obtain a straight pull on the cable.

Fit ratchet plate and spindle.

84. INNER COVER, DISMANTLING

The footchange mechanism having been already dealt with, and the clutch operating parts having been removed in order to enable inner cover to be withdrawn, only the kickstarter mechanism remains.

Lever out return spring end from hole in kickstarter axle when the axle can be withdrawn from its bush. Removal of the pawl pin results in pawl, plunger and spring falling out of position.

If the nose of the pawl is worn or chipped, it should be renewed.

If kickstarter crank has been positioned on its splines in a too near vertical position, a large wadered foot may have inadvertently held the crank far enough back whilst riding for the pawl to run continually in mesh with the ratchet annulus in the 1st gear wheel. Both these parts should therefore, be examined for wear.

85. INNER COVER, ASSEMBLING

Examine pawl cam and stop pieces rivetted to cover, if loose re-rivet.

Fit pawl spring, plunger, pawl and pin.

Insert axle into bush, fit return spring.

NOTE that the clutch operating mechanism cannot be re-assembled until cover is fitted to box.

86. REMOVAL OF GEARS

If the clutch has been removed, it will be

helpful to fit a short length of tubing over the end of the main axle and hold it in place with a clutch nut to retain the axle in position whilst the gears are being removed.

Remove end cover (paras. 78 and 82).

Remove the low gear and kickstarter wheel the large gear on the layshaft which has a bronze bush pressed into its centre.

Remove the small wheel from the end of the main axle.

Remove the mainshaft second gear; this is fitted with a fully floating bush. Unscrew the striker fork shaft by means of the two flats machined on its outer end and remove it together with the layshaft second gear and the striker fork.

Remove the tubular distance piece on clutch and withdraw the main axle together with the third gear and striker fork.

Withdraw the layshaft and the two remaining gears.

Gently warming the box and dropping it face downwards on a wooden block will withdraw the layshaft bearing.

Remove axle sprocket nut which has a left hand thread and is held with a locking washer and screw, and withdraw the main gearwheel. If the gearbox is in the frame and the rear chain in position, obtain assistance to hold rear wheel whilst the nut is being removed.

If the gearbox is removed from the frame, the sprocket may be held by passing a length of old chain around it and holding the ends in a vice.

87. REMOVAL OF CAM PLATE

Remove the domed hexagon nut from beneath the forward side of the gearbox shell. This serves as a bush for the camplate indexing plunger and spring which will come away with it when the nut is unscrewed.

Remove the two hexagon set pins, with washers, from the forward side of the gear box. The cam plate also cam plate quadrant, can now be extracted from inside the gear box shell. Wear on the two bushes for the cam plate and quadrant can cause the gears to disengage due to bad indexing.

Renew the "O" rings on both shafts if oil leakage occurs.

Should these bushes require replacement, they can be pressed or drifted out, preferably heating the shell first.

88. FITTING CAM PLATE

Insert the quadrant through the gear box, secure it with its set pin and washer. Raise the lever portion, until the top radius is in line with the top right hand stud for the case cover (top gear position).

Fit the cam plate to engage with the quadrant so that only the first two teeth are visible through the slot in the cam plate.

Secure the cam plate with its set pin and washer. Put back the plunger, spring, and domed nut.

89. FITTING GEARS INTO GEARBOX

Fit the main gearwheel, make sure spacer which bears on oil seal is in position as the sleeve of the gear passes through the bearing in the wheel. Fit the axle sprocket, tighten the nut *left hand thread*, fit locking washer and set screw.

Check the fit of the layshaft in the ballrace in gearbox shell—it should be a hand push fit. If it is tight, ease the end of the shaft down with emery tape.

Fit third gear wheel (free pinion) 20T to layshaft followed by fixed pinion 18T. This must be fitted with its flat side to the free pinion and its slightly raised centre to the ballrace. Fit layshaft in gearbox. Oil mainshaft on plain portion and fit in sleeve gear.

Set the cam plate in neutral position, i.e. with indexing plunger in the shallow groove. Fit the selector fork to mainshaft third gear (21T) and fit to mainshaft, meshing it with the layshaft gear already in position. Fit the other selector fork to the layshaft second gear (24T). Fit this to layshaft, engage pegs on selector forks with slots in cam plate, fit selector fork spindle and screw home. It is not difficult to fit this spindle, even with the gearbox in the frame, use a screwdriver if necessary to 'lift' the inner selector fork into position whilst the spindle carrying the outer fork is passed through it.

The selector forks are identical and can, therefore, be interchanged but it is advisable to replace them in their original positions.

Fit mainshaft free pinion, mainshaft fixed pinion and low gear wheel to layshaft. There are no shims.

Fit end cover taking care that joint washer is undamaged and properly positioned.

Fit remainder of parts as described in para. 85 inner cover assembling, and para. 83 inner cover fitting.

Finally, remember to refill the gearbox with oil to correct level.

Wheels, Hubs and Brakes

90. FRONT WHEEL REMOVAL

Place machine on centre stand, remove split pin from brake control clevis pin and withdraw pin. Unscrew cable adjuster from brake plate. Unscrew wheel spindle nut (R.H. thread) and release pinch stud nut in L.H. fork end.

Take the weight of the wheel in left hand and withdraw spindle by means of a tommy bar placed through the hole in the head of the spindle. Withdraw spindle and as wheel is removed, take great care not to allow the brake plate to fall from the drum (its bevelled edge can be badly damaged if it is allowed to fall). Place spindle and dust cover in a clean place to avoid contamination with grit.

91. FRONT WHEEL—FITTING

Re-assemble in reverse order, grease spindle lightly. Fit brake plate into drum and as wheel is lifted into forks, position dust cover on L.H. side and make certain that torque stop on brake plate engages slot in R.H. fork leg. Pass spindle through with right hand. Fit and tighten spindle nut. Deflect forks a few times to 'centre' nearside leg on spindle. DO NOT overtighten pinch stud nut on L.H. side. The lug on the leg can be broken if this is overtightened. Re-connect and adjust brake cable.

92. REAR WHEEL—REMOVAL

Place machine on centre stand, on de Luxe models only remove rear number plate.

Remove the three rubber plugs from offside rear hub and with box or socket spanner remove three sleeve nuts then exposed.

Unscrew right hand portion of wheel spindle and withdraw. Remove spacer and speedometer drive gearbox and allow the latter to hang on its cable.

Withdraw wheel from brake drum by pulling to offside when it should come clear of brake drum which is left in position.

The standard models do not now have a detachable rear mudguard portion and one should therefore stand on the nearside and incline the machine slightly towards one on the stand, when the wheel can be withdrawn with the right hand from the offside.

On de Luxe models, if the tyre is deflated the wheel can be withdrawn rearwards through the space left by the removal of the number plate. With the tyre inflated, it may be necessary to incline the machine as for standard models to get the wheel clear.

If it is necessary to remove the wheel complete with brake, remove chaincase or chainguard and disconnect the chain, remove brake rod adjusting nut but **do not** push the brake pedal down to withdraw rod from roller. Disconnect the 'dead' lead from stoplamp switch. Disconnect speedometer drive cable, and slacken both sides of the wheel spindle. The wheel should now slide out of the fork ends and be removed as described above but it may be necessary to remove the offside silencer due to greater width caused by the offside portion of the wheel spindle remaining in the hub.

93. REAR WHEEL—REFITTING

Reverse dismantling operations and if fitting with brake complete make certain torque stop on brake plate properly engages with slot in left hand fork end. Engage brake rod in cam lever roller and push wheel spindle up against adjuster screws. Position speedometer gearbox for correct cable take-off angle and tighten both sides of spindle. Connect speedometer drive cable—do not overtighten gland nut.

Fit rear chain taking care to fit clip to connecting link as described in para. 71—Chain Hints. Check rear chain tension.

Fit chaincase or chainguard. Adjust rear brake. Re-connect stop switch 'dead' lead. On de Luxe models refit number plate.

When fitting rear wheel only with brake drum already in situ, incline machine as necessary to position wheel under mudguard or tail fairing. Turn brake drum by hand so

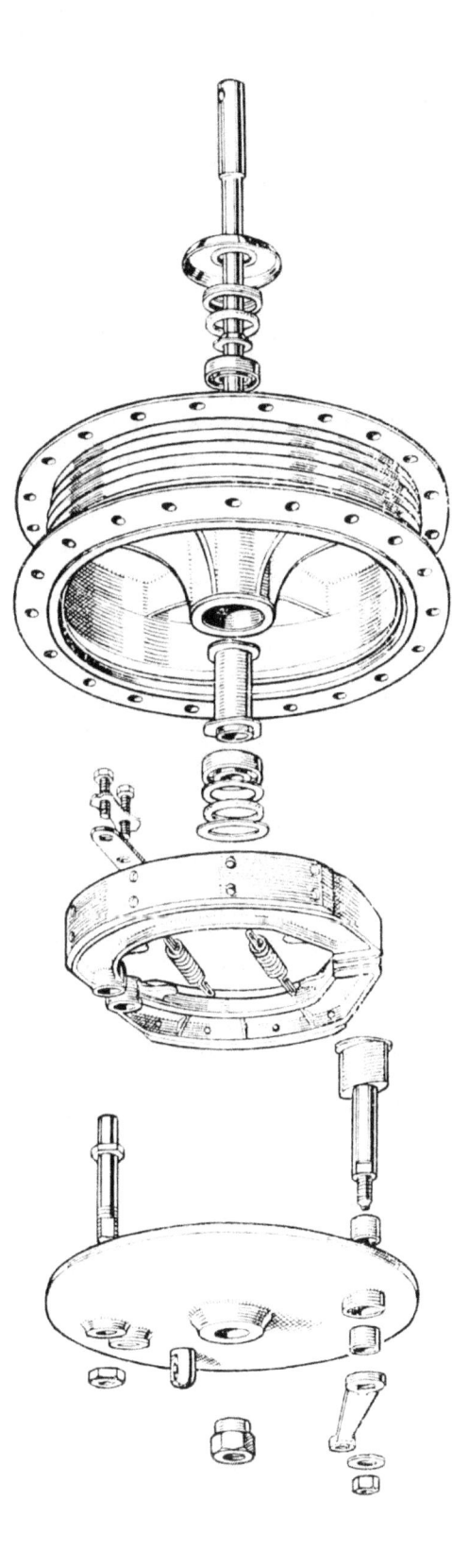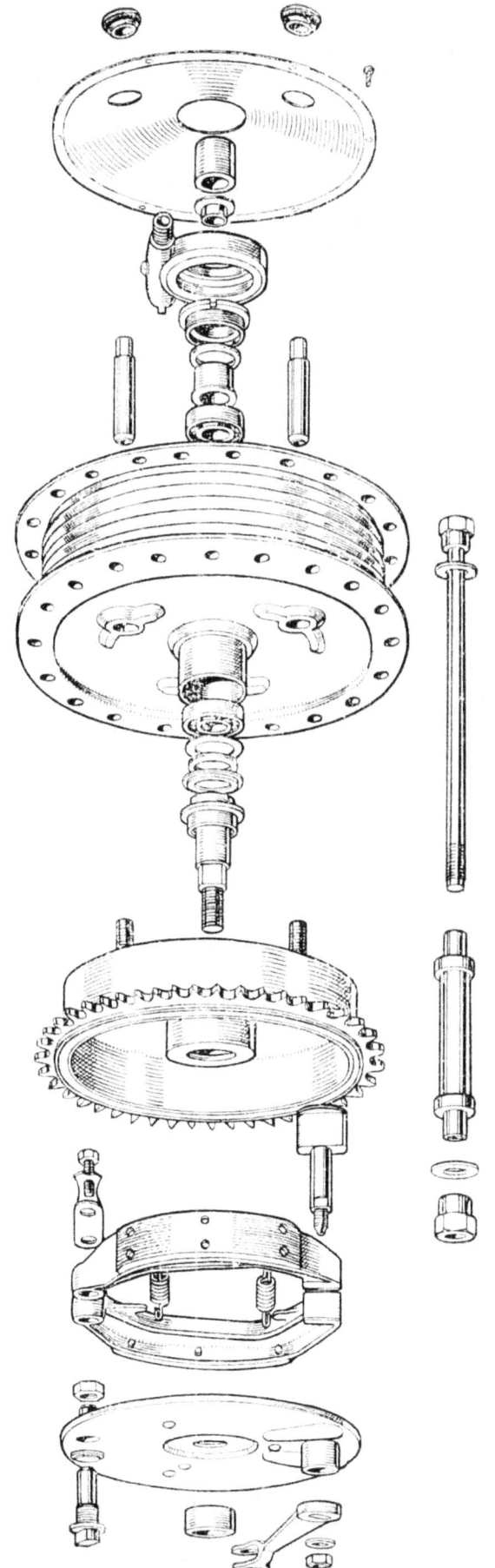

FIG. 20 FRONT HUB   FIG. 21 REAR HUB

that one of the three studs is approximately in line with tubes of pivoted fork (swinging arm). This facilitates getting the bearing boss on the hub past the other two studs and fitting the hub to the brake drum. Fit and tighten three sleeve nuts and replace rubber plugs. Fit speedometer drive gearbox taking great care that its driving dogs properly engage with the slots in the hub bearing lock ring. Position spacer and fit R.H. part of divided spindle. Take care that the washer on this passes the end of the adjuster screw in the fork end and that as the spindle is screwed home its head does not catch on the adjuster screw and bend it.

Tighten spindle and on de Luxe models refit number plate.

94. REAR HUB—DISMANTLING

Remove rear wheel (para. 92). Unscrew very carefully the left hand threaded locking ring which drives the speedometer gearbox. Take out distance piece and felt washer.

Now take the rear wheel spindle, leave on it the thick washer and thread over it the dull plated spacer which fits between speedometer gearbox and fork end.

Insert this assembly through the double row ball race at the opposite side of the hub —the brake drum side. Drive on the end of the spindle with a hide hammer or mallet carefully until a stop is felt. This should have commenced to move the single row bearing out of the lock ring side of the hub. It cannot be moved any further with the spindle and spacer because the double row bearing will have come up against a shoulder in the hub.

Remove spindle and spacer and using front wheel spindle, insert threaded end in double row bearing on brake drum side. Hold square and tap gently with mallet when bearing spacer should be driven from inner race of bearing taking with it the single row bearing from the opposite side.

Now insert rear spindle with dull plated spacer through shouldered bearing spacer and pass into hub from lock ring side.

Carefully centre in double row bearing, hold square and carefully drive out. As this bearing comes out it will bring with it steel cup washer, felt washer and pen steel washer.

95. REAR HUB—RE-ASSEMBLING

Pack bearings with grease (see table of lubricants) with care not to overfill.

Fit the single row bearing into threaded side of hub, fit shouldered bearing spacer with long end into single row bearing. Fit shouldered distance piece, felt washer and locking ring and tighten. (L.H. thread. Do not damage slots which drive speedometer gearbox).

Press double row bearing into position on opposite side of hub. It can be driven home square by using rear spindle and dull plated spacer, as described for removal.

Fit pen steel washer, felt washer and steel cup or dished washer. Lightly rivet the latter washer into position.

96. FRONT HUB—DISMANTLING

Remove front wheel (see para. 90). Remove brake plate. Unscrew lock ring (R.H. thread) using a peg spanner or if not available, a hammer and pin punch. If the ring does not move easily, try tapping from different holes and heat the hub with a soft flame such as a gas ring with a low light.

Remove felt washer and distance washer. Now insert front wheel spindle from brake side and drive with hide hammer or mallet. This will move the double row bearing further into the hub and at the same time drive the single row bearing out.

Drive carefully until this bearing just drops clear, if you drive harder the spacer which fits between the bearings will be damaged. Now withdraw the front wheel spindle, pass it through the bearing spacer still in the hub and holding it central, drive the double row bearing out. This will take with it the large steel washer, felt washer and pen steel washer.

97. FRONT HUB—RE-ASSEMBLING

Pack bearings with grease as for rear hub. Press single row bearing into position, followed by distance washer with flat side to bearing, felt washer and locking ring, which can be tightened up. Insert distance tube small end first into hub, ensuring that it is right home against the bearing just fitted.

Enter double row bearing squarely into hub, pass front wheel spindle through until it enters opposite bearing. Drive on end of spindle until double row bearing comes up against the distance tube and stops. Fit pen steel washer, this is the small one, felt washer and large steel washer and lightly rivet the latter into position.

98. BRAKES, ADJUSTMENT, Front

Clearance between the brake shoes and

drum can be reduced by unscrewing the adjuster on the cable. Continual adjustment causes the expander lever to occupy a position with lost leverage. To restore leverage, take off the cable and reverse the expander lever.

To improve brake efficiency, release the spindle nut a few turns, hold the brake hard on, retighten the spindle nut at the same time. The brake shoes will then centralize. On models before 1964 enlargen spindle hole in brake plate by $\frac{1}{32}''$ to centralize.

Rear

If the rear brake pedal is depressed in excess of its normal travel, the return spring (in the pedal) will stretch and become ineffective. The pedal position can be adjusted, within limits, by releasing the pedal spindle and setting the stop to the desired position. If the brake has been disturbed, centralize the brake shoes, by releasing the left hand spindle nut and press hard on the pedal and tighten the spindle nut at the same time. On machines made before 1964 enlargen spindle hole in brake plate by $\frac{1}{32}''$.

99. BRAKES, DISMANTLING AND ASSEMBLY

Remove brake plate from drum. Remove nut and washer from cam spindle. Remove cam lever.

Remove springs from shoes. This is best done with a screwdriver placed against one of the spring hooks and held in position with one hand, now knock the screwdriver with the palm of the other hand to push the spring off the lug on the shoe. The spring may fly off so care should be taken that it is not lost.

Turn back the tabwasher and unscrew the two hexagon headed set screws which secure the shoes to the pivot pins. Lift off the pivot pin tie plate and remove the brake shoes.

The cam can now be withdrawn. It may be tight in its bush if the cam lever nut has been overtight as this causes the end of the spindle to become swelled. When this happens the end immediately behind the flats should be eased down with emery tape.

If the cam will pass through the bush but is tight, it can be eased down more easily after removal.

On the rear brake plate only, the cam spindle bush can be removed after unscrewing its locknut from the inside.

TO RE-ASSEMBLE

Remove all traces of rust and dirt from the expander cam and pivot pins, apply a slight smear of grease. For ease in working the brake plate can be held in a smooth jaw vice, clamping it by the torque stop. Fit the brake shoes, tie plate and tab washer and set screws. If the tab washer has been used on more than one occasion discard it and use a new one. Fit the shoe springs, by anchoring the end farthest away from the operator, use a length of stout string in the free end of the spring, stretch the spring with one hand and guide the spring onto its anchorage with the other hand. Alternatively use a narrow blade screwdriver. Finally fit the expander lever with its nut and washer. The washer on the rear brake expander, together with the rim on the brake plate, prevents the rear brake shoes being removed from the pivot pins, unless the linings are badly worn. Removing the expander cam will allow the shoes to be detached from the plate.

Front Forks

100. MAINTENANCE

The oil from both fork tubes, which may be contaminated by swarf, should be drained and refilled with fresh oil at the first 1,000 miles and again at 10,000 miles. Use one of the grades shown in the table of lubricants.

Each fork leg has a small cheese headed set screw as a drain plug and with a suitable receptacle placed on the ground, these screws should be removed one at a time, taking care not to lose the small fibre or aluminium washer which makes the seal.

Now hold the front brake on and move the forks up and down to expel the oil. Allow a few minutes for draining and repeat on the other side.

Next refit the drain plugs with their washers and place the machine on the centre stand.

Unscrew the large filler plug on top of each fork leg and 'pull up' the front wheel to expose the springs. Place a block of wood or similar under the wheel to hold the springs clear. Using two spanners, unscrew the filler plug nuts from top of the damper rods.

Remove the block and allow the forks to move to full extension. Pour in a measured 5 fluid ozs. (142 c.c.'s) of 20 grade oil in each leg.

Because these forks have springs inside the main tubes the oil is slow to run down and patience is therefore necessary when refilling.

Before refitting the filler plugs to the damper rods, make certain that their locknuts are screwed down to the end of the thread on the rod. Lock the two together and screw in, and tighten filler plugs.

101. STEERING HEAD ADJUSTMENT

With the machine on its centre stand, and the front wheel clear of the ground, check the steering head bearing for adjustment by:-

Place the fingers of the left hand, round the space between the rear of the handlebar lug and the frame, with the right hand grasp the end of the front mudguard and try to raise and lower the fork assembly. Any movement or slack in the bearing will be apparent. To adjust release the two pinch stud nuts clamping the fork tubes (see fig. 22). Release the domed nut for the fork column which has a $\frac{11}{16}$" Whitworth hexagon. To take up movement use an opened spanner to screw down and turn the nuts on the column below the handlebar lug, retighten the dome nut and recheck. The bearing should be devoid of movement and free from friction. Retighten the fork tube pinch stud nuts.

The steering head bearings for the 1964 models are of the cup and cone type, with 18 loose $\frac{1}{4}$" dia ball bearings in each bearing. The cup portion is a press fit into the head lug. To remove the cups use a piece of steel tubing through the head lug to drive out the cups, shifting the tubing from one side of the cup to the other to eject it square with the lug. Use an old screwdriver, or taper wedge to take off the cone on the fork column.

Thief-proof Lock. A lock is incorporated in the handlebar lug, two keys are supplied with each new machine.

102. REMOVAL OF FRONT FORKS

Place machine on centre stand or on a stout wooden box under engine. Release brake and clutch cables from handlebar levers. Remove handlebar clips and allow bar to rest on tank.

Unscrew both filler plugs on top of fork legs and pull forks and wheel up, placing a block of wood or similar under the tyre to hold the wheel up whilst the filler plugs are unscrewed from the top of the damper rods. A thin $\frac{5}{16}$" Whit. open ended spanner is necessary for this along with the filler plug spanner.

Remove filler plugs and their washers. Remove headlamp and allow to hang by the cables. Disconnect front brake cable from brake plate and remove front wheel.

Remove top column nut and give headclip a sharp jar upwards with hide hammer or mallet to free it from tapers on main tubes. Remove headclip followed by top covers with lamp brackets and their rubber washers. (On some 1960 and 1961 machines it is necessary to remove the steering lock stop plate before the steering column can be withdrawn and this applies to 1962 machines if they are fitted with steering dampers either solo or sidecar). This is secured with a single $\frac{5}{16}$" × 26T bolt with washers, spacer and nut to the trouser plate on the frame immediately below the headlug.

Remove steering column nut and dust cover and carefully withdraw forks.

To remove the steering head bearings (see para 101 for 1964 models) without damage, use a piece of steel strip $1\frac{3}{4}$" long × .9" wide about $\frac{1}{2}$" thick, with a radius on both ends to lay flat across both the inner and outer member of the bearing, when inserted endwise through the bearing. A central hole in the strip for a pilot drift will facilitate removal.

103. REFITTING FRONT FORKS

Apply some heavy grease to the top cone portion of the bearing, fill 18 balls, fit the cone to the cup part.

Load the ball track on the column race by the same method. Introduce the column through the frame, with care not to dislodge the bearings. Fit top shim washer, dust cover, screw down column nut.

Fit lamp brackets, their top rubber washers and headclip. Release nuts on pinch studs in fork crown. Adjust head bearings and tighten top column nut and check that tightening of this does not alter bearing setting.

Pull up forks to expose springs and damper rods. Fit filler plugs and washers to damper rods, first ensuring that the locknuts are already screwed down to the end of the thread on the rod.

Tighten filler plugs to pull main tubes into their tapers in headclip and tighten pinch stud nuts on crown.

It is assumed that the oil in the fork legs has not been drained if the forks were removed complete with mudguard and stays in position. Refit headlamp, handlebars and front wheel and re-connect control cables. Check headlamp for correct height and lateral position of beam.

104. FORK LEG, DISMANTLING

The individual legs may be dismantled either with the forks in position in the frame or otherwise.

Having drained the oil, unscrew the filler plug from the top of the leg and lift it sufficiently for an open ended spanner to be used to slacken the nut which locks the damper rod into the filler plug.

Release the pinch stud nut on the fork crown and pull jerkily on the fork end when the leg should be withdrawn complete.

If necessary partly replace the filler plug without its washer, screwing it down a few threads and tap it smartly with a mallet or hide hammer to release the leg from the taper in the headclip.

The upper ends of the main tubes may be rusty where they pass inside the top covers (lamp brackets) and this may make them difficult to withdraw. It will help to remove the headclip complete and the covers and clean off the rust with emery tape and smear with oil. Additionally, the slot in the crown where the pinch stud passes through can be expanded slightly with an old screwdriver.

Now with the leg removed, the damper unit and spring complete can be withdrawn by unscrewing the $\frac{3}{16}$" Whit. hex. set screw in the bottom end of each fork leg.

Remove the plated bottom cover which is screwed into the fork end and when this is removed, the fork end can be pulled off leaving the flanged top bush and oil seal

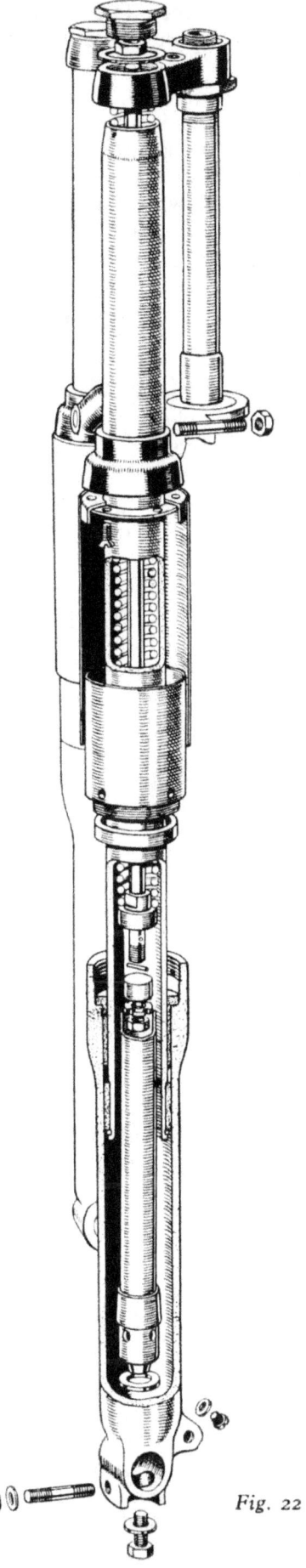

Fig. 22

on the main tube. The steel bush on the bottom end of the tube is attached by a circlip.

If it is desirable to dismantle the damper unit, the top gland nut should be unscrewed and the rod withdrawn from the cylinder, after which removal of the nut from the bottom of the rod will enable the cup, slotted washer and cross pin to be removed.

No difficulty should be experienced in fitting new bushes either to the top of the fork end or the bottom of the main tube.

105. FORK LEG, ASSEMBLY

Thoroughly clean all components and lightly smear each one with oil before placing into position.

Fit crosspin, cup and slotted washer to short screwed end of damper rod. Fit and tighten securing nut.

Insert this assembly into the damper cylinder and screw home the top gland nut. Hold the cylinder whilst this is done with a good fitting tommy bar through the holes in the base.

The cylinder can easily be damaged if it is held in a vice. Place fibre washer over extension on damper cylinder and insert in fork end and secure with set screw and thick washer. Fit fork spring over damper rod followed by aluminium centraliser and screw on filler plug locknut, bevelled edge first, right up to end of thread.

Fit steel bush to bottom end of main tube making certain that circlip is properly fitted and not distorted. Fit bronze bush, paper washer and oil seal to main tube. Oil seal should have its spring towards paper washer and flange of bronze bush. Pass damper rod and spring through main tube from bottom end, carefully entering bush and oil seal into fork leg. Using screwed plated cover, push oil seal in square and screw cover home. Do not overtighten this but it can be tightened best after the wheel spindle has been fitted when the leg cannot turn. Lightly grease upper part of main tube and pass through fork crown. A pull through is available if necessary—part No. 13685, price 10/-. Lightly clamp pinch stud nuts to prevent legs dropping out if necessary. Pour 5 fluid ozs. of 20 grade oil in each leg (142 c.c.).

Push up fork leg to expose damper rod and spring, fit filler plug washer and screw filler plug up to locknut already on damper rod.

Screw up filler plug nuts to pull main tubes hard up into taper in head clip, make certain head bearing adjustment is correct, tighten nuts on pinch studs in crown.

Rear Springing

106. PIVOTTED FORK—REMOVAL AND ASSEMBLY (Swinging arm)

Remove chaincase or chainguard.

Remove rear wheel complete with brake. Remove bottom shock absorber attachment bolts, nuts and washers, and swing the shock absorbers clear. Slacken top bolts if necessary

Remove nut and washer from one end of pivotted fork bolt on frame gusset plate and withdraw bolt from opposite side. Fork or arm should now be pushed forward to clear gusset plates, turned and withdrawn.

If the 'Clayflex' bearings require to be replaced, the fork should be returned to the works for the old bearings to be removed and new ones fitted.

To re-assemble reverse this procedure, fit and tighten the bottom shock absorber bolts before tightening the fork (arm) pivot bolt on the frame. This will ensure that the 'Clayflex' bearings are clamped in approximately the correct rotational position.

107. REAR SUSPENSION UNITS

These fittings embody quite complicated oil damping arrangements which are carefully set to provide the correct suspension characteristics for your machine. They are sealed and are virtually leak proof and should **not be interfered with.** In the unlikely event of any attention being necessary, their removal is quite simple and straightforward and they should be taken to your usual Norton dealer or the nearest Norton distributor.

It is quite permissible to remove the covers in order to grease the spring to promote silent operation.

These units are adjustable to three positions by means of the 'C' spanner provided. The soft or normal solo position is in use when the abutments spot welded to the damper body are in engagement with the topmost positions on the bottom spring collar which has a scroll or face cam, or when this part is rotated as far as possible in an anti-clockwise direction when viewed from above. Rotation in a clockwise direction (by means of the key) will result in the stronger positions being engaged. It is important that both units are adjusted to the same position.

No attempt whatever should be made by the normal rider to dismantle, drain or refill these units.

When these units are fitted to the machine it is important that they should be primed first as they will lose their prime if they have been laid horizontally for only a short time.

To prime mount vertically in a vice by the lower mounting lug, set to the soft position, pull down on top cover and remove split collet. Remove covers and spring and now operate damper rod over its full range until smooth even resistance is felt on extension but none at all on compression. If you cannot get this result the damper is faulty.

Refit covers and spring and collets and refit to machine keeping vertical.

Handlebar Fittings

108. AIR CONTROL LEVER

To remove the control cable from the lever, open the lever as far as possible, hold the outer cable, and as the lever is closed, pull the outer cable from the lever body.

Remove nipple from the lever.

To fit the cable, fit nipple into the lever, close the lever, pull the outer cable away from the lever and fit the cable to the lever body.

109. CLUTCH AND FRONT BRAKE CONTROL LEVERS

The clutch and front brake controls are so simple as to require no instructions for their dismantling or assembly.

The screws on which the levers pivot can be adjusted to reduce side clearance between lever and fulcrum part of clip as the lower side of each lever is threaded and a self locking nut fitted.

To remove the clutch cable from the lever, take off the inspection cap from gearbox end and with a screwdriver, lift up the small operating lever. At the same time pull the outer cable clear of the handlebar lever.

It should be noted that if replacement levers are at any time obtained, the one for clutch operation with an A.M.C. gearbox should have $\frac{7}{8}"$ centres between cable nipple and fulcrum screw.

This is not the same on earlier machines with Norton/Burman gearboxes and these require levers having $1\frac{1}{16}"$ centres.

Now unscrew the cable adjuster from the brake plate and the cable will come clear. Re-assemble in reverse order.

110. TWIST GRIP

The twist grip assembly is shown in Fig. 23.

To assemble the twist grip, grease the portion of the handlebar where grip works.

Fit sleeve to the bar.

Grease the drum on the sleeve.

Fit spring and adjuster bolt and nut to the bottom half clip.

Thread the cable through the hole in the half clip.

Fit the nipple to the drum on the sleeve.

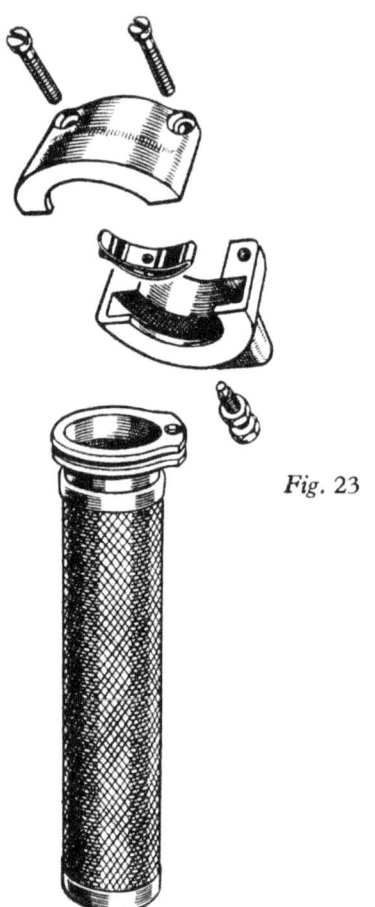

Fig. 23

(Sufficient length of cable can be obtained by lifting the throttle slide and holding in position by piece of soft wood placed in the air intake).

Fit the top half clip.

Adjust the tightness of the grip with the adjusting screw and lock in the desired position.

Dismantle in the reverse order.

Amal Carburetter

111. DISMANTLING OF THE CARBURETTER

The easiest way to remove the carburetter is to turn the petrol tap off and disconnect feed pipe from carburetter, remove the two nuts securing carburetter flange and unscrew the knurled ring immediately below where the control cables enter the top of the mixing chamber body so that the slides may be withdrawn, either before or after the carburetter is removed. The air and throttle valves may be left on the cables unless it is desired to change or renew the cables or valves.

The throttle valve needle may be removed or adjusted for position by removal of the spring clip at the top of the slide.

Remove the float chamber cover by removing the three screws securing it, and withdraw the hinged float and spacer, this will enable the nylon needle which controls the flow of fuel to be withdrawn and cleaned.

Removal of the nut at the base of the mixing chamber gives access to the main jet which may be unscrewed from the jet holder which also carries the needle jet, accessible by removal of jet holder. Removal of these parts enables the jet block to be pushed or tapped out through the large end of the mixing chamber body when the jet block locating screw has been removed. This screw lies to the left of and slightly below the pilot air adjuster which is the horizontal milled headed screw equipped with restricting spring.

112. RE-ASSEMBLY OF CARBURETTER

Re-assembly should present no difficulty but the following points should be watched. The washer fitted to the stub of the jet block should be in good condition, also the one fitted to the needle jet holder. When fitting throttle valve ensure that taper needle really enters the centre hole in the jet block, and throttle works freely when mixing chamber top cap is fitted and secured. Fit float with narrow side of hinge uppermost, replace spacer, and ensure that side cover washer and body are clean and undamaged to obtain a petrol tight joint.

113. CARBURETTER TUNING

There are four distinct phases of tuning and each must be handled separately to obtain best results for any particular set of conditions. For all these positions the air valve should be fully open, the engine should be at its normal working temperature, and the machine should be driven on a slight up gradient to ensure engine pulling the whole time.

1st MAIN JET.

This jet controls the fuel supply when the throttle is more than ¾ open. With the throttle fully open and the engine pulling hard, slightly close the air lever when there should be a slight falling off of speed indicating a reasonably correct mixture. If maximum speed is obtained before the throttle is fully open, then a larger main jet is required; similarly if there is an increase in speed with the air lever slightly closed.

2nd SLOW RUNNING.

Having fixed the main jet, set the throttle

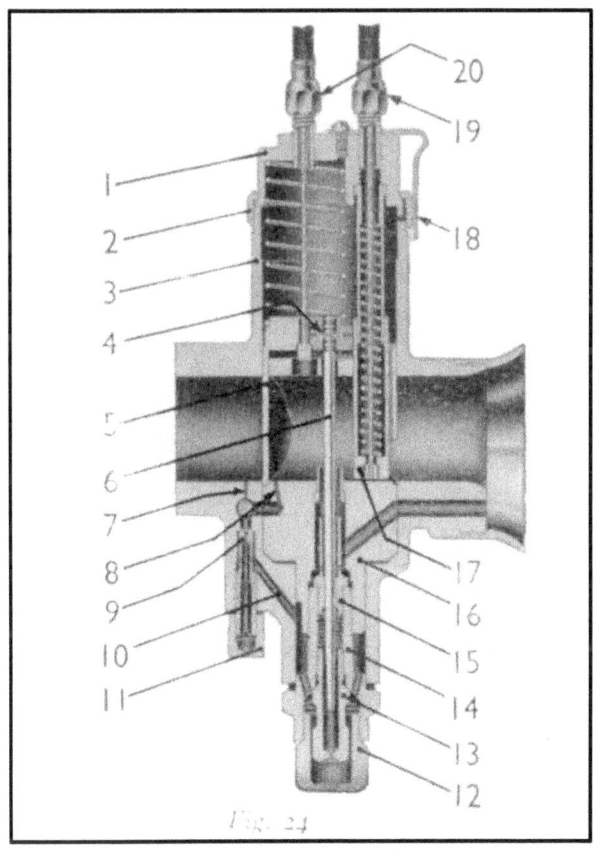

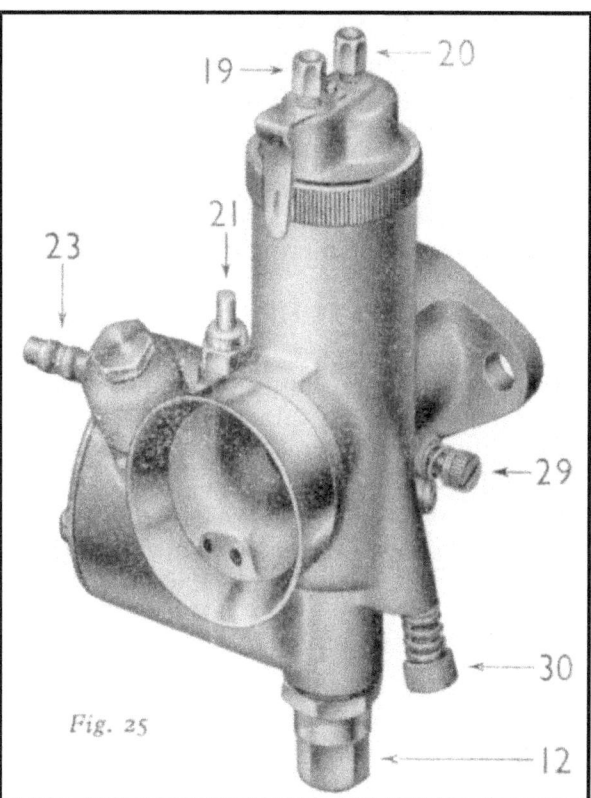

Fig. 25

adjusting screw to provide fairly fast idling with the twist grip in the fully closed position and the ignition (where manually controlled) set for best slow running. Screw out the throttle adjusting screw until engine begins to falter; now adjust the pilot air screw in or out as necessary to make the engine run evenly and faster. Lower the throttle adjusting screw further to reduce engine speed until a position of the pilot air screw is found at which the engine runs evenly and steadily on the smallest throttle opening.

3rd THROTTLE VALVE CUTAWAY.

With the throttle valve about ¼ open (marking the twist grip if necessary in order to readily find this position whilst riding) note whether there is any spitting (indicating weakness) or jerky running under load (indicating richness). In the former event try screwing in the pilot air screw slightly and if this is ineffective, a throttle valve having less cutaway, i.e., stamped with a lower number and the reverse for jerky running.

4th THROTTLE VALVE NEEDLE.

With the throttle about ¾ open and the needle in a low position try the machine for acceleration. If the results are poor and partially closing the lever provides improved conditions, raise the needle a notch or two until the best position is found.

5th RE-CHECK IDLING.

To ensure that subsequent adjustments have not upset the condition.

1—Mixing Chamber Top
2—Mixing Chamber Cap
3—Carburetter Body
4—Jet Needle Clip
5—Throttle Valve
6—Jet Needle
7—Pilot Outlet
8—Pilot by-pass
9—Pilot Jet
10—Petrol feed to pilot jet
11—Pilot Jet Cover Nut
12—Main Jet Cover
13—Main Jet
14—Jet Holder
15—Needle Jet
16—Jet Block
17—Air Valve
18—Mixing Chamber Cap Spring
19—Cable Adjuster (Air)
20—Cable Adjuster (Throttle)
21—Tickler
23—Banjo
29—Pilot Air Adjusting Screw
30—Throttle Adjusting Screw

114. MAINTENANCE

Clean periodically by dismantling and washing in clean petrol, cleaning out all holes by blowing. Whilst dismantled examine throttle valve needle and float needle for wear and all fibre washers, renewing as necessary. Check that throttle valve is not unduly worn in the mixing chamber body.

115. RICH MIXTURE

Indicated by black exhaust smoke, excessive soot on plug, lumpy running, petrol blown back from air intake.

Assuming that carburation has previously been satisfactory, suspect:—flooding due to punctured float, dirt on float needle seating or worn needle or seat. Worn throttle valve needle or needle jet, air cleaner choked.

116. WEAK MIXTURE

Indicated by spitting back, poor acceleration, overheating, erratic slow running or improved performance with air lever partly shut.

Again assuming carburetter has been correctly set, suspect:— fuel blockage, either main supply or within carburetter. Worn inlet valve guide, air leaks at engine carburetter connection, worn throttle valve, loose jets.

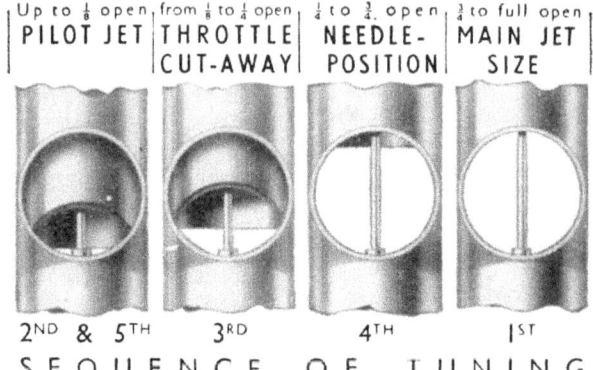

Fig. 26

Tyres

117. MAINTENANCE

Always keep tyres at the correct pressures, (see data page at front of book). Remove any stones which may be embedded in the tread. Replace valve dust cap if lost.

118. REMOVAL

Deflate tube by removing valve cap and core. Remove rim nut and security bolt nut if security bolt fitted. Push the beads of the cover down into the well of the rim at a point opposite to the valve. Insert a small tyre lever between the bead and the rim near to the valve. Ease the bead off the rim using a second lever inserted a short distance away. Repeat until one bead is free of the rim.

Remove security bolt and tube, and remove the second bead in a similar manner.

119. FITTING

Fit rim band. Dust tube, beads and rim with French chalk. Slightly inflate tube and place within cover on top of wheel with valve in line with hole in rim. Fit the underneath bead by hand, completing the operation with levers. Thread valve and stem of security bolt through appropriate holes. Fit second bead starting opposite valve. See that security bolt and tube are not being pinched between cover and rim. Inflate. Fit rim nut and security bolt nut. Adjust pressure to manufacturer's recommendation and fit dust cap. NOTE—All 650 c.c. and S.S. models are fitted with the Avon G.P. rear tyre and special inner tube.

The manufacturers recommend that under no circumstances should anything other than these be fitted to the rear wheel as replacement.

Pressures recommended below must be strictly adhered to:—

For sustained speeds up to 110 m.p.h. and for short bursts of not more than 2 minutes up to 125 m.p.h.—Front 24 p.s.i.; Rear 24 p.s.i.

For sustained speeds above 110 m.p.h.— Front 24 p.s.i. Rear 30 p.s.i.

Pressures given above are for cold tyres and with rider only.

Valve caps must be securely fitted.

Electrical Section

All the machines covered by this book have A.C. generators, and all have coil ignition except Sports Special models.

The essentials of this form of lighting and ignition consist of the following units.

Alternator. For the generation of Alternating Current.

Rectifier. For conversion of A.C. to Direct Current to enable battery to be charged.

Battery. For current storage.

Coil. For conversion of low tension voltage to high tension.

Contact Breaker (and Distributor on Twin Cylinder machines). To control the timing of the high tension voltage to the sparking plugs (ignition timing).

Switch. For control of ignition and lighting.

120. ESSENTIAL MAINTENANCE

Battery. Inspect regularly and frequently and maintain acid level to top of separators by addition of distilled water. The level check should be made after the machine has been standing and not immediately after a run when the electrolyte will be gassing and showing a higher level.

On Lucas PUZ7E batteries, after standing, the acid level should be just to the top of the plates, that is just visible when the filler plugs are removed. On Exide 3EV11 and 3EV9 batteries, again after standing, the level should be to but not above the lower of the two lines marked on the case.

If the levels on either battery are in any way on the high side, there will be risk of overspilling and resultant acid damage to plated and enamelled parts of the machine.

Battery terminals should be kept clean and greased and a periodic check should be made to ensure that the wires themselves are not corroding. On Lucas batteries, clean up the end of the terminal with a smooth file if there is any doubt about the screw on terminal making firm contact. The Exide batteries employ a tag terminal secured with a screw and this must make clean contact with the battery terminal post.

It is well worth while paying attention to these connections as if for any reason, the battery becomes out of circuit, the light bulbs will burn out, even with quite low engine revolutions. ALL BATTERIES TO HAVE POSITIVE TERMINAL CONNECTED TO 'EARTH'.

Wiring. Keep all connections and terminals tight and ensure cables are clear of moving parts. Examine carefully stop and tail lamp leads for being properly positioned in the aluminium clip on the left hand side number plate mounting stud. The clip must hold the connectors themselves, and the longer lead which passes round the inside of the mudguard must also be in the clips and not foul the tyre at the front end of the guard where it passes through the grommet.

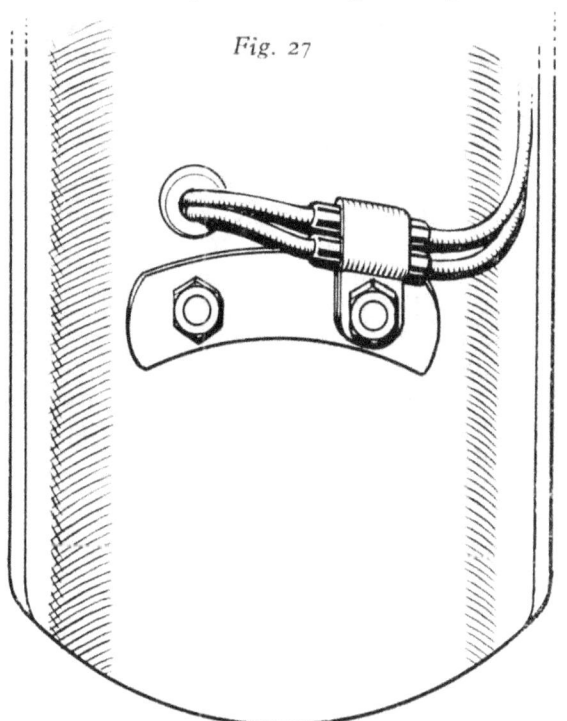

Fig. 27

EARLY MODELS ONLY

Any surplus wire on the lamp side of the snap connectors should be 'fed back' through the grommet into the space between the number plate and outside of mudguard.

These remarks regarding stop/tail lamp leads apply to all Standard models. De luxe machines are slightly different and on these it is important that the leads are clipped or taped to the tubular stay which supports the tail portion of the rear fairing.

Contact Breaker (and distributor on twins).

Check points for correct gap and cleanliness. Gap should be set to .015" plus or minus .001" and on twins the setting should be checked on both cams. If, on a twin cylinder model, the settings vary appreciably on each cam, the ignition timing should be checked on both cylinders and this should not vary more than 2° on one cylinder compared with the other.

To lubricate the A.T.D., it is necessary to remove the cover, the rotor and then the two Phillips head screws which secure the base plate. The timing will not be lost by removing this plate, but the points gap setting should be checked on refitting.

Headlamp. Set the beam so that with the main filament 'on', it is just below horizontal, with the machine loaded as for the larger proportion of night riding. For example, if most of your night riding is done with a passenger, set the beam with the weight of two people up. The main beam should never be set above horizontal. Do not employ bulbs of greater wattage than those normally fitted, as the generator will then not maintain the battery charge state.

Oil the dipper switch pivot and toggle lever periodically, it can be very dangerous, if this switch sticks and does not make an instant changeover from one filament to the other. It is desirable that the switch is connected so that when its lever is lowered, the dipped beam is in use. Keep the glass of the light unit clean, a thin mud covering very much reduces the light. Check that the light unit is properly 'keyed' in the lamp rim ensuring its correct rotational position for angle of dipped beam.

121. IGNITION

In the "OFF" position when key in top of switch in headlamp lies in line with machine. Turn key in clockwise direction for normal "ON" position. Turn key in anti-clockwise direction for emergency starting, i.e., starting with flat battery. Return key to normal "ON" position when engine running.

Ignition timing must be very carefully set if best conditions are to be obtained: the correct figures are:—

Model 88 — 30° Fully advanced; 6° Fully retarded, before T.D.C.
Model 99 — 32° Fully advanced; 8° Fully retarded, before T.D.C.

It should be noted that the auto advance unit has only 12° (24 crankshaft degrees).

See paras. 30A and 59 for timing procedure.

122. ALTERNATOR. Lucas RM15

Since the alternator has no commutator, brush mechanism bearings or oil seals, it requires no maintenance apart from occasionally checking that its leads are intact and its connectors clean and tight. Examine the grommet in the rear half of the chaincase as if this becomes perished, the leads may chafe on the relatively sharp edge of the hole.

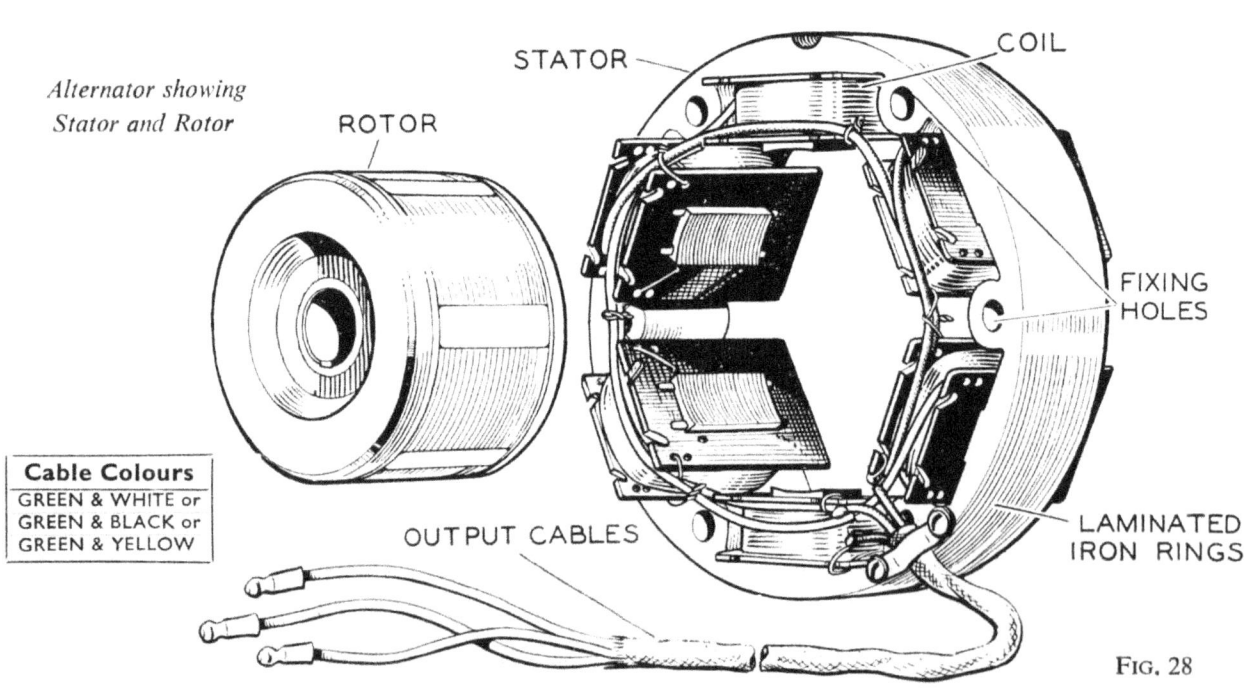

Alternator showing Stator and Rotor

Cable Colours: GREEN & WHITE or GREEN & BLACK or GREEN & YELLOW

FIG. 28

There should always be at least .005″ clearance between the rotor and the pole pieces on the stator and this clearance should be checked whenever the stator is refitted.

Note that the stator should be fitted with the lead taken off side towards the outer primary chaincase and not towards the inner portion of the chaincase.

The rotor is secured to the mainshaft by nut and key and may be withdrawn when the nut is removed. It may be necessary to remove the stator (secured by three nuts and fan disc washers) if the rotor is tight on the shaft but the shaft is parallel.

There is no necessity to fit keepers to the rotor poles when the rotor is removed. Wipe off any metal swarf which may have collected on the pole tips and place the rotor in a clean place.

As mentioned above, the stator is capable of being fitted into the spigot recess either way round, but it will only operate satisfactorily in one position.

123. SWITCH

The switch together with the ammeter and speedometer is carried on the headlamp shell and connections are accessible when headlamp front and light unit assembly are removed. The various cables will be readily recognisable by their coloured sleeving.

Normal Running. Under normal running conditions (i.e. ignition switch in IGN position) electrical energy in the form of rectified alternating current passes to the battery from the alternator — the rate of output depending on the position of the lighting switch. When no lights are in use, the alternator output supplies the ignition coil and trickle charges the battery. When the lighting switch is turned, the output is automatically increased to meet the additional load of parking lights and again when the main bulb is in use.

Emergency Starting (coil ignition models)

An emergency starting position is provided on the ignition switch for use if the battery has become discharged.

Under these conditions, the alternator is connected direct to the ignition coil, allowing the engine to be started independently of the battery.

When kickstarting with the switch in the EMG position, a considerably 'heftier' kick may be necessary than is the case when making a normal start. If the ignition timing is, for any reason, only slightly out, it may not be possible to obtain an EMG start with the kickstarter.

A push start should then be tried, in 2nd gear with the switch in normal IGN position.

A further point which should be noted is that, if the alternator leads have been changed over to obtain the increased charge rate, it may not be possible to obtain a start in the EMG position. In this case the leads should be temporarily changed back or a push start tried as described above.

124. INCREASED CHARGING RATE

Should the battery become run down due to prolonged slow riding in traffic, or during running-in or due to parking with lights on for long periods and whenever a sidecar is fitted an increased charge rate can be obtained by a simple wiring alteration.

The alternator leads after emerging from the primary chaincase, join the main harness by means of a 3-way snap connector. It may be clipped to the H.T. leads where they leave the distributor or higher up near the top of the battery box.

The colours are:—Light green or green and white. Dark green or green and black and green and yellow.

Disconnect the dark green or green and black and the green and yellow and reverse these two connectors.

That is connect the green and black alternator cable to the green and yellow harness cable. Connect the green and black harness cable to the green and yellow alternator cable.

With the light switch in the off position, the ammeter should show approx. twice the previous output. When the lights are switched on to either 'pilot' or 'head' however, the output remains as before.

WHENEVER A SIDECAR IS PERMANENTLY ATTACHED TO ONE OF THESE MACHINES this alteration should be carried out as otherwise the added consumption of the sidecar lamp or lamps will not be compensated for and the battery will slowly run down.

On a solo machine on a long daylight run using the increased output, the battery may become overcharged which can result in damage to the battery and damage to plated and enamelled parts of the machine due to acid spillage.

125. RECTIFIER

The rectifier is a device to allow current to flow in one direction only. It is connected to provide full-wave rectification of the alternator output current.

The Rectifier requires no maintenance beyond checking that the connections are clean and tight.

The nuts clamping the rectifier plates together must not UNDER ANY CIRCUMSTANCES be slackened as the presseure has been carefully set during manufacture to give correct rectifier performance. A separate nut is used to secure the rectifier to the machine and it is important to check periodically that the rectifier is firmly attached to its mounting point. It should make firm metal to metal contact to ensure a good electrical connection.

126. COIL

An ignition coil of orthodox type is attached to a suitable position on the frame by a bolt and clip. Like the rectifier, the coil should only require occasional checking for cleanliness and tightness of mounting and terminals.

127. CONTACT BREAKER AND DISTRIBUTOR (models 88, 99 and 650).

Chain driven from the intermediate timing gear, the driving sprocket is located on the distributor spindle by a parallel peg, upon removal of which the sprocket may be withdrawn. Behind the sprocket there is a tubular spacer and copper washer on the spindle. Care should be taken that these are not misplaced and when refitting the washer goes on the spindle first.

Removal of the single set screw holding the clamping flange to the inside of the timing cover extension, allows the contact breaker/distributor unit complete to be withdrawn from the housing when the distributor cap has been removed.

It may also be necessary to remove the low tension connection to the contact breaker so that the latter can be turned as it is withdrawn in order that the bolt in the clamp will clear the engine plates. Alternatively, the clamping bolt can be released and the unit withdrawn leaving the clip attached to the housing by the set screw. Routine maintenance can be carried out without removing

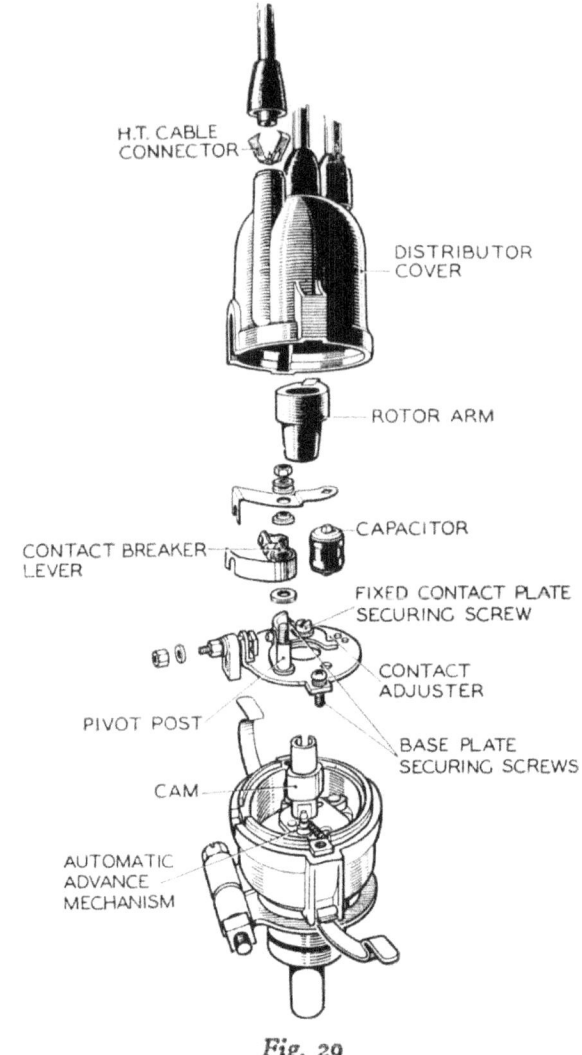

Fig. 29

the unit from the engine.

Contact Breaker setting. Check the contact breaker after the first 500 miles running and subsequently every 6000 miles.

To check the gap, remove the sparking plugs, and rotate the engine slowly until one lobe of the cam is directly under the heel of the rocker arm. In this position the points are wide open and a .015" feeler should be a sliding fit. Take care to enter the feeler square without side influence or an accurate result will not be obtained. The gap should be from .014" to .016" and the setting should be checked on both lobes of the cam.

To adjust the gap, keep the engine in the position giving maximum contact opening and slacken the screw securing the fixed contact plate. Insert a screwdriver between the two studs or pips on the base plate and the notch in the fixed contact plate, and adjust the position of the plate until the correct gap is obtained. Tighten the securing screw and re-check the gap.

Lubrication and cleaning. To be carried out every 6000 miles. Remove and clean the distributor cover. Pay particular attention to the spaces between the metal electrodes in the cover, and check that the small carbon brush moves freely in its holder.

Lift off the rotor arm, and unscrew the two screws securing the contact breaker base plate. Remove the base plate and lubricate the automatic advance mechanism with clean engine oil, paying particular attention to the pivots.

Re-fit the base plate and rotor arm.

Examine the contact breaker. The contacts must be free from grease or oil. If they are burned or blackened, clean with fine carborundum stone or very fine emery cloth, afterwards wiping away any trace of dirt or metal dust with a clean petrol-moistened cloth.

Contact cleaning is made easier if the contact breaker lever carrying the moving contact is removed. Before re-fitting the contact breaker lever, lightly smear the cam and pivot post with clean engine oil.

No grease or oil must be allowed to get on or near the contacts.

After cleaning, check the contact breaker setting.

Renewing High Tension Cables. Replace the high tension cables when these show signs of perishing or cracking, using 7 mm. p.v.c. or neoprene-covered rubber ignition cable. It is advisable to fit new H.T. cable connectors when renewing the ignition cables.

129. BATTERY—Lucas PUZ7E/11

When examining a battery, do not hold naked lights near the vents as there is a danger of igniting the gas coming from the plates.

Remove the vent plugs and see that the ventilating holes in each are quite clear.

Remove any dirt by means of a bent wire.

A clogged vent plug will cause the pressure in the cell to increase, due to gases given off during charging, and this may cause damage.

Make sure that the rubber washer is fitted under each vent plug, otherwise the electrolyte may leak.

Battery — Exide 3EV9. This battery is fitted on de Luxe models and requires similar maintenance to the Lucas one.

All these machines should have the battery positive terminal connected to the frame of the machine, i.e., Positive earth.

See para. 120—Essential Maintenance.

Battery—Topping-up. About once a fortnight or more often in warm climates check the level of the electrolyte in the battery cells and add distilled water as indicated in para. 120.

Wipe dirt and moisture from battery top.

Checking Battery Condition. The state of charge of the battery should be examined by taking hydrometer readings of the specific gravity of the acid in the cells.

The specific gravity readings and their indications are as follows:

1.280—1.300. Battery fully charged.
About — 1.210. Battery about half discharged.
Below—1.150. Battery fully discharged.

These figures are given assuming the temperature of the acid is about 60°F.

Each reading should be appoximately the same.

If one cell gives a reading very different from the rest, it may be that the acid has been spilled or leaked from this particular cell, or there may be a short circuit between the plates.

Fig. 31

This will necessitate its return to a Repair Depot for rectification.

Wipe the top of the battery to remove all dirt or water.

Note. Do not leave the battery in a discharged condition for any length of time.

If a motor cycle is to be out of use, the battery must first be fully charged, and afterwards given a refreshing charge about every two weeks.

Earthing Connections. The positive terminal must be connected to the frame or earth terminal. The Rectifier will be damaged if a battery is only momentarily connected wrong way round.

Charging. If the previous tests indicate that the battery is merely discharged, and if the acid level is correct, the battery must be recharged from an external supply.

130. HEADLAMP

The headlamp which carries also the switch, ammeter, and speedometer, incorporates a Lucas light unit.

Setting headlamp beam. See para. 120.

Bulb Replacement. To remove the headlamp front, slacken the screw at the top of the lamp and pull off the front rim complete with light unit assembly.

The pilot bulb holder is a 'spring' fit in the reflector itself and has a 'cushioning' rubber washer which should not be misplaced or lost when the holder is pulled out of the reflector.

To gain access to the headlamp bulb, push on the adaptor and twist in an anti-clockwise direction to take it off. The bulb can now be removed from the rear of the reflector.

Place the correct replacement bulb in the holder, engage the projections on the inside of the adaptor, noting that they will only engage in one position, press on and secure by twisting to the right (turn clockwise).

Lucas replacement bulbs should always be used, the pilot bulb is No. 988—6v. 3w. with miniature bayonet cap. Main bulb No. 373—6v. 30/24w. with pre-focus cap. Stop/Tail bulb Lucas No. 384—6v. 6/18w.

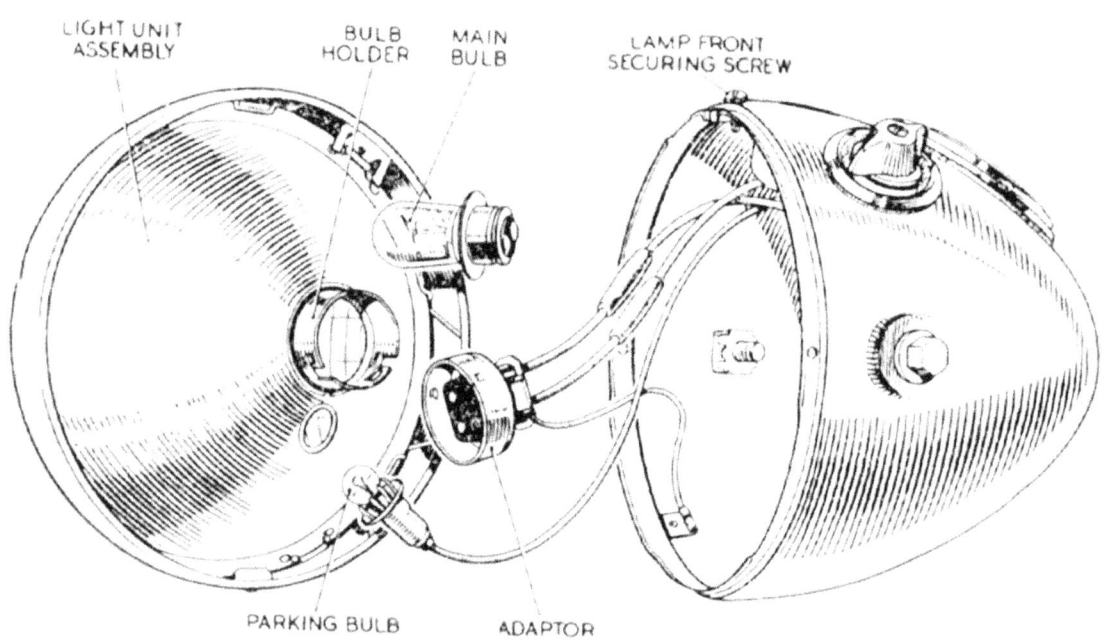

Fig. 32 Light Unit—bulb removal

131. TAIL, STOP AND NUMBER PLATE LAMP

This is Lucas No. 564 which incorporates twin 'Reflex' reflectors, thus eliminating the necessity of fitting a separate reflector.

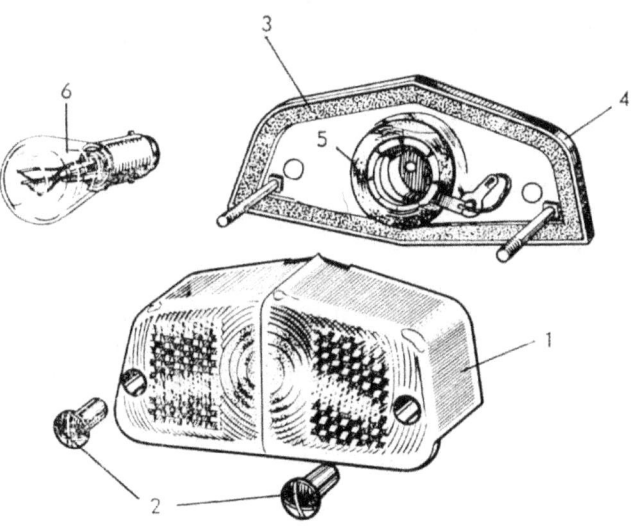

1. Lens and Window
2. Nut
3. Gasket
4. Base Assembly
5. Grommet
6. Bulb

Fig. 33 Tail, Stop and Number Plate Lamp

This lamp is fitted with a double filament bulb having a 6 watt filament for the normal rear and number plate light and an 18 watt controlled by the rear brake.

To obtain access to the bulb, remove the two securing screws and the plastic lens complete. The bulb has unequally positioned bayonet pins so that it cannot be incorrectly fitted into the holder.

132. CABLES

To connect leads to a Lucas battery, unscrew knurled plastic terminal nut and withdraw collet (small thick washer).

Bare the end of the cable (about $\frac{1}{2}''$) and thread the bared end through the knurled nut and collet. Coil up the surplus wire against the end of the collet, feed back collet and wire into knurled terminal nut and screw on to terminal post firmly. Do not overtighten or the nut may burst.

To connect the leads to an Exide battery, the leads on the machine have soldered on tag terminals. The battery terminals incorporate set screws which should be removed, the tags threaded on and the screws firmly replaced.

Snap connectors, i.e. rubber covered push-pull connections are used at many points in the wiring system.

They appear when connected as a small rubber sleeve, or bunch of sleeves when grouped. Disconnect by pulling apart and reconnect by holding in cable pliers, the metal nipple soldered to cable end. Hold rubber covered portion in fingers and press nipple home with pliers. Ensure rubber sleeves are always covering metal portions of connectors when in use.

Special pliers are available from some accessory houses for assembling these fittings and they are so constructed that both nipples can be pressed into the sleeve at the same time.

133. LIGHTING AND IGNITION SWITCH

The switch is carried in the headlamp shell and connections are accessible when headlamp front and light unit assembly is removed. The cables are identified by various colours.

The switch on coil ignition machines—Lucas PRS8—is complicated and should, on no account be dismantled.

With magneto ignition, fewer connections are involved and a switch similar to those employed on earlier D.C. systems is used.

134. HORN

Electric horns are adjusted to give their best performance before leaving the works and will give a long period of service without any attention.

If the horn becomes uncertain in action, or does not vibrate, it has not necessarily broken down.

The trouble may be due to a discharged battery or a loose connection, or short circuit in the wiring of the horn.

The performance of the horn may be upset by the fixing bolt working loose, or by the vibration of some part adjacent to the horn.

To check this, remove the horn from its mounting, hold it firmly in the hand by its bracket, and press the push.

If the note is still unsatisfactory, the horn may require adjustment and should be taken to a Lucas Service Station.

135. SPARKING PLUG

Clean periodically, say every 3000 miles, and if of detachable type, dismantle and clean thoroughly. Never unscrew the gland nut with other than a ring or box spanner and do not hold the plug in a vice by the gland nut. The plug body itself, may be held in a vice whilst the gland nut is unscrewed with a ring spanner. Clean the electrode insulator with glass paper—not emery cloth and clean the inside of the body with emery tape wrapped round a screwdriver or on an arbor in a drilling machine. Clean the earth points on the body with a wire brush and re-assemble making certain that the gas sealing washer is in position on the insulator and that the central electrode is properly centralised when the gland nut is tightened. Reset gap or gaps as necessary—.015" to .020" for magneto ignition. Gaps can usually be a little larger with coil equipment.

Non-detachable plugs should be cleaned with a wire brush and if they are oiled, flushed out with a small quantity of petrol.

136. MAGNETO

Lucas Rotating Armature. Type K2F, K2FC. When a magneto is fitted the sole purpose of the alternator is to charge the battery by way of the rectifier.

Most Norton machines are fitted with a centrifugally operated mechanism that automatically alters the point of firing to suit differing engine speeds. Some model 88 S.S. machines, however, have a manual control of ignition timing. Such a control should be moved to the retard position for starting and when the engine labours on a large throttle opening. At all other times the control should be in the fully advanced position.

Automatic Timing Control. This employs a driving sprocket carrying a plate fitted with two pins. A weight is pivoted on each pin, and the movement of the weight is controlled by a spring connected between the pivot end of the weight and a toggle lever pivoted at approximately the centre of the weight. Holes are provided in each toggle lever in which are located pegs on the underside of a driving plate secured to the magneto spindle.

This plate is also provided with stops which limit the range of the control. When the magneto is stationary, the weights are in the closed position and the magneto retarded for starting purposes. As the speed is increased, centrifugal force acting on the weights overcomes the restraining influence of the springs and the weights move outwards causing relative movement to take place between the driving sprocket and the magneto spindle, so advancing the timing. By careful design of the springs, the characteristics of the control can be arranged to conform more closely with the engine requirements than is the case with other types of control.

At 1600 engine r.p.m. the unit begins to advance the timing. At 2000 r.p.m. there can be from 10 to 20 degrees advance, and at 2500 r.p.m. and above, the unit moves to the fully advanced position giving approximately 24 degrees.

When timing a magneto fitted with one of these units, it should be 'propped' in the advance position with a small wooden wedge or a small nut and the timing set to the advanced figure. Particular care being taken afterwards of course, to remove the wedge, and when the nut securing the unit to the magneto armature spindle has been tightened, check that the unit will still move freely over its advance range. The wedge should be removed whilst this nut is tightened and replaced to check the timing only.

Checking Contact Breaker Gap (every 3000 miles). To check the contact breaker gap, remove the contact breaker cover and turn the engine over slowly until the contacts are fully open. A flat steel gauge of thickness of .012" to .015" (.305 to 381 mm.) should be a sliding fit between the contacts.

Adjusting Contact Breaker Gap. Two types of contact breaker are in service. The present assembly has a fixed contact plate secured by a single screw passing through a slotted hole in the plate. To adjust the gap, slacken this screw and, using a screwdriver move the fixed contact plate until the correct gap is obtained. Tighten the screw and re-check the gap.

NOTE—The present contact breaker is interchangeable with the older pattern, provided the present shorter straight-shanked securing screw is fitted in place of the former longer screw, the shank of which has a 17° taper for $\frac{3}{16}$" (4.76 mm.) below the head.

The earlier assembly has a contact screw and locking nut. To adjust the gap, slacken the locking nut and turn the contact screw by its hexagon head until the correct gap is obtained. Tighten the locking nut and re-check the gap. Do not overtighten this.

Lubrication. The cam ring is supplied with lubricant from a felt strip contained in a recess in the contact breaker housing. Oil reaches the inner surface of the cam ring by way of a small circular wick passing through the thickness of the cam ring.

Remove the contact breaker cover. Take out the central hexagon headed securing screw and carefully withdraw the contact breaker from the tapered magneto spindle. When the screw is completely clear of the threads, but still in the centre of the contact breaker, it can be used to 'break' the taper by 'levering' sideways with the fingers. The breaker should then come out on the screw.

Withdraw the cam ring. It is a sliding fit in the contact breaker housing.

NOTE—If a manual control of ignition timing is fitted, withdrawal and refitting of the cam ring will be made easier if the handle-bar control lever is moved to the half retard position, thus taking the cam ring from its stop peg.

Clean the cam ring both inside and out and lightly smear with Mobilgrease No. 2.

Add a few drops of thin machine oil to the felt strip and to the circular wick.

Remove the contact breaker lever (rocker arm) and smear the pivot with Mobilgrease No. 2 applying sufficient grease to fill the annular groove.

To remove the rocker arm from the present contact breaker, it is necessary to remove the push-on retaining ring and this must not be used again but must be replaced with a new one.

An alternative method of lubrication for this type of rocker arm pivot, is to apply a spot of clean engine oil to the tip of the pivot post. While this will obviate the necessity of removing the arm (lever), great care must be exercised to prevent any oil getting on or near the contacts.

If the arm is removed, care must be taken that the fibre washers fitted on either side of the arm are not misplaced. They are fitted to align the contact points.

The spring should be detached from the 'fixed' end and it has a small buffer spring on the inside and this requires to be fitted with its bent portion towards the centre. Wipe the two leaves of the spring clean and very lightly smear with oil.

To re-assemble, refit in the reverse order. Refit the cam ring, taking care that when manual timing control is fitted that the stop peg in the contact breaker housing and the spring loaded plunger engage with their respective slots.

If an earthing brush is fitted at the back of the contact breaker base plate, see that it is clean and can move freely in its holder before refitting the contact breaker assembly in the cam ring.

Refit the contact breaker assembly, ensuring that the projecting key on the tapered portion of the contact breaker base plate engages correctly with the spindle keyway. Check that the spring does not touch the cam ring.

To remove the rocker arm on the earlier contact breaker, the same remarks regarding the spring and buffer spring apply but to remove the arm from its pivot, it is merely necessary to swing aside the arm or lever retaining spring. There should be a single insulating washer at the base of the pivot post.

Cleaning. Every 6000 miles.

Remove the contact breaker cover and high tension pick-up mouldings. Thoroughly clean the inside and outside of the magneto using a clean, dry, fluffless cloth, if necessary, moistening it with petrol to remove any grease from the H.T. pick-up mouldings and contact breaker contacts. Ensure that the pick-up brush moves freely in its holder. Renew the brush if it is worn to $\frac{1}{8}''$ above the shoulder.

Clean the slip ring track and flanges by pressing the cloth on them while the engine is turned by hand.

Ensure that the gaskets between the pick-up mouldings and the magneto body are in good condition. Examine the contacts when the contact breaker is removed for lubrication. If the contacts are pitted or piled, they should be trimmed with a carborundum stone, silicon carbide paper, or very fine emery cloth.

Contacts do not retain a polished appearance when in use, and if operating correctly, will have a dull grey appearance.

137. RENEWING HIGH TENSION CABLES

When the high tension cable shows signs of cracking or perishing, replace it using 7 mm. P.V.C. covered or Neoprene covered vulcanised rubber insulated ignition cable.

Coil and magneto ignition equipped machines use different connections at the ends opposite the sparking plugs.

The coil and distributor H.T. leads have a clamped on connector which has three spikes. With care these can be removed from the old leads and used again but if their condition is in doubt they should be replaced.

Magneto leads have a split copper washer on the end of the wire itself. The insulation on the new wire should be cut back about ¼" and the split washer passed over the conductor, the strands of which should now be bent back radially. These can be soldered if desired.

Notes

PISTONS

There are two pistons available for model 88 and three for model 99. These give different ratios according to the year of the engine as follows:

Model 88 1955/59
Std. Piston 7.6 to 1   High Comp. app. 9 to 1
Model 88 1960/62
Std. Piston 8.5 to 1   High Comp. app. 9.45 to 1
Model 99 1956/59
Std. Piston 7.4 to 1   High Comp. app. 8.2 to 1
                         Nomad Piston 9 to 1
Model 99 1960/62
Std. Piston 8.2 to 1   High Comp. app. 9 to 1
                         Nomad Piston 10 to 1

It should be understood that the pistons were not altered but that all cylinder heads on 1960 and later engines give one higher ratio.

CAMSHAFTS

The original 'Daytona' camshaft is fitted to every model 99 and all models 88 from 1956.

Quietening ramps were added to this on all 1959 and later models. From 1960 onwards the same camshaft was used but with flat base tappets.

In 1961 a camshaft giving slightly more lift was introduced on 650 c.c. machines for export. This is now fitted to all S.S. models along with tubular pushrods and special valve springs. It is also fitted to 650 c.c. Standard and de Luxe models.

CARBURETTERS

When twin carburetters are fitted to models 88 and 99 they require similar settings to those employed with a single instrument.

Model 88 usually has a Main Jet No. 240 and model 99 a No. 250. These should be regarded as minimum sizes if performance is a first consideration and they should be increased to 260 and 270 respectively before undertaking a full bore run on, for example, a Motorway.

GEAR RATIOS

All machines with A.M.C. gearboxes up to and including 1959, had a rather large drop in ratio from top to third gear.

To bring these gearboxes into line with 1960 and later machines, it is necessary to replace the main sleeve gear, the layshaft free pinion (3rd gear) and the engine sprocket. The net result of this being chiefly, to lower top gear and allow the twin cylinder engines in particular, to more nearly reach maximum r.p.m. in that gear.

FITTING SIDECARS TO 'FEATHERBED' FRAMES

We emphasise that if sidecars are fitted to these models without reducing the trail, they will not handle well.

For this reason a special fork crown and column and head clip are available which, because of different dimensions also require new top fork covers with lamp brackets. These parts reduce the trail and with an outfit properly aligned and set up, give very good steering.

This crown and column employs a steering damper with two friction discs which centre on a large diameter boss on the underside of the crown. These parts will not fit the solo crown.

There is also a steering damper for the solo crown which employs a single friction disc of different dimensions and it is therefore important to state for which crown a damper is required when ordering.

Stronger fork springs and rear shock absorber springs are also available, and should be fitted.

Because of the added electrical consumption of a sidecar lamp or lamps, an A.C. generator may not maintain the battery state unless an increased output is obtained as described in para. 124.

FITTING A FOG OR SPOT LAMP

The correct method is to connect an additional dip switch (i.e. a single pole, two-way switch) in series with the existing dip switch in order to be able to select for operation either the headlamp or the fog/spot lamp, when the main lighting switch is turned on position 'H'. To do this:

1. Disconnect the feed cable (normally blue) from the centre main terminal of the existing dipswitch.
2. Connect this cable to the centre main terminal of the new switch.
3. Connect one of the two remaining terminals of the new switch to the centre main terminal of the existing switch.
4. Connect the 3rd terminal of the new switch to one of the fog or spot lamp terminals.
5. Connect the other terminal of the foglamp to 'earth'—frame of machine.

The advantage of this method of connection is that electrical overloading due to the simultaneous use of headlamp and foglamp is prevented, and, further, the correct distribution of light to suit differing driving conditions is assured.

FITTING RACING FOOTRESTS—REAR SET

Manx type racing footrests, either folding or fixed can be fitted to Standard featherbed frames. To do so it is necessary to drill a $\frac{7}{16}$" hole in the gusset plate of the frame on each side.

Its position is $1\frac{1}{4}$" below and $\frac{3}{8}$" forward of the centre of the pivoted fork (swinging arm) attachment bolt. It is not correct to drill a hole on the offside to match the standard brake pedal mounting hole on the nearside.

VALVE GEAR LUBRICATION

On all the machines covered by this book, an oil feed to the valve gear is taken from the return oil pipe between oil pump and tank.

Because the valve gear is at a higher level than the end of the return pipe in the tank, it is necessary to have a restriction in the end of this pipe to create a pressure to force the oil to this higher level.

This restriction may vary slightly in individual tanks and if for this or any other reason, the valves or rockers of a particular engine appear to obtain insufficient lubrication, an oil tank return union adaptor as is fitted to 250 c.c. twins can be interchanged with the existing one. This has a restriction built into its outlet at the tank end and may thus give an increased supply to the valve gear. The part No. is 22148.

VIBRATION

In cases where vibration seems excessive on single and twin cylinder models, in addition to checking the tightness of all engine/frame attachment bolts, etc., particular attention should be paid to the cylinder head steady attachments.

Due to heat, the enamel may 'give' slightly under the pressure of nuts and washers and lockwashers of the spring or 'fan disc' type also tend to settle down. The nuts and bolts concerned, therefore, should be checked for tightness, especially at the first 500 mile service.

DIFFICULT STARTING—De Luxe Models

This can be brought about by failure of the extended lever on the carburetter float 'tickler' to actually depress the float when moving within the limit of travel imposed by the slot in the side panel. The remedy is to 'set' the lever slightly at the point where it makes contact with the plunger.

SET SCREWS SECURING BRACKETS TO SILENCERS

Due to the enamel on the brackets 'giving' slightly under heat from the silencer pommels, the screws tend to slacken during initial mileage. If they are not well tightened by the time 500 miles have been covered, they may be lost. Check with good fitting ring spanner after say, 200 miles, and again at 500.

SETTING TWIN CARBURETTERS

To do this the engine should be warm and one H.T. lead should be disconnected and the sparking plug removed from the cylinder. When taking the plug out, check that there are not any small stones, grit or dirt in the plug recess in the head which might enter the cylinder.

Now start up the engine on the other cylinder and by means of the pilot air screw and throttle stop, obtain the slowest even tickover. If you start with the pilot air screw fairly well closed, speed will increase as this is unscrewed. The speed should be progressively set down with the throttle stop. (The pilot air screw enters the mixing chamber body horizontally and the throttle stop screw is the larger one which enters at an upwards angle).

Repeat this procedure on the other cylinder and now when you run on both cylinders, the tick-over may be too fast. Set it down by unscrewing both throttle stop screws a similar small amount. In effect the engine is now running with both throttle valves resting on the throttle stops, but if there is an unequal amount of backlash in the short throttle cables between mixing chambers and cable junction block, the engine will not open up properly.

You should stop the engine therefore and carefully set the adjusters in the mixing chamber tops so that there is just a trace of backlash when the twist grip is closed. It is advisable to tape these adjusters afterwards with thin strips of insulating tape to prevent them moving due to vibration. Whilst they are not so important, provided they reach the fully open position, the air valves should have their cables adjusted in the same way. Finally check that both throttle valves reach the fully open position and set the mid-way adjuster in the single throttle cable to give a trace of backlash at the twist grip.

Set the twist grip friction device to suit individual requirements.

STOP/TAIL LAMP LEADS

Reference is made to the Electrical Section of this book under Essential Maintenance—Wiring.

Stop/Tail lamps are not fitted to the number plates when the machines leave the works because of risk of breakage in transit. It therefore falls upon the dealer to fit and connect the lamp. It should be connected and the wires positioned as shown in the diagram. The snap connectors themselves must be in the aluminium clip provided and should be positioned horizontally above the left hand number plate stud. Surplus wire on the lamp side should be fed back through the grommet in the guard and then if the long lead is also positioned in the clips in the mudguard no trouble will be experienced due to the rear tyre chafing the wires (see Fig. 27).

OWNERS SHOULD CHECK THIS WIRING ON TAKING DELIVERY as if it is not properly carried out there is risk of a short circuit which can cause failure of the lights and also ignition in the case of a coil ignition model.

OIL TANKS

Reference is made to Rear Chain Lubrication at the end of para. 71 and the following information given:

Some 1962, 88 and 650 S.S. machines may have a modified oil tank breather system and when fitted, this consists of an oil tank with a vapour tower at the top and the crankcase breather pipe is fed in to the top of the tank so that it discharges downwards away from the top of the tower. A separate connection from the top of the tower is then taken to a welded connection on the rear chainguard. There is thus only a single vent pipe from the oil system feeding the rear chain.

ELECTRICAL WIRING DIAGRAM
for 650 Std. and de Luxe, 99 Std., de Luxe and S.S., 88 Std. and de Luxe

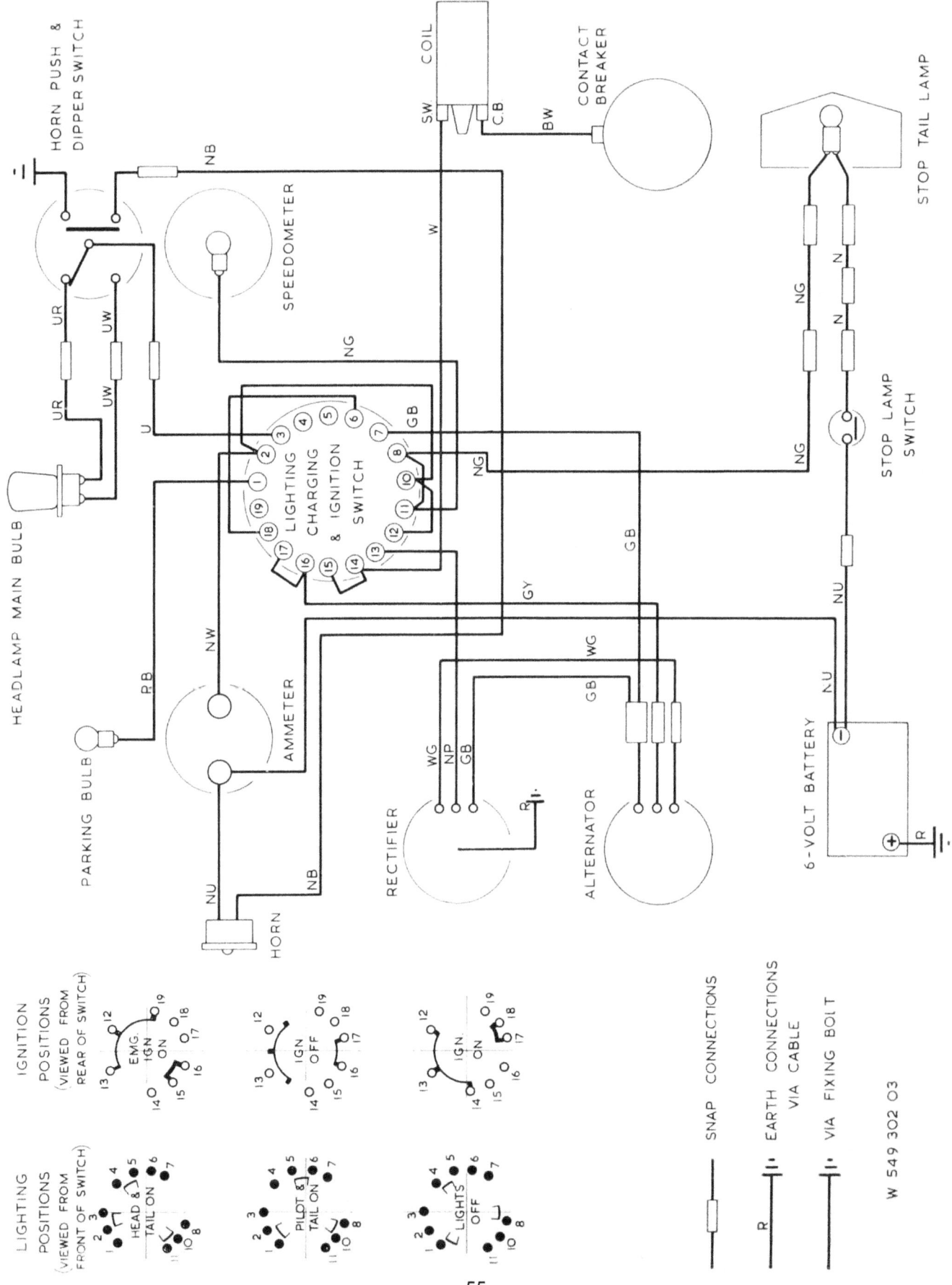

ELECTRICAL WIRING DIAGRAM for models 500 S.S., 650 S.S. and 650 American

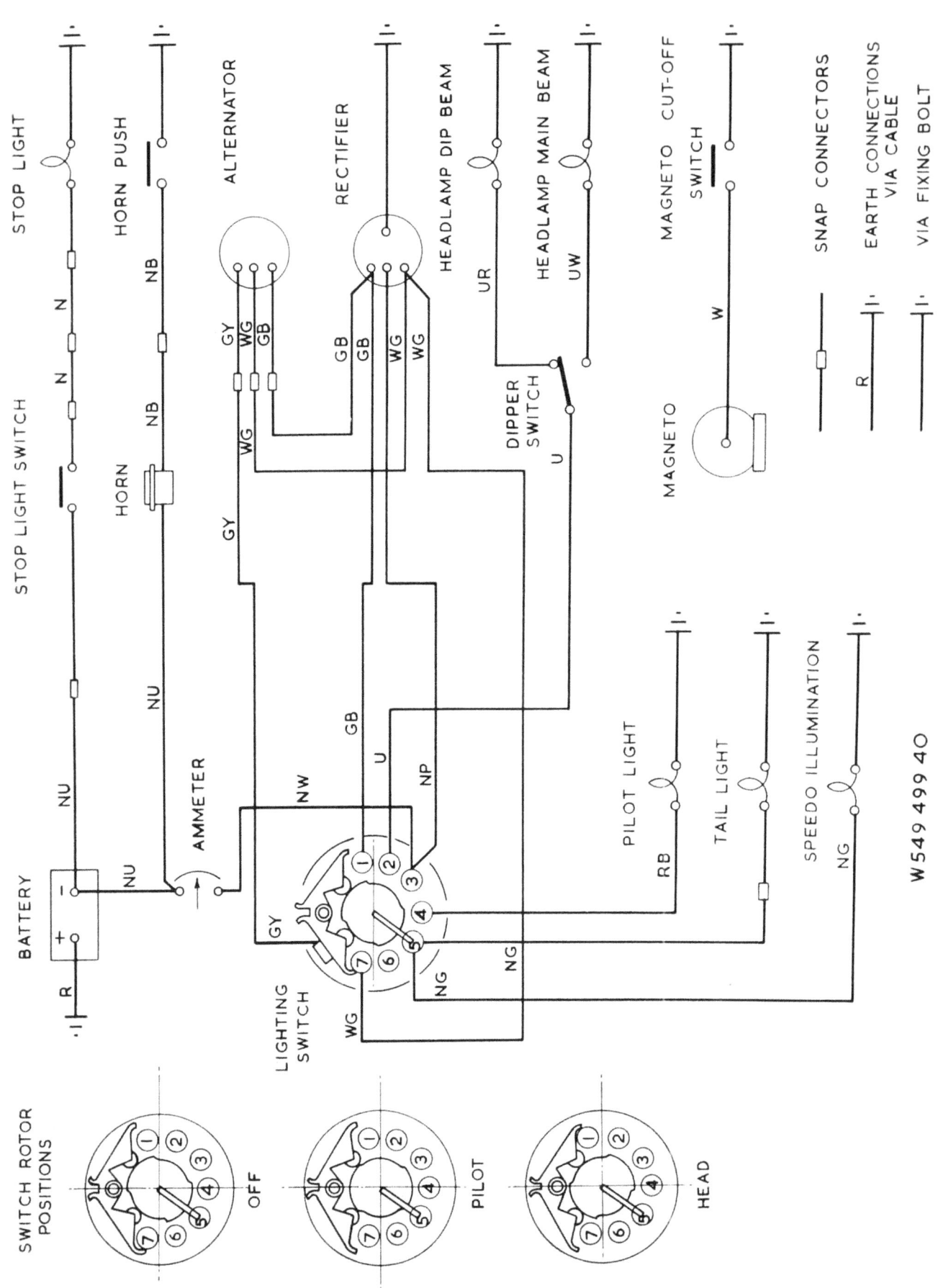

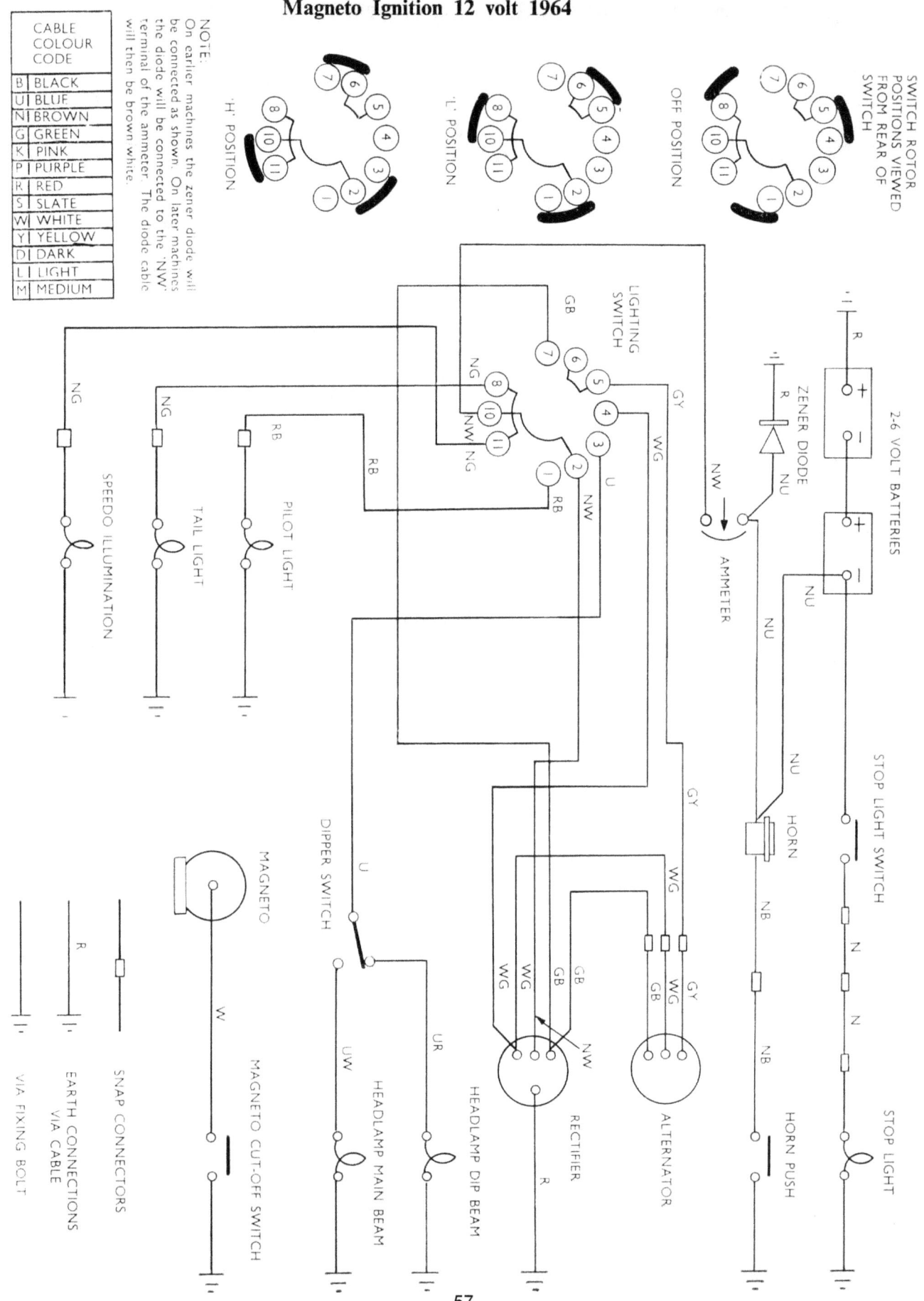

ELECTRICAL WIRING DIAGRAM for Norton 650 cc. Manxman (Export) 650 S.S. and 650 cc. Twin Magneto Ignition 12 volt 1964

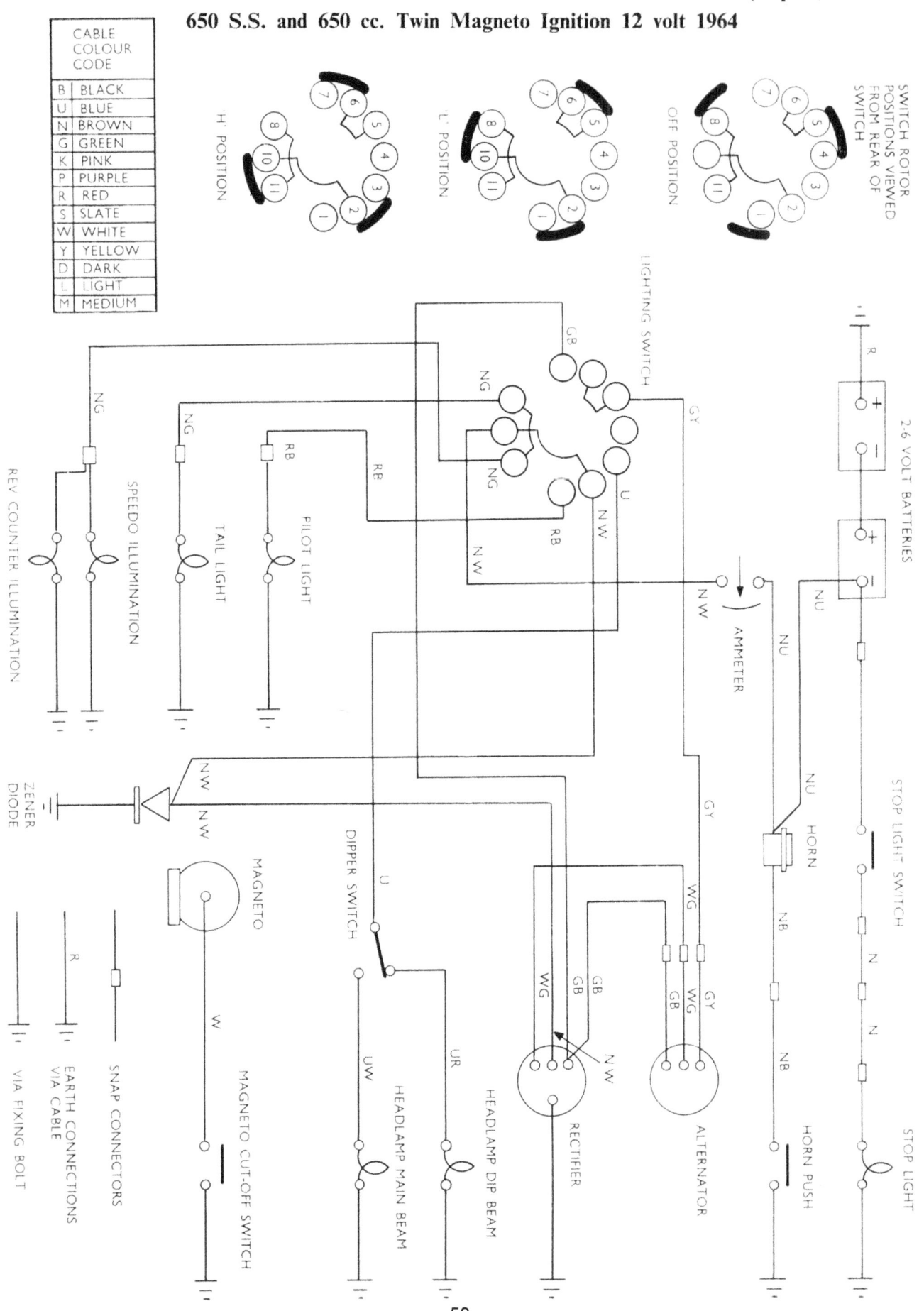

1956-1957 MODELS 88 and 99

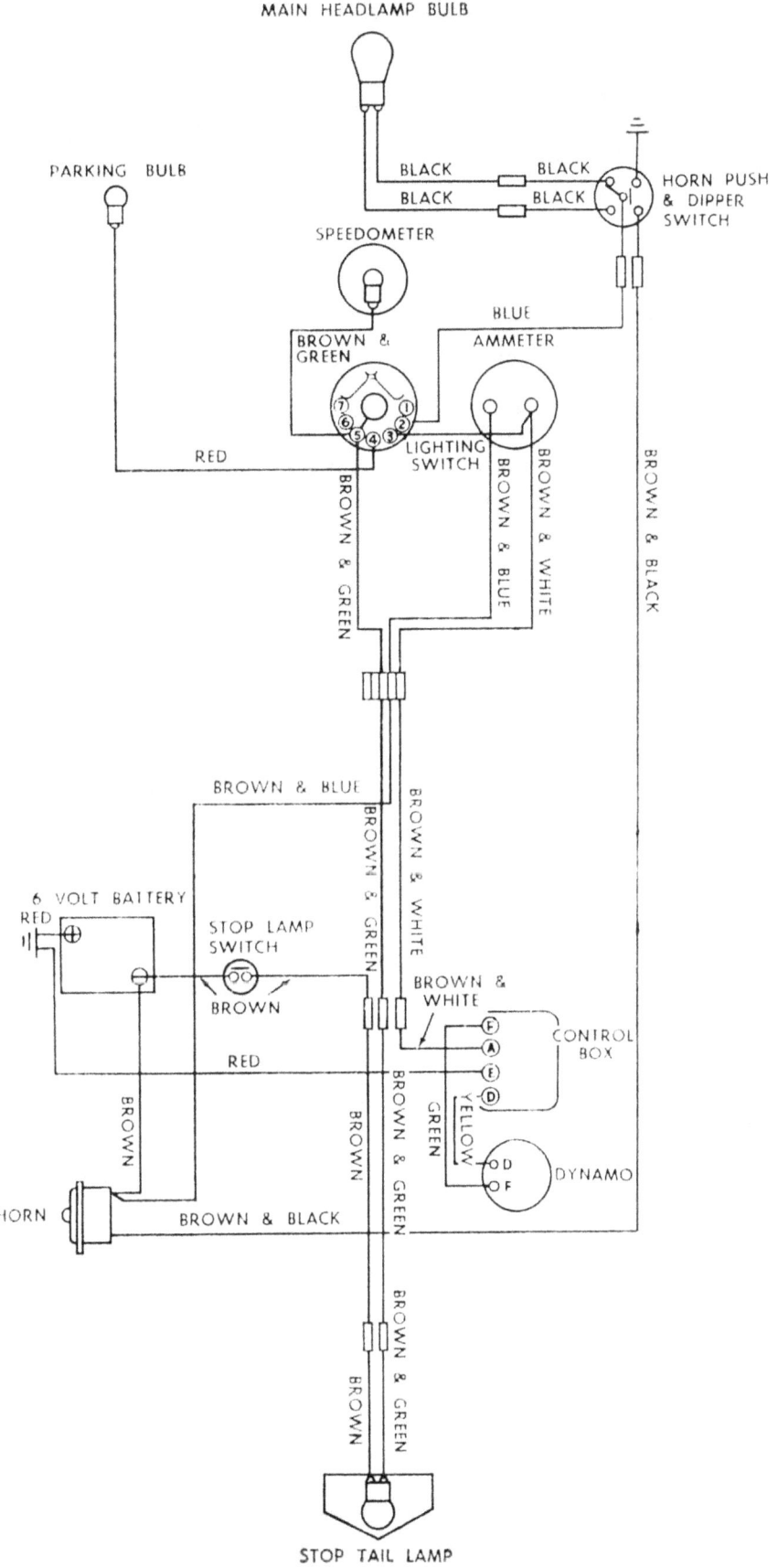

1967 Onwards - 650SS & Mercury Models

CHECKING IGNITION TIMING

For accuracy, the use of a degree plate mounted on the drive side crankshaft to record piston movement, is essential. As an alternative the piston movement can be measured before the cylinder head is re-fitted by using a straight edge on the top face of the cylinder and the use of a short steel rule. The use of a timing rod inserted through the spark plug aperture will be less accurate by reason of the steep angle of the spark plug in relation to the piston crown. First ensure that the point gap for both cylinders is between .014" to .016" at full separation. To adjust the gap release the slotted pillar nut that fixes the small plate with a screwdriver. Use the screwdriver between the edge of the plate and the inside diameter of the contact breaker housing which will move the plate in the required direction. See that the pillar nut is secure when the gap is correct. Take out the left side spark plug also the inlet valve rocker cover. Rotate the engine until the left side inlet rocker goes down and comes up again—the piston will be approximately at the top of the firing stroke. Use a short length of stiff wire through the spark plug hole in contact with the piston crown—rock the engine backwards and forwards to determine when the piston is on the extreme top dead centre position—then set the degree plate with its pointer to register with the zero mark—turn the engine backwards to the extent of eight degrees on the degree plate when the points on the TOP contact set should start to separate. A piece of cigarette paper inserted between the points—when with a light pull on the paper will indicate when the points are about to separate. Eight degrees on the degree plate is equal to .022" in piston travel. The ignition timing for the full advanced position is given in the technical data. The timing given above is with the auto unit in the fully retarded position.

NOTE: If non regular pistons are fitted with a higher compression ratio the ignition must be retarded to prevent detonation.

ADJUSTING THE IGNITION TIMING

The base plate for the contact breaker is moveable, by reason of the two slots in the plate to allow adjustment. To move the base plate, release the two cheese headed screws, which secure the plate—the cam for the contact breaker runs clockwise—looking at the contact breaker—to advance the timing—the base plate is moved counter clockwise.

REMOVING THE BASE PLATE

Take out the two cheese headed screws—disconnect the two wires from the snap connector—the base plate can now be taken away.

NOTES ON IGNITION TIMING

The instructions given to check the ignition timing with the auto advance unit in the retarded position, is satisfactory providing the machine has not covered considerable mileage, for under these circumstances there is a possibility that wear has taken place on the limit stops for the auto unit. This would give a greater range of ignition advance if the ignition timing is checked or set with the auto unit in the full retarded position. To check the timing in the full advance position, take out the bolt in the centre of the contact breaker, use a radio type screwdriver in the slot in the outer edge of the cam, turn the cam with the screwdriver clockwise to get the full advance position. See data for details.

FINDING TOP DEAD CENTRE

With the timing cover removed, the top dead centre position of both pistons can be decided by the position of the timing mark on the sprocket for the camshaft. If this mark is positioned to exactly 12 o'clock, both pistons will be on the top of the stroke.

CAPACITOR IGNITION SYSTEM

The advantage of the capacitor ignition system over the regular coil ignition system is to enable the machine to be used—either with—or without the battery. Starting the engine and lighting is equally effective with or without the battery—excluding supplementary accessories such as parking lights etc. Two separate ignition coils attached to the back of the battery compartment with the ignition switch attached to the oil tank top fixing bolt. The capacitor is mounted on the underside of the tool tray. Two separate contact breakers—the contact points for each contact breaker can be adjusted individually for a balanced firing point—are used in the system.

HOW THE SYSTEM WORKS

The large valve capacitor stores energy impulses from the alternator and supplies the ignition coils with sufficient energy to the spark plugs for easy starting and running at all speeds throughout the operating range of the engine.

The Zener diode takes care of the voltage output from the alternator, the battery is connected across the ammeter to a positive ground connection, when in use.

The wiring diagram shows all connections also the rectifier.

THE CAPACITOR 2MC

The capacitor is an electrolytic-polarised type. It is important that the correct wiring fittings are made, despite the fact that the capacitor connections are dissimilar in size. The small lucar connector $\frac{3}{16}$ inch is the POSITIVE—ground terminal. The rivet on this connection is marked with red paint to identify. The double terminal $\frac{1}{4}$ inch is the NEGATIVE terminal.

SPECIAL NOTE

The capacitor must always be fitted with the terminals DOWNWARDS.

The efficiency of the capacitor can be verified with the use of a voltmeter with a scale reading of at least 12 volts, also a fully charged 12 volt battery.

Connect the battery across the capacitor terminals—POSITIVE to positive and NEGATIVE to negative and leave for five minutes.

When the charging period is completed—take off the two battery wires and use the 12 volt battery properly connected—an instantaneous reading of 8 volts will indicate if the capacitor is serviceable or otherwise.

REMOVING THE BATTERY

With this equipment, if the battery is removed it is vital to insulate the negative battery lead to avoid shorting to engine or chassis. Failure to do so will render the capacitor beyond further use. The part number for the capacitor is 541 700 09. A defective capacitor cannot be detected when the battery is in circuit. To check, take off the battery cables—to determine if the engine will run also with full lights.

ELECTRICAL WIRING DIAGRAM for 650 models

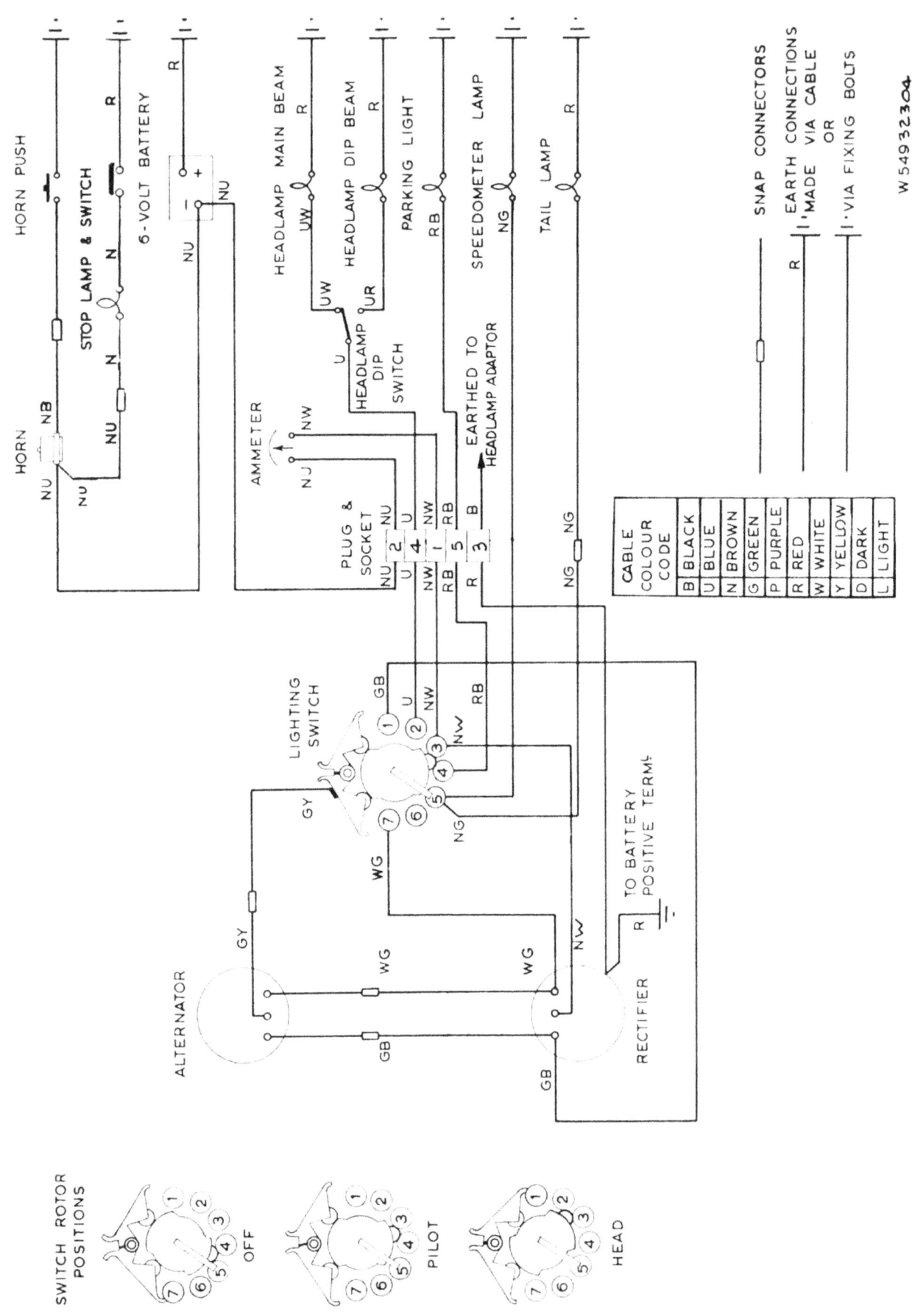

Capacitor-Ignition System
From Engine No. 121307 (May 1967)

The advantage of the capacitor-ignition system over the regular coil-ignition system is that the machine can be used either with or without the battery. Starting the engine and lighting is equally effective with or without the battery, supplementary accessories such as parking lights excepted. Two separate ignition coils are attached to the frame. There are two separate contact breakers and the points for each contact breaker can be adjusted individually for a balanced firing point. The capacitor is attached to the rear frame alongside the battery.

The large-volume capacitor stores energy impulses from the alternator and supplies the ignition coils with sufficient energy for easy starting and high-speed running.

The Zener diode takes care of the voltage output from the alternator and, when in use, the battery is connected across the ammeter to a positive ground connection.

The wiring diagram shows all connections including the rectifier.

Capacitor 2MC

The capacitor is an electrolytic-polarised type and it is important that the correct wiring fittings are made, despite the fact that the capacitor connections are dissimilar in size. The $\frac{3}{16}$ in. connector is the positive ground terminal. The rivet on this connection is marked with red paint. The $\frac{1}{4}$ in. double terminal is the negative.

The capacitor must always be fitted with the terminals DOWNWARDS.

The efficiency of the capacitor can be verified with the use of a fully charged 12-volt battery and voltmeter. Connect the battery across the capacitor terminals, POSITIVE to POSITIVE and NEGATIVE to NEGATIVE, and leave for five minutes.

When the charging period is complete take off the two battery wires and use the 12-volt battery properly connected. An instantaneous reading of 8 volts will indicate that the capacitor is serviceable.

Battery Lucas (PUZ5A)

A 12-volt system with a positive ground connection is used. The battery capacity is 8 ampere/hour rating.

Filling the battery

The specific gravity of the electrolyte must be corrected according to the shade temperature. At 80°F and below add one part of acid (1.835 SG) to 2.8 parts of distilled water to obtain a filling solution with a specific gravity of 1.270 at 60°F.

Where the shade temperature is above 80°F the acid-to-water ratio must be 1.4 to give a specific gravity of 1.270 at 60°F.

Dry-charged batteries are given a four-hour charge at 1.5 to 2.5 amperes.

Battery maintenance

Check the electrolyte level every 14 days and top up with distilled water to the level of the separator guard. If a visible level is not used keep the top of the battery and terminals clean. If the machine is out of service for any length of time recharge the battery every 14 days until each cell is gassing freely. This replaces energy lost during the inactive period.

Removing battery

With this equipment, if the battery is removed it is important to insulate the negative battery lead to avoid shorting to the engine or the frame, which would make the capacitor unserviceable. The part number for the capacitor is 541 700 09. A defective capacitor cannot be detected when the battery is in circuit. To check, take off the battery cables and see if the engine will run with full lights.

Checking ignition timing

For accuracy, use a pointer attached to some part of the engine and a degree plate mounted on the drive-side crankshaft, to record piston movement. Alternatively the piston movement can be measured before the cylinder head is refitted by using a straight edge on the top face of the cylinder and a short steel rule. The method of inserting a timing rod through the spark-plug aperture will be less accurate because of the steep angle of the spark-plug hole in relation to the piston crown.

First ensure that the contact-breaker point gap for both cylinders is between .014 in. to .016 in. If the gap needs adjusting release the pillar nut that fixes the small plate with a screwdriver and with the screwdriver between the edge of the plate and the inside diameter of the contact-breaker housing move the plate in the required direction. Secure the pillar nut when the gap is correct.

Take out the left-side spark plug and the inlet-valve rocker cover. Rotate the engine until the left-side inlet rocker goes down and comes up again. The piston will then be approximately at the top of the firing stroke. Insert a short length of stiff wire through the spark-plug hole until it is in contact with the piston crown. Rock the engine backwards and forwards to determine when the piston is at top dead centre position and set the degree plate so that the pointer registers zero. Turn the engine backwards eight degrees on the degree plate, at which stage the points on the **top** contact set should start to separate.

A simple method of checking the point of separation is to place a cigarette paper between the points. The moment at which the paper can be withdrawn without tearing is the point of separation. Eight degrees on the degree plate is equal to .022 in. in piston travel. The ignition timing for the fully advanced position is 32° or 8.69 mm (.343 in.) B.T.D.C. The timing given above is with the auto unit in the fully retarded position.

Note: If non-regular pistons are fitted, giving a higher compression ratio, the ignition must be retarded to prevent detonation.

Adjusting ignition timing

Two slots in the contact-breaker base plate enable adjustments to be made, the plate being free to move on releasing the two cheese-headed screws. The contact-breaker cam runs clockwise looking at the contact breaker. To advance the timing move the base plate anti-clockwise and to retard it move the plate clockwise.

Removing base plate

To remove the base plate, take out the two cheese-headed screws and disconnect the two wires from the snap connector.

Ignition timing - auto-advance unit

The instructions on checking the ignition timing with the auto-advance unit in the retarded position are satisfactory provided the machine has not covered considerable

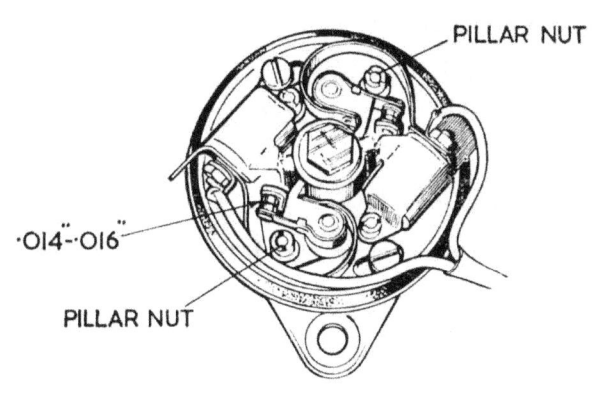
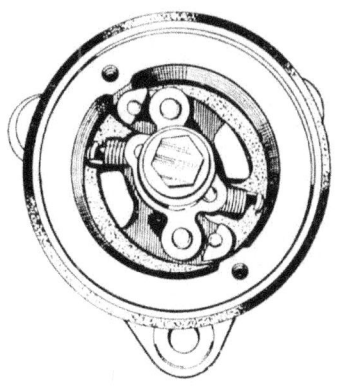

Contact-breaker assembly   *Auto-advance unit*

mileage, in which case there is a possibility that wear will have taken place on the auto-unit limit stops. This would give a greater range of ignition advance if the ignition timing is checked or set with the auto unit in the fully retarded position. To check the timing in the fully advanced position take out the bolt in the centre of the contact breaker and, with a radio-type screwdriver in the slot in the outer edge, turn the cam clockwise to the fully advanced position.

Finding top dead centre

With the timing cover removed, the top dead centre position of both pistons can be decided by the position of the timing mark on the small pinion. If this is positioned at 12 o'clock both pistons will be on the top of their stroke.

Contact-breaker assembly

There are two sets of contact points with a separate H.T. coil for each cylinder. The contact-breaker housing is attached to the timing-side crankcase and houses the automatic timing control.

Note: If the contact-breaker plate or housing is removed the yellow and black wire attached to the top contact set goes to the left-side coil mounted on the rear-frame down tube. The H.T. cable from the left-side coil goes to the left-hand or drive-side cylinder. See electrical section for maintenance.

Refitting contact-breaker cover

Two insulated strips are attached to each condenser and are bent to cover and insulate the condenser terminals to avoid shorting out when the cover is fitted. Make sure that both strips are correctly positioned before fitting the cover. The cable entry is below the housing.

Contact breaker

A few drops of light oil applied periodically on the felt wick will lubricate the cam. Apply a few drops behind the base plate to lubricate the auto mechanism. Check the condenser pillar nuts for security.

Removing drive sprocket

To remove the chain sprocket, which is a parallel fit on the contact-breaker shaft, push out the spring pin which passes through the sprocket and shaft.

To remove automatic control

The cam and automatic control can be withdrawn after removing the drive sprocket, cover and the two screws in the slots in the contact-breaker base plate. To remove the cam, take out the central bolt and with a draw bolt in the thread separate the cam from the taper shaft.

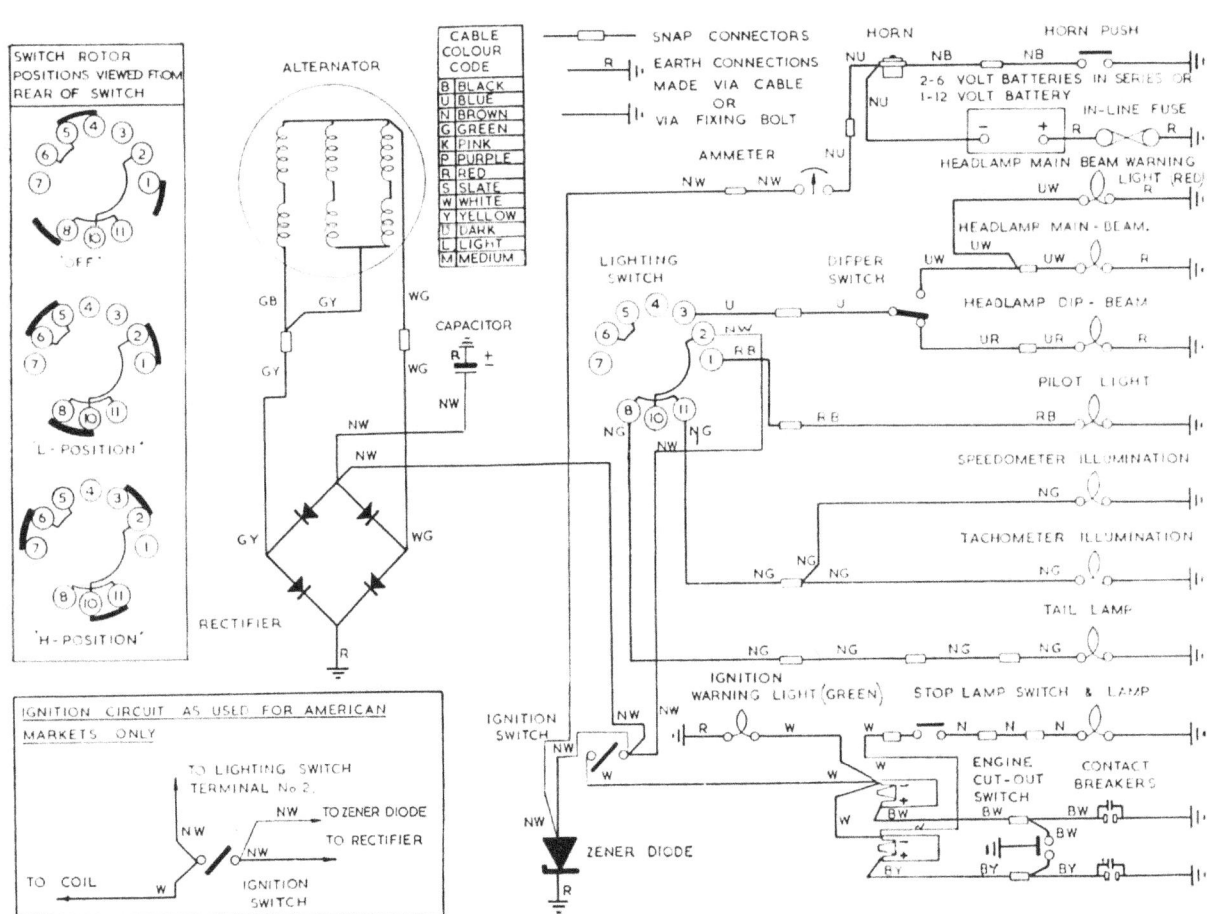

Wiring diagram

Lucas Model 6CA Contact Breaker - From Engine No. 124372 (January 1968)

From engine number 124372 onwards a redesigned Lucas contact breaker is fitted. Each contact set has its own mounting plate held to the circular base plate by two screws (A), each mounting plate being provided with a slot into which an eccentric-headed adjusting screw (B) is fitted. When the securing screws are slackened, rotation of the eccentric screw moves the mounting plate in relation to the ignition cam. This permits a very accurate setting of the ignition timing for each cylinder.

Another eccentric headed screw (C), which is made of brass for easier identification, is located in a slot in each fixed-contact plate and provides adjustment for the contact-breaker points gap.

To adjust the contact-breaker points gap

Remove the sparking plugs so that the engine can be rotated easily. An examination of the cam will reveal a small mark adjacent to the slot which assists in obtaining a uniform gap for each cylinder.

Rotate the engine and when the fibre heel of the moving contact registers with this mark the points will be in the fully open position. Using a .015 in. feeler gauge, check the gap. If the adjustment is correct, the gauge should be an easy sliding fit. When adjustment is necessary, release the fixed contact-plate locking screw (D) and rotate the eccentric adjusting screw (C) until the correct gap is obtained. Retighten the locking screw.

Adjust the other set of contact-breaker points in a similar manner.

Checking the ignition timing

Before checking the ignition timing, the contact-breaker points should be adjusted and the tension of the ignition timing chain checked. The ignition timing can be checked in the static or fully retarded position (8° of crankshaft rotation or .022 in. [.56 mm] of piston travel) but if the engine has covered a considerable mileage, the limit stops of the auto-advance unit may have worn, making it advisable to check the timing at fully advance (32° of crankshaft rotation or .343 in. [8.69 mm] of piston travel). To lock the auto-advance unit in the fully advanced position, remove the central fixing bolt and replace the washer with one having a hole large enough to fit over the cam post and bear on the cam. Replace the bolt loosely, turn the cam to the fully advanced position and tighten the bolt.

Do not forget to refit the original washer after the timing has been checked.

For accuracy, use a degree plate mounted on the drive-side crankshaft, with a pointer attached to a convenient part of the engine to record the crankshaft rotation.

Remove the sparking plugs and the inlet-rocker cover. Rotate the engine until the right-side inlet valve opens and closes again. The right-side piston will then be rising on

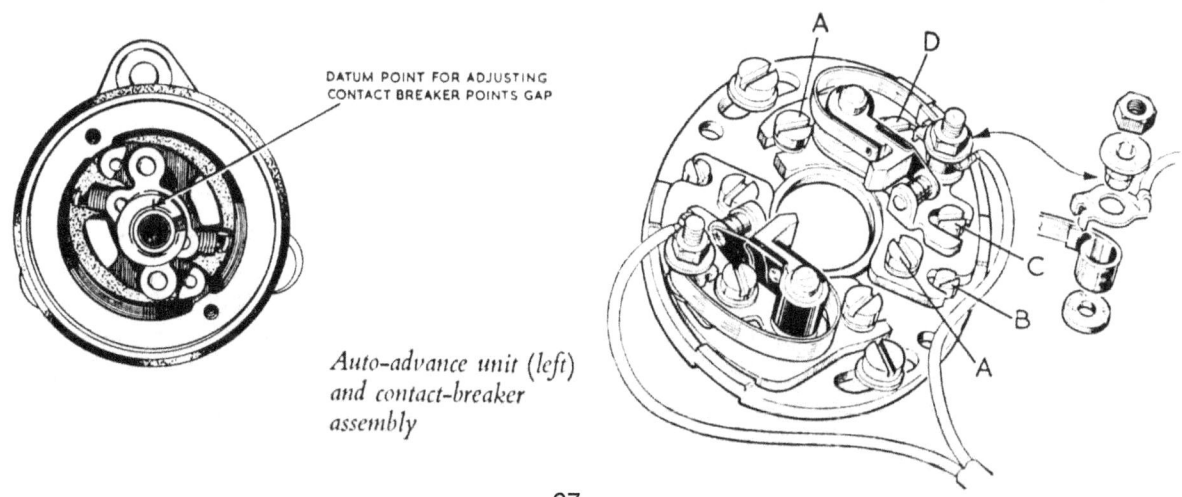

Auto-advance unit (left) and contact-breaker assembly

the compression stroke. Insert a short length of stiff wire through the sparking-plug hole to make contact with the piston crown. Rotate the engine and, by observing the movement of the wire, determine the exact position of top dead centre. Without moving the crankshaft from this position, set the degree plate and the pointer to zero. Turn the engine backwards 32° on the degree plate, at which point the top set of contacts should be just opening.

A simple method of checking the precise opening point is to insert a cigarette paper between the points. When the points are fully closed the paper will be gripped tightly and if pulled gently will come away as the points separate. Ensure that no shreds of paper adhere to the points. If slight adjustment is required, slacken the two contact-breaker-plate securing screws (A) and rotate the eccentric screw (B) until the points are just breaking. Rotate the engine until the other cylinder is 32° from top dead centre on the compression stroke and check the bottom set of points in a similar manner.

If the timing is considerably out, it may be necessary to move the baseplate within the limit of the elongated fixing screw holes. If so, final adjustment should be made on each contact set as described above.

An alternative method of checking the timing is to use a clock gauge to record piston movement with the cylinder head removed. Fit the gauge to the cylinder block with the stylus in contact with the piston crown. Obtain the exact position of top dead centre by observing the movement of the dial pointer as the piston rises and falls and set the dial face to zero.

The engine can be timed on either cylinder and as a guide the drive-side piston is on the compression stroke when the timing mark on the half-time pinion is at 12 o'clock from the cylinder centre line. In this case the bottom set of points will be firing.

Turn the engine backwards until the movement of the dial pointer indicates that the piston has descended .343 in. Check the opening of the contact-breaker points as described above. An alternative method of determining the precise opening point is to use a low wattage 12-volt bulb with a lead soldered to the body of the bulb and another lead attached to the bulb connection. Connect one lead to the contact-breaker spring and the other to a convenient earth point on the engine. With the ignition switched on the bulb will light up at the instant the points separate.

The Condensers

The two condensers are now remote mounted and enclosed in a waterproof case.

Maintenance

Every 5,000 miles the contact-breaker points should be examined to determine their condition. Remove the nut securing the contact-breaker spring to the anchor post and lift off the spring heel together with the terminal, insulating bush and the insulating washer. Remove the fixed contact-plate locking screw and take off the fixed contact plate.

Points which are slightly burnt or pitted should be dressed with a fine carborundum stone and afterwards cleaned with a brush moistened in petrol or white spirit. If they are badly affected they should be renewed.

Before reassembly, smear the contact-breaker pivot post and the cam very sparingly with grease and when reassembling ensure that the insulating washer, contact-breaker spring, terminal and insulating bush are fitted in the order shown in the sketch and that the terminal tags are inside the curve of the spring.

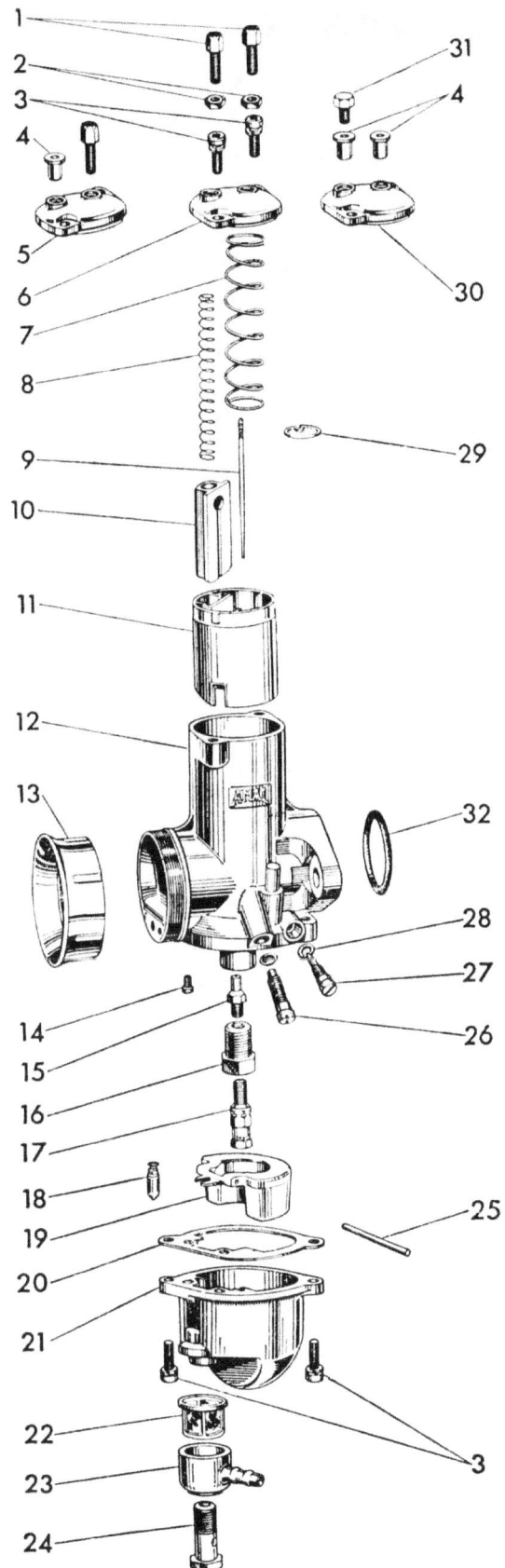

Amal concentric carburettor

1. Cable adjuster
2. Cable-adjuster locknut
3. Float-chamber and mixing-chamber-top securing screws
4. Cable ferrules
5. Mixing-chamber top for adjuster and ferrule
6. Mixing-chamber top (standard)
7. Throttle-valve spring
8. Air-valve spring
9. Throttle needle
10. Air valve
11. Throttle valve
12. Carburettor body and tickler assembly
13. Air-intake tube
14. Pilot jet
15. Needle jet
16. Jet holder
17. Main jet
18. Float needle
19. Float
20. Float-chamber washer
21. Float-chamber body
22. Filter
23. Banjo union
24. Banjo bolt
25. Float spindle
26. Throttle-stop adjusting screw
27. Pilot-air adjusting screw
28. 'O' Rings
29. Needle clip
30. Mixing-chamber top for two ferrules
31. Plug for mixing-chamber top
32. 'O' ring for flange sealing

Amal Concentric Carburettor

This engine is fitted with twin Amal 930 right-and left-hand carburettors with concentric float chambers. To dismantle the carburettor, remove the two float-bowl fixing screws allowing the float bowl to be detached from the mixing chamber and the float and hinge pin to be removed. The main and pilot jets are now accessible and can be removed for cleaning.

To remove the throttle slide, needle and air slide, detach the top plate, which is secured to the mixing chamber by two small screws.

Tuning

Carburettor tuning is carried out in a manner similar to that already described although in some cases one carburettor may require a slightly different setting from the other.

With twin carburettors accurate synchronisation is essential, both throttles must open simultaneously and reach the fully open position together.

To set the carburettors, slacken the throttle-stop screws fully and close the twist-grip control. Adjust the cable adjusters so that with the handlebars in the normal position there is slight and equal backlash on each carburettor and as the twist grip is operated the throttle slides begin to lift simultaneously. This can be checked by removing the air filter and placing the fingers inside the carburettor intake as the twist grip is rotated.

To adjust the idling speed, open the twist grip slightly until the engine idles at the required speed then screw in the throttle-stop screws until they just make contact with the throttle slides, holding them in that position. Return the twist grip control to the fully closed position.

Check that both throttle slides are fully lifted when the twist grip is in the fully open position.

When adjusting the pilot-jet mixture strength and idling speed, accuracy can be obtained by disconnecting one plug lead and tuning each cylinder as a single unit. When both leads are connected, the engine speed will increase and if necessary should be reduced by unscrewing each throttle-stop screw equally.

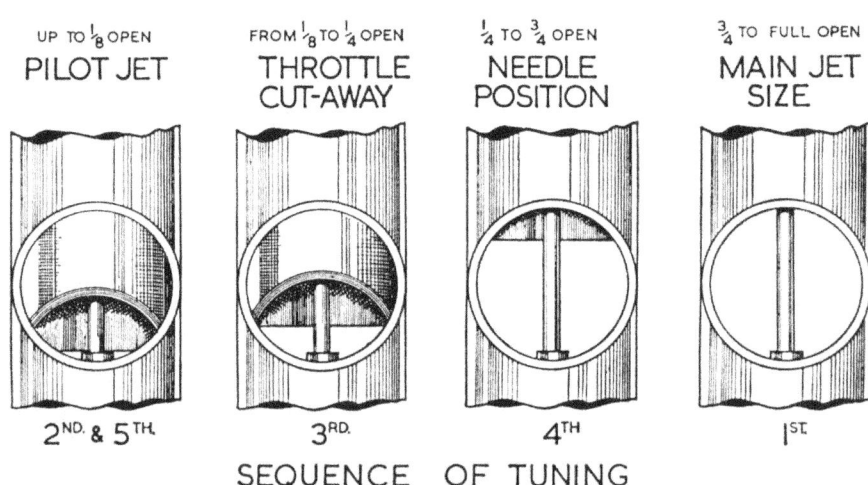

PHASES OF AMAL NEEDLE JET CARBURETTOR THROTTLE OPENINGS

UP TO 1/8 OPEN — PILOT JET — 2ND. & 5TH.
FROM 1/8 TO 1/4 OPEN — THROTTLE CUT-AWAY — 3RD.
1/4 TO 3/4 OPEN — NEEDLE POSITION — 4TH
3/4 TO FULL OPEN — MAIN JET SIZE — 1ST

SEQUENCE OF TUNING

The phases of tuning the Amal needle jet carburettor are shown in Fig. 23, but before tuning ensure that the engine is in in sound mechanical condition and that the ignition timing and contact-breaker points gap are correctly set.

1. **Main jet with throttle fully open.** If at full throttle slightly closing the throttle or air control seems to improve power, the main jet is too small. If the engine runs "heavily" the main jet is too large.

2. **Pilot jet – with throttle up to ⅛ in. open.** Close the throttle, allow the engine to idle fairly fast and set the ignition lever to the best idling position.

Screw out the throttle adjusting screw until the engine runs slower and begins to falter then screw the pilot-jet adjusting screw in or out until the engine runs evenly. If the idling speed is not too fast, regulate it by means of the throttle adjusting screw.

3. **Throttle cut away – with throttle ⅛ in. to ¼ in. open.** If, as the throttle is opened from the idling position, there is spitting back through the carburettor, slightly richen the pilot mixture adjustment. If this is not effective, return to the original adjustment and fit a throttle slide with a smaller cut away, which will richen the mixture at this throttle opening.

If the engine jerks under load, either the jet needle is too high or a throttle slide with a larger cut away is required.

4. **Jet needle – with throttle ¼ in. to ¾ in.** The jet needle controls a wide range of throttle opening and the acceleration. Try the needle in a low position and if the acceleration is poor but improves by partial closure of the air slide raise the needle two grooves. If the results are very much better, try lowering the needle one groove and after tests leave it in the groove giving the best results.

If, with the needle in the top groove, the mixture is still too rich the needle jet should be renewed. If the needle has been in use for a very long period, renew it also.

CARBURETTOR DATA 650SS

Type:	Twin Amal Concentric-Type 930
Choke size:	30 mm
Main jet (Revised settings):	
With air cleaner:	260
Without air cleaner:	280
Pilot jet:	25 c.c.
Throttle slide:	3
Needle jet:	.107
Needle position:	Central notch

CARBURETTOR DATA 650 MERCURY

Type:	Single Amal Concentric-Type 930
Choke size:	30 mm
Main jet:	280
Pilot jet:	25 c.c.
Throttle slide:	3
Needle jet:	.106 (with bleed hole)
Needle position:	Central notch

LOCATING AND RECTIFYING POSSIBLE TROUBLES

TROUBLE	POSSIBLE CAUSE	REMEDY
Failure to start.	Over flooding.	Open twist grip and kick vigorously a few times.
	Weak mixture due to failure to close air lever (if cold).	Ensure that air slide falls as lever is shut.
	Broken throttle cable.	Ensure that throttle slide rises as twist grip is rotated.
	Lack of fuel.	Check that there is petrol in tank.
	Failure of fuel to reach mixing chamber.	Check that petrol taps, or tap, is in the "on" position and that petrol is flowing through
		Clean Carburetter.
	Contact breaker points dirty or out of adjustment	Remove high tension lead from one plug and hold end about $\frac{1}{8}$ in. from cylinder whilst revolving engine. If no spark, examine contact breaker points, clean, check gap. Check lights.
	Battery flat.	
Firing on one cylinder.	Faulty plug.	Change plug.
	Faulty high tension lead.	Examine high tension lead, renew if necessary.
	Water on plug.	
Erratic slow running.	Uneven mixture distribution.	Check and clean carburetter.
	Pilot air screw requires resetting.	Adjust as in para. 113.
	Air leaks from carburetter joint or sparking plug.	Check joint washer and nuts for tightness. Check plug for tightness.
	Faulty valve seats.	Examine and regrind as necessary.
	Worn inlet valve or guides.	Dismantle, check and renew as necessary.
Loss of power.	No tappet clearance.	Check and reset as necessary.
	Broken piston rings.	Examine and replace.
	Tight front chain.	Adjust.
Excessive oil consumption.	Broken piston rings. Worn cylinder block.	Examine and replace as necessary.
	Oil not returning to tank, due to:—Stoppage in oil way; pump drive failed; pump gears fouled by foreign matter.	Examine and make necessary replacements. Trace through and clean out or take any other action necessary.
Engine runs harshly.	Tight chains.	Check and adjust.
Engine cuts out at large throttle openings.	Dirt in carburetter. Dirt in filters.	Dismantle and clean.
	Dirt in petrol tap.	Remove petrol taps and clean.
	Condenser broken down.	Change condenser, clean contacts.
Loss of oil pressure.	Oil overheated or unsuitable.	Drain and refill with fresh oil of correct grade.
	Oil pump nipple washer failed.	Examine and renew.
	Timing side oil seal worn or collapsed.	Examine and renew.
	Pressure release valve plunger stuck.	Examine, clean and free off.
	Pump failed.	Examine for foreign matter.

LOCATING AND RECTIFYING POSSIBLE TROUBLES

TROUBLE	POSSIBLE CAUSE	REMEDY
Inefficient brakes. (Front and Rear)	Grease on lining.	Examine and wash in petrol. Do not wash in paraffin.
	Tightness in mechanism.	Make sure that cam is free in its own bearing and pedal is not binding on spindle due to mud.
Slipping clutch.	Cable adjusted too tightly.	Re-adjust cable until there is some movement on handle bar lever before clutch operates.
	Clutch push rod adjusted 'hard on'.	Re-adjust, para. 72.
	Oil on plates (usually caused by over-filling oil bath).	Dismantle clutch plates and wash in petrol.
	Tightness in operating mechanism.	Examine, clean and free off as necessary.
Clutch hard to free.	Water in cable.	Lubricate.
Gear changing accompanied by excessive noise.	Slack rear chain.	Adjust as necessary.
Failure of footchange lever to return to normal position.	Broken hairpin return spring.	Remove gearbox cover. Examine spring, renew as required.
Steering rolls or wanders.	Loose head adjustment.	Adjust as necessary.
Twist grip closes if released.	Tension requires adjusting.	Screw in adjuster one or two turns.
Steering appears tight on corners.	Steering damper binding, caused by bent frame anchor bracket.	Remove anchor bracket and re-set to correct angle.

NOTES

SPARE PARTS LIST

1949–1950 Model 7
DOMINATOR TWIN

NORTON MOTORS LIMITED
Bracebridge Street, Birmingham 6, England

Phone: Aston Cross 3711 (Private Branch Exchange)

Grams "Nortomo, Birmingham"

INSTRUCTIONS FOR ORDERING SPARE PARTS.

This Spare Parts List deals with replacement parts for 1949-1950 Model 7 Dominator Twin.

It is most essential that the Engine and Frame Number of the machine is stated. The Engine Number is to be found on the transmission side of the Crankcase, and the Frame Number is stamped on the Head Lug of the Frame, below the steering damper anchor plate. It is always advisable to order parts on a separate sheet, and not to include on the same sheet other matter of a different nature; this facilitates prompt despatch.

It is found in a number of instances that money orders and postal orders are sent in parcels containing patterns; this is inadvisable. We strongly recommend parts as patterns being despatched separately, and a covering letter sent containing the remittance for replacement parts.

RETURNING MACHINES FOR OVERHAULING.

When returning machines or parts for repair or overhaul, these should be sent carriage paid, and with the sender's name and address in full **securely** attached. It is also advisable to state on the tally that a letter has been sent respecting the parts, and giving the date. All easily detached fittings should be removed, such as Lamps, Horns, Tool Bags, Speedometers, etc.; these are liable to be lost or damaged in transit, and the Company cannot accept any responsibility for them.

ESTIMATES FOR REPAIRING MACHINES.

We are always prepared to give approximate estimates for the cost of repairs; it is quite impossible to give a firm quotation. Additional parts may be found necessary during the process of repair, unforeseen when preparing an estimate. Should our estimate for repair not be accepted, a charge may be made in accordance with work entailed in dismantling and re-assembling. When we give an estimate for the cost of repairs, and this is curtailed by the owner, we cannot accept any responsibility for the performance of the machine; it is always preferable to accept our estimate in full.

TERMS OF BUSINESS.

Our terms are strictly nett cash with order or cash against prepayment invoice. The exact amount, plus 5% to cover postage or carriage and packing (subject to a minimum of 6d.), packing cases or crates to be extra, must be remitted, or when the cost of the parts required is unknown, a sum likely to cover the cost should be enclosed; if the amount remitted is more than the cost of the parts that are ordered, the balance will be returned. Cheques and postal orders should be made payable to " Norton Motors, Ltd.," and crossed Barclays Bank, Ltd. Prices quoted in this list do not include the cost of carriage or fitting. We reserve the right to alter prices or specification of any parts at any time without notice. Where parts are urgently required, remittance may be sent by Telegraphic Money Order, **but it is absolutely essential that the sender fill in his name and address in the space provided on the Post Office Money Order Form.** Unless this is done, the Post Office do not give us the information in the telegram. It is necessary that all orders given by wire or 'phone should be confirmed by letter at the earliest opportunity.

DEPOSIT ACCOUNT.

We strongly recommend riders of our machines to open a deposit account; this can be done by depositing with us not less than £10. This will ensure goods to that value being despatched with the least possible delay. When ordering by 'phone, wire or post, this often avoids great inconvenience, and for the benefit of the depositor, a monthly statement of account is rendered, showing credit balance. Under no circumstances whatever can parts be despatched without remittance covering same has been sent, unless a deposit account is opened. Should the machine be disposed of at a later date, we are always prepared to remit any amount that may be remaining.

PARTS BY C.O.D. SYSTEM.

Unless remittance is received with order, parts are despatched by C.O.D. System or against proforma invoice at our discretion.

INDEX

	Page
Air control lever	11
Amal carburetter	8
Battery carrier	26
Cable clips (rubber)	27
Carburetter	8
Chain (front)	23
Chain (rear)	23
Chain adjuster (front)	15
Chain adjuster (rear)	23
Chaincase and fittings (front)	21
Chainguard (rear)	21
Clutch control lever	11
Clutch group	17
Connecting rods and fittings	8
Control cable adjuster and nipples	11
Control cables	11
Crankcase and engine plate bolts, nuts and washers	5
Crankcase and fittings	5
Crankcase pressure and breather fittings	5
Crankshaft	5
Cylinder barrel	7
Cylinder head	7
Cylinder head and barrel studs and bolts	7
Dynamo drive parts and securing fittings	6
Electric horn and fittings	27
Engine plates	23
Engine sprocket	23
Engine steady stay and fittings	6
Exhaust pipes and fittings	9
Float chamber and parts	8
Flywheel	5
Footchange parts	19
Forks (front)	9
Frame	23
Frame rear springing	23
Front brake lever	11
Front mudguard, stays and fittings	25
Front number plate	25
Front stand	26
Front wheel and fittings	19
Gearbox axle sprocket	17
Gearbox fixing bolts	15
Gearbox front chain adjuster	15
Gearbox pinions, shafts and bearings	15
Gearbox shell	15
Handlebar and fittings	11
Headlamp and parts	26
Horn and fittings	27
Hub parts (common to front and rear)	21

	Page
Kickstarter parts	17
Lamp (front)	26
Lamp (rear)	27
Magneto and drive parts	7
Main bearings	5
Mudguard (front)	25
Mudguard (rear)	25
Number plate (front)	25
Number plate (rear)	25
Oil gauge and fittings	15
Oil pipes and fittings	13
Oil pump parts	7
Oil tank and fittings	13
Petrol tank and fittings	13
Pillion footrests	26
Pistons and rings	8
Positive footchange parts	19
Prop stand and fittings	25
Push rods and tappets	6
Rear brake pedal and fittings	21
Rear chainguard	21
Rear lamp and fittings	27
Rear mudguard stays and fittings	25
Rear number plate	25
Rear springing	23
Rear wheel and fittings	19
Rings	8
Rocker box fittings	6
Saddle and parts	26
Silencers	9
Speedometer and fittings	26
Spokes	21
Stand (front)	26
Stand (prop)	25
Steering damper	9
Tappets	6
Timing gear and fittings	6
Tools	27
Tool-box	26
Transfers	27
Twist grip	11
Valves, guides, springs, etc.	7
Voltage regulator and fittings	27
Wheel (front)	19
Wheel (rear)	19
Wheel rims and spokes	21

PLATE.T.A.

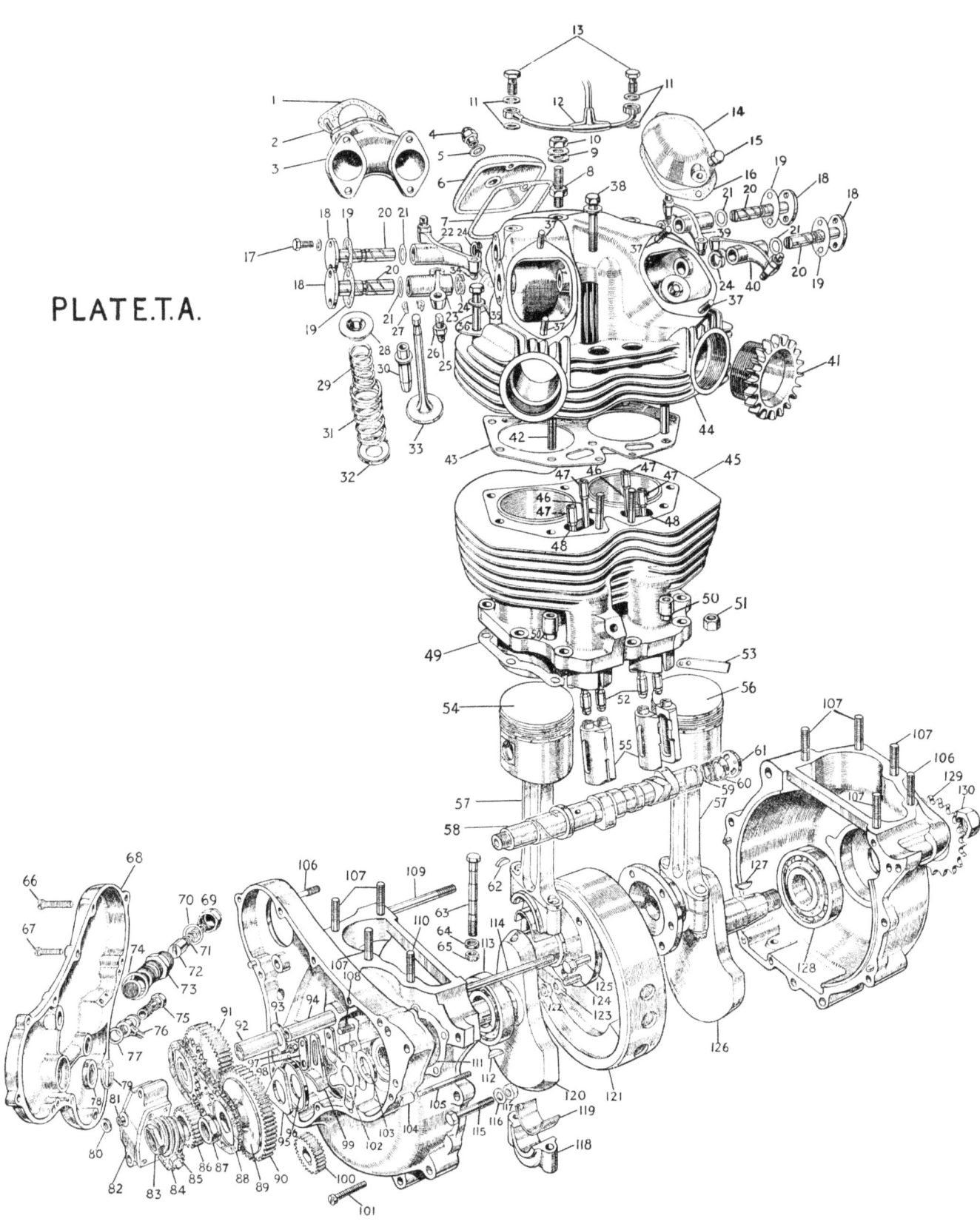

PART No.	PLATE No.	DESCRIPTION	QTY.	£	s.	d.

CRANKCASE AND FITTINGS.

PART No.	PLATE No.	DESCRIPTION	QTY.	£	s.	d.
D12/1	....	Crankcase with timing cover		14	0	0
D12/6	TA/68	Crankcase timing cover		1	17	6
T2236	....	Paper washer for timing cover				9
D12/704	....	Crankcase timing side			7	2 6
D12/703	....	Crankcase driving side			5	0 0

(NOTE.—Half crankcases and timing cover cannot be supplied separately. Therefore, it is necessary to return sound half for matching in the works.)

PART No.	PLATE No.	DESCRIPTION	QTY.	£	s.	d.
D12/18/TS		Crankcase camshaft bush timing side			5	0
D12/18/DS		Crankcase camshaft bush driving side			5	0
D12/2 (L)	TA/107	Crankcase cylinder base stud (⅜in. diam.)	7		1	0
D12/2 (S)	TA/110	Crankcase cylinder base stud (5/16in. diam.)	2			10
D12/3 (L)	TA/51	Crankcase cylinder base stud nut (⅜in.)	7			6
D12/3 (S)	TA/50	Crankcase cylinder base stud nut (5/16in.)	2			5
E3336	....	Crankcase drain plug				8
10009	....	Crankcase drain plug washer				3
D12/912	....	Crankcase and magneto joint washer				3
10940	TA/66	Timing cover screws (long)	6			6
E6980	TA/67	Timing cover screws (short)	5			5
D12/913	TA/78	Timing cover mainshaft oil seal			1	0
D12/914	TA/79	Circlip for mainshaft oil seal				6

CRANKCASE PRESSURE AND BREATHER FITTINGS.

PART No.	PLATE No.	DESCRIPTION	QTY.	£	s.	d.
D12/915	....	Timing cover pressure valve complete			12	6
D12/916	TA/73	Pressure release valve body			7	6
D12/917	TA/72	Piston for release valve			2	0
D12/918	TA/71	Pressure release valve spring				3
D12/919	TA/74	Washer for release valve body				3
D12/920	TA/69	Nut for release valve body			2	6
D12/921	TA/70	Washer for release valve body nut				3
D12/708	....	Crankcase breather pipe with flange			2	0
D12/923	....	Crankcase breather pipe securing bolt				5

FLYWHEEL, CRANKSHAFT AND MAIN BEARINGS.

PART No.	PLATE No.	DESCRIPTION	QTY.	£	s.	d.
D12/24	....	Flywheel and crankshaft assembly with con rods		21	0	0
D12/924	TA/121	Flywheel		3	10	0
D12/705	TA/120	Crankshaft, timing side			6	5 0
D12/706	TA/126	Crankshaft, driving side			6	5 0
D12/925	TA/125	Flywheel and crankshaft bolt	4		2	0
D12/926	TA/124	Flywheel and crankshaft stud	2		1	6
D12/927	TA/122	Flywheel and crankshaft bolt or stud nut	8		1	9
D12/928	....	Dowel for Flywheel			1	0
D12/929	TA/123	Retaining plate for flywheel dowel	2			9
D12/30	TA/113	Mainshaft ball bearing (timing side)		1	5	6
D12/930	TA/96	Mainshaft ball bearing sealing washer			1	0
D12/32	TA/128	Mainshaft roller bearing (driving side)		1	19	0
D12/931	....	Driving side shaft sealing washer			3	9
D12/46	....	Mainshaft packing washer (as necessary)				4

CRANKCASE AND ENGINE PLATE BOLTS, NUTS AND WASHERS.

PART No.	PLATE No.	DESCRIPTION	QTY.	£	s.	d.
T2013	TA/109	Stud crankcase, top rear, ⅜in.	1		2	6
T2015	TA/114	Stud crankcase, top front, 5/16in.	1		2	6
10940	TA/101	Screw crankcase sump	2			6
13870	TA/115	Bolt, short, crankcase boss	1		1	0
E3223	TA/117	Nut for bolt, crankcase boss, 5/16in.	1			4
E5456	TA/116	Washer for bolt	3			4
T2194	....	Nut for top crankcase stud, 5/16in.	1			5
E4262	....	Bolt, crankcase to engine cradle	3		2	6
E5456	....	Washer for bolt, crankcase to engine cradle	6			4
E3223	....	Nut, crankcase to engine cradle	3			4
T2012	....	Stud, crankcase to engine plate, ⅜in.	4		2	6
T2213	....	Stud, crankcase to engine plate (for side prop stand, 1950)			2	6
E5455	....	Washer for stud, crankcase to engine plate	8			3
E3224	....	Nut for stud, crankcase to engine plate	8			4
E4256	....	Bolt, engine plate to frame, front	1		2	6
E3238	....	Nut for bolt, engine plate to frame, front	1			5
E5377	....	Washer for bolt, engine plate to frame, front	8			3
E4268	....	Bolt, engine plate to frame, rear, 7/16in. × ⅞in.	2		1	6

PART No.	PLATE No.	DESCRIPTION	QTY.	£	s.	d.
ENGINE STEADY STAY AND FITTINGS.						
D12/932	....	Engine steady stay			3	6
T12171	TA/8	Stud for steady stay, frame or cylinder head			1	6
E3224	TA/10	Nut for steady stay stud	2			4
E5376	TA/9	Washer for steady stay stud	2			3
TIMING GEAR FITTINGS.						
D12/790	TA/58	Camshaft		4	15	0
D12/774	....	Camshaft washer				3
D12/933	TA/61	Camshaft Breather stationary plate			2	0
D12/934	TA/60	Camshaft breather rotary plate			2	0
D12/935	TA/59	Camshaft breather spring				3
D12/58	TA/86	Half time pinion			10	0
E3683	TA/112	Half time pinion key				3
D12/936	TA/95	Half time pinion backing washer			3	0
D12/937	TA/91	Intermediate gear with sprockets		2	15	0
D12/938	TA/92	Bush for intermediate gear			4	6
D12/939	TA/93	Washer for intermediate gear				3
D12/940	TA/94	Intermediate gear wheel spindle			4	0
D12/941	..	Circlip for gear wheel spindle				6
D12/79	TA/89	Camshaft sprocket		1	10	0
E3683	TA/62	Camshaft sprocket key				3
D12/942	TA/87	Camshaft sprocket nut			2	3
PUSH RODS AND TAPPETS.						
D12/82 (In.)	TA/46	Push rod complete (inlet)	2		9	0
D12/82 (Ex.)	TA/48	Push rod complete (exhaust)	2		9	0
D12/86	TA/47	Push rod top	4		4	0
D12/83	TA/52	Push rod ball end	4		3	6
D12/75	TA/55	Tappet	4		8	6
D12/943	TA/53	Tappet locating plate	2		5	0
D12/944	....	Tappet locating plate screw	4			3
ROCKER BOX FITTINGS.						
D12/99 (R.H.)	TA/22	Rocker, inlet (right hand)			17	6
D12/99 (L.H.)	TA/39	Rocker, inlet (left hand)			17	6
D12/100(R.H.)	TA/23	Rocker, exhaust (right hand)			17	6
D12/100(L.H.)	TA/40	Rocker, exhaust (left hand)			17	6
D12/104	TA/34	Rocker ball end	4		3	6
D12/803	TA/25	Rocker adjuster screw	4		3	0
D12/804	TA/26	Rocker adjuster screw nut	4			6
D12/97	TA/20	Rocker shaft	4		12	0
D12/945	TA/19	Rocker shaft locking plate	4		1	0
D12/946	TA/18	Rocker shaft fixing plate	4		1	0
D12/947	....	Rocker shaft locking plate washer	4			3
D12/948	....	Rocker shaft fixing plate washer	4			3
D12/949	TA/17	Rocker shaft fixing plate bolt	8			4
D12/950	TA/24	Rocker shaft spring washer	4			4
D12/951	TA/21	Rocker shaft thrust washer	4			6
D12/93F	TA/14	Rocker box cover (front)	2		7	6
D12/952	TA/37	Rocker box cover stud (front)	4			6
D12/953	TA/15	Rocker box cover stud nut (front)	4			6
D12/95F	TA/16	Rocker box cover washer (front)	2			6
D12/93R	TA/6	Rocker box cover (rear)			7	6
D12/954	....	Rocker box cover stud (rear)				8
D12/955	TA/4	Rocker box cover stud nut (rear)				8
D12/956	TA/5	Rocker box cover stud nut washer (rear)				3
D12/95R	TA/7	Rocker box cover washer (rear)				6
DYNAMO DRIVE PARTS AND SECURING FITTINGS.						
D12/957	TA/90	Fibre gear for dynamo drive		1	2	6
D12/1012	TA/103	Fibre gear distance piece			2	0
D12/958	TA/102	Friction spring for fibre gear			2	3
D12/959	....	Plate for friction spring				6
D12/960	...	Locating peg for friction spring			1	0
D12/1013	TA/100	Dynamo steel driven pinion			10	0
D12/961	TA/88	Dynamo drive chain			11	8
200737	....	Brush set for dynamo	per set		3	6

PART No.	PLATE No.	DESCRIPTION	QTY.	£	s.	d.
DYNAMO DRIVE PARTS AND SECURING FITTINGS—cont.						
D12/962	....	Dynamo securing strap			2	6
D12/963	....	Dynamo securing strap dowel				6
D12/964	....	Dynamo securing strap roller			1	0
D12/965	....	Dynamo securing strap screw				6
D12/966	TA/105	Stud securing dynamo to crankcase	3		1	0
D12/967	TA/104	Nut for stud securing dynamo to crankcase	3			4
D12/968	TA/99	Tensioner slipper for dynamo chain			2	6
D12/969	TA/108	Stud securing chain tensioner to crankcase	2			6
D12/970	TA/97	Stud nut securing chain tensioner to crankcase	2			4
D12/971	TA/98	Plate for chain tensioner	2			6
T2184	TA/111	Dynamo sealing washer				6
MAGNETO AND DRIVE PARTS.						
D12/113	....	Magneto chain			11	8
T2191	....	Paper washer for magneto				4
47508	....	Magneto sprocket with automatic advance and retard unit		2	10	0
458644	....	Pick up assembly (left hand)			4	4
458643	....	Pick up assembly (right hand)			4	4
451260	....	Brush and spring for pick up	2			10
458619	....	Contact breaker cover			5	9
470534	....	Contact breaker	1		4	2
470609	....	Contact breaker points (set)			8	10
455191	....	Brush spring and holder (magneto to earth)			1	2
455190	....	Brush and spring (magneto to earth)				10
T2089	TA/106	Bolt securing magneto to crankcase	3			6
E3223	....	Nut for bolt securing magneto to crankcase	3			4
E5456	....	Washer for bolt securing magneto to crankcase	3			3
OIL PUMP PARTS.						
D12/128	TA/82	Dry sump gear pump complete		3	0	0
A2/129	TA/85	Dry sump gear pump spindle nut				5
A2/130	TA/84	Pump spindle worm gear wheel			6	6
A2/131	....	Pump spindle worm gear wheel key				3
A2/132	TA/81	Pump body and timing cover connection bush				8
D12/133	TA/80	Pump body and timing cover connection washer				4
D12/134	TA/83	Mainshaft pump driving worm			7	6
E4440	....	Dry sump gear pump crankcase stud	2			9
E3231	....	Dry sump gear pump crankcase stud nut	2			4
VALVES, GUIDES, SPRINGS, ETC.						
D12/142	....	Valve (inlet)	2		12	0
D12/143	TA/33	Valve (exhaust)	2		12	0
D12/140	TA/30	Valve guide	4		6	6
D12/145	TA/29	Valve spring, inner	4		1	0
D12/146	TA/31	Valve spring, outer	4		2	0
D12/148	TA/32	Valve spring cup bottom	4		1	0
D12/147	TA/28	Valve spring cup top	4		3	0
D12/149	TA/27	Valve cotter (2 halves one cotter)	4		1	0
CYLINDER HEAD, BARREL, STUDS AND BOLTS.						
D12/135	TA/45	Cylinder barrel		9	0	0
D12/136	TA/44	Cylinder head		12	0	0
D12/137	TA/43	Cylinder head gasket			5	0
D12/157	TA/49	Cylinder base washer				10
D12/972	TA/36	Cylinder Head and barrel bolt (long), $\frac{3}{8}$in.	4		1	0
D12/973	TA/38	Cylinder Head and barrel bolt (short), 3in.	1			10
D12/974	TA/35	Cylinder head and barrel bolt washer	5			3
D12/975	....	Cylinder head and barrel stud (front), $\frac{5}{16}$in.	2		1	0
D12/976	....	Cylinder head and barrel stud nut (front), $\frac{5}{16}$in.	2			6
D12/977	TA/42	Cylinder head and barrel stud (front and rear), $\frac{3}{8}$in.	3			6
D12/978	....	Cylinder head and barrel stud nut (front), $\frac{3}{8}$in.	2			6
D12/979	....	Cylinder head and barrel stud nut (rear), $\frac{3}{8}$in.	1			6
D12/980	TA/2	Stud for carburetter fixing	2			4
D12/981	....	Stud nut for carburetter fixing	2			3
D12/982	....	Stud washer for carburetter fixing	2			2

PART No.	PLATE No.	DESCRIPTION	QTY.	£	s.	d.
CYLINDER HEAD, BARREL, STUDS AND BOLTS—cont.						
D12/727	TA/1	Paper washer for carburetter flange	1			3
D12/983	TA/3	Cylinder head carburetter manifold			10	0
D12/984		Fibre distance piece for manifold	2		2	6
D12/985		Stud securing manifold to cylinder head	4			6
D12/986		Nut for stud securing manifold	4			3
D12/987		Washer for stud securing manifold	4			2
PISTONS AND RINGS.						
D12/702(L.H.)	TA/56	Piston complete, L.H.		1	17	6
D12/702(R.H.)	TA/54	Piston complete, R.H.		1	17	6
D12/160(L.H.)		Piston only, L.H.		1	5	0
D12/160(R.H.)		Piston only, R.H.		1	5	0
D12/161		Piston ring (compression)	4		2	0
D12/162		Piston ring (scraper)	2		2	6
D12/163		Gudgeon pin	2		5	0
D12/164		Gudgeon pin circlip	4			6
		Pistons and Rings can be supplied in the following oversizes. State size when ordering: .005, .010, .020, .030, .040.				
CONNECTING ROD AND FITTINGS.						
D12/158	TA/57	Connecting rod with small end bush	2	2	15	0
		Big end bearing and bolts				
D12/159		Small end bush	2		3	6
D12/27	TA/119	Big end bearing (2 halves one rod)	2		6	0
D12/988	TA/118	Connecting rod big end cap (not supplied separately)	2			
D12/989	TA/63	Big end cap bolt	4		2	3
D12/990	TA/64	Big end cap bolt washer	4			3
D12/991	TA/65	Big end cap bolt nut	4		2	0
D12/992		Big end cap bolt split cotter	4			2
AMAL CARBURETTER.						
76AK/1AT		Amal-Norton carburetter complete		3	6	0
76/413		Mixing chamber			14	0
6/057		Jet block			7	6
6/423		Mixing chamber top			2	6
6/031		Mixing chamber cap ring			2	6
4/235		Fixing spring for cap				9
4/241		Screw for fixing spring for cap				2
4/035		Cable adjuster				6
6/132		Cable top hat ferrules				3
6/052		Throttle valve (6/3)			6	0
4/263		Throttle valve spring				4
4/060		Throttle Valve Cotter pin				1
6/065		Taper needle			2	0
4/230		Needle clip				6
6/045		Air valve			3	9
6/047		Air valve guide			1	0
4/046		Air valve spring				4
4/061		Needle jet			2	6
4/042		Main jet (170)				8
6/062		Mixing chamber union nut			2	3
6/040		Washer for mixing chamber union nut				2
4/043		Holding bolt for float chamber			3	0
4/053		Washer for holding bolt for float chamber				2
13/129		Pilot air adjusting screw				9
4/148		Pilot air adjusting spring				3
4/063		Throttle stop screw				9
16/010		Throttle stop screw lock nut				2
6/038		Air intake tube			3	0
FLOAT CHAMBER AND PARTS.						
1AT		Float chamber complete		1	3	0
64/192		Float chamber body only			14	0
14/208		Float chamber cover complete			3	9
14/021		Float chamber cover lock screw				4

PART No.	PLATE No.	DESCRIPTION	QTY.	£	s.	d.
FLOAT CHAMBER AND PARTS—cont.						
14/301	....	Tickler complete			1	4
14/209	....	Tickler only				10
14/032	....	Tickler spring				2
14/289	....	Tickler cotter pin				1
14/210	....	Tickler stop				3
14/015	....	Float			3	9
14/014	....	Float bow spring				4
14/024	....	Float needle valve			1	6
13/153	....	Plug screw (body arm)				3
14/039	....	Wash for plug screw (body arm)				1
14/178	....	Seating lock nut				4
14/175	....	Seating washer				2
EXHAUST PIPES, SILENCERS AND FITTINGS.						
D12/169 (R.H.)	....	Silencer (R.H.)		3	5	0
D12/169 (L.H.)	....	Silencer (L.H.)		3	5	0
D12/165 (R.H.)	....	Exhaust pipe (R.H.)		1	12	6
D12/165 (L.H.)	....	Exhaust pipe (L.H.)		1	12	6
D12/167	TA/141	Exhaust pipe locking nut (cylinder head)	2		8	0
D12/166	....	Exhaust pipe nut C. and A. washer	2			6
E3801	....	Silencer clip bolt	2			5
E3231	....	Silencer clip bolt nut	2			4
11796	....	Silencer clip bolt washer	2			3
E4268	....	Silencer rear attachment bolt	2		1	6
E5377	....	Silencer rear attachment bolt washer	2			3
NORTON ROAD-HOLDER FORKS AND STEERING DAMPER.						
D12/170	....	Road-Holder fork complete	1	25	0	0
B2/605	J.7	Main tube	2	2	0	0
B2/606	J.29	Main tube bottom bush	2		6	6
B2/607	J.31	Main tube bottom bush locking nut	2		3	9
B2/608	J.30	Main tube bottom bush locking nut washer	2			3
D12/609	J.28	Fork end (left-hand)	1	5	5	0
13433	J.39	Fork end hub spindle pinch stud, near side	1			6
13434	J.41	Fork end hub spindle pinch stud nut	1			4
11776	J.40	Pinch stud washer	1			3
D12/611	J.27	Fork end (right-hand)	1	5	5	0
B2/612	J.38	Fork end drain plug	2			4
B2/613	J.37	Fork end drain plug washer	2			2
B2/614	J.26	Main tube top sleeve bush	2		12	6
B2/615	J.22	Main tube top sleeve bush locking ring	2		7	6
B2/616	J.24	Super oil seal	2		6	6
B2/617	J.25	Super oil seal paper washer	2			2
B2/618	J.17	Buffer spring	2		6	6
B2/619	J.19	Buffer spring leather washer (top)	2			6
B2/620	J.18	Main spring	2		15	0
B2/621	J.21	Main spring leather washer (bottom)	2			3
B2/622	J.14	Spring cover tube (top)	2		4	0
B2/623	J.15	Spring cover tube top securing plate	2		1	0
B2/624	J.16	Spring cover tube top securing plate screw	6			3
B2/625	J.20	Spring cover tube (bottom)	2		6	6
B2/626	J.23	Spring cover tube (bottom) securing screw	4			2
B2/627	J.33	Oil damper rod	2		15	0
B2/628	J.34	Oil damper rod fibre washer	1			3
C2/629	J.36	Oil damper rod plain washer	1			3
C2/630	J.35	Oil damper rod bolt	1			3
B2/631	J.75	Speedometer panel	1		7	6
B2/632	J.76	Speedometer panel control cable rubber grommett	2			6
B2/633	J.2	Main tube filler and retaining plug	2		5	0
B2/634	J.3	Main tube filler and retaining plug washer	2			9
B2/635	J.6	Main tube top cover (left-hand)	1	1	1	0
B2/636	J.5	Main tube top cover (right-hand)	1	1	1	0
B2/637	....	Main tube top cover name plate	2		1	6
B2/638	....	Main tube top cover name plate rivet (per set 2)	2			3
B2/639	J.4	Main tube top cover rubber ring	2		1	6
B2/201	J.42	Steering damper adjuster	1		6	0
B2/203	J.46	Steering damper adjuster rod	1		2	0
B2/202	J.45	Steering damper adjuster rod spring	1		1	0
B2/640	J.47	Steering damper adjuster rod spring lock-nut	1			4

PLATE. J

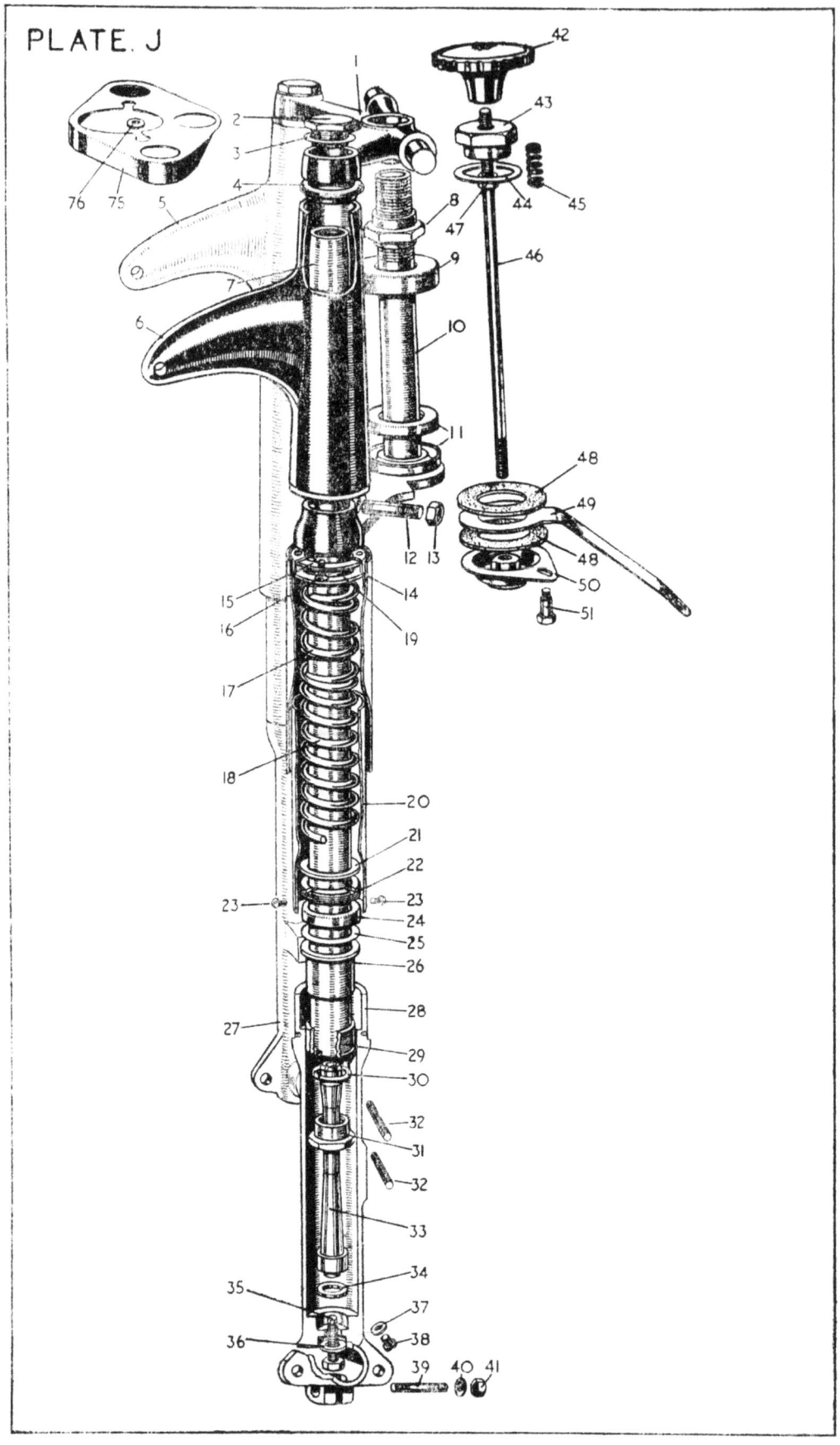

PART No.	PLATE No.	DESCRIPTION	QTY.	£	s.	d.
NORTON ROAD-HOLDER FORKS AND STEERING DAMPER—cont.						
B2/207	J.48	Steering damper friction disc	2		3	0
D12/206	J.49	Steering damper friction and anchor plate	1		6	6
B2/208	J.50	Steering damper bottom plate	1		4	0
B2/641	J.51	Steering damper bottom plate bolt	1			6
B2/172	J.10	Fork crown and column	1	3	0	0
B2/642	J.12	Fork crown main tube clamping stud	2			6
B2/643	J.13	Fork crown main tube clamping stud nut	2			4
B2/173	J.11	Fork crown or head clip ballrace	1		7	6
B2/644	J.9	Fork head clip ballrace cover	1		1	0
D2/174	J.1	Fork head clip	1	1	12	0
D2/175		Handlebar half clip	2		2	0
D2/176		Handlebar half clip pin	4			10
B2/645	J.8	Fork head race adjuster nut	1		9	0
B2/205	J.43	Fork crown and column locknut	1		5	0
B2/646	J.44	Fork crown and column locknut washer	1		1	0
HANDLEBAR AND FITTINGS.						
D12/211	K.48	Handlebar bend		1	14	7
AIR CONTROL LEVER.						
A2/216		Air control lever assembly complete			16	8
A2/217	K.33	Air control lever only			6	0
A2/218	K.32	Air control lever body			5	0
A2/219	K.18	Air control lever top screw			1	0
A2/220	K.19	Air control lever cap			1	8
A2/221	K.20	Air control lever cap spring washer				4
A2/222	K.21	Air control lever clip			1	0
A2/223	K.22	Air control lever clip screw	2			5
FRONT BRAKE AND CLUTCH CONTROL LEVERS.						
D12/224		Front brake lever assembly complete			19	0
D12/225	K.38	Front brake lever only			9	0
D12/226		Clutch lever assembly complete			19	0
D12/227	K.1	Clutch lever only			9	0
A2/228	K.4	Front brake or clutch lever body			7	0
A2/222	K.11	Front brake or clutch lever clip	2		1	0
A2/223	K.15	Front brake or clutch lever clip screw	4			5
A2/229	K.12	Front brake or clutch lever pivot pin	2		1	0
A2/230	K.14	Front brake or clutch lever pivot pin nut	2			3
A2/873	K.13	Front brake or clutch lever pivot pin washer	2			2
TWIST GRIP.						
A2/237		Twist grip complete		1	2	3
A2/238	K.41	Twist grip top half clip			6	0
A2/239	K.44	Twist grip bottom half clip			6	0
A2/240	K.45	Twist grip clip fixing pin	2			8
A2/241	K.43	Twist grip control barrel			7	0
A2/242	K.40	Twist grip control barrel adj. screw				5
A2/236	K.39	Twist grip control barrel adj. screw nut				4
A2/243	K.42	Twist grip control barrel adj. screw spring			1	0
A2/244	K.79	Twist grip cable stop				8
A2/245	K.46	Twist grip rubber			3	8
A2/246	K.47	Dummy grip to match twist grip			3	8
CONTROL CABLE ADJUSTERS AND NIPPLES.						
A2/247	K.23	Front brake or clutch cable adjuster	2		5	0
A2/249	K.27	Air or throttle control cable nipple (handlebar end)	2			3
A2/251		Air or throttle control cable nipple (carburetter end)	2			3
A2/252	K.2	Clutch or front brake control cable nipple (handlebar end)	2		1	0
A2/253		Clutch control cable nipple (gearbox end)				3
A2/254		Front brake cable nipple ("U" clip end)				3
CONTROL CABLES.						
D12/265		Clutch control cable complete			8	6
D12/266	K.5	Clutch control cable (outer)			5	0
D12/267	K.3	Clutch control cable (inner)			3	6

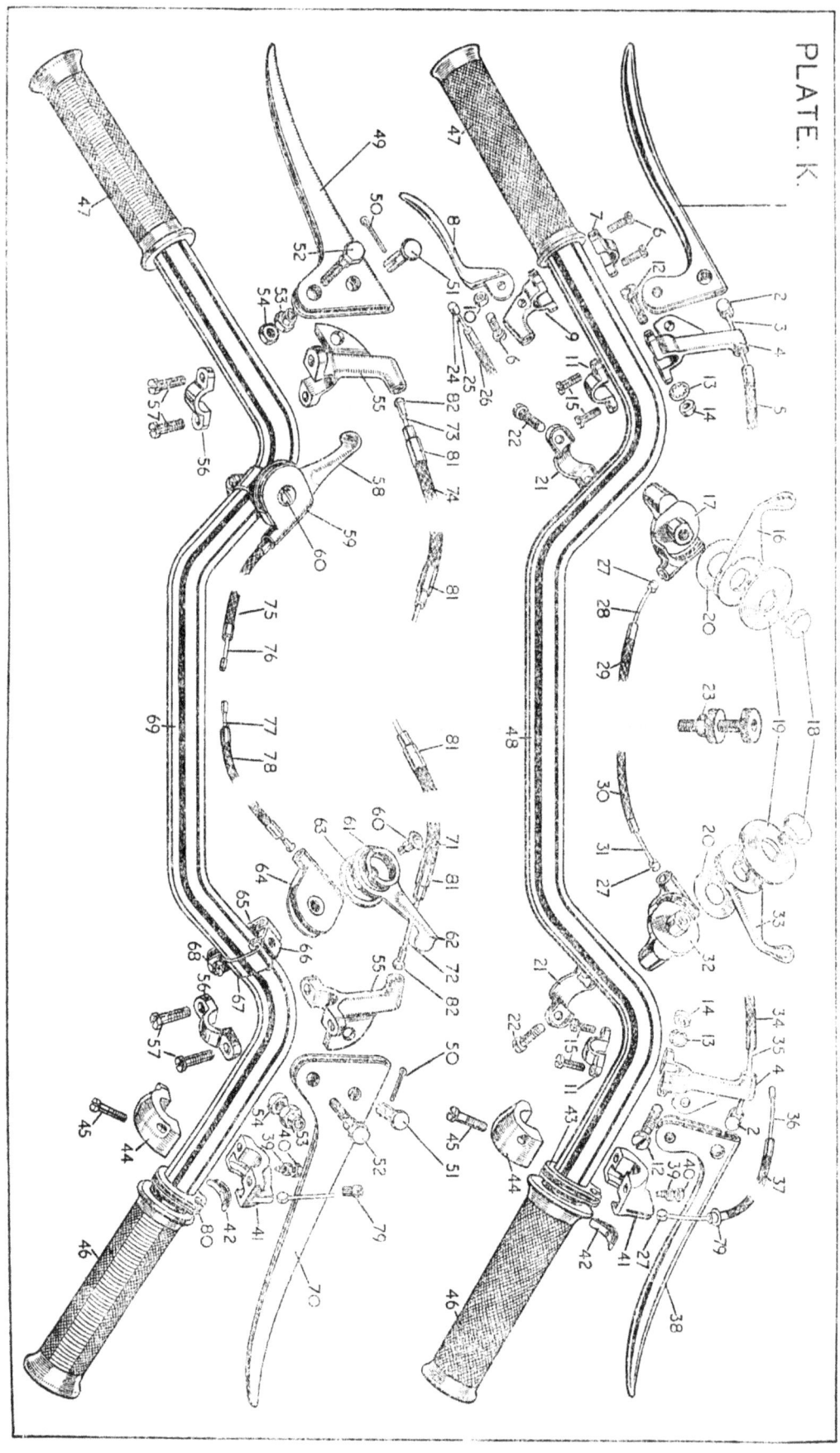

PART No.	PLATE No.	DESCRIPTION	QTY.	PRICE EACH. £ s. d.

CONTROL CABLES—cont.

Part No.	Plate No.	Description	Qty.	£	s.	d.
D12/268	....	Front brake control cable complete			12	6
A11M/269	K.71	Front brake control cable (outer)			9	0
D12/270	K.35	Front brake control cable (inner)			3	6
A2/259	....	Air control cable complete (inner and outer)			4	6
A2/260	K.30	Air control cable (outer)			2	6
A2/261	K.31	Air control cable (inner)			2	0
D12/262	....	Throttle control cable complete (inner and outer)			7	6
D12/263	K.37	Throttle control cable (outer)			5	6
D12/264	K.36	Throttle control cable (inner)			2	0
A2/709	....	Front brake cable "U" clip				6
A2/427	....	Front brake cable "U" clip pin				4
A2/195	....	Front brake cable "U" clip pin cotter				2

PETROL TANK AND FITTINGS.

Part No.	Plate No.	Description	Qty.	£	s.	d.
D12/274	....	Petrol tank		13	15	0
D12/841	TL/5	Rubber buffers front mounting	2		1	0
D12/279F	TL/4	Rubber buffer cup front mounting	2		1	6
14356	TL/6	Distance tube front mounting				9
D12/837	TL/1	Bolt tank front mounting			1	6
E3224	TL/2	Nut for front mounting bolt				4
E5376	TL/3	Washer for front mounting bolt	2			3
D12/838	TL/7	Rear tank mounting bolt			1	6
E3223	TL/11	Nut for rear tank mounting bolt				4
14357	TL/9	Rear tank mounting rubbers (shouldered)	2			6
A2/278	TL/10	Rear tank mounting rubber, plain	2			4
A2/279	TL/8	Cup washer for plain rubber washer	4			6
D12/289	....	Petrol tank frame top tube packing rubbers	2		2	6
D12/282 (L.H.)	....	Knee grip (L.H.)			6	6
D12/282 (R.H.)	....	Knee grip (R.H.)			6	6
14434	....	Knee grip fixing pin	4			5
A11/285	....	Petrol tap	2		7	0
E5264	....	Petrol tap washer	2			3
D12/283 (L.H.)	....	Petrol pipe (L.H.)			11	0
D12/283 (R.H.)	....	Petrol pipe (R.H.)			11	0
A2/280	....	Petrol tank filler cap			17	0
A2/710	....	Petrol tank filler cap washer			2	0
A2/281	....	Petrol tank filler cap cotter pin				2

OIL TANK AND FITTINGS.

Part No.	Plate No.	Description	Qty.	£	s.	d.
D12/290	....	Oil tank, less fittings		4	10	0
A2/291	....	Oil tank filler cap			17	0
A2/711	....	Oil tank filler cap washer			1	0
A2/281	....	Oil tank filler cap cotter pin				2
E3798	....	Oil tank fixing bolt	2			4
11796	....	Washer for oil tank fixing bolt	2			3
D12/297	....	Oil tank top fixing clip			2	0
E3801	....	Oil tank bottom fixing bolt				5
11796	....	Oil tank bottom fixing bolt washer				3
E3336	....	Oil tank drain plug				8
E5264	....	Oil tank drain plug washer				3
D12/292	....	Oil tank union with filter			7	0
A2/293	....	Oil tank union washer				6

OIL PIPES AND FITTINGS.

Part No.	Plate No.	Description	Qty.	£	s.	d.
D12/993	....	Junction block for oil pipes			6	0
D12/994	....	Hollow dowel for junction block				9
D12/995	....	Paper washer for junction block				3
D12/996	....	Sleeve nut for junction block			1	6
D12/997	....	Washer for sleeve nut				3
D12/295	....	Oil delivery pipe to junction box			3	6
D12/296	....	Oil return pipe from junction box			3	6
D12/699	TA/12	Oil pipe to rocker box			7	6
D12/700	TA/13	Oil pipe to rocker box banjo bolt	2		2	0
D12/701	TA/11	Washer for banjo bolt	4			3
D12/998	TA/76	Pipe from crankcase to oil gauge			5	0
D12/700	TA/75	Banjo bolt for oil gauge pipe			2	0
D12/701	TA/77	Washer for banjo bolt	2			3

PLATE T.L.

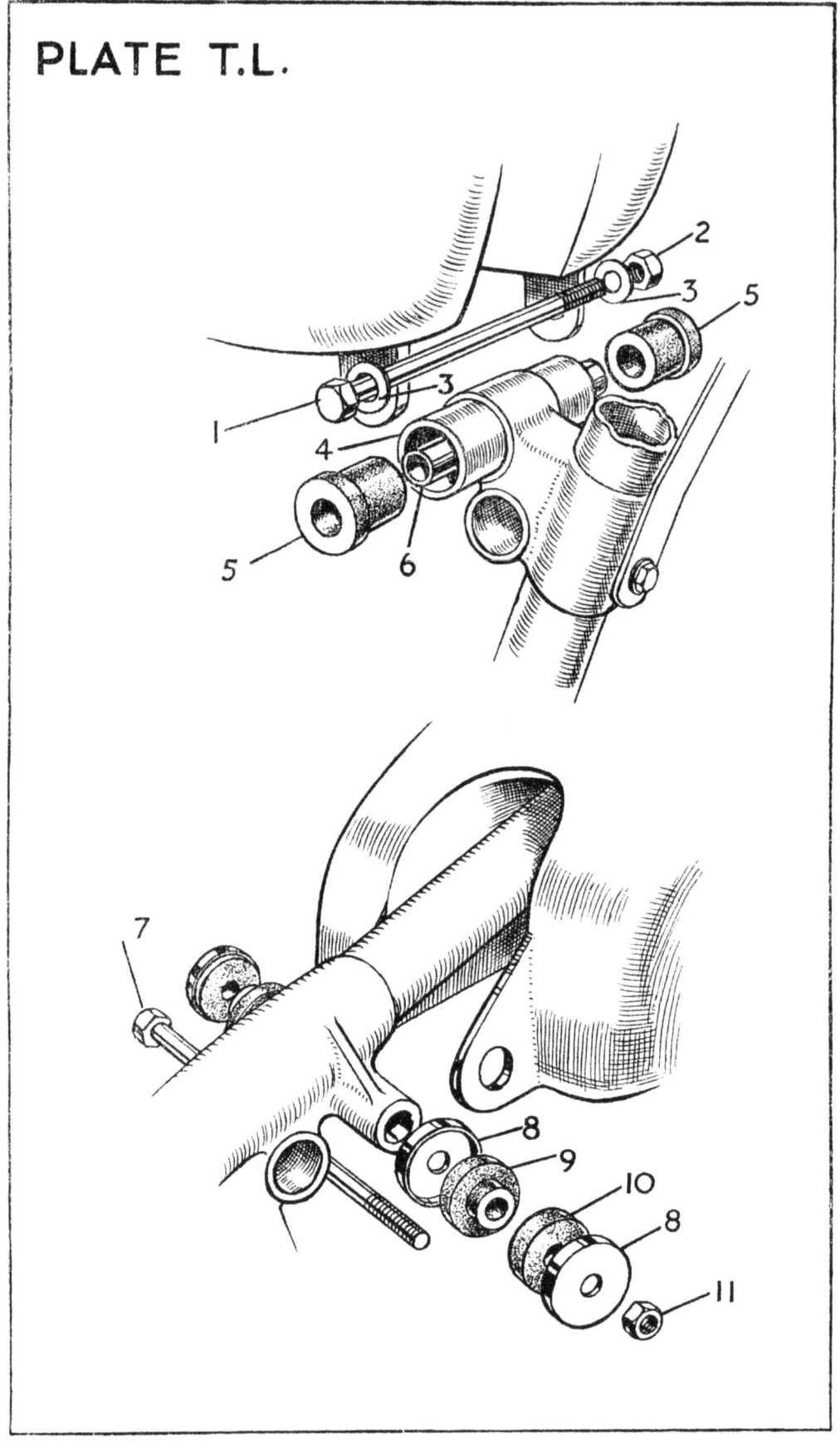

PART No.	PLATE No.	DESCRIPTION	QTY.	£	s.	d.
OIL GAUGE AND FITTINGS.						
D12/999	....	Oil gauge		1	12	6
D12/1000	....	Oil gauge fixing rod with adaptor			2	0
D12/1001	....	Oil gauge securing strap			1	6
D12/1002	....	Steel washer for oil gauge				6
D12/1003	....	Rubber washer for oil gauge				9
D12/1004	....	Oil gauge connection pipe			3	6
GEARBOX SHELL.						
D12/299	TN/21	Gearbox shell with studs		6	19	0
D12/300	TN/73	Gearbox end cover (inner)		2	15	0
D12/301	TN/53	Gearbox end cover (outer)		1	15	0
D12/302	TN/42	Gearbox clutch worm inspection cover			5	0
D12/647	....	Clutch worm inspection cover screw	2			6
D12/1005	TN/19	Paper washer between shell and inner cover				6
D12/1006	TN/72	Paper washer for outer cover				6
D12/1007	TN/43	Joint washer for inspection cover				4
D12/304	TN/20	Gearbox cover stud	8			5
A2/307	....	Gearbox cover stud nut (plain)	5			4
A11M/307	....	Gearbox cover stud nut (dome)	3			4
A2/308	....	Gearbox stud spring washer	8			3
A2/309	....	Gearbox outer plate fixing screw	7			5
E3336	....	Gearbox oil drain plug				8
13765	....	Oil level plug				8
13833	....	Washer for oil level plug				3
GEARBOX FIXING BOLTS.						
D12/310	....	Gearbox suspension bolt and nut			6	0
D12/313	....	Gearbox suspension bolt nut			1	0
E5454	....	Gearbox suspension bolt washer				4
A2/312	....	Gearbox bottom bolt and nut			3	0
A2/313	....	Gearbox bottom bolt nut			1	0
GEARBOX FRONT CHAIN ADJUSTER.						
D12/314	....	Gearbox front chain adjuster bolt and nut			5	0
D12/1008	....	Gearbox front chain adjuster bolt only			4	0
D12/1009	....	Gearbox front chain adjuster bolt nut			1	0
GEARBOX PINIONS, SHAFTS AND BEARINGS.						
A2/316	TN/18	Main gear wheel bearing complete		1	7	0
A2/317	TN/16	Main gear wheel oil retaining washer between main gear wheel and bearing				4
A2/318	....	Main gear wheel sleeve bearing rollers (per set 13)			5	0
A2/319	TN/12	Main gear wheel sleeve bearing roller retaining washer			2	0
A2/320	....	Main gear wheel bearing oil retaining washer between gearbox shell and bearing				4
A2/321	TN/15/77	Mainshaft R.H. bearing or layshaft L.H. bearing			16	0
A2/323	TN/78	Mainshaft bearing packing washer (end cover end)				3
D12/324	TN/1	Main axle		2	0	0
A2/325	TN/35	Layshaft		1	16	8
A2/326	TN/13	Main gear wheel with bronze bush (1949)		2	0	0
E12/326	....	Main gear wheel with bronze bush (1950)		2	0	0
A2/327	TN/17	Main gear wheel bush (per pair) (1949)			4	8
E12/327	....	Main gear wheel bush (per pair) (1950)			4	8
A2/328	TN/11	Main axle thrust washer			5	0
A2/329	TN/8	Main axle sliding pinion		1	10	0
A2/330	TN/6	Main axle free pinion		1	6	0
A2/331	TN/2	Main axle pinion			12	0
A2/332	TN/14	Layshaft pinion			14	0
A2/333	TN/9	Layshaft free pinion		1	3	4
A2/334	TN/7	Layshaft sliding pinion		1	10	0
A2/335	TN/4	Bush for main axle free pinion			4	0
A2/336	TN/10	Bush for layshaft free pinion			5	0
A2/337	TN/3	Low gear and kickstart wheel with bronze bush		1	13	4
A2/338	TN/5	Bronze bush for kickstart and low gear wheel			4	8
A2/339	TN/37	Striker fork	2	1	0	0
A2/340	TN/36	Striker fork shaft			5	0

15

PLATE T.N.

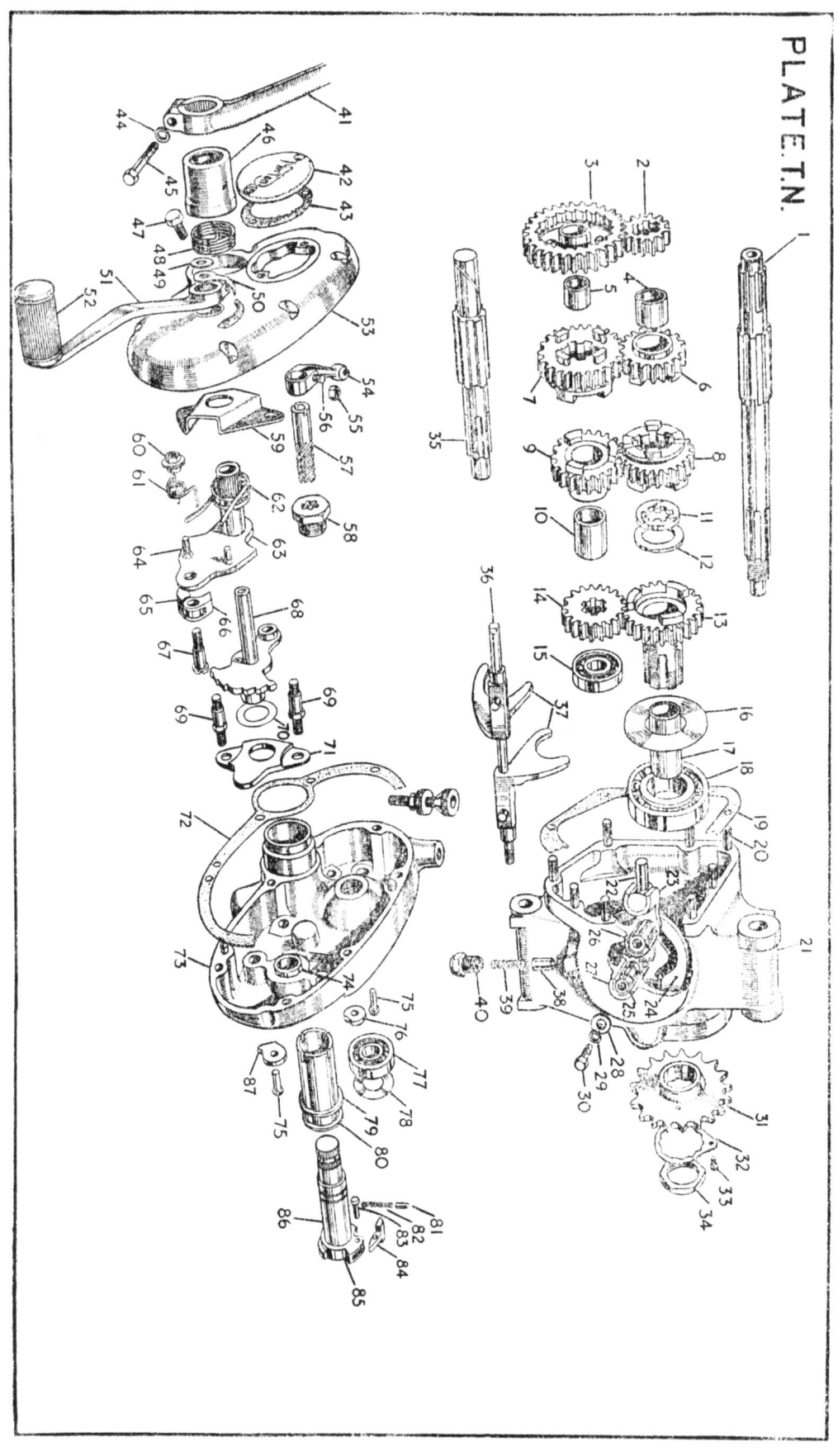

PART No.	PLATE No.	DESCRIPTION	QTY.	£	s.	d.
GEARBOX PINIONS, SHAFTS AND BEARINGS—cont.						
D12/341	TN/24	Cam plate		1	0	0
D12/342	TN/25	Cam plate spindle			13	4
D12/343	TN/23	Cam plate quadrant with spindle			16	8
D12/344	TN/26/27	Cam plate or quadrant spindle bush			5	0
A2/346	TN/28	Cam plate or quadrant spindle washer	2			5
A2/347	TN/29	Cam plate or quadrant spindle spring washer	2			3
D12/348	TN/30	Cam plate or quadrant spindle bolt	2			5
D12/349	TN/22	Knuckle pin with head			10	0
A2/350	TN/38	Indexing plunger for cam plate				8
A2/351	TN/40	Indexing plunger bush			2	4
A2/352	TN/39	Indexing plunger spring				4
A2/372		Main axle nut			1	0
A2/373		Axle nut lock washer				3
KICK-STARTER PARTS.						
A2/353	TN/86	Kickstarter axle with bronze bush		2	0	0
A2/354	TN/85	Bronze bush for K.S. end of layshaft			5	0
A2/355	TN/79	Kickstarter axle cork washer				4
A2/356	TN/84	Kickstarter pawl			2	8
A2/357	TN/83	Kickstarter pawl pin				5
A2/358	TN/46	Kickstarter return spring cover			2	4
A2/359	TN/45	Kickstarter crank bolt				5
A2/308	TN/44	Kickstarter crank bolt washer				3
A2/360	TN/41	Kickstarter crank		1	6	8
A2/367	TN/48	Kickstarter return spring			2	4
B2/648		Kickstarter crank rubber			2	0
A2/361	TN/76	Kickstarter cam				8
A2/362	TN/75	Kickstarter cam or stop piece rivet				3
A2/363	TN/87	Kickstarter stop piece				10
A2/364	TN/80	Kickstarter bush			6	0
A2/365	TN/82	Kickstarter pawl spring				4
A2/366	TN/81	Kickstarter pawl spring plunger				8
GEARBOX AXLE SPROCKET.						
D12/368	TN/31	Axle sprocket (1949)		1	2	0
E12/368		Axle sprocket (1950)		1	2	0
A2/369	TN/34	Axle sprocket locking nut			1	8
A2/370	TN/32	Axle sprocket nut locking plate				8
A2/371	TN/33	Axle sprocket locking plate screw				3
CLUTCH GROUP.						
D12/374		Clutch assembly complete		12	5	0
D12/375	TN/57	Clutch worm			5	0
D12/376	TN/58	Clutch worm nut			13	4
D12/377	TN/54	Clutch worm lever			5	0
D12/378	TN/56	Clutch worm lever stud				6
GT158	TN/55	Clutch worm lever stud nut				3
A2/379		Clutch rod			2	0
A2/380		Thrust pin			2	0
D12/381	Q.2	Clutch back plate			7	6
A2/382	Q.3	Clutch roller cage			3	6
A2/383	Q.4	Clutch rollers (per set 13)			6	6
A2/384	Q.13	Clutch sprocket with inserts		2	5	0
A2/385	Q.7	Clutch body		1	17	0
A2/386	Q.5	Clutch body back cover plate			4	8
D12/387	Q.10	Clutch body centre			17	0
A2/388	Q.8	Clutch body centre rubber buffers, large (per set 3)			4	6
A2/389	Q.9	Clutch body centre rubber buffers, small (per set 3)			4	6
A2/390	Q.11	Clutch body front cover plate			6	0
A2/391	Q.12	Clutch body front cover plate screw	3			3
A2/392	Q.14	Clutch plate steel	6		5	6
A2/393	Q.15	Clutch friction plate with inserts	5		11	0
A2/394		Clutch friction plate inserts (per doz.)	100		3	0
A2/395		Clutch sprocket inserts (per doz.)	20		3	0
A2/396	Q.18	Clutch plate cover			4	6
A2/397	Q.17	Clutch outer plate			5	6
A2/398	Q.16	Clutch plate retaining ring			1	4
D2/399	Q.20	Clutch spring	3			8

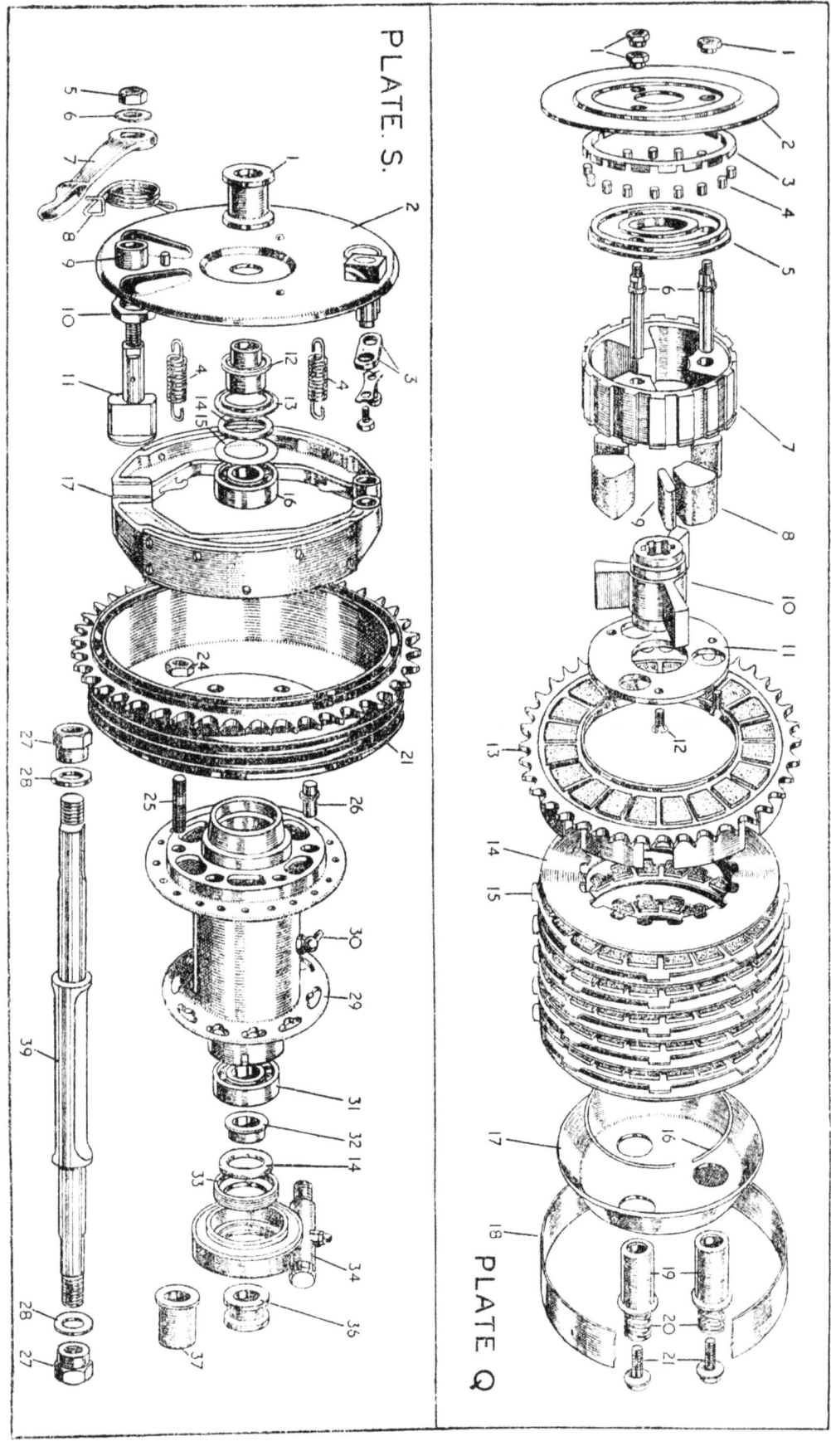

PART No.	PLATE No.	DESCRIPTION	QTY.	£	s.	d.
CLUTCH GROUP—cont.						
D2/400	Q.19	Clutch spring box	3		1	6
D2/401	Q.6	Clutch spring stud	3		1	6
A2/402	Q.1	Clutch spring stud nut	3			4
A2/403	Q.21	Clutch spring screw	3			4
POSITIVE FOOTCHANGE PARTS.						
D12/404	TN/50	Gearbox change speed indicator			1	6
D12/405	TN/47	Gearbox speed indicator bolt				6
D12/864	TN/49	Change speed indicator bolt washer				3
D12/406	TN/51	Gear lever		1	0	0
D12/407	TN/52	Gear lever rubber			2	0
A2/408		Gear lever securing bolt				8
D12/409	TN/59	Return spring cover plate			6	8
D12/410	TN/62	Return spring for pawl carrier			1	4
D12/411	TN/69	Stop stud for pawl carrier	2		1	4
A2/412F		Stop stud nut for pawl carrier	2			8
A2/413	TN/64	Peg for pawl carrier	2			4
D12/414	TN/63	Pawl carrier			13	0
D12/415	TN/70	Pawl carrier spacing washer				3
A2/417	TN/65	Pawl (plain)			4	0
A2/418	TN/66	Pawl (forked)			4	0
A2/419	TN/61	Pawl return spring			1	0
A2/420	TN/67	Pawl pin			1	6
A2/421	TN/60	Pawl pin nut				8
D12/422	TN/68	Ratchet plate with spindle		1	0	0
D12/423	TN/71	Cam plate			4	0
D12/1010	TN/74	Bronze bush inner for gear change			5	0
D12/1011		Bronze bush outer for gear change			5	0
FRONT WHEEL AND FITTINGS.						
D12/714		Front wheel complete with bearings and brake, less tyre		13	10	0
D12/428		Front wheel with hub shell only		6	10	0
B2/655	R.26	Front wheel hub shell with brake drum		3	12	0
B2/452	R.31	Front hub spindle			15	0
B2/453	R.8	Front hub spindle distance piece			2	0
B2/454	R.7	Front hub spindle nut			2	2
B2/455	R.15	Front hub brake plate distance piece			4	0
B2/457	R.6	Front brake plate			15	6
A2/459	R.9	Front hub brake cam lever			2	0
B2/657	R.5	Front hub brake shoe fulcrum pin			2	6
B2/658	R.4	Front hub brake shoe fulcrum pin nut				6
B2/441	R.28	Hub bearing distance piece, plain side			1	0
C2/656	R.25	Hub shell bearing distance tube			1	6
B2/439	R.16	Hub bearing felt washer steel plate (brake side)				6
B2/442	R.30	Hub bearing dust cover			3	0
D12/443	R.21	Hub brake shoe with lining (each)	2		18	0
D12/444	R.23	Hub brake shoe linings (per pair)			12	0
REAR WHEEL AND FITTINGS.						
D12/715		Rear wheel complete with bearings and brake (less tyre)		17	5	0
D12/649		Rear wheel with hub shell only		6	6	0
B4/433	S.29	Hub shell only		2	15	0
A2/441	S.32	Hub bearing distance, plain side (rear)			2	0
A2/439	S.13	Hub bearing felt washer steel cup (brake side)			1	0
D12/460	S.39	Rear hub spindle		2	10	0
B2/659	S.28	Rear hub spindle washer				3
B2/660		Rear hub spindle shouldered washer, plain side (for speedometer gearbox)			1	6
D12/461	S.36	Rear hub spindle distance piece (plain side)			2	6
B4/462	S.2	Rear hub brake plate			15	6
D12/468	S.21	Rear hub brake drum and sprocket		3	5	0
D12/465	S.1	Rear hub brake plate distance piece (outer)			2	6
B4/661	S.12	Rear hub brake plate distance piece (inner)			3	0
A2/454	S.27	Rear hub spindle nut	2		2	2
D11M/469	S.7	Rear hub brake cam lever			3	0
D11M/470	S.8	Rear hub brake cam lever return spring			1	0

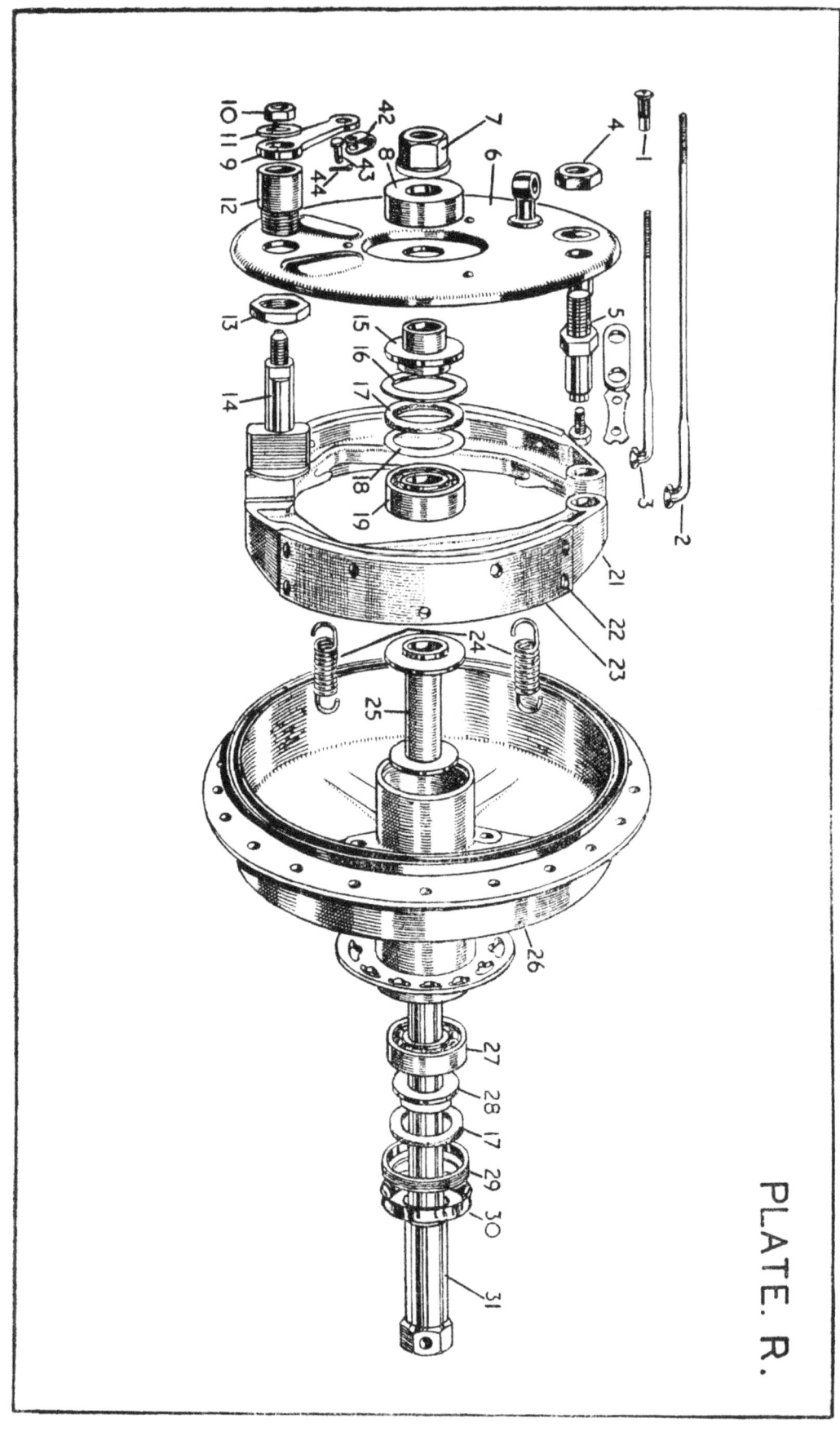

PLATE. R.

PART No.	PLATE No.	DESCRIPTION	QTY.	£	s.	d.
REAR WHEEL AND FITTINGS—cont.						
B4/662	S.26	Rear hub shell brake drum dowel	3		2	0
B4/663	S.25	Rear hub brake drum stud	3		1	0
B4/664	S.24	Rear hub shell brake drum stud nut	3			4
A11M/443	S.17	Rear hub brake shoes with linings (each)	2		18	0
A11M/444 (R)		Rear hub brake shoe linings (per pair)			12	0
PARTS COMMON TO FRONT AND REAR HUBS.						
A2/435	R.27/S.31	Hub bearing (plain side)	2		16	6
A2/436	R.19/S.16	Hub bearing (brake side)	2	1	11	4
A2/440	R.29/S.33	Hub bearing lock ring (plain side)	2		2	0
A2/437	R.17/S.14	Hub bearing felt washer	2			8
A2/438	R.18/S.15	Hub bearing pen steel washer	2			4
A2/198	S.30	Hub grease nipple	2		1	0
A2/446	R.24/S.4	Hub brake shoe return spring	4		1	0
A2/447	R.20/S.3	Hub brake shoe circlip	4			6
A2/448	R.14/S.11	Hub brake cam with nut and washer	2		7	0
E3224	R.10/S.5	Hub brake cam nut	2			4
E5455	R.11/S.6	Hub brake cam nut washer	2			2
A2/449	R.11/S.9	Hub brake cam bush	2		2	0
A2/450	R.13/S.10	Hub brake cam bush locknut	2		1	0
A2/445	R.22/S.30	Hub brake shoe lining rivet (per set 14)	2		1	0
WHEEL RIMS AND SPOKES.						
B11/654		Front wheel rim WM1-21		1	7	6
A2/432		Rear wheel rim WM2-19		1	5	0
A11/650	R.3	Wheel spoke, front (brake side) (per set 20)			4	0
A11/651	R.2	Wheel spoke, front (plain side) (per set 20)			4	0
B2/652		Wheel spoke, rear (brake drum side) (per set 20)			4	0
B2/653		Wheel spoke, rear (plain side) (per set 20)			4	0
A2/431	R.1	Wheel spoke nipples (per set 40)	2		4	6
FRONT CHAINCASE AND FITTINGS.						
D12/484	T.5	Front chaincase, inner portion (1949)		3	4	0
E12/484	T.5	Front chaincase, inner portion (1950)		3	4	0
D12/485	T.9	Front chaincase, outer portion		3	10	0
A2/486	T.11	Front chaincase sealing washer			9	0
E3336	T.18	Front chaincase drain plug				8
E5264	T.17	Front chaincase drain plug washer				3
A2/487	T.14	Front chaincase inspection disc			2	0
A2/488	T.13	Front chaincase inspection disc washer			1	0
A2/489	T.12	Front chaincase inspection disc spring clip			1	0
E6354	T.7	Front chaincase inner portion crankcase attachment pin				5
A2/490	T.6	Front chaincase pin locking plate				4
D12/491	T.3	Front chaincase inner portion engine plate attachment bolt			3	6
E3223	T.2	Nut for inner portion attachment bolt	2			4
E5456	T.10	Washer for inner portion attachment bolt	2			4
A2/493	T.4	Front chaincase inner portion gearbox felt washer				8
A2/494	T.8	Front chaincase inner portion footrest tube felt washer				4
A2/495	T.16	Front chaincase outer portion securing nut			2	4
A2/496	T.15	Front chaincase outer portion securing nut washer			2	0
REAR CHAINGUARD.						
D12/497	T.19	Rear chainguard		1	8	0
14455	T.22	Rear chainguard attachment bolt, front end	2			8
E3229	T.20	Rear chainguard attachment bolt nut	2			4
E5379	T.21	Rear chainguard attachment bolt washer	4			3
(For rear attachment see rear springing member bolt.)						
REAR BRAKE PEDAL AND FITTINGS.						
D12/498		Rear brake pedal		1	4	0
A2/500		Rear brake pedal grease nipple			1	0
A2/501		Rear brake pedal adjuster and locknut			1	6
D12/502		Rear brake pedal pivot bolt			2	0
E3223		Rear brake pedal pivot bolt nut				4

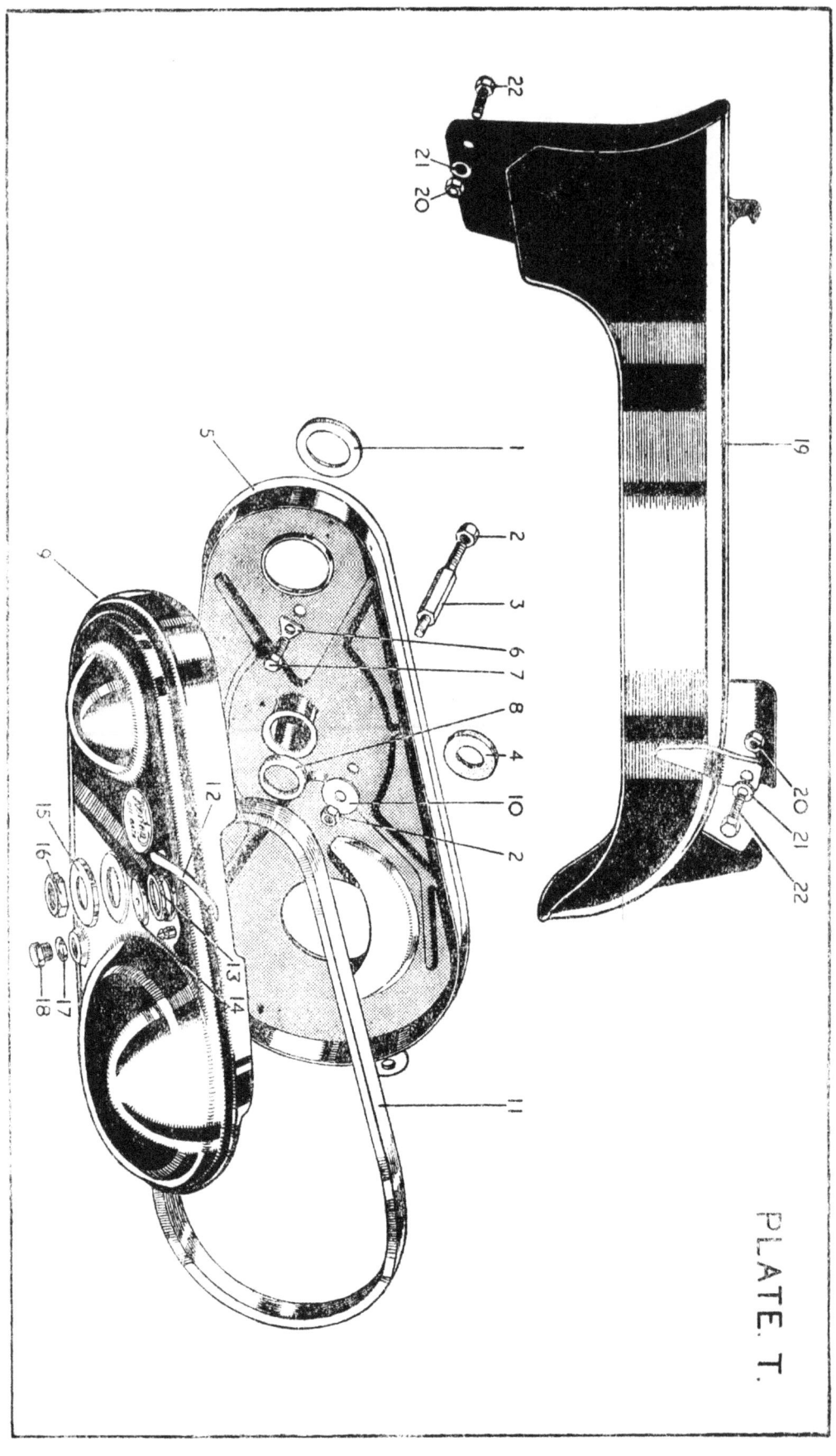

PLATE T.

PART No.	PLATE No.	DESCRIPTION	QTY.	£	s.	d.
REAR BRAKE PEDAL AND FITTINGS—cont.						
E5456	....	Rear brake pedal pivot bolt washer				3
B4/503	....	Rear brake rod			6	0
A2/504	....	Rear brake rod jaw joint			4	6
D12/505	....	Rear brake rod adjuster			3	0
A2/506	....	Rear brake rod jaw joint pin				5
A2/195	....	Rear brake rod jaw joint split pin				2
FOOTRESTS AND FITTINGS.						
A2/507	....	Footrest rubber	2		2	6
A2/508	....	Footrest rubber bolt and nut	4			10
A2/509	....	Footrest pad holder	2		5	6
D12/510	....	Footrest rod			4	0
E3226	....	Footrest rod nut (plain)				5
E3220	....	Footrest rod nut (domed)				10
E5377	....	Footrest rod washer	2			3
A2/512 (L.H.)	....	Footrest hanger with spindle (left hand)			12	0
D12/512 (R.H.)	....	Footrest hanger with spindle (right hand)			15	0
A2/513 (L.H.)	....	Footrest hanger only (left hand)			9	8
D12/513 (R.H.)	....	Footrest hanger only (right hand)			12	6
A2/514	....	Footrest hanger spindle only	2		2	4
A2/515	....	Footrest hanger spindle nut	2			5
E5376	....	Footrest hanger spindle washer	2			3
ENGINE PLATES.						
D12/522	....	Front engine plate, L.H. or R.H.	2		8	0
D12/516	....	Rear engine plate with footrest tube (L.H.) (1949)			19	0
E12/516	....	Rear engine plate with footrest tube (L.H.) (1950)			19	0
D12/517	....	Rear engine plate (R.H.)			12	6
ENGINE SPROCKET.						
D12/473	TA/129	Engine sprocket	1		2	0
A2/474	TA/127	Engine sprocket key				3
A2/475	TA/130	Engine sprocket locknut			1	0
FRONT AND REAR CHAINS.						
D12/477	....	Front chain (76 link)	1		5	0
D12/478	....	Rear chain (89 link)	2		3	0
A2/479	....	Front chain spring link			1	9
A2/480	....	Front chain cranked link			3	0
A2/481	....	Rear chain spring link			1	9
A2/482	....	Rear chain cranked link			3	0
REAR CHAIN ADJUSTERS.						
B4/483	....	Rear chain adjuster complete	2		6	0
B4/665	Y.14	Rear chain adjuster stirrup	2		3	0
B4/666	Y.15	Rear chain adjuster bolt	2		1	6
B4/667	Y.12	Rear chain adjuster bolt nut	2			6
B4/668	Y.13	Rear chain adjuster fork end cap	2		1	0
FRAMES.						
D12/518	....	Frame only with head races	1	30	0	0
A2/519	....	Frame head race, top	1		7	6
A2/520	....	Frame head race, bottom	1		7	6
A2/521	....	Frame head balls (per set 34)	1		4	0
13195	....	Frame fork stop bolt	2			8
11796	....	Frame fork stop bolt washer	4			3
B2/877	....	Frame fork stop bolt distance piece	2			6
FRAME REAR SPRINGING.						
D12/669	....	Frame fork end, left hand	1	5	0	0
B4/670	Y.19	Frame fork end, right hand	1	5	0	0
A2/500	Y.20	Frame fork end grease nipple	2		1	0
B4/671	Y.28	Frame fork end main rod	2	3	0	0
B4/672	Y.30	Frame fork end main rod bottom bolt	2		1	0
11181	Y.29	Frame fork end main rod bottom bolt washer	2			3
B4/673	Y.24	Frame fork end main rod plug	2		2	0

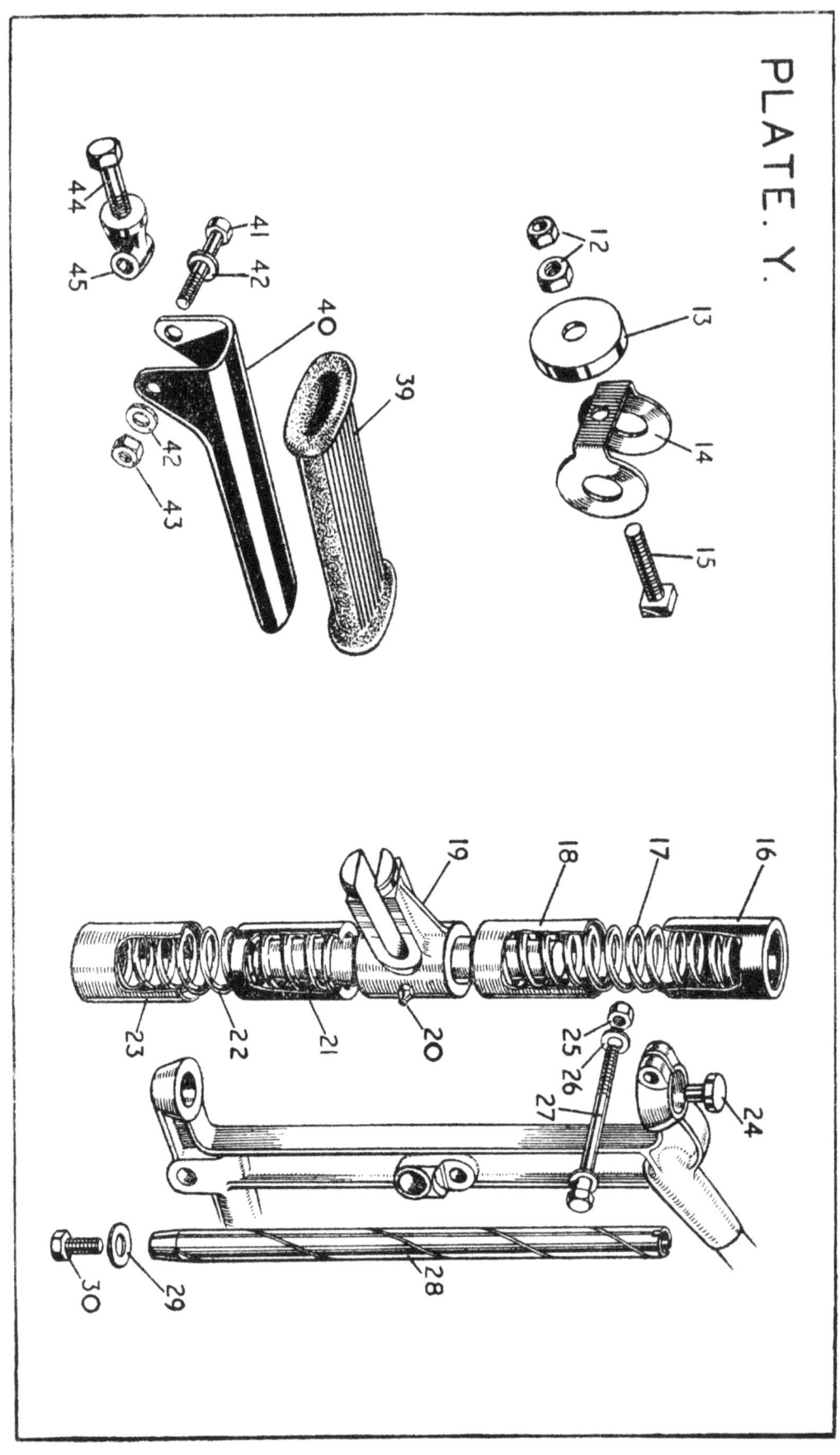

PLATE. Y.

PART No.	PLATE No.	DESCRIPTION	QTY.	£	s.	d
FRAME REAR SPRINGING—cont.						
E4261	Y.27	Rear frame member pinch bolt (nearside)	1			9
11304		Rear frame member pinch bolt (offside)	1			9
E3223	Y.25	Rear frame member pinch bolt nut	2			4
11796	Y.26	Rear frame member pinch bolt washer	4			3
B4/674	Y.17	Frame fork end top spring	2		15	0
B4/675	Y.16	Frame fork end top spring cover, outer	2		9	0
B4/676	Y.18	Frame fork end top spring cover, inner	2		12	6
B4/677	Y.22	Frame fork end bottom spring	2		12	6
B4/678	Y.23	Frame fork end bottom spring cover, outer	2		9	0
B4/679	Y.21	Frame fork end bottom spring cover, inner	2		12	6

PROP STAND AND FITTINGS.

PART No.	PLATE No.	DESCRIPTION	QTY.	£	s.	d
B4/524		Prop stand		1	5	0
A11/525		Prop stand bolt	2			9
A2/527		Prop stand return spring			2	0
E12/1014		Side prop stand	1	1	1	0
E2/1015		Side prop stand spring			2	0
E12/1016		Side prop stand fixing plate			5	0
E6706		Side prop stand head bolt				9
12079		Side prop stand head bolt nut				4

FRONT MUDGUARD, STAYS AND FITTINGS.

PART No.	PLATE No.	DESCRIPTION	QTY.	£	s.	d
D12/529		Front mudguard with number plate studs		1	15	0
D12/530		Front mudguard stay, left or right hand	2		3	6
E3223		Front mudguard stay nut	2			4
E5456		Front mudguard stay washer	2			3
14455		Front mudguard stay fork end bolt	2			8
E5379		Front mudguard stay fork end bolt washer	2			3
T1085		Front mudguard centre stay fork attachment stud	4			6
E3229		Front mudguard centre stay stud nut	4			4
E5379		Front mudguard centre stay stud washer	4			3
E3262		Front mudguard stand attachment bolt				8
E3223		Front mudguard stand attachment bolt plain nut				4
E3218		Front mudguard stand attachment bolt domed nut				6
E5456		Front mudguard stand attachment bolt washer	2			3

REAR MUDGUARD, STAYS AND FITTINGS.

PART No.	PLATE No.	DESCRIPTION	QTY.	£	s.	d
D12/534		Rear mudguard complete		2	5	0
D12/535 (F.)		Rear mudguard, front half			15	0
D12/535 (R.)		Rear mudguard, rear half		1	10	0
12135		Bolt attaching front and rear halves of mudguard	2			6
E3223		Nut attaching front and rear halves of mudguard	2			4
E5456		Washer attaching front and rear halves of mudguard	2			3
E6354		Bolt attaching mudguard to bottom frame lug				5
E3223		Nut attaching mudguard to bottom frame lug				4
E5456		Washer attaching mudguard to bottom frame lug	2			3
E6354		Bolt attaching mudguard to top frame lug	2			5
E3223		Nut attaching mudguard to top frame lug	2			4
E5456		Washer attaching mudguard to top frame lug	2			3
D12/536 (L.H.)		Rear mudguard stay and handle (L.H.)		1	0	0
D12/536 (R.H.)		Rear mudguard stay and handle (R.H.)		1	0	0
E3223		Nut for mudguard stay	4			4
E5456		Washer for mudguard stay	4			3

NUMBER PLATES, FRONT AND REAR.

PART No.	PLATE No.	DESCRIPTION	QTY.	£	s.	d
A2/531		Front number plate			2	0
A2/533		Front number plate pin and nut	2			3
A2/875		Front mudguard number plate clip and nut	2		1	0
D2/532		Rear number plate			5	0
14468		Rear number plate pins (top)	2			6
14455		Rear number plate pins (bottom)	2			8
E3229		Rear number plate pin nuts	4			4
E5379		Rear number plate pin washer	4			3

PART No.	PLATE No.	DESCRIPTION	QTY.	£	s.	d

TOOL-BOX.

Part No.		Description	QTY	£	s	d
D12/538	....	Tool box		1	5	0
A2/539	....	Tool box knob			2	4
A2/281	....	Tool box knob cotter pin				2
14455	....	Tool box bolt attaching to mudguard	2			8
E3229	....	Nut for bolt	2			4
E5379	....	Washer for bolt	4			3

(Rear of tool box attached to frame by pillion footrest lug bolt.)

SADDLE.

Part No.		Description	QTY	£	s	d
D12/540	....	Saddle		2	17	0
D12/541	....	Saddle spring	2		7	6
14425	....	Saddle spring frame stud	2		2	0
E3223	....	Nut for saddle spring stud	8			4
E5456	....	Washer for saddle spring stud	4			3
12080	....	Saddle front anchor bolt			1	8
E3223	....	Saddle front anchor bolt nut				4
E5379	....	Saddle front anchor bolt washer				3

FRONT STAND.

Part No.		Description	QTY	£	s	d
A2/544	....	Front stand		1	0	0
E6354	....	Front stand attachment pin	2			5
E5379	....	Front stand attachment pin washer	2			3
E3223	....	Front stand attachment pin nut	2			4

BATTERY CARRIER.

Part No.		Description	QTY	£	s	d
D12/586	....	Battery carrier (1949)			15	0
E12/586	....	Battery carrier (1950)			15	0
E6354	....	Battery carrier top fixing bolt	2			5
E3798	....	Battery carrier bottom fixing bolt	2			4
11796	....	Washer for battery carrier bolt	3			3

SPEEDOMETER AND FITTINGS.

Part No.		Description	QTY	£	s	d
D12/545	....	Speedometer head		3	0	0
B2/681	....	Speedometer head rubber washer				6
B2/555	....	Speedometer head attachment bracket			1	6
B2/556	....	Speedometer head securing nut	2			4
B2/557	....	Speedometer head securing washer	2			3
B2/552	....	Speedometer cable complete		1	5	0
B2/553	....	Speedometer cable, outer			12	6
B2/554	....	Speedometer cable, inner			12	6
B2/564	....	Speedometer gearbox complete		1	10	0

PILLION FOOTRESTS.

Part No.	Plate	Description	QTY	£	s	d
A2/582	Y.40	Pillion footrest hanger, L.H. or R.H.			4	0
A2/583	Y.39	Pillion footrest rubber, L.H. or R.H.			3	0
E3801	Y.41	Pillion footrest attachment bolt	2			5
5790A	Y.42	Pillion footrest attachment bolt spring washer	2			4
E3223	Y.43	Pillion footrest attachment bolt nut	2			4
A2/584	....	Pillion footrest complete (per pair)			17	0
B4/686	Y.45	Frame pillion footrest lug	2		2	6
11601	Y.44	Frame pillion footrest lug bolt	2			6

HEADLAMP AND PARTS.

Part No.		Description	QTY	£	s	d
50788	....	Headlamp complete (SSU.700P)		5	14	6
112201	....	Headlamp fixing bolt	2			8
506860	....	Headlamp rim			11	8
507586	....	Headlamp glass			5	5
508736	....	Headlamp glass cork washer			1	0
364455	....	Ammeter			11	8
351551	....	Switch complete			10	3
SK49	....	Headlamp switch lever and screw			2	1
380501	....	Headlamp dipper switch			6	7

(State size of headlamp when ordering parts.)

PART No.	PLATE No.	DESCRIPTION	QTY.	£	s.	d.

REAR LAMP AND FITTINGS.

PART No.	PLATE No.	DESCRIPTION	QTY.	£	s.	d.
53056	....	Rear lamp complete (MT211)			16	10
526232	....	Rear lamp cover assembly			7	2
526239	....	Rear lamp flange assembly			6	4

VOLTAGE REGULATOR AND FITTINGS.

PART No.	PLATE No.	DESCRIPTION	QTY.	£	s.	d.
37097	....	Voltage regulator MCR2		1	19	0
12343	....	Voltage regulator fixing pin	2			8
E3229	....	Voltage regulator fixing pin nut	4			4
E5379	....	Voltage regulator fixing pin washer	4			3

ELECTRIC HORN AND FITTINGS.

PART No.	PLATE No.	DESCRIPTION	QTY.	£	s.	d.
069343	....	Electric horn and bracket		1	15	8
701686	....	Electric horn bracket			3	4
13299	....	Electric horn frame attachment bolt				6

TOOLS.

PART No.	PLATE No.	DESCRIPTION	QTY.	£	s.	d.
A2/561	....	Tyre inflator with connection			8	0
A2/562	....	Tyre inflator connection			3	6
D12/563	....	Tool roll complete with tools		2	17	6
A2/565	....	Double ended spanner, $\frac{3}{16}$in. × $\frac{1}{4}$in.			2	0
A2/566	....	Double ended spanner, $\frac{5}{16}$in. × $\frac{3}{8}$in.			2	8
A2/567	....	Screwdriver			2	6
D12/568	....	Tappet spanners (per pair)			2	0
A2/570	....	Wheel nut box spanner			2	0
A3/571	....	Sparking plug spanner			4	0
A2/573	....	Tyre lever	2		2	0
A2/574	....	Wheel spindle spanner			2	8
A2/578	....	Single ended spanner, $\frac{1}{8}$in.			1	0
A3/579	....	Exhaust pipe "C" spanner			3	0
A2/581	....	Tommy bar			1	0
B2/682	....	Front fork crown and column locknut spanner			2	6
B2/683	....	Front fork filler plug and head adjuster nut spanner			3	0
B2/684	....	Front fork main tube top bush lockring spanner			2	0
B2/685	....	Pull through for road holder fork			7	6

TRANSFERS.

PART No.	PLATE No.	DESCRIPTION	QTY.	£	s.	d.
A2/865	....	Petrol tank name transfer	2		1	2
A2/866	....	Petrol tank name transfer top panel			1	2
A2/867	....	Front chaincase transfer			1	2
A2/868	....	Oil tank transfer (minimum oil level)			1	2
A2/869	....	Rear mudguard transfer			1	2

(PLEASE NOTE.—Panels, Red and Black lines cannot be supplied. These are painted by hand.)

RUBBER CABLE CLIPS.

PART No.	PLATE No.	DESCRIPTION	QTY.	£	s.	d.
Size "A"	....	For clutch, air throttle mag. cables and headlamp cable harness to top frame tube				4
Size "D"	....	For tail lamp lead				4
Size "S"	....	For speedometer cable and battery lead				4

NOTES

SPARE PARTS LIST FOR 1957

PRICES SUBJECT TO 15% UNLESS STATED NETT

Models 77, 88 and 99

NORTON MOTORS LTD.

BRACEBRIDGE ST., BIRMINGHAM, 6, ENGLAND

Phone: Aston Cross 3711 (Private Branch Exchange)

Grams: "Nortomo, Birmingham"

INSTRUCTIONS FOR ORDERING SPARE PARTS

This Spare Parts List deals with replacement parts for Models 88, 99 and 77 of 1957 manufacture.

It is most essential that the Engine and Frame Number of the machine is stated. The Engine Number is to be found on the transmission side of the Crankcase directly below cylinder base. The frame number is stamped on the nearside of the frame gusset plate on 88 and 99 models and on the petrol tank front mounting lug on the Model 77. It is always advisable to order parts on a separate sheet, and not to include on the same sheet other matter of a different nature; this facilitates prompt despatch.

It is found in a number of instances that money orders and postal orders are sent in parcels containing patterns ; this is inadvisable. We strongly recommend parts as patterns being despatched separately, and a covering letter sent containing the remittance for replacement parts.

RETURNING MACHINES FOR OVERHAULING

When returning machines or parts for repair or overhaul, these should be sent carriage paid, and with the sender's name and address in full **securely** attached. It is also advisable to state on the tally that a letter has been sent respecting the parts, and giving the date. All easily detached fittings should be removed, such as Lamps, Horns, Tool Bags, Speedometers, etc. ; these are liable to be lost or damaged in transit, and the Company cannot accept any responsibility for them.

ESTIMATES FOR REPAIRING MACHINES

We are always prepared to give approximate estimates for the cost of repairs ; it is quite impossible to give a firm quotation. Additional parts may be found necessary during the process of repair, unforeseen when preparing an estimate. Should our estimate for repair not be accepted, a charge may be made in accordance with work entailed in dismantling and re-assembling. When we give an estimate for cost of repairs, and this is curtailed by the owner, we cannot accept any responsibility for the performance of the machine ; it is always preferable to accept our estimate in full.

PURCHASE OF SPARE PARTS

Norton Dealers throughout the British Isles generally carry a very comprehensive stock of Norton spare parts and it is recommended that owners should obtain any spare parts required through them.

The name of the nearest Norton dealer will be supplied on request and if any difficulty whatever is experienced in obtaining spare parts through a Norton Dealer, if we are advised, we shall be very pleased to investigate the matter.

It is our desire that replacement parts are available to Norton owners with the least possible delay.

Please note we reserve the right to alter the prices in the list at any time without notice.

FOR ENAMELLED PARTS—PLEASE STATE COLOUR

INDEX

	Page		Page
Air cleaner and fittings	32	Headlamp and fittings (all prices Retail nett)	30
Amal carburetter	11	Kickstarter parts	19
Battery (price Retail nett)	30	Lapel badges (this price Retail nett)	32
Brake shoe linings and shoes	23	Magneto and drive parts (all prices Retail nett)	8
Cable clips	32	Norton road holder front forks and fittings	13
Centre stand and fittings	28	Number plates	29
Clutch	21	Oil pipes and fittings	18
Connecting rods and big end bearings	11	Oil pump parts	9
Control cable, adjusters and nipples	15	Oil tank and fittings	16
Crankcase, engine plate bolts, etc.	6	Parts common to front and rear hubs	23
Crankcase and fittings	5	Petrol tank and fittings	15
Crankcase pressure and breather fittings	5	Pillion footrests	25
Cylinder head, barrel, studs and nuts	9	Pistons and rings	9
Dual seat and fittings	31	Positive footchange	19
Dynamo drive parts and securing fittings	8	Push rods and tappets	7
Electric horn and fittings	31	Rear brake pedal and fittings	25
Enamel (this price Retail nett)	32	Rear chain adjusters	27
Engine plates	25	Rear chainguard and fittings	24
Engine sprockets	27	Rear suspension	27
Engine steady stay and fittings	7	Rear wheel and fittings	23
Exhaust pipe, silencer and fittings	13	Rear mudguard and fittings	29
Flywheels, crankshaft and main bearings	5	Rocker box fittings	7
Footrests and fittings	25	Side prop stand and fittings	28
Frame	27	Speedometer and fittings (all prices Retail nett)	31
Front and rear chains	27	Swinging arm and fittings	27
Front chaincase and fittings	24	Tail and stop lights	29
Front wheel and fittings	21	Timing gear fittings	7
Front mudguard, stays and fittings	28	Tool box, tool tray and fittings	30
Gearbox fixing bolts	18	Tool kit	31
Gearbox front chain adjuster	18	Transfers	32
Gearbox pinions, shafts and bearings	19	Valves, guides, springs, etc.	9
Gearbox shell	18	Voltage control and fittings	31
Handlebars and fittings	15	Wheel rims and spokes	24

146

PLATE.T.A.

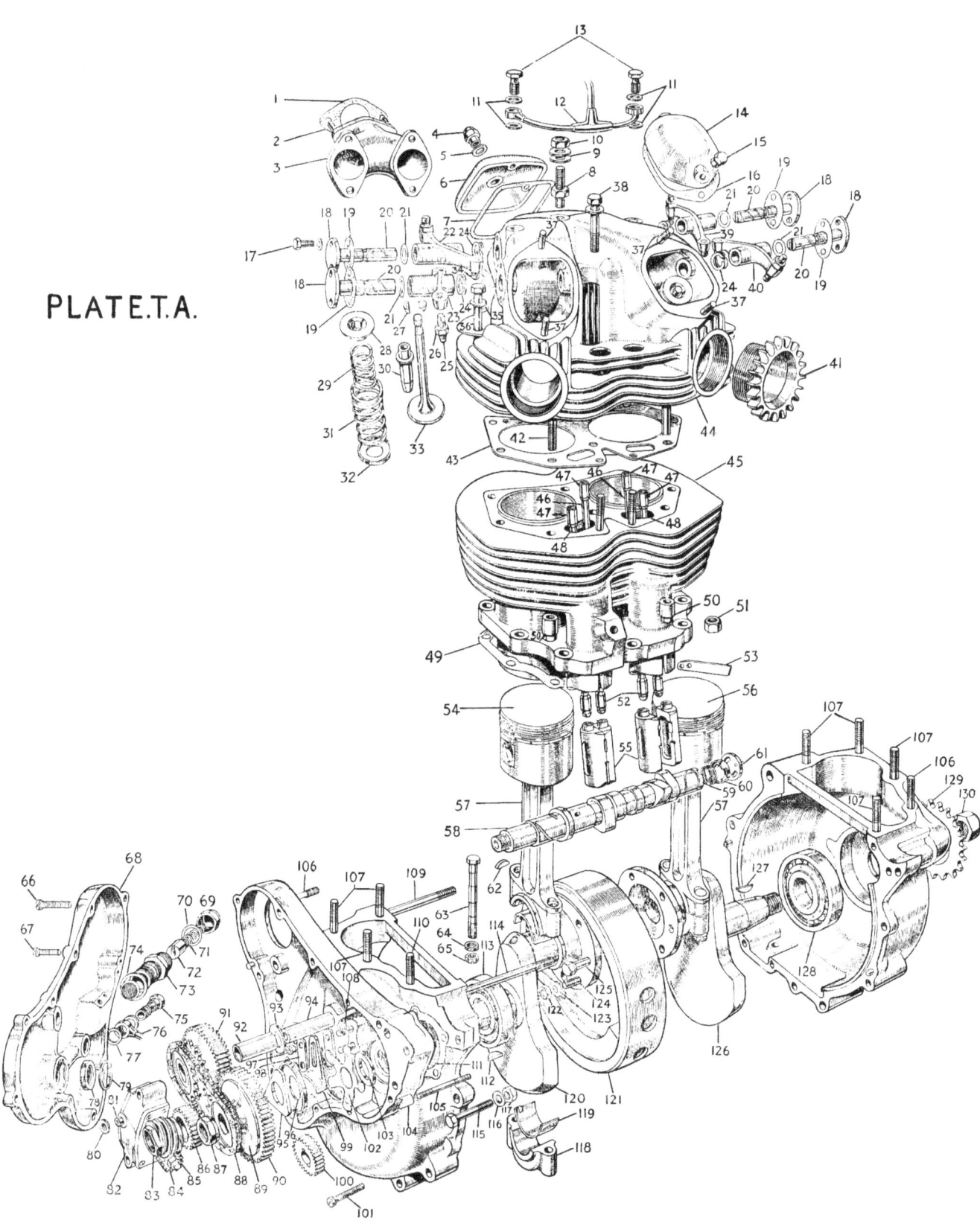

4

PART No.	SUPERSEDED No.	PLATE No.	DESCRIPTION	QTY.	MODEL	PRICE EACH

CRANKCASE AND FITTINGS

£ s. d.

PART No.	SUPERSEDED No.	PLATE No.	DESCRIPTION	QTY.	MODEL
50235	—	—	Crankcase with timing cover	1	88, 99, 77
19257	—	TA68	Timing cover	1	88, 99, 77
T2236	—	—	Crankcase timing cover paper washer	1	88, 99, 77
19228	—	—	Timing cover badge	1	88, 99, 77
50234	H12/704	—	Crankcase, driving side	1	88, 99, 77
50177	H12/703	—	Crankcase, timing side	1	88, 99, 77
			NOTE.—Half crankcases and timing cover cannot be supplied separately. Therefore it is necessary to return the sound half for matching at the works.		
T2036	D12/18/TS	—	Crankcase camshaft bush timing side	1	88, 99, 77
T2037	D12/18/DS	—	Crankcase camshaft bush driving side	1	88, 99, 77
T2018	D12/2(L)	TA107	Crankcase cylinder base stud $\frac{3}{8}''$ dia.	6	88, 99, 77
T2209	D12/2(S)	TA110	Crankcase cylinder base stud $\frac{5}{16}''$ dia.	2	88, 99, 77
18943	—	—	Crankcase cylinder base stud $\frac{3}{8}''$ dia. (front centre)	1	88, 99, 77
T2016	D12/3(L)	—	Crankcase cylinder base stud nut $\frac{3}{8}''$ dia.	7	88, 99, 77
T2210	D12/3(S)	—	Crankcase cylinder base stud nut $\frac{5}{16}''$ dia.	2	88, 99, 77
T2211	—	—	Crankcase cylinder base stud washer	2	88, 99, 77
T2191	D12/912	—	Crankcase and magneto joint washer	1	88, 99, 77
10940	—	TA66	Crankcase timing cover screws (long)	8	88, 99, 77
11775	—	—	Crankcase timing cover washer	16	88, 99, 77
E6980	—	TA67	Crankcase timing cover screws (short)	6	88, 99, 77
T2124	D12/913	TA78	Timing cover mainshaft oil seal	1	88, 99, 77
17841	D12/914	TA79	Timing cover mainshaft oil seal circlip	1	88, 99, 77
E4591	—	—	Timing cover oilway plug	1	88, 99, 77
16945	H12/16945	—	Crankcase oil sump filter body	1	88, 99, 77
16949	H12/16949	—	Filter body copper and asbestos washer	1	88, 99, 77
16946	H12/16946	—	Filter body gauze	1	88, 99, 77
16947	H12/16947	—	Filter body gauze retaining plate	1	88, 99, 77
16948	H12/16948	—	Filter body gauze retaining plate circlip	1	88, 99, 77
15399	—	—	Name plate for drive side of crankcase	1	88, 99, 77
17842	—	—	Screws for name plate	2	88, 99, 77

CRANKCASE PRESSURE AND BREATHER FITTINGS

PART No.	SUPERSEDED No.	PLATE No.	DESCRIPTION	QTY.	MODEL
D12/915	—	—	Timing cover pressure release valve complete	1	88, 99, 77
T2059	D12/916	TA73	Timing cover pressure release valve body	1	88, 99, 77
T2060	D12/920	TA69	Timing cover pressure release valve body nut	1	88, 99, 77
T2057	D12/921	TA70	Timing cover pressure release valve body nut washer	1	88, 99, 77
T2054	D12/917	TA72	Timing cover pressure release valve piston	1	88, 99, 77
T2061	D12/918	TA71	Timing cover pressure release valve spring	1	88, 99, 77
T2056	D12/919	TA76	Timing cover pressure release valve body washer	1	88, 99, 77
T2058	—	—	Timing cover pressure release valve union washer	1	88, 99, 77
19382A	D12/708	—	Crankcase breather pipe with flange	1	88, 99, 77
T2213	D12/923	—	Crankcase breather pipe securing bolt	1	88, 99, 77
19383	—	—	Oil pipe rubber	1	88, 99, 77
16902	—	—	Set pin for oil gauge hole	1	88, 99, 77
T1084	—	—	Set pin washer	1	88, 99, 77

FLYWHEELS, CRANKSHAFT AND MAIN BEARINGS

PART No.	SUPERSEDED No.	PLATE No.	DESCRIPTION	QTY.	MODEL
D12/24	—	—	Flywheel and crankshaft assembly with con rods	1	88
L14/24	—	—	Flywheel and crankshaft assembly with con rods	1	99, 77
18246	D12/924	TA126	Flywheel	1	88
18744	L14/924	—	Flywheel	1	99, 77

PART No.	SUPERSEDED No.	PLATE No.	DESCRIPTION	QTY.	MODEL	PRICE EACH
FLYWHEELS, CRANKSHAFT AND MAIN BEARINGS—cont.						£ s. d.
18247	D12/705	TA120	Crankshaft, timing side	1	88	
18746	L14/705	—	Crankshaft, timing side	1	99, 77	
18248	D12/706	TA126	Crankshaft, driving side	1	88	
18745	L14/706	—	Crankshaft, driving side	1	99, 77	
T2033A	—	TA125	Flywheel and crankshaft bolt	3	88, 99, 77	
T2033	D12/925	—	Flywheel and crankshaft bolt	1	88, 99, 77	
T2086	D12/926	TA124	Flywheel and crankshaft stud	2	88, 99, 77	
T2031	D12/927	TA122	Flywheel and crankshaft bolt or stud nut	8	88, 99, 77	
T2105	D12/928	—	Dowel for flywheel	1	88, 99, 77	
T2032	D12/929	TA123	Retaining plate for dowel	2	88, 99, 77	
17822	D12/30	TA113	Mainshaft ball bearing, timing side	1	88, 99, 77	nett
T2008	D12/930	TA96	Mainshaft ball bearing timing side sealing washer	1	88, 99, 77	
17824	D12/32	TA128	Mainshaft roller bearing, driving side	1	88, 99, 77	nett
T2187	D12/931	—	Driving side shaft oil seal	1	88, 99, 77	
T2196A	—	—	Mainshaft packing shim	A.R.	88, 99, 77	
T2196B	—	—	Mainshaft packing shim	A.R.	88, 99, 77	
CRANKCASE AND ENGINE PLATE BOLTS, NUTS AND WASHERS						
E4256	—	—	Stud, engine plate to frame front	1	77	
E5377	—	—	Washer, engine plate to frame	2	77	
E3223	—	—	Engine plate to frame nuts	1	77	
E3224	—	—	Nuts, engine plate to frame	2	77	
T2012	—	—	Crankcase to engine plate stud (bottom)	2	77	
E5376	—	—	Washer, crankcase to engine plate stud	5	77	
E3224	—	—	Nuts, crankcase to engine plate stud	6	77	
E4262	—	—	Studs, crankcase to bottom frame tube	2	77	
17696	—	—	Washers, crankcase to bottom frame tube stud	4	77	
E3223	—	—	Nuts, crankcase to bottom frame tube stud	3	77	
E4268	—	—	Bolt, engine	2	77	
E5377	—	—	Washers, crankcase to engine plate	5	77	
E3224	—	—	Nuts, crankcase to engine plate studs	6	77	
E4268	—	—	Bolts, engine plate to frame	2	77	
E5377	—	—	Washers, engine plate to frame bolt	2	77	
T2231	—	—	Crankcase and prop stand stud	1	77	
E4262	—	—	Crankcase and prop stand stud	1	77	
T2012	—	—	Crankcase to engine plate stud (top)	1	88, 99	
E5376	—	—	Washer to engine plate stud	1	88, 99	
E3224	—	—	Nuts to engine plate stud	2	88, 99	
18649	—	—	Bolts, bottom fixing frame to engine plates	2	88, 99	
E5456	—	—	Washers, bottom fixing frame to engine plate bolts	4	88, 99	
T2017	—	—	Nuts, bottom fixing frame to engine plate bolts	2	88, 99	
E4261	—	—	Crankcase to engine plate bolt (bottom)	1	88, 99	
E3223	—	—	Crankcase to engine plate bolt nut	1	88, 99	
T2012	—	—	Crankcase to engine plate bolt stud	1	88, 99	
E5376	—	—	Crankcase to engine plate bolt washer	2	88, 99	
E3224	—	—	Crankcase to engine plate bolt nuts	2	88, 99	
T2012	—	—	Crankcase to engine plate stud (top)	1	88, 99	
E5376	—	—	Crankcase to engine plate bolt washers	2	88, 99	
E3224	—	—	Crankcase to engine plate bolt nuts	2	88, 99	
16317	—	—	Front and rear engine plate to frame bolts	6	88, 99	
E5376	—	—	Washers for bolts	12	88, 99	
E3224	—	—	Nuts for bolts	6	88, 99	
13870	—	—	Crankcase bolts (short)	1	88, 99, 77	
E3223	—	—	Crankcase bolt nuts	1	88, 99, 77	
E5456	—	—	Crankcase bolt washers	1	88, 99, 77	
T2013	—	—	Crankcase top studs (rear)	1	88, 99	
19077	—	—	Crankcase top studs (front)	1	88, 99	
E3224A	—	—	Crankcase top stud nuts (rear)	1	88, 99	

PART No.	SUPERSEDED No.	PLATE No.	DESCRIPTION	QTY.	MODEL	PRICE EACH
CRANKCASE AND ENGINE PLATE BOLTS, NUTS AND WASHERS—cont.						£ s. d.
E3229	—	—	Crankcase top stud nuts (front)	1	88, 99	
E5376	—	—	Crankcase top stud washers (rear)	1	88, 99	
T2221	—	—	Crankcase top stud washers (front)	1	88, 99	
E3214	—	—	Crankcase top stud	1	88, 99	
E3231	—	—	Crankcase stop stud nuts	2	88, 99	
10940	—	—	Screws, T.S. to D.S.	2	88, 99, 77	
11775	—	—	Washers for screws	2	88, 99, 77	
ENGINE STEADY STAY AND FITTINGS						
18637	H12–2/932	—	Head steady Plate	1	88, 99	
15315	—	—	Head steady plate	1	77	
18032	—	—	Head steady stay stud	1	88, 99, 77	
E3224	—	—	Head steady stay stud nut	1	88, 99, 77	
E5376	—	—	Head steady stay stud nut washer	1	88, 99, 77	
E3798	—	—	Steady stay fixing bolts	2	88, 99	
11796	—	—	Steady stay fixing bolt washers	2	88, 99	
E3223	—	—	Steady stay fixing bolt nuts	2	88, 99	
18202	—	—	Steady stay fixing bolt washers	2	88, 99	
TIMING GEAR FITTINGS						
17413	D12/790	TA58	Camshaft	1	88, 99, 77	
T2043	D12/774	—	Camshaft washer	1	88, 99, 77	
T2078	D12/933	TA61	Camshaft breather stationary plate	1	88, 99, 77	
T2075	D12/934	TA60	Camshaft breather rotary plate	1	88, 99, 77	
T2108	D12/935	TA59	Camshaft breather spring	1	88, 99, 77	
T2035	D12/58	TA86	Half time pinion	1	88, 99, 77	
T2007	D12/936	TA95	Half time pinion backing plate	1	88, 99, 77	
E3683	—	TA112	Half time pinion driving key	1	88, 99, 77	
50008	D12/937	TA91	Intermediate gear with sprockets	1	88, 99, 77	
T2026	D12/938	TA92	Intermediate gear bush	1	88, 99, 77	
T2080	D12/939	TA93	Intermediate gear washer	1	88, 99, 77	
T2021	D12/940	TA94	Intermediate gear spindle	1	88, 99, 77	
17823	D12/941	—	Intermediate gear spindle circlip	1	88, 99, 77	
E3683	—	TA62	Cam shaft sprocket key	1	88, 99, 77	
T2044	D12/79	TA89	Cam shaft sprocket	1	88, 99, 77	
T2046	D12/942	TA87	Cam shaft sprocket nut	1	88, 99, 77	
T2043	D12/774	—	Cam shaft sprocket washer	1	88, 99, 77	
PUSH RODS AND TAPPETS						
M12/82 In.	—	TA46	Push rod complete, inlet	2	88	
M12/82 Ex.	—	TA48	Push rod complete, exhaust	2	88	
M14/82 In.	—	TA46	Push rod complete, inlet	2	99, 77	
M14/82 Ex.	—	TA48	Push rod complete, exhaust	2	99, 77	
20130	—	—	Push rod only, inlet	2	88	
20131	—	—	Push rod only, exhaust	2	88	
20132	—	—	Push rod only, inlet	2	99, 77	
20133	—	—	Push rod only, exhaust	2	99, 77	
T2064	D12/86	TA47	Push rod top	4	88, 99, 77	
T2182	D12/83	TA52	Push rod ball end	4	88, 99, 77	
18784A	H12/75A	TA55	Tappets, right-hand	2	88, 99, 77	
18784B	H12/75B	TA55	Tappets, left-hand	2	88, 99, 77	
T2142	D12/943	TA53	Tappet location plates	2	88, 99, 77	
T2143	D12/944	—	Tappet location plate screws	4	88, 99, 77	
ROCKER BOX FITTINGS						
18249	D12/99RH	TA22	Rocker, inlet, R.H.	1	88, 99, 77	
18250	D12/99LH	TA39	Rocker, inlet, L.H.	1	88, 99, 77	
18252	D12/100LH	TA40	Rocker, exhaust, L.H.	1	88, 99, 77	
18251	D12/100RH	TA23	Rocker, exhaust, R.H.	1	88, 99, 77	
T2074	D12/803	TA25	Rocker adjuster	4	88, 99, 77	
T232	D12/804	TA26	Rocker adjuster nuts	4	88, 99, 77	
T2063	D12/104	—	Rocker ball ends	4	88, 99, 77	
T2237	D12/97	TA20	Rocker shafts	4	88, 99, 77	
18102	D12/951	TA21	Rocker shaft thrust washer	4	88, 99, 77	
18103	D12/950	TA24	Rocker shaft spring	4	88, 99, 77	
T2083	D12/947	—	Rocker shaft washers	4	88, 99, 77	

PART No.	SUPERSEDED No.	PLATE No.	DESCRIPTION	QTY.	MODEL	PRICE EACH

ROCKER BOX FITTINGS—cont.

PART No.	SUPERSEDED No.	PLATE No.	DESCRIPTION	QTY.	MODEL
T2240	D12/948	—	Rocker shaft joint washers	4	88, 99, 77
T2238	D12/945	TA19	Rocker shaft locking plates	4	88, 99, 77
T2239	D12/946	TA18	Rocker shaft retaining plate	4	88, 99, 77
T2256	K12/949	—	Rocker shaft bolts	8	88, 99, 77
18094	D12/93R	TA6	Rocker box rear cap	1	88, 99, 77
T2084	D12/95R	TA7	Rocker box rear cap washer	1	88, 99, 77
T2082	D12/956	TA5	Rocker box rear cap washer	1	88, 99, 77
T2162	D12/955	TA1	Rocker box rear cap acorn nuts	1	88, 99, 77
18093	D12/93F	TA14	Rocker box front caps	2	88, 99, 77
T2088	D12/95F	TA16	Rocker box front joint washer	2	88, 99, 77
T2252	K12/952	TA37	Rocker box front cap studs	4	88, 99, 77
T2085	D12/953	TA15	Rocker box front cap nuts	4	88, 99, 77
18033	K12/954	—	Rocker box rear cap studs	1	88, 99, 77
13937	—	—	Rocker box rear cap dowel	1	88, 99, 77
18380	K12/985	—	Inlet manifold fixing studs	4	88, 99, 77

DYNAMO DRIVE PARTS AND SECURING FITTINGS

PART No.	SUPERSEDED No.	PLATE No.	DESCRIPTION	QTY.	MODEL
20167	—	—	Dynamo	1	88, 99, 77 nett
T2243	D12/1013	TA100	Dynamo steel driven pinion	1	88, 99, 77
T2244	F12/957	TA90	Dynamo fibre gear wheel	1	88, 99, 77
19280	—	TA105	Dynamo to crankcase securing pins	3	88, 99, 77
T2184	—	TA111	Dynamo sealing washer	1	88, 99, 77
T2027	D12/962	—	Dynamo fixing strap	1	88, 99, 77
T2029	D12/963	—	Dynamo fixing strap dowel	1	88, 99, 77
T2028	D12/964	—	Dynamo fixing strap roller	1	88, 99, 77
T2030	D12/965	—	Dynamo fixing strap bolt	1	88, 99, 77
T2039	D12/958	TA102	Friction spring for fibre gear wheel	1	88, 99, 77
T2242	D12/960	—	Locating peg for friction spring	1	88, 99, 77
T2224	D12/959	—	Plate for friction spring	1	88, 99, 77
17806	D12/961	TA86	Dynamo chain, 38-link	1	88, 99, 77 nett
T2217	D12/968	TA99	Dynamo chain tensioner slipper	1	88, 99, 77
T247	D12/969	TA108	Dynamo chain tensioner stud	2	88, 99, 77
T2218	D12/971	TA98	Plate for chain tensioner (thick)	1	88, 99, 77
T2218A	—	—	Plate for chain tensioner (thin)	1	88, 99, 77
E3231	—	—	Chain tensioner stud nuts	2	88, 99, 77
200737	—	—	Brushes for dynamo	1 set	88, 99, 77 per set nett

MAGNETO AND DRIVE PARTS (all prices RETAIL NETT)

PART No.	SUPERSEDED No.	PLATE No.	DESCRIPTION	QTY.	MODEL
20201	—	—	Magneto	1	88, 99 nett
18256	—	—	Magneto	1	77 nett
47508	—	—	Magneto sprocket with automatic advance and retard unit	1	88, 99, 77
18257	D12/113	—	Magneto chain	1	88, 99, 77
458368	—	—	Pick-up assembly, left-hand	1	88, 99, 77
458367	—	—	Pick-up assembly, right-hand	1	88, 99, 77
458638	—	—	Magneto contact breaker cover	1	88, 99, 77
470534	—	—	Magneto contact breaker	1	88, 99, 77
104244	—	—	Magneto contact breaker cover nuts	2	88, 99, 77
470609	—	—	Magneto contact breaker points	1 set	88, 99, 77 per set
455191	—	—	Brush spring and holder (magneto to earth)	1	88, 99, 77
455190	—	—	Brush spring (magneto to earth)	1	88, 99, 77
T2245	—	TA106	Crankcase T.S. to magneto, studs	3	88, 99, 77
E3231	—	—	Crankcase T.S. to magneto, stud nuts	3	88, 99, 77
11796	—	—	Crankcase T.S. to magneto, stud washers	3	88, 99, 77
18464	—	—	Sparking plug cover	2	88, 99, 77
18465	—	—	Sparking plug cover with suppressor	2	88, 99, 77
20347	—	—	Magneto cut-out lead and button	1	88, 99, 77

PART No.	SUPERSEDED No.	PLATE No.	DESCRIPTION	QTY.	MODEL	PRICE EACH
OIL PUMP PARTS						£ s. d.
15522	D12/128	TA82	Oil pump assembly	1	88, 99, 77	
15511A	A2/129	TA85	Oil pump spindle nut	1	88, 99, 77	
T2077	D12/130	TA84	Oil pump spindle gear wheel	1	88, 99, 77	
17697	A2/131	—	Oil pump spindle gear wheel key	1	88, 99, 77	
15515	A2/132	TA81	Body and timing cover connection bush	1	88, 99, 77	
T272	D12/133	TA80	Body and timing cover connection bush washer	1	88, 99, 77	
T2076	D12/134	TA83	Mainshaft pump driving worm	1	88, 99, 77	
E4440	—	—	Pump crankcase studs	2	88, 99, 77	
E3231	—	—	Pump crankcase stud nuts	2	88, 99, 77	
E4590	—	—	Grub screw oil stop	1	88, 99, 77	
VALVES, GUIDES, SPRINGS, ETC.						
T2010	D12/142	—	Valve inlet	2	88, 99, 77	
T2204	D12/143	TA33	Valve exhaust	2	88, 99, 77	
T2011	K12/140	TA30	Valve guides	4	88, 99, 77	
T186	D12/148	TA32	Valve collars	4	88, 99, 77	
T2073	D12/147	TA28	Valve spring cups	4	88, 99, 77	
T187	D12/149	TA27	Valve cotters	4 pr.	88, 99, 77	
19302	K12/145	TA29	Valve springs (inner)	4	88, 99, 77	
19303	K12/146	TA31	Valve springs (outer)	4	88, 99, 77	
16339	H12/16339	—	Heat resisting washers	4	88, 99, 77	
CYLINDER HEAD, BARREL, STUDS AND NUTS						
18244	H12/135	TA45	Cylinder barrel	1	88	
18743	L14/135	—	Cylinder barrel	1	99, 77	
50166	K12/136	TA44	Cylinder head	1	88, 99, 77	
T2141	D12/137	TA43	Cylinder head gasket	1	88, 99, 77	
T2093	D12/157	TA49	Cylinder base washer	1	88, 99, 77	
T2096	D12/972	TA36	Cylinder barrel and head bolts (long)	4	88, 99, 77	
T2097	D12/973	TA38	Cylinder barrel and head bolts (short)	1	88, 99, 77	
E5376	D12/974	TA35	Cylinder barrel and head bolt washers	4	88, 99, 77	
T2161	D12/975	—	Cylinder head fixing studs	2	88, 99, 77	
T2017	D12/976	—	Cylinder head and barrel stud nuts $\frac{5}{16}''$	2	88, 99, 77	
18756	K12/977	TA42	Cylinder head studs	3	88, 99, 77	
T2034	D12/978	—	Cylinder head stud nut (front)	2	88, 99, 77	
E3224	D12/979	—	Cylinder head stud nuts (rear)	1	88, 99, 77	
E5376	D12/974	—	Cylinder head stud washer	1	88, 99, 77	
20344	—	—	Carburetter to manifold studs	2	88, 99, 77	
E3231	—	—	Carburetter to manifold stud nuts	2	88, 99, 77	
T2221	—	—	Carburetter to manifold stud washers	2	88, 99, 77	
18242	D12/983	TA3	Cylinder head and carburetter manifold	1	88, 99, 77	
T2241	D12/984	—	Cylinder head and carburetter manifold fibre distance piece	1	88, 99, 77	
18380	K12/985	—	Studs, securing to manifold cyl. head	4	88, 99, 77	
T2220	D12/986	—	Securing manifold to cyl. head stud nuts	4	88, 99, 77	
T2224	D12/987	—	Securing manifold to cyl. head stud washers	4	88, 99, 77	
PISTONS AND RINGS						
19785	—	TA54	Piston assembly, L.H.	1	88	
19786	—	TA56	Piston assembly, R.H.	1	88	
19406	L14/702LH	—	Piston assembly, L.H.	1	99, 77	
19407	L14/702RH	—	Piston assembly, R.H.	1	99, 77	
19789	D12/161	—	Piston ring (compression)	2	88	
L14/161	—	—	Piston ring (compression)	2	99, 77	
L14/162	—	—	Piston ring (scraper)	1	99, 77	
19790	D12/162	—	Piston ring (scraper)	1	88	
19791	D12/163	—	Gudgeon pin	1	88, 99, 77	
L14/164	—	—	Gudgeon pin circlip	4	88, 99, 77	

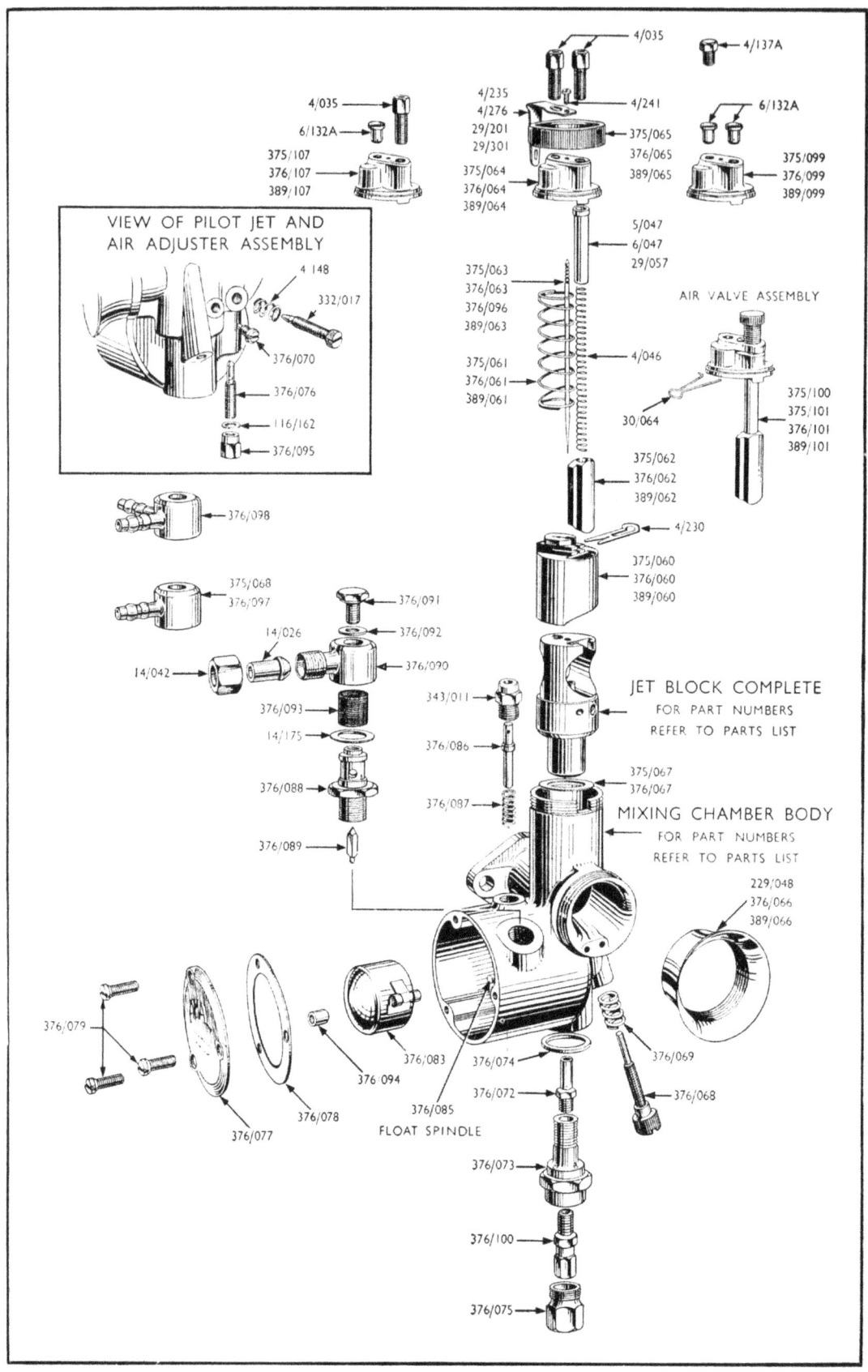

PART No.	SUPERSEDED No.	PLATE No.	DESCRIPTION	QTY.	MODEL	PRICE EACH
						£ s. d.

CONNECTING RODS AND BIG END BEARINGS

PART No.	SUPERSEDED No.	PLATE No.	DESCRIPTION	QTY.	MODEL
50023	D12/158	TA57	Connecting rod with small end bush, big end bearing and bolts	2	88, 99, 77
T2160	D12/159	—	Small end bush	2	88, 99, 77
17828	D12/27	TA119	Big end bearing (2 halves)	2	88, 99, 77
T2150	D12/989	TA63	Big end cap bolts	4	88, 99, 77
T2152	D12/990	TA64	Big end cap bolt washers	4	88, 99, 77
17827	—	TA65	Big end cap bolt nuts	4	88, 99, 77

AMAL CARBURETTER (all prices RETAIL NETT)

PART No.	SUPERSEDED No.	PLATE No.	DESCRIPTION	QTY.	MODEL
376/66	—	—	Carburetter complete with cables less twist grip	1	88
376/67	—	—	Carburetter complete with cables less twist grip	1	99, 77
376/1 1/16"	—	—	Mixing chamber body	1	99, 77
376/1"	—	—	Mixing chamber body	1	88
376/056	—	—	Jet block	1	88
376/057	—	—	Jet block	1	99, 77
376/070	—	—	Locating peg for jet block	1	88, 99, 77
376/067	—	—	Washer	1	88, 99, 77
376/064	—	—	Mixing chamber top	1	88, 99, 77
376/065	—	—	Mixing chamber top cap ring	1	88, 99, 77
4/235	—	—	Cap ring for top	1	83, 99, 77
4/241	—	—	Fixing screw for cap spring	1	88, 99, 77
4/035	—	—	Cable adjuster	1	88, 99, 77
6/132A	—	—	Cable ferrule (top hat)	1	88, 99, 77
4/137A	—	—	Plug screw	1	88, 99, 77
376/060	—	—	Throttle valve	1	88, 99, 77
376/061	—	—	Throttle valve spring	1	88, 99, 77
376/063	—	—	Taper needle	1	88, 99, 77
4/230	—	—	Taper needle clip	1	88, 99, 77
376/062	—	—	Air valve	1	88, 99, 77
6/047	—	—	Air valve guide	1	88, 99, 77
4/046	—	—	Air valve spring	1	88, 99, 77
376/101	—	—	Rod control air valve assembly	1	88, 99, 77
30/064	—	—	Click spring for rod control air valve assembly	1	88, 99, 77
376/072	—	—	Needle jet	1	88, 99, 77
376/100	—	—	Main jet (specify size)	1	88, 99, 77
376/073	—	—	Main jet holder	1	88, 99, 77
376/074	—	—	Main jet holder washer	1	88, 99, 77
376/075	—	—	Main jet cover nut	1	88, 99, 77
376/076	—	—	Pilot jet	1	88, 99, 77
376/095	—	—	Pilot jet cover nut	1	88, 99, 77
116/162	—	—	Pilot jet cover nut washer	1	88, 99, 77
332/017	—	—	Air adjusting screw	1	88, 99, 77
4/148	—	—	Air adjusting screw spring	1	88, 99, 77
376/068	—	—	Throttle stop screw	1	88, 99, 77
376/069	—	—	Throttle stop screw spring	1	88, 99, 77
376/066	—	—	Air intake tube	1	88, 99, 77
376/083	—	—	Float complete	1	88, 99, 77
376/085	—	—	Float hinge spindle	1	88, 99, 77
376/094	—	—	Float spindle bush	1	88, 99, 77
376/089	—	—	Float needle	1	88, 99, 77
376/088	—	—	Float needle seating	1	88, 99, 77
14/175	—	—	Float needle seating washer	1	88, 99, 77
376/097	—	—	Banjo single	1	88, 99, 77
14/175	—	—	Banjo washer	1	88, 99, 77
376/091	—	—	Banjo bolt	1	88, 99, 77
376/092	—	—	Banjo bolt washer	1	88, 99, 77
376/086	—	—	Tickler	1	88, 99, 77
343/011	—	—	Tickler body	1	88, 99, 77
376/087	—	—	Tickler spring	1	88, 99, 77
376/077	—	—	Float chamber cover	1	88, 99, 77
376/078	—	—	Float chamber cover joint	1	88, 99, 77
376/079	—	—	Float chamber cover screws	1	88, 99, 77
376/093	—	—	Filter gauze	1	88, 99, 77
20000	—	—	Carburetter sealing ring	1	88, 99, 77

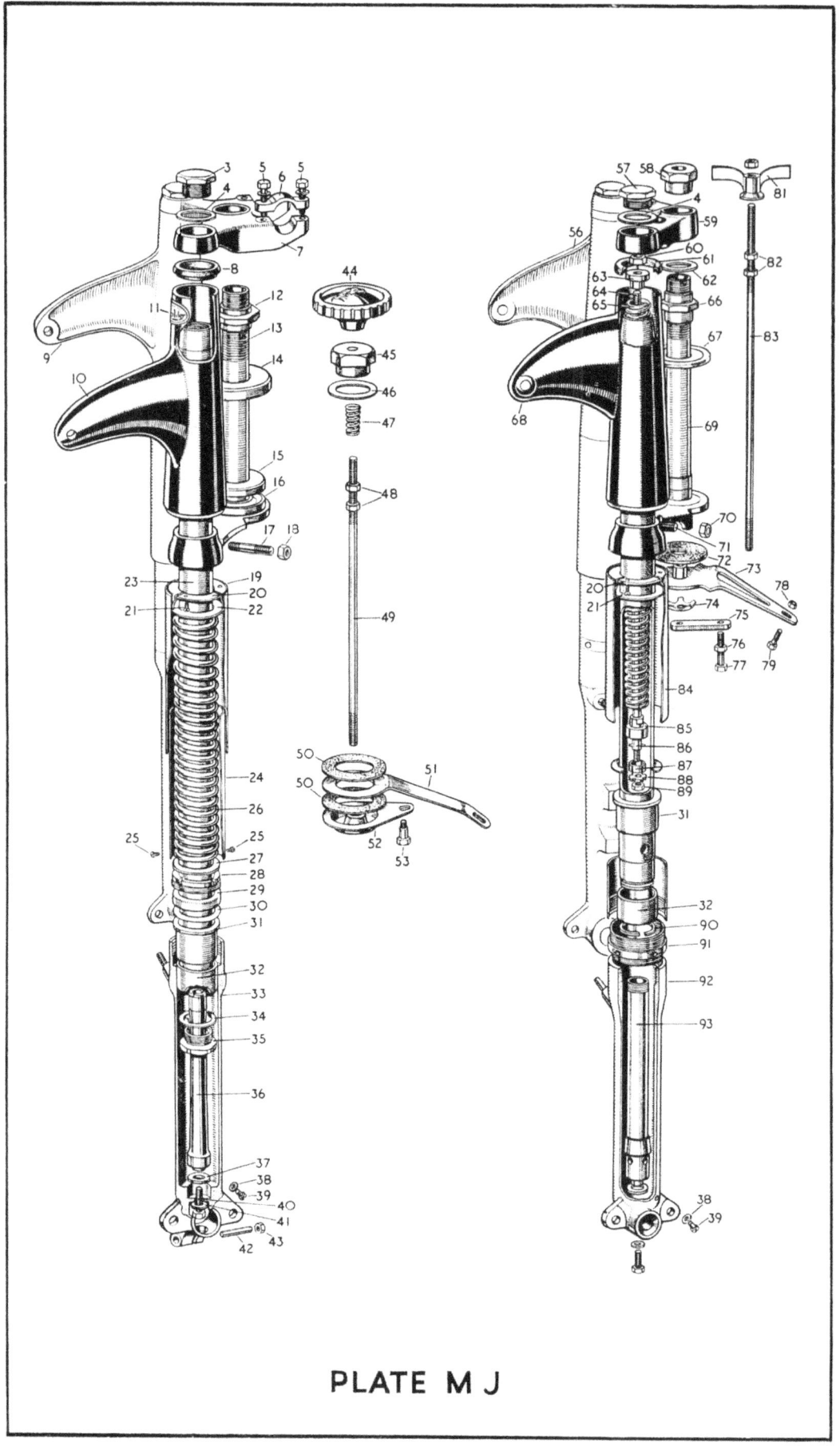

PLATE M J

PART No.	SUPERSEDED No.	PLATE No.	DESCRIPTION	QTY.	MODEL	PRICE EACH
						£ s. d.

EXHAUST PIPE, SILENCER AND FITTINGS

PART No.	SUPERSEDED No.	PLATE No.	DESCRIPTION	QTY.	MODEL
19464	—	—	Exhaust pipe, L.H.	1	88
19466	—	—	Exhaust pipe, L.H.	1	99
20310	—	—	Exhaust pipe, L.H.	1	77
19465	—	—	Exhaust pipe, R.H.	1	88
19467	—	—	Exhaust pipe, R.H.	1	99
20311	—	—	Exhaust pipe, R.H.	1	77
18092	D12/167	—	Exhaust pipe locking ring	2	88, 99, 77
T2166	D12/166	—	Exhaust pipe locking washer	2	88, 99, 77
20110	—	—	Silencer, R.H.	1	88, 99, 77
20111	—	—	Silencer, L.H.	1	88, 99, 77
20064	—	—	Silencer fixing bracket, L.H.	1	88, 99
19473	—	—	Silencer fixing bracket, R.H.	1	88, 99
17075	—	—	Silencer fixing bolts	4	77
E.5456	—	—	Silencer fixing bolt washers	4	77
16255	H12/168	—	Silencer to exhaust pipe clips	2	88, 99, 77
E3154	—	—	Silencer to exhaust pipe clip bolts	2	88, 99, 77
E3231	—	—	Silencer to exhaust pipe clip bolt nuts	2	88, 99, 77
20307	—	—	Silencer fixing brackets	2	77

NORTON ROAD HOLDER FRONT FORKS AND FITTINGS

PART No.	SUPERSEDED No.	PLATE No.	DESCRIPTION	QTY.	MODEL
M12-2/170	—	—	Road-holder forks complete	1	88, 99
M15/170	—	—	Road-holder forks complete	1	77
18482	H12-2/605	—	Fork main tube	2	88, 99
18467	B2/605	—	Fork main tube	2	77
T1055	B2/606	MJ32	Fork main tube bottom bush	2	88, 99, 77
T1048	B2/614	MJ35	Fork main tube top bush	2	88, 99, 77
14298	E11M/1044	MJ90	Fork main tube circlips	2	88, 99
19299	—	MJ92	Fork end (left-hand)	1	88, 99
19310	—	MJ33	Fork end (left-hand)	1	77
19298	—	—	Fork end (right-hand)	1	88, 99
19309	—	—	Fork end (right-hand)	1	77
16664	—	MJ42	Fork end hub spindle pinch stud	1	88, 99, 77
13434	—	MJ43	Fork end hub spindle pinch stud nut	1	88, 99, 77
T387	B2/612	MJ29	Fork end drain plug	2	88, 99, 77
11775	B2/613	MJ38	Fork end drain plug washer	2	88, 99, 77
T1090	B2/608	MJ34	Tab locking washers	2	77
T1047	B2/607	MJ35	Main tube bush retaining washer	2	77
17713	D3T/616	MJ29	Oil seals	2	88, 99, 77
T1054	B2/615	—	Oil seal locking rings	2	77
T1049	B2/617	MJ30	Oil seal paper washer	2	88, 99, 77
50177	F11M/615	MJ91	Main tube lock ring with cup	2	88, 99
18491	B2/625	MJ24	Bottom cover tubes	2	77
19816	—	MJ25	Bottom cover tube screws	4	77
18809	E2/620	MJ22	Fork spring	2	77
18813	F11M2/620	MJ65	Fork spring	2	88, 99
16880	—	—	Fork spring locating bushes	2	88, 99
T595	B2/621	MJ27	Fork spring bottom leather washer	2	77
T594	B2/619	MJ22	Fork spring top leather washer	2	77
18490	B2/622	MJ19	Spring top cover tube	2	77
19307	L12-2/622	MJ84	Spring top cover tube	2	88, 99
T831	B2/623	MJ20	Spring top cover tube securing plate	2	88, 99
T702	B2/624	MJ21	Spring top cover tube securing plate screws	6	88, 99
13197	B2/627	MJ36	Oil damper pegs	2	77
16001	F11M/627	MJ93	Oil damper tubes	2	88, 99
15801	F11M/1049	MJ64	Oil damper rods	2	88, 99
17075	C2/630	MJ40	Oil damper peg bolts	2	77
14275	F11M2/630	—	Oil damper tube bolts	2	88, 99
T814	B2/628	MJ37	Oil damper peg washers	2	88, 99, 77
T1009	C2/629	MJ41	Oil damper peg bolt washer	2	88, 99, 77
14119	E11M/1048	MJ86	Piston locating pegs	2	88, 99
14118B	E11M/1046	MJ87	Oil damper valve cup	2	88, 99
14117	E11M/1047	MJ88	Oil damper valve cup slotted ring	2	88, 99
E3231	—	—	Oil damper rod bottom nuts	2	88, 99
14605	E11M/1045	MJ85	Oil damper tube cap	2	88, 99
E3224A	—	MJ60	Oil damper rod nuts (top)	2	88, 99

PART No.	SUPERSEDED No.	PLATE No.	DESCRIPTION	QTY.	MODEL	PRICE EACH

NORTON ROAD HOLDER FRONT FORKS AND FITTINGS—cont.

£ s. d.

PART No.	SUPERSEDED No.	PLATE No.	DESCRIPTION	QTY.	MODEL
50259	—	MJ13	Crown lug complete with column	1	88, 99
50001	B2/172	—	Crown lug complete with column	1	77
13457	B2/642	MJ17	Pinch stud for crown lug	1	77
16164	F11M2/642	—	Pinch stud for crown lug	1	88, 99
16187	F11M2/643	—	Pinch stud nuts	2	88, 99
13459	B2/643	—	Pinch stud nuts	2	77
15628	F11M2/644	MJ67	Fork head clip ball race cover	1	88, 99
15630	F11M2/645	MJ58	Fork head race adjuster nut	1	88, 99
19275	L12-2/635	MJ68	Top cover tube, complete with lamp bracket, L.H.	1	88, 99
19276	L12-2/636	MJ56	Top cover tube, complete with lamp bracket, R.H.	1	88, 99
19340	L4/635	MJ10	Top cover tube, complete with lamp bracket, L.H.	1	77
19339	L4/636	MJ9	Top cover tube, complete with lamp bracket, R.H.	1	77
15398	B2/637	MJ11	Top cover tube name plate	2	88, 99, 77
T1081	B2/638	—	Top cover tube name plate rivets	4	77 per set
18810	—	—	Top cover tube name plate rivets	4	88, 99 per set
19272	—	—	Lamp bracket distance pieces	2	88, 99
T597	F11M2/639	MJ61	Main tube top cover rubber ring	2	88, 99
T1079	B2/639	—	Main tube top cover rubber ring	2	77
T347	B2/207	MJ50	Steering damper friction washer	1	77
T838	B2/206	MJ51	Steering damper anchor plate	1	77
5002	B2/208	MJ52	Steering damper friction plate	1	77
19537	—	—	Bolt for friction plate and cable clip	1	77
19530	—	—	Cable clip for brake cable	1	77
11796	—	—	Washer between cable clip and friction plate bolt	1	77
12342	—	—	Bolt for anchor plate to frame	1	77
E5379	—	—	Washer for anchor plate to frame bolt	1	77
16725	—	MJ16	Headrace (bottom)	1	77
T358	—	MJ15	Headrace (top)	1	77
17714	A2/521	—	Headrace ball bearings (top or bottom)	34	77 per set
14365	B2/644	—	Headrace cover	1	77
T355	B2/645	—	Fork head race adjuster nut	1	77
19015	L4/174	MJ7	Head clip	1	77
T695	B2/646	—	Fork crown and column lock nut washer	1	77
T352A	B2/205	—	Fork crown and column lock nut	1	77
19019	L12-2/174	MJ59	Head clip	1	88, 99
15627	—	—	Fork crown and column lock nut washer	1	88, 99
19490	L12-2/205	—	Fork crown and column lock nut	1	88, 99
T830	B2/203	MJ49	Steering damper rod	1	77
E3231	B2/640	MJ48	Steering damper rod nuts	2	77
E4563	B2/202	MJ47	Steering damper rod spring	1	77
E4643	B2/201	MJ81	Steering damper adjuster	1	77
T816	B2/633	MJ3	Fork main tube filler and retaining plug	2	77
16998	H12-2/633	MJ57	Fork main tube filler and retaining plug	2	88, 99
T320	B2/634	MJ54	Fork main tube filler and retaining plug washer	2	88, 99, 77
18769	H12-2/206	MJ74	Front fork stop and anchor plate	1	88, 99
16008	H12-2/207	MJ72	Front fork stop and anchor plate friction disc	1	88, 99
12343	—	—	Front fork stop and anchor plate bolt	1	88, 99
E3229	—	—	Front fork stop and anchor plate bolt nut	1	88, 99
E5379	—	—	Front fork stop and anchor plate bolt washer	1	88, 99
15686	—	—	Front fork stop and anchor plate distance piece	1	88, 99
19021A	L4/175	MJ6	Caps for handlebar top clip	2	88, 99, 77
19437	L4/176	MJ3	Handlebar top slip securing screws	4	88, 99, 77

PART No.	SUPERSEDED No.	PLATE No.	DESCRIPTION	QTY.	MODEL	PRICE EACH
HANDLEBARS AND FITTINGS						£ s. d.
19396	L4/211	—	Handlebar bend	1	77	
19405	L12-2/211	—	Handlebar bend	1	88, 99	
19410	—	—	Front brake lever and air control lever, complete	1	88, 99, 77	
19414	—	—	Throttle grip (plastic)	1	88, 99, 77	
20267	—	—	Dummy grip	1	88, 99, 77	
M122/216	—	—	Air lever complete	1	88, 99, 77	
M122/217	—	—	Air lever only	1	88, 99, 77	
M122/218	—	—	Air lever body	1	88, 99, 77	
M122/219	—	—	Air lever cap screw	1	88, 99, 77	
M122/220	—	—	Air lever cap	1	88, 99, 77	
A2/221	—	—	Air lever cap spring washer	1	88, 99, 77	
M122/223	—	—	Air lever clip screw	2	88, 99, 77	
M12-2/224	—	—	Front brake control lever, complete	1	88, 99, 77	
M12-2/225	—	—	Front brake control lever only	1	88, 99, 77	
M12-2/226	—	—	Clutch lever complete	1	88, 99, 77	
M12-2/227	—	—	Clutch lever only	1	88, 99, 77	
M12-2/228RH	—	—	Front brake lever body	1	88, 99, 77	
M122/226LH	—	—	Clutch lever body	1	88, 99, 77	
A2/222	—	—	Clutch lever body clip	1	88, 99, 77	
A2/223	—	—	Clutch lever body clip pins	2	88, 99, 77	
M122/229	—	—	Clutch or front brake lever pivot pin	2	88, 99, 77	
M122/230	—	—	Clutch or front brake pivot pin nut	2	88, 99, 77	
M12-2/238	—	—	Twist grip top half clip	1	88, 99, 77	
M12-2/239	—	—	Twist grip bottom half clip	1	88, 99, 77	
A2/240	—	—	Twist grip clip fixing pins	2	88, 99, 77	
M12-2/241	—	—	Twist grip control barrel	1	88, 99, 77	
A2/242	—	—	Twist grip control barrel adjusting screw	1	88, 99, 77	
A2/236	—	—	Twist grip control barrel adjuster nut	1	88, 99, 77	
M12-2/243	—	—	Twist grip control barrel adjuster spring	1	88, 99, 77	
M12-2/244	—	—	Twist grip cable stop	1	88, 99, 77	
M12-2/237	—	—	Twist grip complete	1	88, 99, 77	
CONTROL CABLE, ADJUSTERS AND NIPPLES						
19828	—	—	Clutch cable	1	88, 99	
19827	—	—	Clutch cable	1	77	
A2/267	—	—	Clutch cable inner	1	77	
M12-2/267	—	—	Clutch cable inner	1	88, 99	
M12-2/266	—	—	Clutch cable outer	1	88, 99	
M15/266	—	—	Clutch cable outer	1	77	
20295	B2/268	—	Front brake cable inner and outer	1	88, 99, 77	
B2/270	—	—	Front brake cable inner	1	88, 99, 77	
B2/269	—	—	Front brake cable outer	1	88, 99, 77	
20276	—	—	Air control cable complete	1	88, 99, 77	
M12-/260	—	—	Air control cable inner	1	88, 99, 77	
M12-2/261	—	—	Air control cable outer	1	88, 99, 77	
20277	—	—	Throttle control cable complete	1	88, 99, 77	
18881	A2/247	—	Front brake cable adjuster	1	88, 99, 77	
18889	A2/248	—	Clutch cable adjuster	1	88, 99, 77	
A2/249	—	—	Air or throttle cable nipple (handlebar end)	1	88, 99, 77	
19987	A2/253	—	Clutch cable nipple (gear box end)	1	88, 99, 77	
14759	A2/709	—	Front brake U clip	1	88, 99, 77	
A2/427	—	—	Front brake U clip pin	1	88, 99, 77	
A2/195	—	—	Front brake U clip cotter pin	1	88, 99, 77	
PETROL TANK AND FITTINGS						
200072	—	—	Petrol Tank	1	88, 99	
20154	—	—	Petrol tank	1	77	
18524	K12/280	—	Petrol Tank filler cap	1	88, 99, 77	
16256	H12-2/1070	—	Petrol Tank fixing strap	1	88, 99	
16238	H12-2/1071	—	Petrol tank fixing strap rubber	1	88, 99	
16372	H12-2 1072	—	Petrol tank fixing strap roller (front)	1	88, 99	
16257	H12-2/1073	—	Fulcrum pin for strap	1	88, 99	

PART No.	SUPERSEDED No.	PLATE No.	DESCRIPTION	QTY.	MODEL	PRICE EACH
						£ s. d.

PETROL TANK AND FITTINGS—cont.

PART No.	SUPERSEDED No.	PLATE No.	DESCRIPTION	QTY.	MODEL
18291	A2/281	—	Fulcrum pin split pin	2	88, 99
16365	H12-2/1074	—	Petrol tank strap roller (tool tray end)	1	88, 99
18747	—	—	Roller bracket	1	88, 99
16413	—	—	Roller bracket pins	2	88, 99
17013	—	—	Petrol tank strap roller fixing bolt	1	88, 99
E5380	—	—	Petrol tank strap roller fixing bolt washer	2	88, 99
E3223	—	—	Petrol tank strap roller fixing bolt nut	1	88, 99
16237	H12-2/289	—	Petrol tank mounting rubbers	6	88, 99
20262	—	—	Petrol tank side panels, L.H.	1	88, 99
20261	—	—	Petrol tank side panels, R.H.	1	88, 99
20231	—	—	Petrol tank side panel fixing screws	4	88, 99
20233	—	—	Petrol tank side panel plastic bead	2	88, 99
18727	L12-2/283	—	Petrol pipe complete	1	88, 99
16294	H12-2/285	—	Petrol tap	1	88, 99
13786	—	—	Petrol tap washer	1	88, 99
E5264	—	—	Petrol tap wash	1	88, 99
E6745	A2/277	—	Petrol tank attachment bolt	4	77
E6744	A2/276	—	Petrol tank platform rubber washer	4	77
E6743	A2/278	—	Petrol tank attachment bolt rubber washer	4	77
E6742	A2/279	—	Petrol tank attachment bolt rubber washer steel cup	4	77
10914	A2/275	—	Petrol tank platform packing washer (steel)	4	77
20197	—	—	Petrol tank side panel, L.H.	1	77
20196	—	—	Petrol tank side panel, R.H.	1	77
20231	—	—	Petrol tank side panel fixing pins	4	77
20232	—	—	Petrol tank side panel plastic bead	2	77
E3073	A2/289	—	Petrol tank top tube packing	2	77
20309	—	—	Petrol pipe assembly	1	77
19388A	—	—	Petrol pipe rubber (short)	1	77
19388B	—	—	Petrol pipe rubber (long)	2	77
19439	—	—	Petrol pipe T piece	1	77
19325	L4/285	—	Petrol tap with filter and banjo	2	77
18700	—	—	Petrol tap washer	2	77
11208/3	L4/287	—	Nut for petrol tap	2	77
18678	—	—	Petrol tank badge	2	88, 99, 77
20230	—	—	Petrol tank badge screws	4	88, 99, 77
18786	—	—	Petrol tank badge washers	4	88, 99, 77
20222	—	—	Petrol tank knee grip, L.H.	1	88, 99, 77
20223	—	—	Petrol tank knee grip, R.H.	1	88, 99, 77

OIL TANK AND FITTINGS

PART No.	SUPERSEDED No.	PLATE No.	DESCRIPTION	QTY.	MODEL
19208E	—	—	Oil tank complete	1	88, 99
20290	—	—	Oil tank complete	1	77
18526	K12/291	—	Oil tank filler cap	1	88, 99, 77
12342	—	—	Oil tank top fixing bolt	1	88, 99, 77
E5379	—	—	Oil tank top fixing bolt washer	2	88, 99, 77
17698	—	—	Oil tank to fixing bolt washer	1	88, 99
E3229	—	—	Oil tank top fixing bolt nut	1	88, 99
19678	—	—	Oil tank fixing bolt	1	77
E5456	—	—	Oil tank fixing bolt washer	1	77
E6453	—	—	Oil tank bottom fixing studs	2	88, 99, 77
E3223	—	—	Oil tank bottom fixing stud nuts	2	88, 99, 77
14867	E2/1050	—	Oil tank bottom fixing plate	1	77
19201	L12-2/1075	—	Oil tank and battery box platform	1	88, 99
19212	L12/1076	—	Oil tank and battery box platform rubber mat	1	88, 99
14481	—	—	Oil tank platform fixing bolts	4	88, 99
E3229	—	—	Oil tank platform fixing bolt nuts	4	88, 99
E5379	—	—	Oil tank platform fixing bolt washers	8	88, 99
17014	L12-2/298	—	Oil tank breather pipe	1	88, 99, 77
19380	L4/1055	—	Oil tank return pipe adapter	1	88, 99, 77
13786	E3/1056	—	Oil tank return pipe adapter washers	2	88, 99, 77
13765	—	—	Oil tank drain plug	1	88, 99, 77

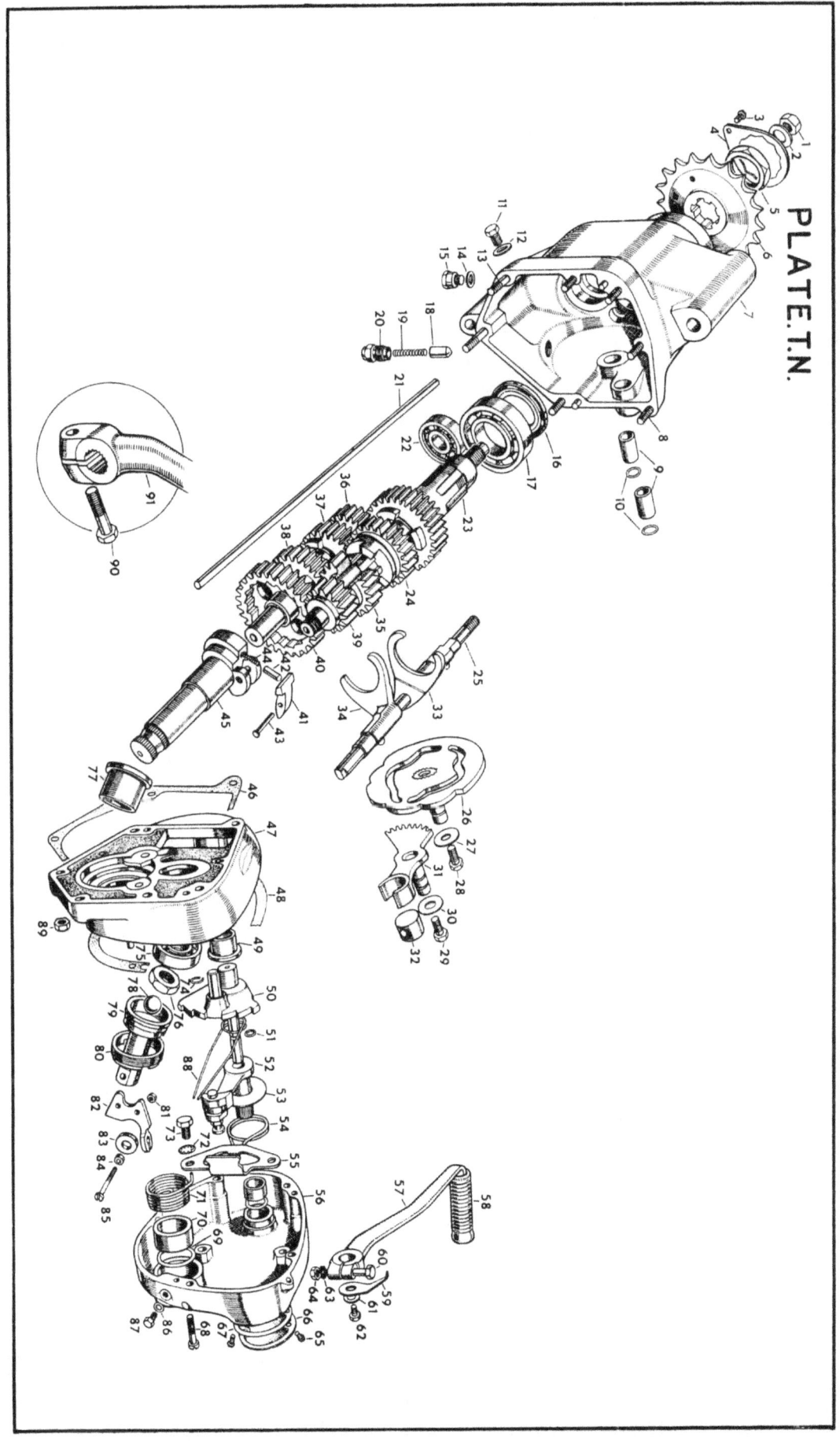

PLATE.T.N.

PART No.	SUPERSEDED No.	PLATE No.	DESCRIPTION	QTY.	MODEL	PRICE EACH
OIL TANK AND FITTINGS—cont.						£ s. d.
13833	—	—	Oil tank drain plug washer	1	88, 99, 77	
19379	L4292	—	Oil tank filter union with gauze	1	88, 99, 77	
E6640	A2/293	—	Oil tank filter union washer	1	88, 99, 77	
OIL PIPES AND FITTINGS						
20316	—	—	Junction box with oil pipes	1	77	
19457	D12/993	—	Junction box with oil pipes	1	88, 99	
T2100	D12/995	—	Junction box washer	1	88, 99, 77	
T2106	D12/994	—	Junction box dowel	1	88, 99, 77	
T2006	—	—	Junction box stud	1	88, 99, 77	
E5377	D12/997	—	Junction box stud washer	1	88, 99, 77	
T2101	D12/996	—	Junction box stud nut	1	88, 99, 77	
19542	L4/295/6	—	Oil pipes, feed and return	2	88, 99, 77	
19425	L12-2/699	TA12	Rocker box oil feed pipe	1	88, 99	
18716	—	—	Rocker box oil feed pipe	1	77	
18101	D12/700	TA13	Rocker box banjo bolts	2	88, 99, 77	
T1084	D12/701	TA11	Rocker box banjo bolt washers	4	88, 99, 77	
GEARBOX SHELL						
040097	—	TN7	Gearbox shell assembly	1	88, 99, 77	
040056	—	—	Gearbox bush	2	88, 99, 77	
000577	—	—	Gearbox dowel pins	2	88, 99, 77	
040064	—	TN8	Gearbox studs (short)	2	88, 99, 77	
000271	—	TN13	Gearbox studs (long)	5	88, 99, 77	
000004	—	—	Gearbox stud nuts	7	88, 99, 77	
040030	—	TN46	Gearbox shell gasket	1	88, 99, 77	
040403	—	TN47	Gearbox inner cover	1	88, 99, 77	
040072	—	TN77	Gearbox inner cover K/S	1	88, 99, 77	
040042	—	—	Gearbox inner cover K/S stop	1	88, 99, 77	
040071	—	—	Gearbox inner cover K/S cam	1	88, 99, 77	
040041	—	—	Kickstarter cam and stop rivets	2	88, 99, 77	
040061	—	TN49	Inner bush for gear change	1	88, 99, 77	
000577	—	—	Dowel pins	2	88, 99, 77	
040063	—	—	Bush for gear change	1	88, 99, 77	
040058	—	TN70	Bush for kickstarter	1	88, 99, 77	
040133	—	TN56	Gearbox outer cover	1	88, 99, 77	
040055	—	TN48	Outer cover gasket	1	88, 99, 77	
000482	—	—	Outer cover screws	5	88, 99, 77	
040138	—	TN11	Drain plug	1	88, 99, 77	
000200	—	TN12	Drain plug washer	1	88, 99, 77	
040053	—	TN66	Inspection cover	1	88, 99, 77	
040057	—	TN67	Inspection cover washer	1	88, 99, 77	
000450	—	TN65	Inspection cover pins	2	88, 99, 77	
000348	—	TN87	Oil level plug	1	88, 99, 77	
000203	—	TN86	Oil level plug washer	1	88, 99, 77	
GEARBOX FIXING BOLTS						
14367	D12/310	MJ25	Gearbox top bolt	1	88, 99, 77	
15170	D12/313	MJ17	Gearbox top bolt nut	1	88, 99, 77	
16410	H12-2/312	—	Gearbox bottom stud less nut	1	88, 99	
18495	A2/312	—	Gearbox bottom bolt less nut	1	77	
E4533	A2/311	—	Gearbox bottom bolt nut	1	77	
11809	—	MJ28	Gearbox bottom bolt washer	1	88, 99, 77	
E3227	—	MJ27	Gearbox bottom bolt nut	1	88, 99	
GEARBOX FRONT CHAIN ADJUSTER						
H2/314	—	MJ16	Gearbox front chain adjuster eye bolt and nut	1	88, 99, 77	
E3231	—	MJ18	Gearbox front chain adjuster nuts	2	88, 99, 77	
16997	H2/1008	—	Gearbox front chain adjuster bolt only	1	88, 99, 77	

PART No.	SUPERSEDED No.	PLATE No.	DESCRIPTION	QTY.	MODEL	PRICE EACH
						£ s. d.

GEARBOX PINIONS, SHAFTS AND BEARINGS

PART No.	SUPERSEDED No.	PLATE No.	DESCRIPTION	QTY.	MODEL
040128	—	—	Gearbox complete less clutch	1	88, 99, 77
040098	—	TN17	Ballrace, mainshaft (large)	1	88, 99, 77
040099	—	TN75	Ballrace, mainshaft (small)	1	88, 99, 77
040100	—	TN22	Ballrace, layshaft	1	88, 99, 77
040131	—	—	Axle sprocket spacer	1	88, 99, 77
040132	—	TN16	Sleeve gear oil seal	1	88, 99, 77
040116	—	TN23	Sleeve gear assembly	1	88, 99, 77
040062	—	—	Sleeve gear bushes	2	88, 99, 77
040010	—	TN6	Axle sprocket	1	88, 99, 77
040076	—	TN4	Axle sprocket locking plate	1	88, 99, 77
000450	—	TN3	Axle sprocket locking plate screw	1	88, 99, 77
040070	—	TN1	Axle sprocket nut	1	88, 99, 77
040108	—	TN26	Cam plate assembly	1	88, 99, 77
040018	—	—	Cam plate bare	1	88, 99 77
040015	—	—	Cam plate spindle	1	88, 99, 77
040109	—	TN31	Quadrant assembly	1	88, 99, 77
040129	—	—	Quadrant O ring	1	88, 99, 77
000174	—	TN27	Washer for cam and quadrant	2	88, 99, 77
040136	—	TN28-30	Screw for cam and quadrant	2	88, 99, 77
040022	—	TN34	Selector fork	2	88, 99, 77
040035	—	TN23	Selector fork shaft	1	88, 99, 77
040001	—	—	Mainshaft	1	88, 99, 77
040023	—	TN74	Mainshaft nut	1	88, 99, 77
040012	—	TN24	Mainshaft, 3rd gear	1	88, 99, 77
040021	—	TN35	Mainshaft, 2nd gear	1	88, 99, 77
040048	—	—	Mainshaft, 2nd gear bush	1	88, 99, 77
040026	—	TN39	Mainshaft, bottom gear	1	88, 99, 77
040025	—	—	Layshaft	1	88, 99, 77
040020	—	TN36	Layshaft pinion	1	88, 99, 77
040016	—	TN37	Layshaft, 3rd gear	1	88, 99, 77
040047	—	—	Layshaft, 3rd gear bush	1	88, 99, 77
040019	—	TN38	Layshaft, 2nd gear	1	88, 99, 77
040115	—	TN40	Layshaft, bottom gear	1	88, 99, 77
040046	—	—	Layshaft, bottom gear bush	1	88, 99, 77
040078	—	TN32	Roller for knuckle pin	1	88, 99, 77
040036	—	TN20	Index plunger bush	1	88, 99, 77
040045	—	TN19	Index plunger spring	1	88, 99, 77
040034	—	TN18	Index plunger	1	88, 99, 77

KICKSTARTER PARTS

PART No.	SUPERSEDED No.	PLATE No.	DESCRIPTION	QTY.	MODEL
040114	—	TN45	Kickstarter axle assembly	1	88, 99, 77
040032	—	TN77	Kickstarter axle assembly bush	1	88, 99, 77
040017	—	TN41	Kickstarter pawl	1	88, 99, 77
040033	—	TN43	Kickstarter pawl pin	1	88, 99, 77
040044	—	TN44	Kickstarter pawl spring	1	88, 99, 77
040069	—	TN42	Kickstarter pawl plunger	1	88, 99, 77
040269	—	—	Kickstarter crank, folding type	1	88, 99, 77
041315	—	—	Pedal for folding kickstarter crank	1	88, 99, 77
041817	—	—	Securing bolt for pedal	1	88, 99, 77
041318	—	—	Spring for folding pedal	1	88, 99, 77
040101	—	TN91	Kickstarter crank	1	88, 99, 77
040102	—	TN90	Kickstarter crank bolt	1	88, 99, 77
040043	—	TN71	Kickstarter return spring	1	88, 99, 77
040005	—	TN69	Kickstarter O ring	1	88, 99, 77
N8081	—	—	Kickstarter rubber	1	88, 99, 77

POSITIVE FOOTCHANGE

PART No.	SUPERSEDED No.	PLATE No.	DESCRIPTION	QTY.	MODEL
040004	—	TN57	Footchange lever	1	88, 99, 77
040086	—	TN58	Footchange lever rubber	1	88, 99, 77
040105	—	TN60	Footchange lever bolt	1	88, 99, 77
000191	—	TN63	Footchange lever bolt washer	1	88, 99, 77
000005	—	TN64	Footchange lever bolt nut	1	88, 99, 77
040051	—	TN59	Footchange gear indicator	1	88, 99, 77
040137	—	TN62	Footchange gear indicator screw	1	88, 99, 77
000012	—	TN61	Footchange gear indicator washer	1	88, 99, 77
040111	—	TN50	Footchange ratchet plate with spindle	1	88, 99, 77

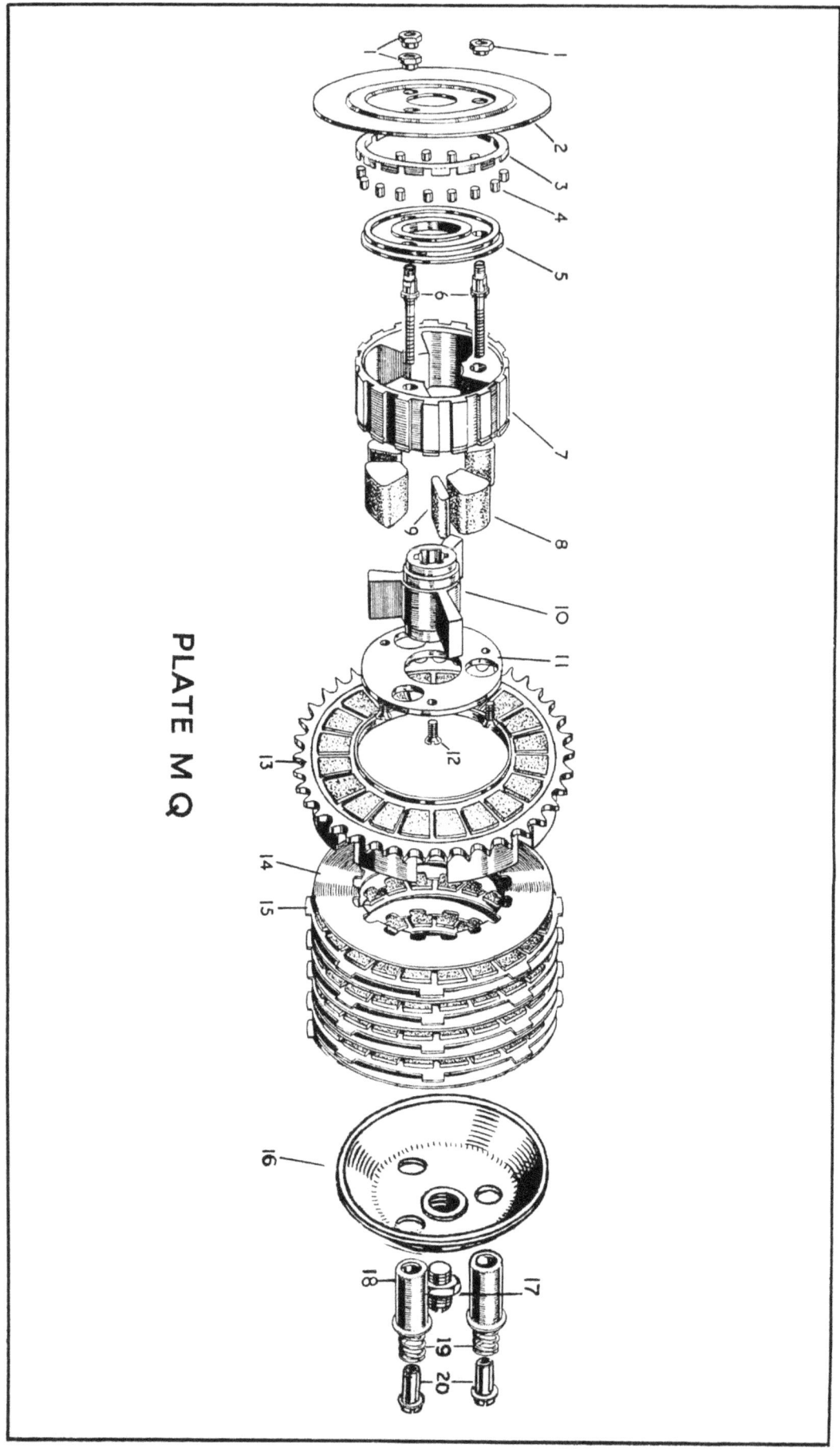

PLATE M Q

PART No.	SUPERSEDED No.	PLATE No.	DESCRIPTION	QTY.	MODEL	PRICE EACH
						£ s. d.

POSITIVE FOOTCHANGE—cont.

PART No.	SUPERSEDED No.	PLATE No.	DESCRIPTION	QTY.	MODEL
040066	—	—	Footchange ratchet plate spindle	1	88, 99, 77
040052	—	TN55	Footchange stop plate	1	88, 99, 77
041400	—	TN73	Footchange stop plate screw	2	88, 99, 77
014117	—	TN72	Footchange stop plate spring washer	2	88, 99, 77
040079	—	—	O ring for ratchet spindle	1	88, 99, 77
04006	—	—	O ring for footchange	1	88, 99, 77
040038	—	TN88	Footchange pawl return spring	1	88, 99, 77
040110	—	TN52	Footchange pawl carrier assembly	1	88, 99, 77
040002	—	—	Footchange pawl carrier only	1	88, 99, 77
040024	—	—	Footchange pawl	1	88, 99, 77
040067	—	—	Footchange pawl carrier pin	1	88, 99, 77
040049	—	—	Footchange pawl circlip	1	88, 99, 77
040075	—	TN54	Footchange pawl return spring	1	88, 99, 77
040135	—	TN53	Footchange pawl return spring washer	1	88, 99, 77
040061	—	—	Footchange inner bush	1	88, 99, 77

CLUTCH

PART No.	SUPERSEDED No.	PLATE No.	DESCRIPTION	QTY.	MODEL
040390	—	—	Clutch complete	1	88, 99, 77
040031	—	TN78	Clutch operating ball	1	88, 99, 77
040059	—	TN79	Clutch operating body	1	88, 99, 77
040003	—	TN80	Clutch operating body locking ring	1	88, 99, 77
040029	—	TN82	Clutch operating lever	1	88, 99, 77
040060	—	TN83	Clutch operating roller	1	88, 99, 77
040065	—	TN84	Clutch roller sleeve	1	88, 99, 77
000457	—	TN85	Clutch roller screw (2BA)	1	88, 99, 7i
011846	—	TN81	Clutch roller screw nut	1	88, 99, 77
040084	—	TN.21	Clutch rod	1	88, 99, 77
040353	—	MQ2	Clutch back plate	1	88, 99, 77
040367	A2/382	MQ3	Clutch roller cage	1	88, 99, 77
000075	A2/383	MQ4	Clutch rollers (15 per set)	1 set	88, 99, 77
040351	—	MQ5	Clutch race plate	1	88, 99, 77
040384	—	MQ6	Clutch spring stud	3	88, 99, 77
040356	A2/402	MQ1	Clutch spring stud nut	3	88, 99, 77
040366	—	MQ7	Clutch body only	1	88, 99, 77
040386	A2/388	MQ8	Clutch shock absorber rubbers (large)	3	88, 99, 77
040387	A2/389	MQ9	Clutch shock absorber rubbers (small)	3	88, 99, 77
040362	—	MQ11	Clutch shock absorber cover plate	1	88, 99, 77
040363	—	MQ12	Clutch shock absorber cover plate pins	3	88, 99, 77
040354	—	MQ10	Clutch body centre	1	88, 99, 77
040392	—	MQ13	Clutch sprocket and inserts	1	88, 99, 77
040371	—	—	Clutch sprocket inserts (thick)	18 per doz.	88, 99, 77
040391	—	MQ15	Clutch friction plate and inserts	4	88, 99, 77
040370	—	—	Clutch friction plate inserts (thin)	80 per doz.	88, 99, 77
040355	—	MQ14	Clutch plate (plain)	4	88, 99, 77
040365	—	MQ16	Clutch pressure plate	1	88, 99, 77
040360	—	MQ7	Clutch adjuster	1	88, 99, 77
040376	—	—	Clutch adjuster lock nut	1	88, 99, 00
040388	—	MQ18	Clutch spring cup	3	88, 99, 77
040385	—	MQ19	Clutch spring	3	88, 99, 77
040389	—	MQ20	Clutch spring adjuster nut	3	88, 99, 77
040373	E6254	—	Main axle nut	1	88, 99, 77
040374	E6266	—	Main axle nut washer	1	88, 99, 77

FRONT WHEEL AND FITTINGS

PART No.	SUPERSEDED No.	PLATE No.	DESCRIPTION	QTY.	MODEL
M12-2/714	—	—	Front wheel complete with bearings and brake less tyre	1	88, 99
K12-2/714	—	—	Front wheel complete with bearings and brake less tyre	1	77
K12-2/428	—	—	Front wheel with hub shell only	1	77
M12-2/428	—	—	Front wheel with hub shell only	1	88, 99
13716	—	KR21	Front wheel hub shell with brake drum	1	77
19664	—	—	Front wheel hub shell with brake drum	1	88, 99
18214	—	—	Front wheel brake drum to hub studs	3	77
E6183	—	KR19	Front wheel brake drum to hub stud nuts	3	77

164

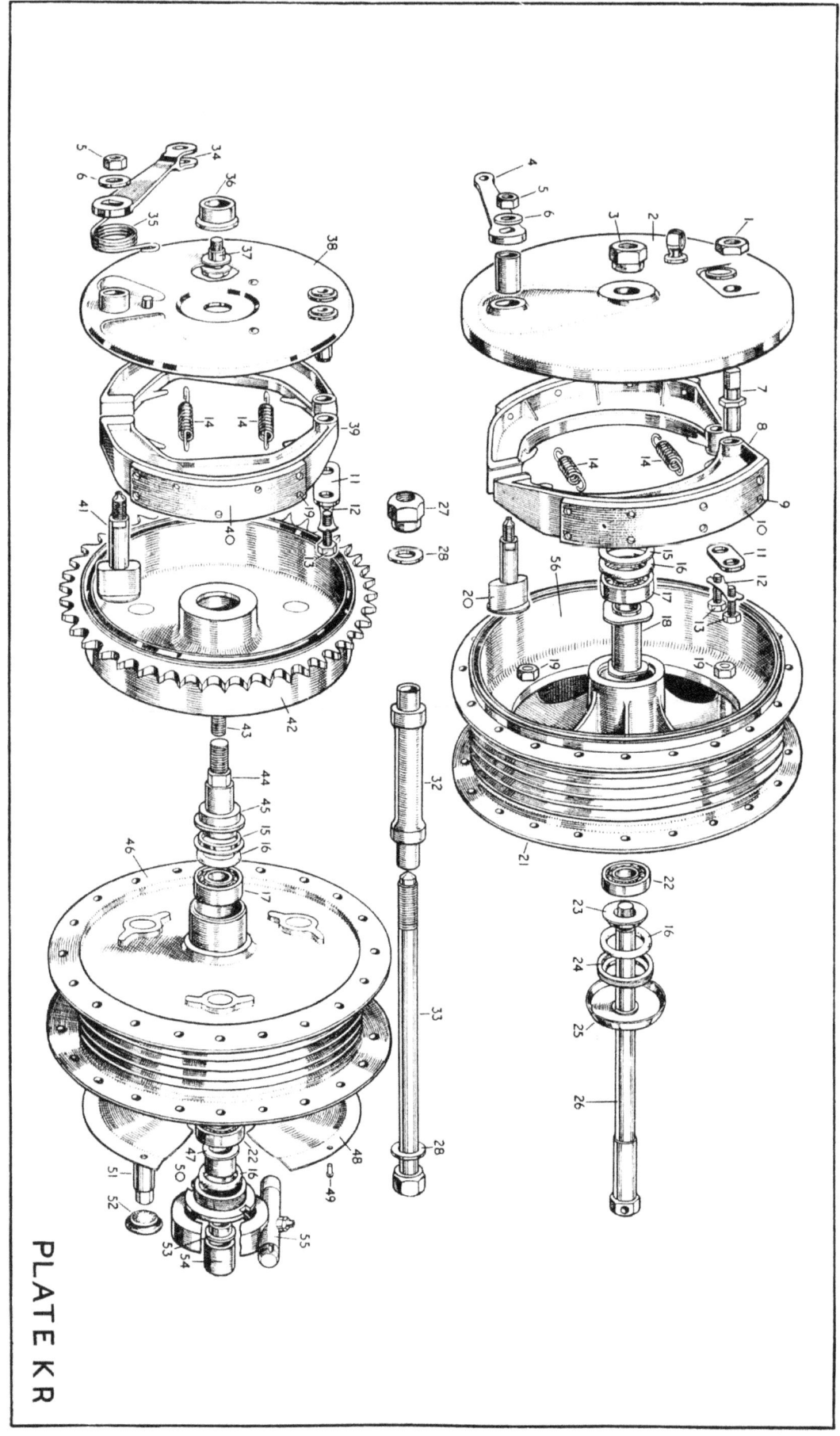

PLATE KR

PART No.	SUPERSEDED No.	PLATE No.	DESCRIPTION	QTY.	MODEL	PRICE EACH
FRONT WHEEL AND FITTINGS—cont.						£ s. d.
16783	J2/441	KR23	Front wheel hub bearing distance piece...	1	88, 99, 77	
E6888	A2/440	KR24	Front wheel hub bearing locking ring ...	1	88, 99, 77	
19719	—	KR15	Front wheel hub bearing oil retaining washer	1	88, 99, 77	
19646	—	KR18	Front wheel hub bearing distance tube ...	1	88, 99	
50036	C2/656	—	Front wheel hub bearing distance tube...	1	77	
18551	K12-2/442	KR25	Front wheel hub bearing dust cap ...	1	88, 99, 77	
20249	B2/452	KR26	Front wheel hub spindle	1	88, 99, 77	
E4768	B2/454	KR3	Front wheel hub spindle nut ...	1	88, 99, 77	
50257	—	KR2	Front wheel brake plate	1	88, 99	
50127	J2/457	—	Front wheel brake plate	1	77	
50249	—	—	Front wheel brake shoe cam and washer	1	88, 99	
50121	J2/448F	—	Front wheel brake shoe cam and washer	1	77	
19653	—	KR7	Front wheel brake plate pivot pin ...	1	88, 99, 77	
13079	B2/658	KR1	Front wheel brake plate pivot pin nut...	1	88, 99, 77	
20052	—	KR4	Front wheel brake cam lever	1	88, 99	
16781	J2/459	—	Front wheel brake cam lever ...	1	77	
E3255	—	—	Front wheel brake cam lever pin ...	1	88, 99, 77	
18942	—	—	Front wheel brake cam lever nut ...	1	88, 99, 77	
E5455	—	—	Front wheel brake cam lever pin whasher	1	88, 99, 77	
17735	A2/195	—	Front wheel brake cam lever split cotter	1	88, 99, 77	
E5944A	—	—	Front wheel brake plate packing washer	1	88, 99, 77	
PARTS COMMON TO FRONT AND REAR HUBS						
17719	A2/435	KR22	Hub bearing (nearside front, offside rear)	2	88, 99, 77 nett	
17721	A2/436	KR17	Hub bearing (offside front, nearside rear)	2	88, 99, 77 nett	
E6885	A2/437	KR16	Hub bearing felt washer	4	88, 99, 77	
E6889	A2/438	KR15	Hub bearing pen steel washer	2	88, 99, 77	
E5832	A2/446	KR14	Brake shoe return spring	4	88, 99, 77	
14454	—	KR11	Brake shoe pivot pin retaining plate ...	2	88, 99, 77	
14506	—	KR12	Brake shoe picot pin retaining plate tab washer	2	88, 99, 77	
14455	—	KR13	Brake plate bolts	2	88, 99, 77	
BRAKE SHOE LININGS AND SHOES						
18502	T2/443F	KR8	Hub brake shoe and linings (front) ...	2	88, 99, 77	
19584	H2/443R	KR39	Hub brake shoe and linings (rear) ...	2	88, 99, 77	
16547	H2/444R	KR40	Hub brake shoes linings (R)	1 pr.	88, 99, 77 per pair nett	
16782	J2/444F	KR10	Hub brake shoe linings (F)	1 pr.	88, 99, 77 per pair nett	
E5061	A2/445	KR9	Hub brake shoe lining rivets (per set 14)	2 set	88, 99, 77 per set	
REAR WHEEL AND FITTINGS						
M12-2/715	—	—	Rear wheel complete with bearings and brakes less tyre	1	88, 99, 77	
M12-2/649	—	—	Rear wheel with hub shell only ...	1	88, 99, 77	
19689	—	KR46	Rear hub only	1	88, 99, 77	
18348	—	KR48	Rear hub diaphragm	1	88, 99, 77	
18396	—	KR49	Rear hub diaphragm drive screws ...	3	88, 99, 77	
18731A	—	KR52	Rear hub rubber grommets	3	88, 99, 77	
50245	—	KR42	Rear hub brake drum with studs 43T ...	1	88, 99, 77	
18233	K12-2/451	KR51	Rear hub brake drum stud sleeve nuts ...	3	88, 99, 77	
18234	K12-2/441	KR47	Rear hub bearing distance piece ...	1	88, 99, 77	
18232	K12-2/440	KR50	Rear hub bearing locking ring ...	1	88, 99, 77	
19714	—	KR45	Rear hub felt washer cup retaining washer	1	88, 99, 77	
18231	K12-2/434	KR32	Rear hub inner sleeve	1	88, 99, 77	
E4760	K12-2/464	KR43	Rear hub brake drum attachment piece...	1	88, 99, 77	
13270	B2/660	KR53	Speedometer drive distance piece ...	1	88, 99, 77	
18235	K122/461	KR54	Hub spindle distance piece	1	88, 99, 77	
19265	A2/460	KR33	Hub spindle	1	88, 99, 77	
19266	B2/659	KR28	Hub spindle washers	2	88, 99, 77	
19267	A2/454	KR29	Hub spindle nut	1	88, 99, 77	

PART No.	SUPERSEDED No.	PLATE No.	DESCRIPTION	QTY.	MODEL	PRICE EACH
						£ s. d.
REAR WHEEL AND FITTINGS—cont.						
19852	—	KR38	Rear brake plate	1	88, 99	
50069	A2/462	—	Rear brake plate	1	77	
50011	—	KR41	Rear brake shoe cam with washer	1	88, 99, 77	
18338	—	—	Rear brake drum stud locating	1	88, 99, 77	
18339	—	—	Rear brake drum stud non-locating	2	88, 99, 77	
13684	H12/470	KR35	Brake lever return spring	1	77	
18177	H12/469	KR34	Brake cam lever	1	77	
19765	—	—	Brake cam lever	1	88, 99	
E5455	—	KR6	Brake cam lever washer	1	88, 99, 77	
18942	—	KR5	Brake cam lever nut	1	88, 99, 77	
19268	A2/465	KR36	Brake plate distance piece	1	88, 99, 77	
15704	A2/466	—	Rear brake torque arm	1	77	
15703	—	—	Bolt to frame	1	77	
E3224A	—	—	Nut to plate	1	77	
E5375	—	—	Washer	1	77	
18923	—	—	Nut	1	77	
T5276	—	—	Brake plate washers	AR	88, 99, 77	
WHEEL RIMS AND SPOKES						
18350	K12-2/432	—	Wheel Rim	2	88, 99, 77	
20063	—	—	Spokes (long head) (per set)	20	88, 99, 77 per set	
20061	—	—	Spokes (short head) (per set)	20	88, 99, 77 per set	
17717	A2/431	—	Nipples (per set)	40	88, 99, 77 per set	
17724	—	—	Security Bolts (rear)	1	88, 99	
FRONT CHAINCASE AND FITTINGS						
20224A	—	—	Front chaincase inner, complete	1	77	
19655	—	—	Front chaincase inner, complete	1	88, 99	
15639	H12/485	—	Front chaincase outer	1	88, 99, 77	
14855	D12/492	—	Crankcase spigot washer	1	88, 99, 77	
E6354	—	—	Crankcase to chaincase bolt	1	88, 99, 77	
E6202	A2/490	—	Chaincase locking washer	1	88, 99, 77	
14371	D12/491	—	Chaincase support stud	1	77	
E3231	—	—	Chaincase support stud nut	1	77	
E3223	—	—	Chaincase support stud nut	1	77	
E5456	—	—	Chaincase support stud washer	1	77	
10914	A2/275	—	Chaincase support stud washer	1	88, 99, 77	
13185	A2/486	—	Chaincase sealing washer	1	88, 99, 77	
E6207	A2/494	—	Chaincase footrest tube felt washer	1	88, 99, 77	
E3336	—	—	Chaincase oil drain plug	1	88, 99, 77	
E5264	—	—	Chaincase oil drain plug washer	1	88, 99, 77	
14837	A2/487	—	Chaincase inspection cover	1	88, 99, 77	
E6085	A2/488	—	Chaincase inspection cover washer	1	88, 99, 77	
E6055	A2/495	MZ47	Chaincase attachment nut	1	88, 99, 77	
E6056	A2/496	MZ46	Chaincase attachment nut washer	1	88, 99, 77	
REAR CHAINGUARD AND FITTINGS						
19846	—	—	Rear chainguard	1	88, 99	
16810	H12/497	—	Rear chainguard	1	77	
12342	—	—	Rear chainguard front fixing bolts	2	88, 99	
12342	—	—	Rear chainguard front fixing bolt	1	77	
E5379	—	—	Rear chainguard front fixing bolt washers	4	88, 99	
E5379	—	—	Rear chainguard front fixing bolt washers	2	77	
E3229	—	—	Rear chainguard front fixing bolt nut	1	77	
E3229	—	—	Rear chainguard front fixing bolt nuts	2	88, 99	
15817	—	—	Rear chainguard rear fixing bolt	1	88, 99, 77	
E5379	—	—	Rear chainguard rear fixing bolt washers	2	88, 99, 77	
E3229	—	—	Rear chainguard rear fixing bolt nut	1	88, 99, 77	
15186	—	—	Rear chainguard distance piece	1	88, 99	
16879	—	—	Rear chainguard distance piece	1	77	
18285	—	—	Rear chainguard grommet	1	88, 99	

PART No.	SUPERSEDED No.	PLATE No.	DESCRIPTION	QTY.	MODEL	PRICE EACH
REAR BRAKE PEDAL AND FITTINGS						£ s. d.
19995	—	MZ62	Rear brake pedal	1	88, 99	
20308	—	—	Rear brake pedal	1	77	
19996	—	MZ69	Rear brake pedal spindle	1	88, 99	
14374	D12/502	—	Rear brake pedal spindle	1	77	
E5456	—	—	Rear brake pedal spindle washer	1	77	
E3223	—	—	Rear brake pedal spindle nut	1	77	
15820	H12/504	MZ66	Rear brake pedal jaw joint	1	77	
E3227	—	MZ67	Rear brake spindle nut	1	88, 99	
11809	—	MZ68	Rear brake spindle washer	1	88, 99	
19997	—	—	Rear brake spindle distance piece	1	88, 99	
19976	—	MZ74	Rear brake spindle stop	1	88, 99	
E3808	—	MZ72	Rear brake pedal adjusting screw	1	77	
13145	—	—	Rear brake pedal adjusting screw lock nut	1	77	
19929	—	—	Rear brake pedal return spring	1	88, 99	
19978	—	MZ63	Rear brake pedal grease nipple	1	88, 99	
17727	A2/500	—	Rear brake pedal grease nipple	1	77	
18929	—	—	Rear brake lever roller	1	88, 99, 77	
15819	H12-2/503	MZ73	Rear brake rod	1	88, 99	
16847	H12/503	—	Rear brake rod	1	77	
20134	—	MZ66	Rear brake rod jaw joint assembly	1	88, 99	
E3255	—	MZ64	Rear brake rod jaw joint pin	1	88, 99	
17043	H12/506	—	Rear brake rod jaw joint pin	1	77	
17735	A2/195	MZ65	Rear brake rod jaw joint split pin	1	88, 99, 77	
15821	H12/505	MZ75	Rear brake rod adjuster	1	88, 99, 77	
FOOTRESTS AND FITTINGS						
18772	D12/513RH	MZ52	Footrest hanger right-hand	1	88, 99, 77	
18149	A2/513LH	MZ16	Footrest hanger left-hand	1	88, 99, 77	
19984	—	—	Footrest hanger spindle	2	88, 99, 77	
19983	—	MZ24	Footrest rubber	2	88, 99, 77	
15641	—	—	Distance piece	1	88, 99	
E5377	—	MZ40	Footrest rod washer	2	88, 99, 77	
E3238	—	MZ51	Footrest rod plain nut	1	88, 99, 77	
E3220	—	MZ39	Footrest rod domed nut	1	88, 99, 77	
14366	D12/510	MZ38	Footrest rod	1	88, 99, 77	
18268	H12-2/1078	MZ50	Footrest tube serrated end, right-hand	1	88, 99	
15640	H12-2/1077	MZ49	Footrest tube serrated end, left-hand	1	88, 99	
PILLION FOOTRESTS						
H12/584	—	—	Pillion footrest complete (per pair)	1	88, 99, 77	
18254	H12/1086	MZ54	Pillion footrest bar	1	88, 99, 77	
16244	H12/1087	MZ57	Pillion footrest lug	1	88, 99, 77	
16841	—	—	Pillion footrest and silencer fixing studs	2	77	
16842	—	—	Pillion footrest and silencer fixing stud, L.H.	1	88, 99	
16246	—	—	Pillion footrest and silencer fixing stud, R.H.	1	88, 99	
16248	—	MZ55	Pillion footrest bar pins	2	88, 99, 77	
16250	—	—	Pillion footrest bar pin spring washers	2	88, 99, 77	
E5376	—	MZ59	Pillion footrest lug fixing washers	2	88, 99, 77	
E3224	—	MZ60	Pillion footrest lug fixing nuts	2	88, 99, 77	
16249	M12/583	MZ53	Pillion footrest rubbers	2	88, 99, 77	
16247	—	—	Pillion footrest bar pin lock nuts	2	88, 99, 77	
ENGINE PLATES						
16816A	—	—	Rear engine plate R.H. with footrest tube	1	77	
14854A	—	—	Rear engine plate L.H. with footrest tube	1	77	
50229	L12-2/517	MZ22	Rear engine plate R.H.	1	88, 99	
19177	L12-2/516	MZ24	Rear engine plate L.H.	1	88, 99	
19100	—	—	Rear engine plate cover	1	88, 99	
15621	H12-2/522	MZ6	Front engine plates	2	88, 99	
14341	D12/522	—	Front engine plates	2	77	
19255	H12-2/491	—	Centre stand spring anchor stud	1	88, 99	
E5456	—	—	Centre stand spring anchor stud washer	1	88, 99	
E3223	—	—	Centre stand spring anchor stud nut	1	88, 99	
E6354	—	—	Rear engine plate bolt R.H.	1	88, 99	
E5456	—	—	Rear engine plate bolt washer R.H.	1	88, 99	
E3223	—	—	Rear engine plate bolt nut R.H.	1	88, 99	

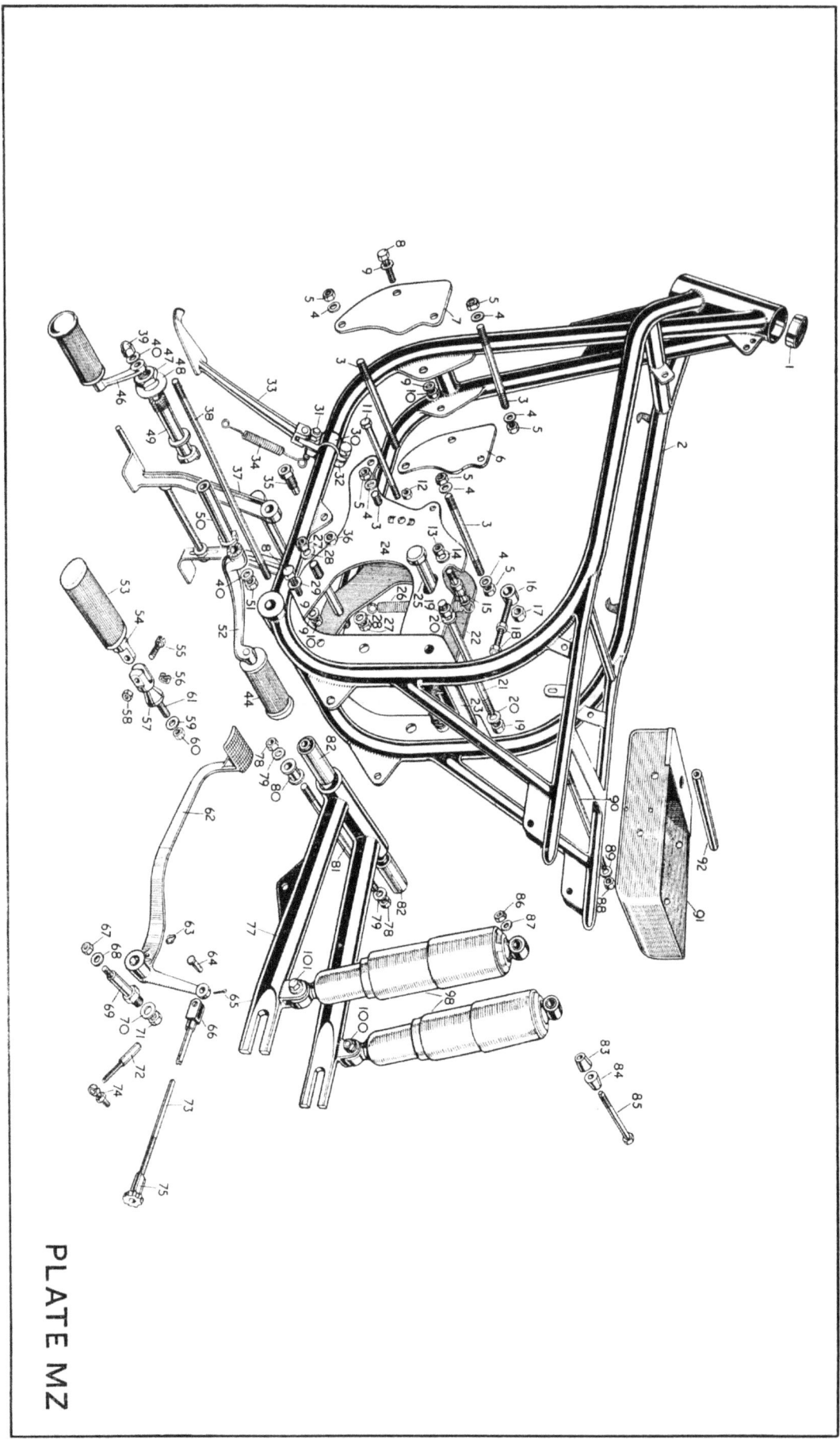

PLATE MZ

PART No.	SUPERSEDED No.	PLATE No.	DESCRIPTION	QTY.	MODEL	PRICE EACH
ENGINE SPROCKETS						£ s. d.
T2180D	D12/473/20T	TA129	Engine sprocket 20T	1	88	
T2180E	D12/473/21T	—	Engine sprocket 21T	1	99, 77	
E3682	A2/474	—	Engine sprocket key	1	88, 99, 77	
E4210	—	TA130	Engine sprocket nut	1	88, 99, 77	
FRONT AND REAR CHAINS						
18265	—	—	Front chain 75L	1	88	nett
17835	—	—	Front chain 76L	1	99	nett
17730	—	—	Front chain 77L	1	77	nett
17729	—	—	Rear chain 90L	1	77	nett
18095	—	—	Rear chain 98L	1	88	nett
18563	—	—	Rear chain 97L	1	99	nett
A2/480	—	—	Front chain crank link	1	88, 99, 77	nett
A2/479	—	—	Front chain spring link	1	88, 99, 77	nett
A2/481	—	—	Rear chain spring link	1	88, 99, 77	nett
A2/482	—	—	Rear chain crank link	1	88, 99, 77	nett
REAR CHAIN ADJUSTERS						
19264	—	—	Fork end rear wheel adjuster	2	88, 99, 77	
E3229	—	—	Fork end rear wheel adjuster lock nuts	2	88, 99, 77	
FRAME						
20060	—	MZ2	Frame complete	1	88, 99	
20237	—	—	Frame complete	1	77	
17727	A2/500	—	Frame head lug grease nipple	1	77	
E3744	—	—	Frame head race bearings	2	77	
18263	125AC	—	Frame head lug bearings (top and bottom)	2	88, 99	nett
15631	—	—	Frame head lug bearing felt washers	2	88, 99	
17429	—	—	Frame head lug bearing washers	2	88, 99	
16825	H12/1091	—	Frame bridge piece assembly	1	77	
17075	—	—	Frame bridge piece fixing screws	2	77	
15893	—	MZ21	Rod for rear engine cross tube	1	88, 99	
E5377	—	MZ20	Rear engine cross tube rod washers	2	88, 99	
13459	—	MZ19	Rear engine cross tube rod nuts	2	88, 99	
15844	H12-2/1091	MZ23	Rear mudguard and engine plate support tube	1	88, 99	
19351	—	—	Fork lock stop bolt	2	77	
16247	—	—	Fork lock stop bolt nut	1	77	
SWINGING ARM AND FITTINGS						
L12-2/1088	—	MZ72	Swinging arm with bushes and bolt	1	88, 99	
M15/1088	—	—	Swinging arm with bushes and bolt	1	77	
20083	—	MZ82	Swinging arm silent bloc bearing	2	88, 99, 77	
20126	—	—	Gusset plate cover	1	88, 99	
15894	—	MZ81	Swinging arm rod	1	88, 99	
16809	—	—	Swinging arm rod	1	77	
11809	—	MZ79	Swinging arm rod washer	2	88, 99	
11809	—	—	Swinging arm rod washer	1	77	
16840	—	—	Swinging arm rod nut	1	77	
15356	—	MZ78	Swinging arm rod nut	2	88, 99	
18578	H12-2/1090	—	Silent bloc bearing spacer tube	1	88, 99	
16790	H12/1090	—	Silent bloc bearing spacer tube	1	77	
REAR SUSPENSION						
20184	—	MZ98	Rear shock absorber units	2	88, 99, 77	nett
18704	—	MZ101	Rear shock absorber bolts	2	88, 99, 77	
11796	—	—	Rear shock absorber bolt washers	4	88, 99, 77	
E3223	—	MZ100	Rear shock absorber bolt nuts	2	77	

PART No.	SUPERSEDED No.	PLATE No.	DESCRIPTION	QTY.	MODEL	PRICE EACH £ s d
REAR SUSPENSION—cont.						
19421	—	—	Rear shock absorber and mudguard fixing bolts	2	77	
19504	—	MZ85	Rear shock absorber and mudguard fixing bolts	2	88, 99	
18537	—	MZ84	Rear shock absorber and mudguard fixing distance piece	2	88, 99	
19420	—	—	Rear shock absorber and mudguard fixing distance piece	2	77	
E5456	—	MZ87	Rear shock absorber and mudguard fixing bolt washers	2	88, 99, 77	
E3223	—	MZ86	Rear shock absorber and mudguard fixing bolt nuts	2	88, 99, 77	
CENTRE STAND AND FITTINGS						
17175	H12-2/524	MZ37	Centre stand complete	1	88, 99	
16813	H12/524	—	Centre stand complete	1	77	
11466	—	—	Centre stand bolts	2	77	
16763	—	MZ35	Centre stand bolts	2	88, 99	
16764	—	MZ36	Centre stand bolt nuts	2	88, 99	
16411	H12-2/527	MZ26	Centre stand spring	1	88, 99	
16937	H2/527	—	Centre stand spring	1	77	
14392	H12/1082	—	Centre stand spring slip	1	88, 99, 77	
E3135	—	—	Centre stand spring clip bolt	1	88, 99, 77	
E3223	—	—	Centre stand spring clip bolt nut	1	88, 99, 77	
E5456	—	—	Centre stand spring clip bolt washer	2	88, 99, 77	
17591	—	—	Centre stand rubber stop	1	88, 99	
E5278	—	—	Centre stand rubber stop pin	1	88, 99	
SIDE PROP STAND AND FITTINGS						
18750	H12-2/1014	MZ23	Side prop stand	1	88, 99	
14791	H12/1014	—	Side prop stand	1	77	
18275	—	MZ30	Side prop stand clip lug front	1	88, 99	
18605	—	MZ32	Side prop stand clip lug rear	1	88, 99	
16373	—	MZ31	Side prop stand clip lug and spring fixing stud	1	88, 99	
16374	—	—	Side prop stand clip lug fixing stud	1	88, 99	
16174	—	—	Side prop stand leg fulcrum pin	1	88, 99	
16176	H12-2/1015	MZ34	Side prop stand spring	1	88, 99	
11824	—	—	Side prop stand clip lug and spring fixing stud nut	1	88, 99	
E3224	—	—	Side prop stand clip lug stud nut	1	88, 99	
14783	E2/1015	—	Side prop stand spring	1	77	
E6706	—	—	Side prop stand head bolt	1	77	
12079	—	—	Side prop stand head bolt lock nut	1	77	
50071	—	—	Side prop stand fixing plate	1	77	
FRONT MUDGUARD STAYS AND FITTINGS						
19286	L4/529	—	Front mudguard complete with number plate stanchions and brake cable guide	1	77	
19362	L12-2/529	—	Front mudguard complete with number plate stanchions and brake cable guide	1	88, 99	
19291	L12/530	—	Front mudguard stays	4	88, 99	
19287	L4/530	—	Front mudguard stays	2	77	
19285	L4/544	—	Front stand	1	77	
E3262	—	—	Front stand fixing stud	1	77	
E3223	—	—	Front stand fixing stud nut	1	77	
E5456	—	—	Front stand fixing stud washer	2	77	
E3218	—	—	Front stand nut	1	77	
19283	L4/680	—	Front mudguard centre stay	1	77	
19282	L12-2/680	—	Front mudguard centre stay	1	88, 99	
18710	—	—	Front mudguard stay bolts	4	88, 99	
18710	—	—	Front mudguard stay bolts	2	77	
18711	—	—	Front mudguard stay bolt washers	2	77	
18711	—	—	Front mudguard stay bolt washers	4	88, 99	
E5379	—	—	Front mudguard stay bolt washers	4	88, 99	
E5379	—	—	Front mudguard stay bolt washers	2	77	
13192	—	—	Front mudguard stay bolt packing washer	2	77	

PART No.	SUPERSEDED No.	PLATE No.	DESCRIPTION	QTY.	MODEL	PRICE EACH
FRONT MUDGUARD, STAYS AND FITTINGS—cont.						£ s. d.
13192	—	—	Front mudguard stay bolt packing washer	4	88, 99	
E3229	—	—	Front mudguard stay bolt nuts	4	88, 99	
E3229	—	—	Front mudguard stay bolt nuts	2	77	
18854	—	—	Front mudguard stay bolts (fork end)	2	77	
18854	—	—	Front mudguard stay bolts (fork end)	4	88, 99	
11940	—	—	Front stand bolt	2	77	
11796	—	—	Front stand bolt washers	4	88, 99, 77	
18709	—	—	Front mudguard centre stay bolts	2	88, 99, 77	
18711	—	—	Front mudguard centre stay bolt washer	2	88, 99, 77	
E5379	—	—	Front mudguard centre stay bolt washer	2	88, 99, 77	
11796	—	—	Front mudguard centre stay bolt washer	2	88, 99, 77	
E3229	—	—	Front mudguard centre stay bolt nuts	4	88, 99, 77	
T1085	—	—	Front mudguard centre stay studs (fork end)	4	88, 99, 77	
E5379	—	—	Front mudguard centre stay stud washers	4	88, 99, 77	
E3229	—	—	Front mudguard centre stay stud nuts	4	88, 99, 77	
REAR MUDGUARD AND FITTINGS						
19363	—	—	Rear mudguard complete	1	77	
20159	L12-2/534	—	Rear mudguard complete	1	88, 99	
19361R	—	—	Rear mudguard tail portion	1	77, 88, 99	
20159F	—	—	Rear mudguard front portion	1	88, 99	
19363F	—	—	Rear mudguard front portion	1	77	
19486	L12-2/536L	—	Rear mudguard lifting handle L.H.	1	88, 99	
19484	L4/536LH	—	Rear mudguard lifting handle L.H	1	77	
19485	L4/536RH	—	Rear mudguard lifting handle R.H.	1	77	
19487	L12-2/536R	—	Rear mudguard lifting handle R.H.	1	88, 99	
19432	—	—	Lifting handle and rear portion fixing bolts	3	88, 99, 77	
19433	—	—	Lifting handle and rear portion fixing bolt washers	3	88, 99, 77	
19434	—	—	Lifting handle to mudguard fixing bolts	2	88, 99, 77	
19435	—	—	Lifting handle to mudguard fixing bolt bolt washers	2	88, 99, 77	
E3229	—	—	Lifting handle to mudguard fixing bolt nuts	2	88, 99, 77	
12342	—	—	Mudguard bottom fixing bolts	2	88, 99, 77	
E3229	—	—	Mudguard bottom fixing bolt nuts	2	88, 99, 77	
E5379	—	—	Mudguard bottom fixing bolt nut washers	2	88, 99, 77	
19429	—	—	Rubber grommets for mudguard	2	88, 99, 77	
14490	—	—	Clip for tail and stop light lead	1	88, 99, 77	
NUMBER PLATES						
18706	K12/531	—	Front number plate	1	88, 99, 77	
18755	—	—	Front number plate rubber	1	88, 99, 77	
18708	—	—	Front number plate stanchion	2	88, 99, 77	
E3229	—	—	Front number plate stanchion nuts	2	88, 99, 77	
E5379	—	—	Front number plate stanchion washers	2	88, 99, 77	
18712	—	—	Front number plate fixing screws	2	88, 99, 77	
13053	—	—	Rear number plate fixing studs	2	88, 99, 77	
11796	—	—	Rear number plate fixing stud washers	2	88, 99, 77	
E3231	—	—	Rear number plate fixing stud nuts	2	88, 99, 77	
19343	L4/532	—	Rear number plate with cuff	1	88, 99, 77	
20965	—	—	Rear number plate plastic bead	1	88, 99, 77	
TAIL AND STOP LIGHT						
53432B	—	—	Tail lamp and stop light with reflector	1	88, 99, 77	nett
573839	—	—	Stop and tail lamp lens	1	88, 99, 77	nett
575200	—	—	Stop and tail lamp window	1	88, 99, 77	nett
575219	—	—	Lens fixing nuts	2	88, 99, 77	nett
166014	—	—	Stop and tail lamp fixing nuts	2	88, 99, 77	nett

PART No.	SUPERSEDED No.	PLATE No.	DESCRIPTION	QTY.	MODEL	PRICE EACH
						£ s. d.
TAIL AND STOP LIGHT—cont.						
188327	—	—	Stop and tail lamp fixing nut washers	2	88, 99, 77 nett	
20165	—	—	Stop lamp switch	1	88, 99 nett	
17749	—	—	Stop lamp switch	1	77 nett	
17008	—	—	Stop lamp switch bracket	1	77	
20129	—	—	Stop lamp switch bracket	1	88, 99	
E5278	—	—	Stop lamp switch fixing pins	2	88, 99, 77	
17904	—	—	Stop lamp switch fixing washers	2	88, 99, 77	
E3221	—	—	Stop lamp switch fixing nuts	2	88, 99, 77	
17005	—	—	Stop lamp switch spring	1	77	
19580	—	—	Stop lamp brake switch lead	1	77 nett	
20248	—	—	Stop lamp brake switch lead	1	88, 99 nett	
19582	—	—	Tail lamp extension lead	1	88, 99, 77 nett	
HEADLAMP AND FITTINGS (all prices RETAIL NETT)						
51954A	—	—	Head lamp complete	1	88, 99	
51876B	—	—	Head lamp complete	1	77	
36084F	—	—	Ammeter	1	88, 99, 77	
31626A	—	—	Switch	1	88, 99	
31340A	—	—	Switch	1	77	
351788	—	—	Switch handle	1	88, 99	
351567	—	—	Switch handle	1	77	
105751	—	—	Switch handle screw	1	88, 99	
101893	—	—	Switch handle screw	1	77	
516798	—	—	Light unit	1	88, 99, 77	
553248	—	—	Headlamp rim	1	88, 99, 77	
31563A	—	—	Dipper and horn switch	1	88, 99, 77	
18733	—	—	Dipper switch rubber	1	88, 99, 77	
18734	—	—	Dipper switch fixing screws	2	88, 99, 77	
112201	—	—	Headlamp fixing bolts	2	88, 99, 77	
137141	—	—	Headlamp fixing bolt washers	2	88, 99, 77	
517079	—	—	Headlamp panel	1	77	
106491	—	—	Headlamp panel fixing screws	3	77	
185026	—	—	Headlamp panel screw washers (3 in set)	1 set	77 **per set**	
BATTERY (price RETAIL NETT)						
4084107	—	—	Battery	1	88, 99, 77	
TOOL BOX, TOOL TRAY AND FITTINGS						
19281	L4/538	—	Tool box and battery box complete	1	77	
19190	L12-2/586	—	Battery box body complete	1	88, 99	
19189	—	—	Tool box and battery box lid	1	88, 99	
19241	—	—	Tool box and battery box lid	1	77	
20069A	—	—	Tool tray complete	1	88, 99	
19195	—	—	Tool box and battery box lid knob	2	88, 99	
19290	L4/539	—	Tool box and battery box lid knob	1	77	
E4764	—	—	Tool box and battery box lid knob circlip	1	77	
11796	—	—	Tool box and battery box lid knob washers	2	88, 99	
17735	—	—	Tool box and battery box lid knob split pin	2	88, 99	
19289	—	—	Battery box support bracket	1	77	
19086	—	—	Platform for battery	1	88, 99	
19093	—	—	Battery fixing U bolt	1	88, 99	
19249	—	—	Battery fixing U bolt	1	77	
19248	—	—	Battery fixing retaining strap	1	77	
19101	—	—	Battery fixing retaining strap	1	88, 99	
E3221	—	—	U bolt nuts	2	88, 99, 77	
17707	—	—	U bolt washers (spring)	2	88, 99, 77	
15689	—	—	Toolbox and battery box rubber grommets	2	88, 99, 77	
14481	—	—	Battery box top fixing bolt	1	88, 99	

PART No.	SUPERSEDED No.	PLATE No.	DESCRIPTION	QTY.	MODEL	PRICE EACH
TOOL BOX, TOOL TRAY AND FITTINGS—cont.						£ s. d.
E5379	—	—	Battery box top fixing bolt washer	3	88, 99	
E3229	—	—	Battery box top fixing bolt nuts	1	88, 99	
13053	—	—	Tool box top fixing stud	1	77	
E5456	—	—	Tool box top fixing stud washer	1	77	
E3223	—	—	Tool box top fixing stud nut	1	77	
18709	—	—	Tool box and battery box fixing bolt	1	77	
18711	—	—	Tool box and battery box fixing bolt washers	1	77	
E5379	—	—	Tool box and battery box fixing bolt washers	2	77	
E3229	—	—	Tool box and battery box fixing bolt nut	1	77	
19092	—	—	Tool box and battery box fixing bolt	1	77	
19092	—	—	Tool box and battery box fixing bolt	2	88, 99	
E5456	—	—	Tool box and battery box fixing bolt washers	2	88, 99, 77	
12342	—	—	Tooltray fixing bolts	4	88, 99	
E5379	—	—	Tooltray fixing bolt washers	8	88, 99	
E3229	—	—	Tooltray fixing bolt nuts	4	88, 99	
VOLTAGE CONTROL AND FITTINGS						
37127M	—	—	Voltage control unit	1	88, 99, 77 nett	
19991	—	—	Voltage control unit waterproof cover	1	77	
12342	—	—	Voltage control unit fixing bolts	2	88, 99, 77	
E5379	—	—	Voltage control unit fixing bolt washers	2	88, 99, 77	
E3229	—	—	Voltage control unit fixing bolt nuts	2	88, 99, 77	
DUAL SEAT AND FITTINGS						
19445	L4/540	—	Dual seat complete	1	77	
20123	H12-2/540	—	Dual seat complete	1	88, 99	
16765	—	—	Seat fixing wing nuts	2	88, 99	
8052	—	—	Seat fixing wing nut washers	2	88, 99	
18538	—	—	Seat sorbo strip	2	88, 99	
15857	—	—	Seat fixing strap rubber grommets	2	88, 99	
13053	—	—	Seat front fixing studs	2	77	
E5456	—	—	Seat front fixing stud washers	2	77	
E3223	—	—	Seat front fixing stud nuts	2	77	
19488	—	—	Seat rubber	2	77	
ELECTRIC HORN AND FITTINGS						
70140A	—	—	Electric horn	1	88, 99, 77 nett	
E3229	—	—	Electric horn fixing bolt nuts	2	88, 99	
E5379	—	—	Electric horn fixing bolt nut washers	2	88, 99	
20155	—	—	Electric horn fixing plate tapped	1	77	
SPEEDOMETER AND FITTINGS (all prices RETAIL NETT)						
19364	L4/545	—	Speedometer head (120 m.p.h.)	1	88, 99, 77	
19367	L4/552	—	Speedometer cable complete	1	88, 99, 77	
L4/554	—	—	Speedometer cable inner	1	88, 99, 77	
L4/553	—	—	Speedometer cable outer	1	88, 99, 77	
19366	L4/564	—	Speedometer gearbox	1	88, 99, 77	
TOOL KIT						
M15/563	—	—	Tool kit complete	1	77	
D12/563	—	—	Tool kit complete with tools	1	88, 99	
SPU1/49	B2/684	—	Headlug bearing and filler cap spanner	1	88, 99	
SPU1/30	B2/682	—	Fork column lock nut spanner	1	77	
SPU2/22	—	—	Fork filler plug and head adjuster nut spanner	1	77	
DWU/01	A2/567	—	Screw driver	1	88, 99, 77	
SPU2/02	A2/565	—	$\frac{1}{4}'' \times \frac{3}{16}''$ spanner	2	77	
SPU2/02	A2/565	—	$\frac{1}{4}'' \times \frac{3}{16}''$ spanner	1	88, 99	
SHU/29	A3/579	—	Exhaust pipe spanner	1	88, 99, 77	

PART No.	SUPERSEDED No.	PLATE No.	DESCRIPTION	QTY.	MODEL	PRICE EACH
						£ s. d.
TOOL KIT cont.						
LTU/07	A2/573	—	Tyre levers...	2	88, 99, 77	
SBU2/88	—	—	Sparking splug spanner	1	88, 99, 77	
SBU2/76	—	—	$\frac{7}{16}''$ x $\frac{1}{2}''$ Box spanner	1	88, 99, 77	
TBU/01	A2/581	—	Tommy bar $\frac{5}{16}''$ x $6\frac{1}{2}''$	1	88, 99, 77	
TBU/47	—	—	Tommy bar $\frac{7}{16}''$ x $8''$	1	88, 99, 77	
SPU2/20	D12/568	—	Rocker adjuster spanner	1	88, 99, 77	
SPU2/04	A2/566	—	$\frac{5}{16}''$ x $\frac{3}{8}''$ open ended spanner	1	88, 99, 77	
SPU1/01	A2/578	—	Cable adjuster spanner	1	88, 99, 77	
19438	—	—	Allen key	1	88, 99, 77	
18672	—	—	Magneto spanner	1	88, 99, 77	
17756	—	—	Tyre inflator	1	77	
18240	—	—	Tyre inflator	1	88, 99	
18976	—	—	Shock absorber adjusting spanner	1	88, 99, 77	
20648	—	—	Box spanner for rear wheel nuts	1	88, 99, 77	
13685	B2/685	—	Fork pull through	1	88, 99, 77	
CABLE CLIPS						
19091	—	—	Cable clip (size C) (speedo cable to frame)	1	88, 99	
19091	—	—	Cable clip (size C) (speedo cable to frame)	4	77	
17752	—	—	Cable clip (size S) (stop lamp and tail lamp leads to frame	12	88, 99	
19090	—	—	Cable clip (size F) (throttle, air and clutch cables to frame)	2	88, 99	
19090	—	—	Cable clip (size F) (throttle, air and clutch cables to frame)	2	77	
18489	—	—	Cable clip (size D) (throttle and air cables, handlebar end)	1	88, 99	
TRANSFERS						
17773	A2/868	—	Oil tank transfer (minium oil level)	1	88, 99, 77	
17731	A2/867	—	Oil bath transfer	1	88, 99, 77	
19958	—	—	Rear mudguard transfer	1	88	
19559	—	—	Rear mudguard transfer	1	99	
20293	—	—	Rear mudguard transfer	1	77	
17755	—	—	Petrol tank panel transfer	1	77	
AIR CLEANER AND FITTINGS						
19667	—	—	Air cleaner	1	88, 99,	
18684	K12-2/1058	—	Air cleaner	1	77	
19518	—	—	Air cleaner connecting hose	1	88, 99	
19729	—	—	Air cleaner fixing clips	1	88, 99	
18484	—	—	Air cleaner fixing clip	1	77	
E3229	—	—	Air cleaner pin nuts	2	88, 99	
E5379	—	—	Air cleaner pin nut washers	2	88, 99	
18483	—	—	Air cleaner carburetter sleeve	1	77	
LAPEL BADGES (this price RETAIL NETT)						
341	—	—	Lapel badge	1		
ENAMEL (this price RETAIL NETT)						
			Polychromatic Grey Touch-up Applicator	1		

All prices subject to 15% increase unless stated as Nett

Please note we reserve the right to alter the above prices or specification of any parts at any time without notice.

REGD. TRADE MARK

SPARE PARTS LIST
for 1964

Models
88ss, 650ss, 650/99 & Atlas
also covers
G15P "N"   G15CS "N"
G15P "M"   G15CS "M"

NORTON MOTORS LTD.
PLUMSTEAD ROAD
WOOLWICH, LONDON S.E. 18

INSTRUCTIONS FOR ORDERING SPARE PARTS

It is most essential that the Engine and Frame Number of the machine is stated. The Engine Number is to be found on the transmission side of the Crankcase directly below cylinder base. The frame number is stamped on the nearside of the frame gusset plate on all models. It is always advisable to order parts on a separate sheet, and not to include on the same sheet other matter of a different nature; this facilitates prompt despatch.

It is found in a number of instances that money orders and postal orders are sent in parcels containing patterns; this is inadvisable. We strongly recommend parts as patterns being despatched separately, and a covering letter sent containing the remittance for replacement parts.

RETURNING MACHINES FOR OVERHAULING

When returning machines or parts for repair or overhaul, these should be sent carriage paid, and with the sender's name and address in full, **securely** attached. It is also advisable to state on the tally that a letter has been sent respecting the parts, and giving the date. All easily detached fittings should be removed, such as Lamps, Horns, Tool Bags, Speedometers, etc.; these are liable to be lost or damaged in transit, and the Company cannot accept any responsibility for them.

ESTIMATES FOR REPAIRING MACHINES

We are always prepared to give approximate estimates for the cost of repairs; it is quite impossible to give a firm quotation. Additional parts may be found necessary during the process of repair, unforseen when preparing an estimate. Should our estimate for repair not be accepted, a charge may be made in accordance with work entailed in dismantling and re-assembling. When we give an estimate for cost of repairs, and this is curtailed by the owner, we cannot accept any responsibility for the performance of the machine; it is always preferable to accept our estimate in full.

PURCHASE OF SPARE PARTS

Norton Dealers throughout the British Isles generally carry a very comprehensive stock of Norton spare parts and it is recommended that owners should obtain any spare parts required through them.

The name of the nearest Norton dealer will be supplied on request and if any difficulty whatever is experienced in obtaining spare parts through a Norton Dealer, if we are advised, we shall be very pleased to investigate the matter.

It is our desire that replacement parts are available to Norton owners with the least possible delay.

Please note we reserve the right to alter the prices in the list at any time without notice.

INDEX

A	Page
Air cleaner	50
Air lever	31
Alternator	46
Ammeter	45
Axle sprocket	18

B

Battery	46
Battery box and mounting	39
Big end bearing	18
Brake lever	31
Brake pedal	43

C

Cable clip	32
Camshaft bushes	6
Carburetter	13
Centre stand	24
Chains	17
Clutch	20
Clutch lever	32
Connecting rods	5
Control cables	33
Crankcase fittings	5
Crankshaft	5
Crash bars	48
Crown and column	28
Cylinder, cylinder head	6

D

Dualseat	33

E

Electrical equipment	47
Engine	5
Engine sprocket	12
Exhaust pipe	15

F

Footchange	18
Footrests	25
Frames	21
Front chaincase, inner and outer	36
Front forks	27
Front wheels	40

G

Gasket sets	48
Gearbox	17
Gudgeon pin	8

H

Half time pinion	9
Handlebars and controls	31
Headlamps	34

	Page
Head steady stay	11
Horn	45

I

Inflator	48

K

Kickstarter	21
Knee grips	34

M

Main bearings	9
Mudguards, front and rear	28 & 30

N

Number plates	30

O

Oil pump	10
Oil tanks and pipes	33 & 35
Optional equipment	50

P

Petrol tank	34
Pillion footrests	36
Pistons and rings	7
Power unit fixing studs	5
Pressure release valve	6
Push rods	9

R

Rear chaincase	38
Rear chainguard	37
Rear suspension	24
Rear wheels	42
Rectifier	46
Rockers and rocker covers	10
Rotor	46
Revolution counter and fittings	49

S

Shock absorbers	24
Side prop stand	25
Silencers	15
Sparking plugs and covers	47
Speedometers	44
Stator	11
Stop and tail lamp	45
Swinging arm	22

T

Tappets	9
Timing cover	6
Timing gear	9
Tools	47
Tool tray	38
Twist grip	32

V

Valves, guides, springs, etc.	7

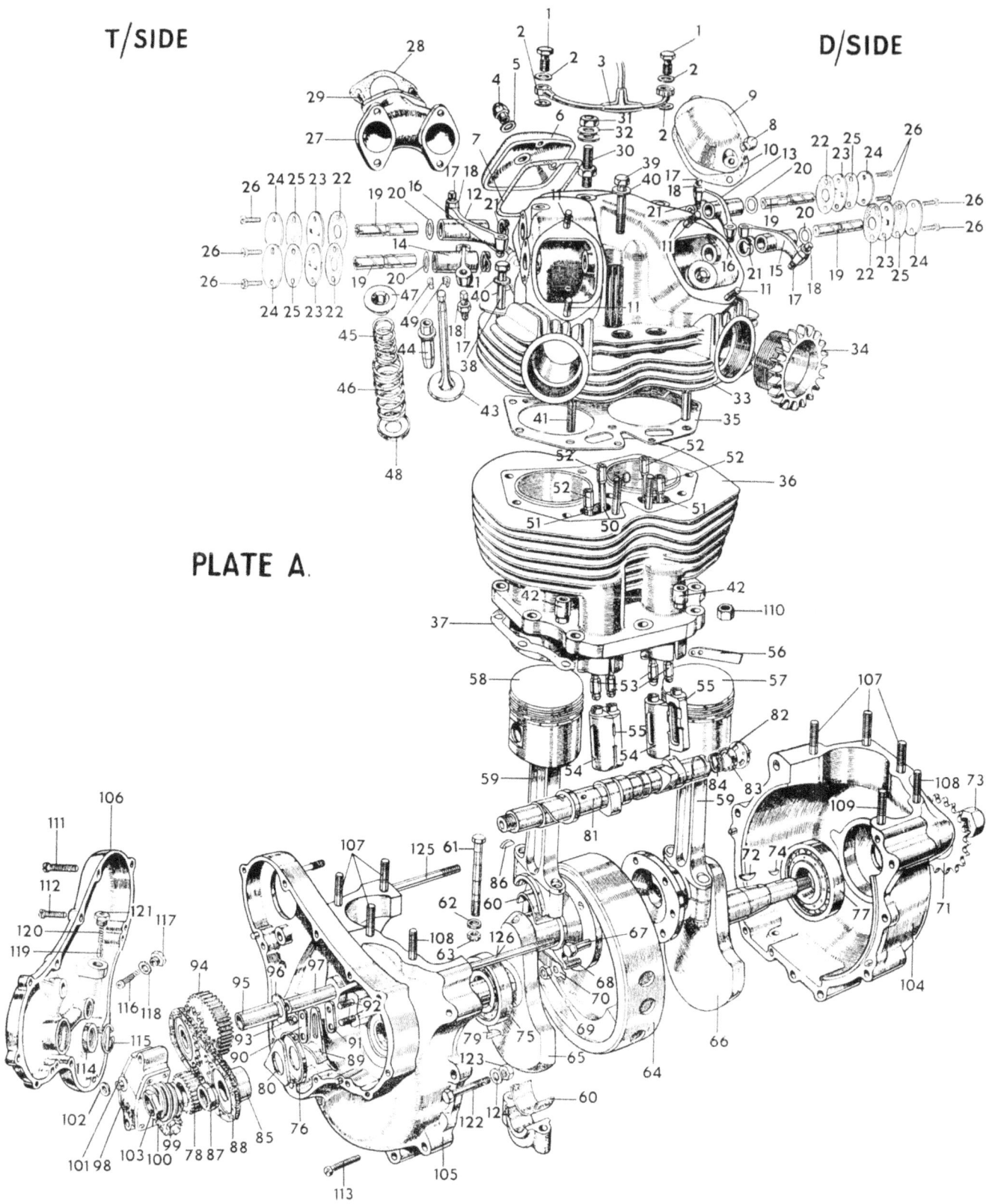

PLATE A.

PLATE No.	PART No.	DESCRIPTION	QTY.	MODEL	PRICE EACH
		CRANKSHAFT			
—	23742	Crankshaft, assembled, less connecting rods	1	88ss	
—	23286	Crankshaft, assembled, less connecting rods	1	650ss and 99	
—	24276	Crankshaft, assembled, less connecting rods	1	All 750	
A65	23636	Crankcheek, timing side	1	88ss	
A65	23262	Crankcheek, timing side	1	650ss and 750	
A66	23637	Crankcheek, driving side	1	88ss	
A66	23261	Crankcheek, driving side	1	650ss and 750	
A64	23820	Flywheel, only	1	88ss	
A64	23315	Flywheel, only	1	650ss and 99	
A64	24248	Flywheel, only	1	All 750	
—	T2105	Dowel, flywheel, crankcheek	1	All	
A67	T2033	Bolt, crankcheek	4	All	
—	T2086	Stud, crankcheek	2	All	
A69	T2031	Nut, for stud and bolt	8	88ss	
A70	T2032	Plate, retaining dowel	2	All	
A69	T2031	Nut, for crankcheek stud	6	All except 88ss	
—	23280	Nut, for crankcheek bolt	2	All except 88ss	
—	E4591	Plug, crankshaft	1	All	
		CONNECTING ROD AND SHELLS			
A59	50023	Connecting rod, with cap	2	88ss	
A59	23297	Connecting rod, with cap	2	650 and 750	
A61	T2150	Bolt, connecting rod cap	4	88ss	
A61	23254	Bolt, connecting rod cap	4	650 and 750	
A63	17827	Nut, for cap bolt	4	88ss	
A63	23253	Nut, for cap bolt	4	650 and 750	
A62	T2152	Washer, for cap bolt	4	88ss	
A60	17828	Shell, connecting rod (two halves)	2	88ss } two halves	
A60	23255	Shell, connecting rod (two halves)	2	650 and 750	
—	T2160	Bush, gudgeon pin	2	88ss	
		CONNECTING ROD SHELLS — OVERSIZE			
—	24914	Shell, connecting rod .005" (two halves)	2	88ss	
—	24915	Shell, connecting rod .010" (two halves)	2	88ss	
—	24916	Shell, connecting rod .020" (two halves)	2	88ss	
—	24917	Shell, connecting rod .030" (two halves)	2	88ss } two halves	
—	25165	Shell, connecting rod .010" (two halves)	2	650 and 750	
—	25166	Shell, connecting rod .020" (two halves)	2	650 and 750	
—	25167	Shell, connecting rod .030" (two halves)	2	650 and 750	
—	25168	Shell, connecting rod .040" (two halves)	2	650 and 750	
		CRANKCASE			
—	25113	Crankcase, complete, with timing cover	1	88ss and 650	
—	25109	Crankcase, complete, with timing cover	1	G15	
—	25115	Crankcase, complete, with timing cover	1	Atlas	
A104	21011	Crankcase, drive side, only	1	88ss and 650	
A104	25043	Crankcase, drive side, only	1	G15	
A104	24278	Crankcase, drive side, only	1	Atlas	

PLATE No.	PART No.	DESCRIPTION	QTY.	MODEL	PRICE EACH
A105	25111	Crankcase, timing side, only	1	88ss and 650	
A105	25107	Crankcase, timing side, only	1	All 750	
A106	18245/RC	Cover, timing gear	1	All	
—	T2236	Gasket, timing cover	1	All	
A107	T2018	Stud, cylinder barrel	6	88ss and 650	
—	24251	Stud, cylinder barrel	6	All 750	
A108	T2209	Stud, cylinder barrel (stepped)	2	All	
A109	18943	Stud, cylinder barrel (front)	1	All	
A111	10940	Screw, timing cover	6	All	
A112	E6980	Screw, timing cover	6	All	
—	20621A	Washer, timing cover screw	12	All	
A113	10940	Screw, for sump	2	All	
—	11775	Washer, for sump screw	2	All	
—	T2036	Bush, camshaft, timing side	1	All	
—	T2037	Bush, camshaft, driving side	1	All	
A114	048023	Seal, oil, timing side shaft	1	All	
A115	048079	Circlip, oil seal	1	All	
—	16945	Body, sump filter	1	All	
—	16949	Washer, filter body	1	All	
—	16948	Circlip, filter body	1	All	
—	16946	Gauze, sump filter	1	All	
—	16947	Washer, filter gauze	1	All	
—	E4591	Plug, oilway, timing cover	1	All	
—	16902	Pin set, oilway	1	All	
—	T1084	Washer, set pin	1	All	

CRANKCASE BREATHER

PLATE No.	PART No.	DESCRIPTION	QTY.	MODEL	PRICE EACH
—	24313	Pipe, crankcase breather	1	88ss and 650	
—	22240	Gasket, breather flange	1	88ss and 650	
—	T2213	Screw, breather flange	1	88ss and 650	
—	24309B	Pipe, rubber, breather	1	88ss and 650	
—	24302	Pipe, rubber, breather	1	All 750	
—	24300	Elbow, breather pipe	1	All 750	
—	13786	Washer, elbow	1	All 750	
—	24303	Nut, elbow	1	All 750	

PRESSURE RELEASE

PLATE No.	PART No.	DESCRIPTION	QTY.	MODEL	PRICE EACH
—	T2059A	Body, assembled, pressure release	1	All	
—	T2054	Piston, release body	1	All	
—	T2061	Spring, release body piston	1	All	
—	15404	Shim, packing	A/R	All	
—	T2060	Nut, release body	1	All	
—	T2058	Washer, release union	1	All	
—	T2057	Washer, release union nut	1	All	

CYLINDER BARREL AND HEAD

PLATE No.	PART No.	DESCRIPTION	QTY.	MODEL	PRICE EACH
A36	20712B	Barrel, cylinder	1	88ss	
A36	23263	Barrel, cylinder	1	650ss and 99	
A36	24237A	Barrel, cylinder	1	All 750	
A37	T2093	Gasket, cylinder base	1	88ss and 650	
A37	24249	Gasket, cylinder base	1	All 750	
—	T2016	Nut, cylinder barrel stud, $\tfrac{3}{8}''$	7	88ss and 650	

PLATE No.	PART No.	DESCRIPTION	QTY.	MODEL	PRICE EACH
—	T2016	Nut, cylinder barrel stud	1	All 750	
—	24250	Nut, cylinder barrel stud	6	All 750	
—	T2210	Nut, cylinder barrel stud, $\frac{5}{16}''$	2	All	
—	000011	Washer, cylinder barrel stud (stepped stud)	2	All	
—	24252	Washer, cylinder barrel stud	6	All 750	
A33	S650/136	Head, cylinder, with valve guides	1	88ss and 650	
A33	25290	Head, cylinder, with valve guides	1	All 750	
A35	T2141	Gasket, cylinder head	1	88ss and 650	
A35	24255	Gasket, cylinder head	1	All 750	
—	T2161	Stud, cylinder head to barrel, $\frac{5}{16}''$	2	All	
A41	18756	Stud, cylinder head to barrel	3	88ss and 650	
A41	24389	Stud, cylinder head to barrel	3	All 750	
A42	T2034	Nut, for stud	2	88ss and 650	
—	24260	Nut, for stud	2	All 750	
—	T2017	Nut, for stud, $\frac{5}{16}''$	2	All	
—	10637	Nut, for stud	1	88ss and 650	
—	24250	Nut, for stud (rear)	1	All 750	
A38	T2096	Bolt, cylinder head, long	4	88ss and 650	
A38	24253	Bolt, cylinder head, long	4	All 750	
A39	T2097	Bolt, cylinder head, short	1	All	
A40	16213	Washer, for bolt	4	88ss and 650	
A40	E5456	Washer, for bolt	4	All 750	

VALVES, GUIDES AND SPRINGS

PLATE No.	PART No.	DESCRIPTION	QTY.	MODEL	PRICE EACH
—	17221	Valve, inlet	2	88ss and 650	
—	24330	Valve, inlet	2	All 750	
A43	T2204	Valve, exhaust	2	All	
A44	T2011	Guide, valve	4	All	
—	23392	Washer, heat insulating	4	All	
A48	T2073	Cup, valve spring	4	All	
A45	22839	Spring, valve, inner	4	All	
A46	22838	Spring, valve, outer	4	All	
A47	T186	Collar, valve, spring	4	All	
A49	T187	Cotter, valve ... pair	4	All	

PISTONS AND RINGS, STANDARD

PLATE No.	PART No.	DESCRIPTION	QTY.	MODEL	PRICE EACH
A57	23185	Piston, complete, left hand	1	88ss	
A57	24022	Piston, complete, left hand	1	650ss and 99	
A57	24246	Piston, complete, left hand	1	All 750	
A58	23186	Piston, complete, right hand	1	88ss	
A58	24023	Piston, complete, right hand	1	650ss and 99	
A58	24247	Piston, complete, right hand	1	All 750	
—	23181	Ring, piston, top, chrome	2	88ss	
—	23272	Ring, piston, top, chrome	2	650	
—	24284	Ring, piston, top, chrome	2	All 750	
—	22797	Ring, piston, plain	2	88ss	
—	23273	Ring, piston, plain	2	650	
—	24285	Ring, piston, plain	2	All 750	
—	22509	Ring, piston, scraper	2	88ss	
—	24024	Ring, piston, scraper	2	650	
—	24286	Ring, piston, scraper	2	All 750	

PLATE No.	PART No.	DESCRIPTION	QTY.	MODEL	PRICE EACH
—	21580	Pin, gudgeon	2	88ss	
—	23275	Pin, gudgeon	2	650	
—	24287	Pin, gudgeon	2	All 750	
—	22798	Circlip, gudgeon, pin	4	88ss	
—	23276	Circlip, gudgeon, pin	4	All except 88ss	

PISTONS, OVERSIZE

PLATE No.	PART No.	DESCRIPTION	QTY.	MODEL	PRICE EACH
—	25125	Piston, complete, left, .010″	1	88ss	
—	25145	Piston, complete, left, .010″	1	650	
—	25238	Piston, complete, left, .010″	1	All 750	
—	25126	Piston, complete, left, .020″	1	88ss	
—	25146	Piston, complete, left, .020″	1	650	
—	25239	Piston, complete, left, .020″	1	All 750	
—	25127	Piston, complete, left, .030″	1	88ss	
—	25147	Piston, complete, left, .030″	1	650	
—	25240	Piston, complete, left, .030″	1	All 750	
—	25128	Piston, complete, left, .040″	1	88ss	
—	25148	Piston, complete, left, .040″	1	650	
—	25241	Piston, complete, left, .040″	1	All 750	
—	25129	Piston, complete, right, .010″	1	88ss	
—	25149	Piston, complete, right, .010″	1	650	
—	25242	Piston, complete, right, .010″	1	All 750	
—	25130	Piston, complete, right, .020″	1	88ss	
—	25150	Piston, complete, right, .020″	1	650	
—	25243	Piston, complete, right, .020″	1	All 750	
—	25131	Piston, complete, right, .030″	1	88ss	
—	25151	Piston, complete, right, .030″	1	650	
—	25244	Piston, complete, right, .030″	1	All 750	
—	25132	Piston, complete, right, .040″	1	88ss	
—	25152	Piston, complete, right, .040″	1	650	
—	25245	Piston, complete, right, .040″	1	All 750	
—	25133	Ring, piston, top, chrome, .010″	2	88ss	
—	25153	Ring, piston, top, chrome, .010″	2	650	
—	25246	Ring, piston, top, chrome, .010″	2	All 750	
—	25134	Ring, piston, top, chrome, .020″	2	88ss	
—	25154	Ring, piston, top, chrome, .020″	2	650	
—	25247	Ring, piston, top, chrome, .020″	2	All 750	
—	25135	Ring, piston, top, chrome, .030″	2	88ss	
—	25155	Ring, piston, top, chrome, .030″	2	650	
—	25248	Ring, piston, top, chrome, .030″	2	All 750	
—	25136	Ring, piston, top, chrome, .040″	2	88ss	
—	25156	Ring, piston, top, chrome, .040″	2	650	
—	25249	Ring, piston, top, chrome, .040″	2	All 750	
—	25137	Ring, piston, plain, .010″	2	88ss	
—	25157	Ring, piston, plain, .010″	2	650	
—	25250	Ring, piston, plain, .010″	2	All 750	
—	25138	Ring, piston, plain, .020″	2	88ss	
—	25158	Ring, piston, plain, .020″	2	650	
—	25251	Ring, piston, plain, .020″	2	All 750	
—	25139	Ring, piston, plain, .030″	2	88ss	
—	25159	Ring, piston, plain, .030″	2	650	
—	25252	Ring, piston, plain, .030″	2	All 750	
—	25140	Ring, piston, plain, .040″	2	88ss	
—	25160	Ring, piston, plain, .040″	2	650	
—	25213	Ring, piston, plain, .040″	2	All 750	

PLATE No.	PART No.	DESCRIPTION	QTY.	MODEL	PRICE EACH
—	25141	Ring, piston, scraper, .010"	2	88ss	
—	25161	Ring, piston, scraper, .010"	2	650	
—	25254	Ring, piston, scraper, .010"	2	All 750	
—	25142	Ring, piston, scraper, .020"	2	88ss	
—	25162	Ring, piston, scraper, .020"	2	650	
—	25255	Ring, piston, scraper, .020"	2	All 750	
—	25143	Ring, piston, scraper, .030"	2	88ss	
—	25163	Ring, piston, scraper, .030"	2	650	
—	25256	Ring, piston, scraper, .030"	2	All 750	
—	25144	Ring, piston, scraper, .040"	2	88ss	
—	25164	Ring, piston, scraper, .040"	2	650	
—	25257	Ring, piston, scraper, .040"	2	All 750	

MAIN BEARINGS

PLATE No.	PART No.	DESCRIPTION	QTY.	MODEL	PRICE EACH
A75	17822	Bearing, ball, timing side	1	All	
A76	T2008	Washer, sealing, timing side bearing	1	All	
A77	17824	Bearing, roller, driving side	1	All	
—	T2187	Oil seal, driving side bearing	1	All	

TIMING GEAR

PLATE No.	PART No.	DESCRIPTION	QTY.	MODEL	PRICE EACH
A78	T2035	Pinion, half-time	1	All	
A79	E3683	Key, for pinion	1	All	
A80	T2007	Plate, backing, for pinion	1	All	
A81	22729	Camshaft	1	All	
A82	T2078	Plate, stationary, for camshaft breather	1	All	
A83	24301	Rotary plate, for breather	1	All	
A84	T2108	Spring, for breather	1	All	
A85	20829	Sprocket, camshaft	1	All	
A86	E3683	Key, for sprocket	1	All	
A87	17211	Nut, for sprocket and r/c drive	1	All	
A88	17806	Chain, camshaft (38 link endless)	1	All	
A89	T2217	Slipper, chain tension	1	All	
A90	T2218	Plate, chain tensioner, thick	1	All	
A91	T2218A	Plate, chain tensioner, thin	1	All	
A92	T247	Stud, chain tensioner	2	All	
A93	E3231	Nut, for stud	2	All	
—	18202	Washer, for stud (fan disc ¼")	2	All	
A94	23819	Gear, intermediate, with sprockets	1	88ss	
A94	50008	Gear, intermediate, with sprockets	1	All except 88ss	
A95	T2026	Bush, intermediate gear	1	All	
A96	T2080	Washer, intermediate gear	1	All	
A97	T2021	Spindle, intermediate gear	1	All	
—	17823	Circlip, for spindle	1	All	

TAPPETS AND PUSH RODS

PLATE No.	PART No.	DESCRIPTION	QTY.	MODEL	PRICE EACH
A55	22771	Tappet, left hand	2	All	
A54	22772	Tappet, right hand	2	All	
A56	T2142	Plate, locating tappet	2	All	
—	T2143	Screw, for Plate	4	All	
A50	88/ss-82 in	Push rod, complete, inlet	2	88ss	
A50	S650-82 in	Push rod, complete, inlet	2	All except 88ss	
A51	88/ss-82 ex	Push rod, complete, exhaust	2	88ss	
A51	S650-82 ex	Push rod, complete, exhaust	2	All except 88ss	

PLATE No.	PART No.	DESCRIPTION	QTY.	MODEL	PRICE EACH
—	23740	Push rod, tube only, inlet	2	88ss	
—	23352	Push rod, tube only, inlet	2	All except 88ss	
—	23741	Push rod, tube only, exhaust	2	88ss	
—	23354	Push rod, tube only, exhaust	2	All except 88ss	
A52	T2064	End, push rod, top	4	All	
A53	T2182	End, push rod, bottom	4	All	

ROCKERS, COVERS, ETC.

PLATE No.	PART No.	DESCRIPTION	QTY.	MODEL	PRICE EACH
A12	18249	Rocker, inlet, right hand	1	All	
A13	18250	Rocker, inlet, left hand	1	All	
A14	18251	Rocker, exhaust, right hand	1	All	
A15	18252	Rocker, exhaust, left hand	1	All	
A16	T2063	Ball end, rocker	4	All	
A17	T2074	Adjuster, rocker	4	All	
A18	T232	Nut, adjuster	4	All	
A19	T2237	Shaft, rocker	4	All	
A20	18102	Washer, thrust, for shaft	4	All	
A21	18103	Washer, spring, for shaft	4	All	
A22	T2083	Washer, joint, for shaft	4	All	
A23	T2238	Plate, locking, for shaft	4	All	
A24	T2239	Plate, retaining, for shaft	4	All	
A25	T2240	Washer, joint, for plate	4	All	
A26	T2256	Set pin, for retaining plate	8	All	
A4	T2162	Nut, domed, rear cap	1	All	
A5	T2082	Washer, domed nut	1	All	
A6	18094	Cap, rocker, rear	1	All	
A7	T2084	Washer, sealing, rear cap	1	All	
—	18033	Stud, rear cap	1	All	
—	000579	Dowel, rear cap	1	All	
A8	T2085	Nut, front cap stud	4	All	
A9	18093	Cap, rocker, front	2	All	
A10	T2088	Washer, sealing, front cap	2	All	
A11	T2252	Stud, front cap	4	All	
A3	25192	Pipe, rocker box oil feed	1	All	
—	22167	Hose, rocker feed pipe	1	All	
A1	18101	Bolt, banjo, feed pipe	2	All	
A2	T1084	Washer, fibre, banjo bolt	4	All	

OIL PUMP

PLATE No.	PART No.	DESCRIPTION	QTY.	MODEL	PRICE EACH
A98	15522	Oil pump, complete	1	88ss	
A98	23111	Oil pump, complete	1	All except 88ss	
A99	15511A	Nut, oil pump spindle	1	All	
A100	T2077	Worm gear wheel (on pump)	1	All	
—	17697	Key, for gear wheel	1	All	
A101	15515	Bush, feed, for pump	1	All	
—	21146	Shim, packing, for feed bush	1	All	
A102	T272	Washer, sealing feed bush	1	All	
A103	T2076	Driving worm, on mainshaft	1	All	
—	E4440	Stud, pump to crankcase	2	All	
—	E3231	Nut, for stud	2	All	
—	E4590	Grub screw, oil stop	1	All	

PLATE No.	PART No.	DESCRIPTION	QTY.	MODEL	PRICE EACH
		STATOR HOUSING			
—	20885	Housing, for stator	1	88ss, 650 and Atlas	
—	20693	Screw, for housing	3	88ss, 650 and Atlas	
—	21411	Washer, for screw	3	88ss, 650 and Atlas	
		HEAD STEADY STAY			
—	23868	Plate, head steady	1	88ss, 650 and Atlas	
A30	18032	Stud, for plate, in head	1	88ss, 650 and Atlas	
A32	000010	Washer, for stud	1	88ss, 650 and Atlas	
A31	E3224	Nut, for stud	1	88ss, 650 and Atlas	
—	E3798	Bolt, steady plate to frame	2	88ss, 650 and Atlas	
—	11796	Washer, for bolt	2	88ss, 650 and Atlas	
—	18202	Washer, for bolt	2	88ss, 650 and Atlas	
—	E3223	Nut, for bolt	2	88ss, 650 and Atlas	
—	030420	Head steady, assembled	1	All G15 models	
—	030424	Bolt, head steady	1	All G15 models	
—	000010	Washer, for bolt	1	All G15 models	
		CRANKCASE BOLTS			
A122	13870	Bolt, crankcase, short	1	All	
A124	E5456	Washer, for bolt	1	All	
A123	E3223	Nut, for bolt	1	All	
A125	T2013	Stud, crankcase, top, rear	1	All	
—	E5376	Washer, for stud	1	All	
—	E3224	Nut, for stud	1	All except 650/99 and Atlas	
—	E3224A	Nut, for stud	1	650/99 and Atlas	
A126	19077	Stud, crankcase, top, front	1	All	
—	T2221	Washer, for stud	1	All	
—	E3229	Nut, for stud	1	All	
—	E3214	Stud, crankcase	1	88ss, 650 and Atlas	
—	E3231	Nut, for stud	2	88ss, 650 and Atlas	
		ENGINE PLATES AND BOLTS			
H49	15621	Plate, engine, front	2	88ss, 650 and Atlas	
H50	20999	Cover, front engine plate	1	88ss, 650 and Atlas	
H1	T2012	Stud, crankcase/engine plate, top and centre, front	1	88ss, 650 and Atlas	
—	000010	Washer, for stud	2	88ss, 650 and Atlas	
H2	E3224A	Nut, for stud	2	88ss, 650 and Atlas	
H5	22694	Stud, crankcase/engine plate and frame, bottom	1	88ss, 650 and Atlas	
H6	000010	Washer, for stud	2	88ss, 650 and Atlas	
H7	E3224	Nut, for stud	2	88ss, 650 and Atlas	
—	T2012	Stud, crankcase/engine plate, top, rear	1	88ss, 650 and Atlas	
—	000010	Washer, for stud	2	88ss, 650 and Atlas	
—	E3224A	Nut, for stud	2	88ss, 650 and Atlas	
H8	T2012	Stud, crankcase/engine plate, centre, rear	1	88ss, 650 and Atlas	
H9	000010	Washer, for stud	2	88ss, 650 and Atlas	
H10	E3224	Nut, for stud	2	88ss, 650 and Atlas	
H3	E4261	Bolt, crankcase/engine plate, bottom, rear	1	88ss, 650 and Atlas	
H4	E3223	Nut, for bolt	1	88ss, 650 and Atlas	
—	000371	Bolt, engine plate/frame, bottom	2	88ss, 650 and Atlas	

PLATE No.	PART No.	DESCRIPTION	QTY.	MODEL	PRICE EACH
—	E5456	Washer, for bolt	4	88ss, 650 and Atlas	
—	000004	Nut, for bolt	2	88ss, 650 and Atlas	
H11	16317	Bolt, engine plate/frame, front and rear	6	88ss, 650 and Atlas	
H12	000010	Washer, for bolt	12	88ss, 650 and Atlas	
H13	E3224	Nut, for bolt	6	88ss, 650 and Atlas	
H52	20700	Plate, engine, rear, left hand	1	88ss, 650 and Atlas	
H51	50229	Plate, engine, rear, right hand	1	88ss, 650 and Atlas	
H53	19100	Cover, rear engine plate	1	88ss, 650 and Atlas	
—	19678	Bolt, rear engine plate, right hand ...	1	88ss, 650 and Atlas	
—	E5456	Washer, for bolt	1	88ss, 650 and Atlas	
—	E3223	Nut, for bolt	1	88ss, 650 and Atlas	

ENGINE PLATES AND BOLTS

PLATE No.	PART No.	DESCRIPTION	QTY.	MODEL	PRICE EACH
—	030216	Plate, engine, front, assembled, left hand	1	All G15 models	
—	030219	Plate, engine, front, assembled, right hand	1	All G15 models	
—	000303	Stud, crankcase/engine plate	2	All G15 models	
—	000010	Washer, for stud	4	All G15 models	
—	000003	Nut, for stud	4	All G15 models	
—	010823	Stud, front engine plate to frame ...	1	All G15 models	
—	000003	Nut, for stud	2	All G15 models	
—	000010	Washer, for stud	2	All G15 models	
—	000277	Stud, front engine plate to engine ...	1	All G15 models	
—	000004	Nut, for stud	2	All G15 models	
—	030221	Spacer, front engine plate	2	All G15 models	
—	030227	Plate, engine, rear, left hand	1	All G15 models	
—	030231	Plate, engine, rear, right hand ...	1	All G15 models	
—	000304	Stud, rear engine plate, top	2	All G15 models	
—	000288	Stud, rear engine plate, bottom ...	1	All G15 models	
—	000010	Washer, for 000304 stud	4	All G15 models	
—	000011	Washer, for 000288 stud	2	All G15 models	
—	000003	Nut, for 000304 stud	4	All G15 models	
—	000004	Nut, for 000288 stud	2	All G15 models	
—	030238	Cover, engine plate	1	All G15 models	

ENGINE SPROCKET

PLATE No.	PART No.	DESCRIPTION	QTY.	MODEL	PRICE EACH
A71	T2180A	Sprocket, 17 teeth (alternative)	1	All	
A71	T2180B	Sprocket, 18 teeth, normal	1	88ss	
A71	T2180C	Sprocket, 19 teeth (alternative)	1	All	
A71	T2180D	Sprocket, 20 teeth (alternative)	1	All	
A71	T2180E	Sprocket, 21 teeth (Home and Export), normal	1	650 and Atlas	
A71	T2180E	Sprocket, 21 teeth (Export), normal ...	1	G15 CS "M" and G15 CS "N"	
A71	T2180F	Sprocket, 22 teeth (Export), normal ...	1	G15 P "M" and G15 P "N"	
A71	T2180G	Sprocket, 23 teeth (Home), normal ...	1	G15 P "M" and G15 P "N"	
A72	E3682	Key, for sprocket	1	All	

MAGNETO

PLATE No.	PART No.	DESCRIPTION	QTY.	MODEL	PRICE EACH
—	42379B	Magneto (Lucas K2F)	1	All	
—	47508D	Sprocket, with auto advance	1	All	

PLATE No.	PART No.	DESCRIPTION	QTY.	MODEL	PRICE EACH
—	458865	Pick-up, with brush and spring, right hand	1	All	
—	458866	Pick-up, with brush and spring, left hand	1	All	
—	451260	Brush and spring, for pick-up	2	All	
—	410600	Nut, H.T. cable	2	All	
—	459269	Cover, contact breaker	1	All	
—	455190	Brush and spring, ignition cut-out	1	All	
—	492854	Contact breaker	1	All	
—	54440888	Contact set	1	All	
—	455191	Brush and spring, earthing, with holder	1	All	
—	498157	Spring set, auto-advance	1	All	pair
—	T2191	Washer, joint, magneto	1	All	
—	T2245	Stud, fixing magneto	2	All	
—	11796	Washer, fixing stud	2	All	
—	E3231	Nut, fixing stud	2	All	
—	25105	Bolt, fixing magneto	1	All	
—	010706	Washer, fibre, for bolt	1	All	
—	015306	Washer, shakeproof, for bolt	1	All	
—	E3229	Nut, for bolt	1	All	
—	14490	Clip, H.T. lead	1	All	
—	18257	Chain, magneto	1	All	

CARBURETTER

PLATE No.	PART No.	DESCRIPTION	QTY.	MODEL	PRICE EACH
—	23874	Sleeve, inlet port	2	88ss and 650	
—	23358	Spacer, carburetter, thin	2	All	
—	23872	Spacer, carburetter, thick	2	88ss, 650 and Atlas	
—	030561	Spacer, carburetter	2	All G15	
—	23873	Union, balance	2	All	
—	11775	Washer, for union	2	All	
—	23875	Hose, balance pipe, 5¾"	1	All	
—	23395	Screw, fixing carburetter	1	88ss, 650 and Atlas	
—	030343	Screw, fixing carburetter	1	All G15	
—	11796	Washer, for screw	1	All	
—	23563	Stud, fixing carburetter	3	88ss, 650 and Atlas	
—	21999	Stud, fixing carburetter	3	All G15	
—	E3231	Nut, fixing stud	3	All	
—	11796	Washer, shakeproof, for stud	3	All	
—	000581	Gasket, carburetter	2	All G15	
—	000952	Petrol pipe float chamber to carb., 2"	1	All	
—	20000	'O' ring, sealing carburetter	1	All	
—	24018	Carburetter, complete, less cables, left hand	1	88ss	
—	25199	Carburetter, complete, less cables, left hand	1	650ss	
—	23406	Carburetter, complete, less cables, left hand	1	650/99	
—	25222	Carburetter, complete, less cables, left hand	1	Atlas	
—	24598	Carburetter, complete, less cables, left hand	1	G15P	
—	25121	Carburetter, complete, less cables, left hand	1	G15CS	
—	24019	Carburetter, complete, less cables, right hand	1	88ss	
—	25200	Carburetter, complete, less cables, right hand	1	650ss	

PLATE No.	PART No.	DESCRIPTION	QTY.	MODEL	PRICE EACH
—	23407	Carburetter, complete, less cables, right hand	1	650/99	
—	25223	Carburetter, complete, less cables, right hand	1	Atlas	
—	25499	Carburetter, complete, less cables, right hand	1	G15P	
—	25122	Carburetter, complete, less cables, right hand	1	G15CS	
—	376-003	Body, only, left hand	1	88ss, 650ss & 650/99	
—	389-002	Body, only, left hand	1	All 750	
—	376-164	Body, only, right hand	1	88ss, 650ss & 650/99	
—	389-028	Body, only, right hand	1	All 750	
—	376-077	Cover, float chamber	2	All	
—	376-078	Washer, side cover	2	All	
—	376-079	Screw, side cover	6	All	
—	376-083	Float, only	1	All	
—	376-094	Bush, float spindle	1	All	
—	376-089	Needle, float	1	All	
—	376-088	Seating, float needle	1	All	
—	376-065	Ring, mixing chamber cap	2	88ss, 650ss & 650/99	
—	389-065	Ring, mixing chamber cap	2	All 750	
—	4-235	Spring, for ring	2	88ss, 650ss & 650/99	
—	29-201	Spring, for ring	2	All 750	
—	4-241	Screw, for spring	2	All	
—	376-064	Cap, mixing chamber	2	88ss, 650ss & 650/99	
—	389-064	Cap, mixing chamber	2	All 750	
—	4-035	Adjuster, control cables	4	All	
—	376-062	Valve, air	2	88ss, 650ss & 650/99	
—	389-062	Valve, air	2	All 750	
—	6-047	Guide, air valve	2	88ss, 650ss & 650/99	
—	29-057	Guide, air valve	2	All 750	
—	376-060	Valve, throttle, size $3\frac{1}{2}$	2	88ss, 650ss & 650/99	
—	389-060	Valve, throttle, size 3	2	All 750	
—	4-046	Spring, air valve	2	All	
—	376-132	Spring, throttle valve	2	88ss, 650ss & 650/99	
—	389-092	Spring, throttle valve	2	All 750	
—	376-068	Screw, throttle stop	2	All	
—	376-069	Spring, stop screw	2	All	
—	332-017	Screw, pilot air adjusting	2	All	
—	4-148	Spring, adjusting screw	2	All	
—	376-063	Needle, jet, taper	2	88ss, 650ss & 650/99	
—	389-063	Needle, jet, taper	2	All 750	
—	4-230	Clip, jet needle	2	All	
—	376-072	Jet, needle, size .1065	2	All	
—	376-100	Jet, main, size 250	2	88ss and 650/99	
—	376-100	Jet, main, size 270	2	650ss	
—	376-100	Jet, main, size 350	2	Atlas	
—	376-100	Jet, main, size 420	2	G15P	
—	376-100	Jet, main, size 380	2	G15CS	
—	376-073	Holder, main jet	2	All	
—	376-074	Washer, jet holder	2	All	
—	376-075	Cover, main jet	2	All	
—	376-076	Jet, pilot, size 25	2	88ss, 650ss & 650/99	
—	376-076	Jet, pilot, size 20	2	All 750	
—	376-095	Nut, pilot jet cover	2	All	
—	116-162	Washer, jet cover nut	2	All	

PLATE No.	PART No.	DESCRIPTION	QTY.	MODEL	PRICE EACH
—	376-057	Choke, or jet block, $1\frac{1}{16}"$	2	88ss, 650ss & 650/99	
—	389-056	Choke, or jet block, $1\frac{1}{8}"$	2	All 750	
—	376-067	Washer, jet block	2	All	
—	376-070	Peg, locating jet block	2	All	
—	376-097	Banjo, petrol feed, left hand	1	650/99 and all 750	
—	244-1730	Banjo, petrol feed, left hand	1	88ss and 650ss	
—	376-141	Banjo, petrol feed, right hand	1	All	
—	376-091	Bolt, for banjo, left hand	1	All	
—	376-140	Bolt, for banjo, right hand	1	All	
—	376-092	Washer, banjo bolt	2	All	
—	14-175	Washer, seating banjo bolt	2	All	
—	373-093	Gauze, filter	2	All	
—	343-011	Body, tickler	1	All	
—	376-086	Plunger, tickler	1	All	
—	376-087	Spring, tickler	1	All	
—	376-066	Venturi, intake	1	88ss, 650ss & 650/99	
—	389-066	Venturi, intake	1	All 750	

EXHAUST PIPE

PLATE No.	PART No.	DESCRIPTION	QTY.	MODEL	PRICE EACH
—	24020	Pipe, only, left hand	1	88ss, 650ss, Atlas and 650/99	
—	23432	Pipe, only, left hand	1	650/99 and Atlas (U.S.A. only)	
—	24021	Pipe, only, right hand	1	88ss, 650ss, Atlas and 650/99	
—	23433	Pipe, only, right hand	1	650/99 and Atlas (U.S.A. only)	
—	030262	Pipe, only, left hand	1	G15P	
—	030264	Pipe, only, left hand	1	G15CS	
—	030266	Pipe, only, right hand	1	G15P	
—	030268	Pipe, only, right hand	1	G15CS	
A34	18092	Ring, locking exhaust pipe	2	All	
—	T2166	Washer, locking ring	2	All	
—	000363	Bolt, clamping	2	G15CS	
—	000011	Washer, for bolt	4	G15CS	
—	000004	Nut, for bolt	2	G15CS	
—	000368	Bolt, support	2	G15CS	
—	000011	Washer, for bolt	4	G15CS	
—	000004	Nut, for bolt	2	G15CS	
—	028247	Bracket, for silencer	2	G15CS	
—	030449	Clip, exhaust pipe	2	G15CS	

SILENCER

PLATE No.	PART No.	DESCRIPTION	QTY.	MODEL	PRICE EACH
—	23768	Silencer, left hand	1	88ss, 650 and Atlas	
—	23767	Silencer, right hand	1	88ss, 650 and Atlas	
—	22804	Bracket, silencer, left hand	1	88ss, 650 and Atlas	
—	22805	Bracket, silencer, right hand	1	88ss, 650 and Atlas	
—	22475	Bolt, for bracket	4	88ss, 650 and Atlas	
—	18202	Washer, for bolt	8	88ss, 650 and Atlas	
—	16255	Clip, silencer	2	88ss, 650 and Atlas	
—	E3154	Bolt, for clip	2	88ss, 650 and Atlas	
—	E3231	Nut, for clip bolt	2	88ss, 650 and Atlas	
—	029727	Silencer, left hand	1	G15P	
—	029728	Silencer, right hand	1	G15P	

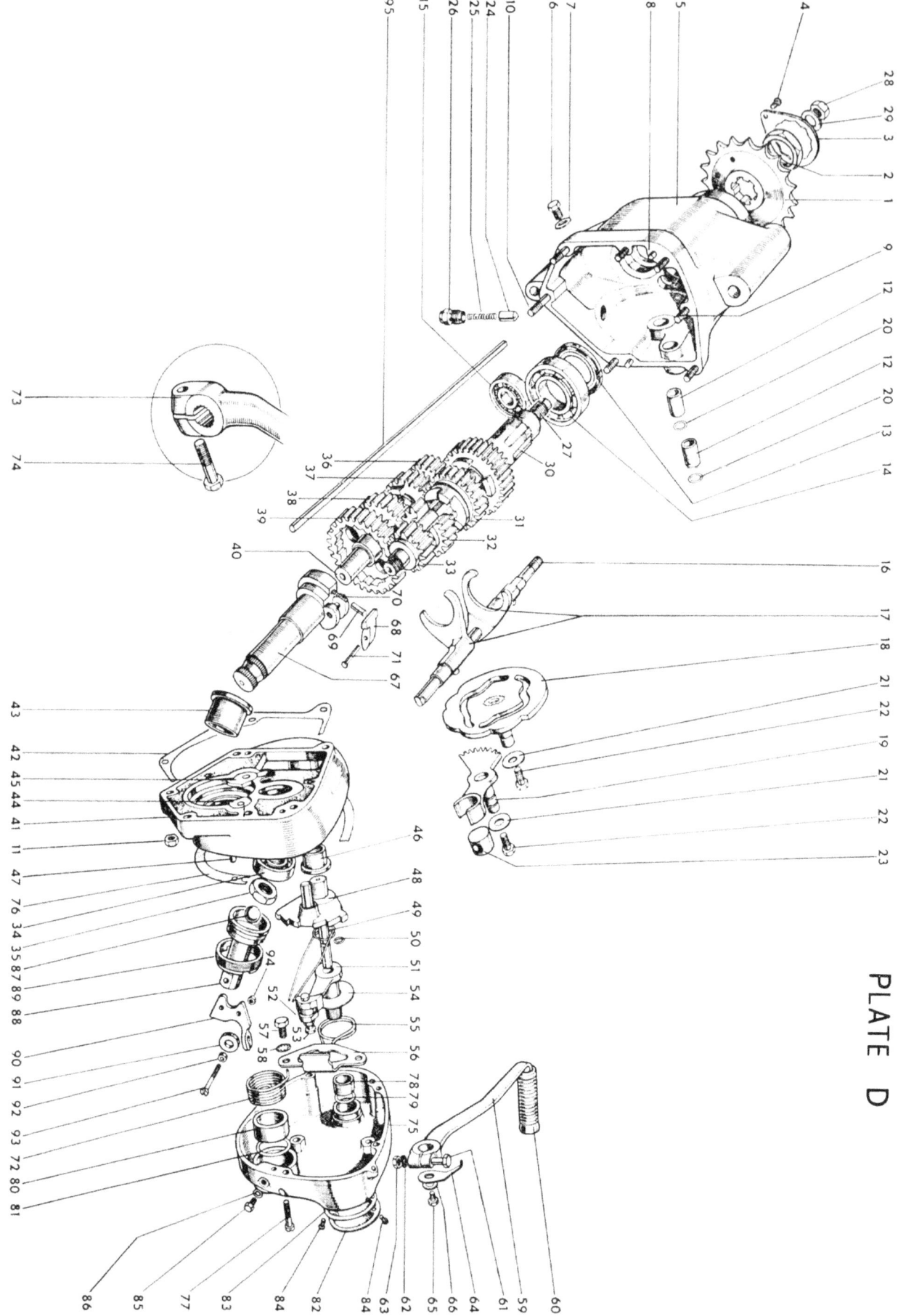

PLATE D

PLATE No.	PART No.	DESCRIPTION	QTY.	MODEL
—	000347	Bolt, clamping silencer	2	G15P
—	024558	Washer, clamping bolt	4	G15P
—	000005	Nut, clamping bolt	2	G15P
—	000367	Bolt, fixing silencer	2	G15P
—	000011	Washer, plain, fixing bolt	2	G15P
—	000192	Washer, spring, fixing bolt	2	G15P
—	000004	Nut, fixing bolt	2	G15P

CHAINS

PLATE No.	PART No.	DESCRIPTION	QTY.	MODEL
—	18265	Chain, front, 75 link, $\frac{1}{2}'' \times .305''$	1	88ss
—	17835	Chain, front, 76 link, $\frac{1}{2}'' \times .305''$	1	650 and Atlas
—	022870	Chain, front, 68 link, $\frac{1}{2}'' \times .305''$	1	All G15
—	18563	Chain, rear, 97 link, $\frac{5}{8}'' \times \frac{1}{4}''$	1	88ss, 650 and Atlas
—	022876	Chain, rear, 97 link, $\frac{5}{8}'' \times \frac{3}{8}''$	1	All G15

GEARBOX FIXING PARTS

PLATE No.	PART No.	DESCRIPTION	QTY.	MODEL
H14	14367	Bolt, fixing, top	1	88ss, 650 and Atlas
H14	030234	Bolt, fixing, top	1	All G15
H15	15170	Nut, top fixing bolt	1	88ss, 650 and Atlas
H15	000002	Nut, top fixing bolt	1	All G15
—	000177	Washer, top fixing bolt	2	All G15
—	030250	Spacer, top fixing bolt	1	All G15
—	16410	Stud, pivot, bottom	1	88ss, 650 and Atlas
—	024276	Stud, pivot, bottom	1	All G15
—	000008	Washer, pivot stud	2	88ss, 650 and Atlas
—	E3227	Nut, pivot stud	2	88ss, 650 and Atlas
—	000002	Nut, pivot stud	2	All G15
H17	16997	Adjuster, gearbox	1	88ss, 650 and Atlas
—	023259	Adjuster, gearbox	1	All G15
H16	E3231	Nut, adjuster	2	88ss, 650 and Atlas
—	000004	Nut, adjuster	1	All G15
—	022504	Crosshead, adjuster	1	All G15
—	000402	Bolt, crosshead	1	All G15
—	000010	Washer, for bolt	1	All G15

GEARBOX SHELL

PLATE No.	PART No.	DESCRIPTION	QTY.	MODEL
D5	040097	Shell, with two bushes	1	88ss, 650 and Atlas
D5	040144	Shell, with two bushes	1	All G15
D41	028534	Case, inner, kickstart	1	All
D75	028535	Cover, outer, kickstart	1	All
D42	040030	Gasket, inner case	1	All
D76	040055	Gasket, outer cover	1	All
D6	040138	Plug, drain	1	All
D7	000200	Washer, for plug	1	All
D85	040137	Plug, oil level	1	All
D86	000203	Washer, for plug	1	All
D82	040053	Cover, inspection	1	All
D83	040057	Gasket, inspection cover	1	All
D84	000450	Screw, for cover	2	All
D8	000577	Dowel, kickstart case	2	All
D9	040064	Stud, kickstart case	2	All
D10	000271	Stud, kickstart case	5	All
D11	000004	Nut, for stud	7	All

PLATE No.	PART No.	DESCRIPTION	QTY.	MODEL	PRICE EACH
D47	000577	Dowel, kickstart cover	2	All	
D77	000482	Screw, kickstart cover	5	All	

SHAFTS AND GEARS

PLATE No.	PART No.	DESCRIPTION	QTY.	MODEL	PRICE EACH
D27	040001	Mainshaft, gearbox	1	All	
D40	040025	Layshaft, gearbox	1	All	
D30	040422	Gear, driving, main, with bushes, 23 teeth	1	All	
D33	040026	Gear, first, mainshaft	1	All	
D32	040418	Gear, second, mainshaft	1	All	
D31	040012	Gear, third, mainshaft	1	All	
D39	040115	Gear, first, layshaft	1	All	
D38	040019	Gear, second, layshaft	1	All	
D37	040420	Gear, third, layshaft	1	All	
D36	040284	Gear, pinion, top, layshaft	1	All	
—	040062	Bush, main driving gear	2	All	
—	040048	Bush, mainshaft second gear	1	All	
—	040047	Bush, layshaft third gear	1	All	
—	040046	Bush, layshaft first gear	1	All	

GEARBOX BEARINGS AND SEALS

PLATE No.	PART No.	DESCRIPTION	QTY.	MODEL	PRICE EACH
D14	040098	Bearing, ball, main gear	1	All	
D34	040099	Bearing, ball, mainshaft in kickstart case	1	All	
D15	040100	Bearing, ball, layshaft in shell	1	All	
D12	040056	Bush, in shell, camplate/quadrant	2	All	
D13	040132	Seal, oil, main gear bearing	1	All	
D20	040129	Seal "O" ring, quadrant and camplate	1	All	
D43	040473	Bush, in kickstart case, for kickstart spindle	1	All	
D46	040061	Bush, in kickstart case, for footchange spindle	1	All	
D80	040472	Bush, in cover, for kickstart spindle	1	All	
D78	040063	Bush, in cover, for footchange spindle	1	All	
D50	040079	Seal, "O" ring, ratchet spindle	1	All	
D79	040006	Seal, "O" ring, footchange spindle	1	All	
D81	040005	Seal, "O" ring, kickstart	1	All	
D26	040036	Bush, camplate plunger	1	All	

GEARBOX SPROCKET

PLATE No.	PART No.	DESCRIPTION	QTY.	MODEL	PRICE EACH
D1	040451	Sprocket, gearbox, 17 teeth, $\frac{5}{8}'' \times \frac{3}{8}''$	1	All G15	
D1	040010	Sprocket, gearbox, 16 teeth, $\frac{5}{8}'' \times \frac{1}{4}''$	1	88ss, 650 and Atlas	
D2	040070	Nut, gearbox sprocket	1	All	
D3	040076	Plate, locking nut	1	All	
D4	000450	Screw, locking plate	1	All	
—	040131	Spacer, for sprocket	1	All	

FOOTCHANGE

PLATE No.	PART No.	DESCRIPTION	QTY.	MODEL	PRICE EACH
D18	040018	Camplate, only	1	All	
D18	040015	Spindle, only	1	All	
D19	040109	Quadrant assembly	1	All	
D21	000174	Washer, for camplate and quadrant spindle	2	All	
D22	040136	Screw, for camplate and quadrant spindle	2	All	

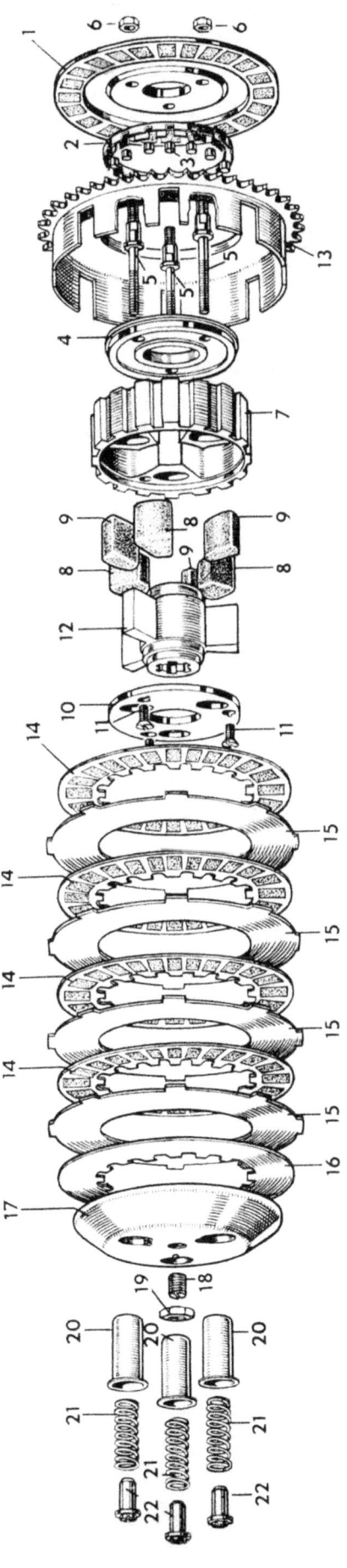

PLATE E

PLATE No.	PART No.	DESCRIPTION	QTY.	MODEL	PRICE EACH
D17	040022	Fork, selector	2	All	
D16	040035	Shaft, selector fork	1	All	
D48	040111	Gear, ratchet assembly	1	All	
D23	040078	Roller, knuckle pin	1	All	
D49	040038	Spring, pawl, gear change	1	All	
—	040110	Carrier, pawl assembly	1	All	
D51	040002	Carrier, pawl, only	1	All	
D53	040067	Pin, pawl carrier	1	All	
D52	040024	Pawl, footchange	1	All	
—	040049	Circlip, for pawl	1	All	
—	040066	Spindle, ratchet	1	All	
D55	040479	Spring, return, gear change	1	All	
D54	040135	Washer, return spring	1	All	
D56	040052	Plate, stop, gear change	1	All	
D57	041400	Screw, stop plate	2	All	
D58	014117	Washer, shakeproof, for screw	2	All	
D59	041311	Pedal, footchange	1	All	
D60	040086	Rubber, footchange pedal	1	All	
D61	040105	Bolt, for pedal	1	All	
D62	045062	Washer, for bolt	1	All	
D63	000005	Nut, for bolt	1	All	
D64	040051	Indicator, gear	1	All	
D65	040137	Screw, gear indicator	1	All	
D66	000012	Washer, indicator screw	1	All	
D24	040034	Plunger, camplate	1	All	
D25	040442	Spring, for plunger	1	All	

CLUTCH

PLATE No.	PART No.	DESCRIPTION	QTY.	MODEL	PRICE EACH
—	040478	Clutch, complete	1	All	
E7	040366	Centre, clutch	1	All	
E1	040584	Plate, back, for clutch	1	All	
E4	040351	Plate, race	1	All	
E2	040367	Cage, roller	1	All	
E3	000075	Roller, clutch	15	All	
E13	040359	Sprocket, clutch	1	All	
E12	043443	Centre, shock absorber	1	All	
E10	043445	Plate, cover, shock absorber centre	1	All	
E11	043446	Screw, cover plate	3	All	
E8	040386	Rubber, large, for centre	3	All	
E9	040387	Rubber, small, for centre	3	All	
E15	043191	Plate, clutch, plain	5	All	
E14	043192	Plate, clutch, friction, double sided	5	All	
E16	043193	Plate, clutch, friction, single sided	1	All	
E17	043362	Plate, pressure, bare	1	All	
E5	043441	Stud, clutch spring	3	All	
E21	040358	Spring, clutch	3	All	
E20	040388	Cup, clutch spring	3	All	
E22	040389	Nut, clutch spring adjustment	3	All	
E6	040356	Nut, clutch stud to centre	3	All	
E18	040360	Adjuster, in pressure plate	1	All	
E19	040376	Nut, locking adjuster	1	All	
D28	040373	Nut, retaining clutch	1	All	
D29	040374	Washer lock, clutch nut	1	All	

PLATE No.	PART No.	DESCRIPTION	QTY.	MODEL	PRICE EACH
		CLUTCH OPERATING PARTS			
D95	040607	Rod, clutch	1	88ss, 650 and Atlas	
D95	040084	Rod, clutch	1	All G15	
D90	040029	Lever, operating	1	All	
D88	040059	Body, operating lever	1	All	
D89	040003	Ring, locking body	1	All	
D87	040031	Ball, operating	1	All	
D91	040060	Roller, operating	1	All	
D92	040065	Sleeve, for roller	1	All	
D93	000457	Screw, for roller	1	All	
D94	011846	Nut, for screw	1	All	
		KICKSTART			
D67	040477	Axle, with bush	1	All	
—	040146	Bush, for axle	1	All	
D68	040017	Pawl, for axle	1	All	
D71	040033	Pin, for pawl	1	All	
D70	040044	Spring for pawl	1	All	
D69	040069	Plunger, for pawl	1	All	
D45	040042	Stop, for axle	1	All	
D44	040071	Cam, for axle	1	All	
—	040041	Rivet, for axle cam	1	All	
—	040474	Rivet, for axle stop	1	All	
D35	040023	Nut, mainshaft, kickstart end	1	All	
D73	040101	Crank, kickstart, with integral pin (Home)	1	88ss and 650ss	
—	040434	Crank, kickstart (folding type) assembly (Home)	1	650/99 and Atlas	
—	040434	Crank, kickstart (folding type) assembly (Export)	1	All	
—	040429	Crank, kickstart only (folding type)	1	All	
—	040431	Pin, pedal, for folding crank	1	All	
—	040432	Nut, domed, for pedal pin	1	All	
—	040433	Washer, spring, for pedal pin	1	All	
—	000010	Washer, plain, for pedal pin	1	All	
D74	040102	Bolt, clamping crank to axle	1	All	
D72	040475	Spring, return, kickstart	1	All	
		FRAME			
H54	24990	Frame, only	1	88ss, 650ss, 650/99 and Atlas	
—	18940	Transfer, registered design	1	88ss, 650ss, 650/99 and Atlas	
H62	20126	Cover, gusset plate	1	88ss, 650ss, 650/99 and Atlas	
H63	15844	Tube assembly, rear engine fixing	1	88ss, 650ss, 650/99 and Atlas	
H64	15893	Rod, engine tube assembly	1	88ss, 650ss, 650/99 and Atlas	
H66	E5377	Washer, for rod	2	88ss, 650ss, 650/99 and Atlas	
H65	13459	Nut, for rod	2	88ss, 650ss, 650/99 and Atlas	
H55	21099	Tube, distance, top, rear	1	88ss, 650ss, 650/99 and Atlas	

PLATE No.	PART No.	DESCRIPTION	QTY.	MODEL	PRICE EACH
H56	21134	Stud, distance tube	1	88ss, 650ss, 650/99 and Atlas	
H57	000010	Washer, for stud	4	88ss, 650ss, 650/99 and Atlas	
H58	E3224	Nut, for stud	2	88ss, 650ss, 650/99 and Atlas	
—	030097	Race, frame head lug	2	88ss, 650ss, 650/99 and Atlas	
—	000021	Ball, steering	36	88ss, 650ss, 650/99 and Atlas	
—	17429	Washer, head lug bearing	2	88ss, 650ss, 650/99 and Atlas	
—	030211	Frame, front only	1	All G15	
—	000051	Nipple, grease	1	All G15	
—	023250	Stud, seat lug	1	All G15	
—	016873	Washer, seat lug stud	2	All G15	
—	000292	Nut, seat lug stud	2	All G15	
—	000306	Stud, rear engine lug, top and bottom	2	All G15	
—	000004	Nut, engine lug stud	4	All G15	
—	026161	Stud, rail junction lug	1	All G15	
—	000010	Washer, junction stud	2	All G15	
—	000003	Nut, junction stud	2	All G15	
—	030315	Loop, rear frame	1	All G15	
—	022248	Stud, frame loop, bottom	1	All G15	
—	029833	Spacer, frame loop stud	1	All G15	
—	000009	Washer, loop stud	1	All G15	
—	000002	Nut, loop stud	1	All G15	
		SWINGING ARM			
H67	22586	Arm, swinging, only	1	88ss, 650ss, 650/99 and Atlas	
H68	20083	Bearing, "Silent Bloc"	2	88ss, 650ss, 650/99 and Atlas	
H70	15894	Rod, swinging arm	1	88ss, 650ss, 650/99 and Atlas	
H72	000008	Washer, for rod	2	88ss, 650ss, 650/99 and Atlas	
H71	15356	Nut, for rod	2	88ss, 650ss, 650/99 and Atlas	
—	19264	Adjuster, rear wheel	2	88ss, 650ss, 650/99 and Atlas	
—	E3229	Nut, wheel adjuster	4	88ss, 650ss, 650/99 and Atlas	
H69	18578	Tube, bearing spacer	2	88ss, 650ss, 650/99 and Atlas	
—	030001	Arm, swinging, only	1	All G15	
—	010096	Cap, bearing end, left hand	1	All G15	
—	010095	Cap, bearing end, right hand	1	All G15	
—	000485	Plug, oil screw	1	All G15	
—	000203	Washer, for plug	1	All G15	
—	010098	Gasket, bearing end cap	2	All G15	
—	010094	Bearing, spoke	1	All G15	
—	012472	Nipple, bearing spoke	1	All G15	
—	010093	Washer, felt	2	All G15	
—	010116	Tube, bearing	1	All G15	

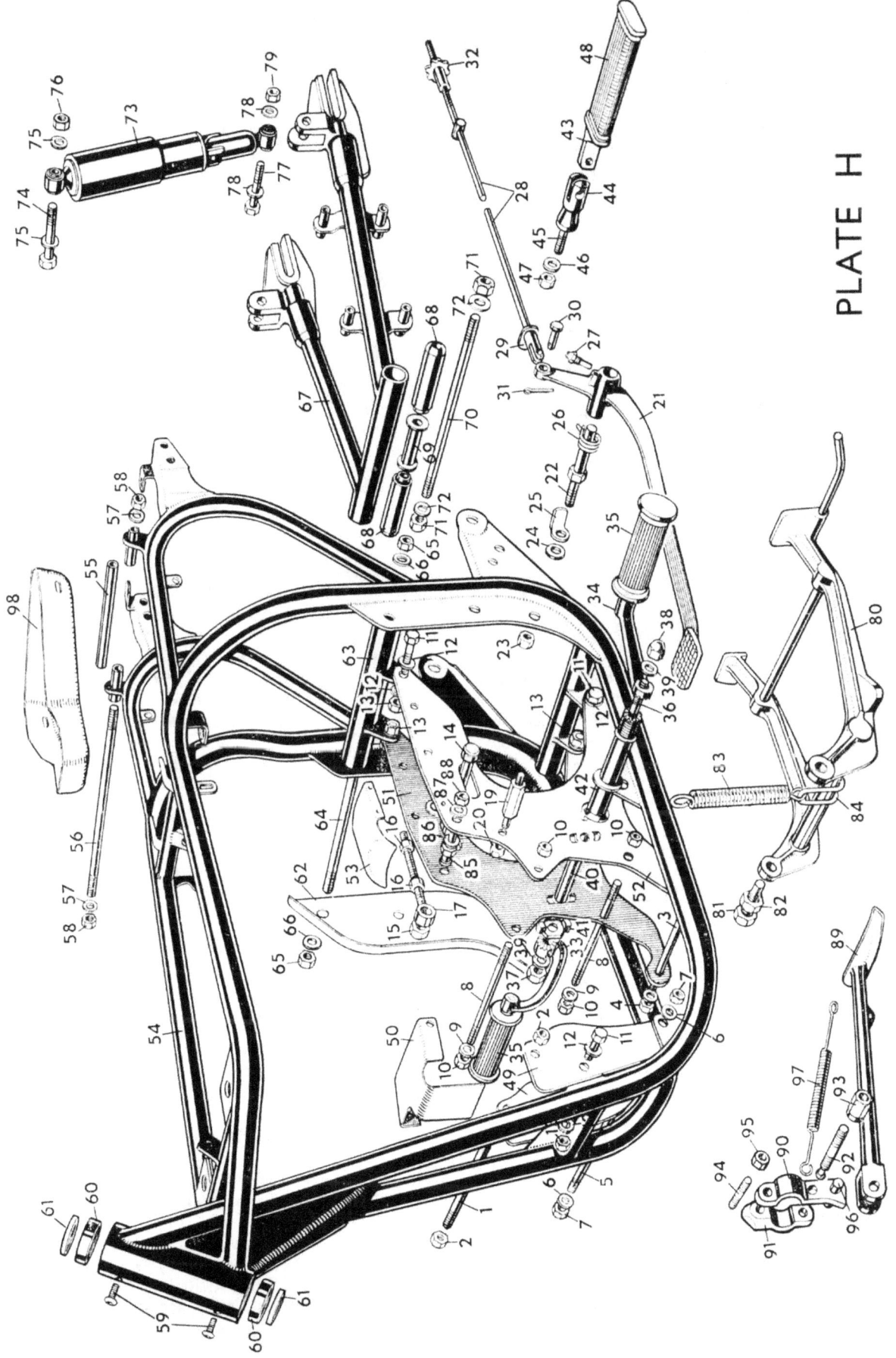

PLATE H

PLATE No.	PART No.	DESCRIPTION	QTY.	MODEL	PRICE EACH
—	022879	Pin, cotter, for tube	1	All G15	
—	014117	Washer, shakeproof, for cotter pin	1	All G15	
—	000004	Nut, cotter pin	1	All G15	
—	014746	Sleeve, assembly, bushed	2	All G15	
—	21843	Adjuster, rear wheel	2	All G15	
—	029245	Nut, for adjuster	2	All G15	

REAR SUSPENSION UNIT

PLATE No.	PART No.	DESCRIPTION	QTY.	MODEL	PRICE EACH
H73	24036	Unit, rear suspension	2	88ss, 650ss, 650/99 and Atlas	
—	043312	Spring, rear suspension, (solo)	2	88ss, 650ss, 650/99 and Atlas	
—	023372	Spring, rear suspension, (sidecar)	2	88ss, 650ss, 650/99 and Atlas	
H74	22674	Bolt, top, rear suspension	2	88ss, 650ss, 650/99 and Atlas	
H75	000010	Washer, top bolt	4	88ss, 650ss, 650/99 and Atlas	
H76	E3224	Nut, top bolt	2	88ss, 650ss, 650/99 and Atlas	
H77	22655	Bolt, bottom, rear suspension	2	88ss, 650ss, 650/99 and Atlas	
H78	11796	Washer, bottom bolt	4	88ss, 650ss, 650/99 and Atlas	
H79	E3223	Nut, bottom bolt	2	88ss, 650ss, 650/99 and Atlas	
H73	029612	Unit, rear suspension	2	All G15P only	
H73	030248	Unit, rear suspension	2	G15CS	
—	029786	Spring, rear suspension (solo)	2	All G15P only	
—	029787	Spring, rear suspension (sidecar)	2	All G15P only	
H74	018648	Bolt, top, rear suspension	2	All G15P only	
H74	012263	Bolt, top, rear suspension	2	G15CS only	
H75	000010	Washer, top bolt	2	All G15	
—	016712	Nut, top bolt	2	All G15P only	
H77	029627	Bolt, bottom, rear suspension	2	All G15	
H78	000010	Washer, bottom bolt	4	All G15	
H79	000003	Nut, bottom bolt	2	All G15	
—	22636	Washer, bottom bolt (outer)	2	G15CS only	

CENTRE STAND

PLATE No.	PART No.	DESCRIPTION	QTY.	MODEL	PRICE EACH
H80	17175	Stand, assembled	1	88ss and 650ss	
H80	23882	Stand, assembled	1	650/99 and Atlas	
H81	16763	Bolt, centre stand	2	88ss, 650ss, 650/99 and Atlas	
H82	16764	Nut, centre stand bolt	2	88ss, 650ss, 650/99 and Atlas	
H83	24074	Spring, for stand	1	88ss, 650ss, 650/99 and Atlas	
H84	24078	Clip, stand spring	1	88ss, 650ss, 650/99 and Atlas	
—	17591	Stop, rubber, for stand	1	88ss, 650ss, 650/99 and Atlas	
—	E5278	Pin, rubber, stop	1	88ss, 650ss, 650/99 and Atlas	

PLATE No.	PART No.	DESCRIPTION	QTY.	MODEL	PRICE EACH
H85	24151	Stud, anchor	1	88ss, 650ss, 650/99 and Atlas	
H86	000011	Washer, for stud	1	88ss, 650ss, 650/99 and Atlas	
H87	E5456	Washer, for stud	1	88ss, 650ss, 650/99 and Atlas	
H88	E3223	Nut, for stud	1	88ss, 650ss, 650/99 and Atlas	
—	029490	Stand, assembled	1	All G15P	
—	022620	Stand, assembled	1	G15CS only	
—	014629	Rod, centre stand	1	All G15	
—	000009	Washer, for rod	2	All G15	
—	000002	Nut, for rod	2	All G15	
—	014626	Bush, centre stand	2	All G15	
—	014630	Spacer, centre stand	1	All G15	
—	014627	Spring, return	1	All G15	
—	029488	Spring, stop	1	All G15	
—	012565	Bolt, stop spring	2	All G15	
—	000039	Washer, for Bolt	2	All G15	

PROP STAND

PLATE No.	PART No.	DESCRIPTION	QTY.	MODEL	PRICE EACH
H89	18750	Leg, prop stand	1	88ss and 650ss	
H89	23877	Leg, prop stand	1	650/99 and Atlas	
H90	25175	Lug, prop stand	1	88ss, 650ss, 650/99 and Atlas	
H91	25176	Lug, back, prop stand	1	88ss, 650ss, 650/99 and Atlas	
H92	25179	Stud, for lug and spring	1	88ss, 650ss, 650/99 and Atlas	
H93	11824	Nut, for stud	1	88ss, 650ss, 650/99 and Atlas	
H94	16374	Stud, for lug	1	88ss, 650ss, 650/99 and Atlas	
H95	E3224	Nut, for stud	1	88ss, 650ss, 650/99 and Atlas	
H96	16174	Pin, fulcrum	1	88ss, 650ss, 650/99 and Atlas	
H97	16176	Spring, return	1	88ss, 650ss, 650/99 and Atlas	
H89	014719	Leg, prop stand	1	All G15	
—	014713	Bolt, prop stand	1	All G15	
—	014139	Nut, for bolt	1	All G15	
—	000049	Pin, split, for bolt	1	All G15	
—	021261	Spring, return	1	All G15	

FOOTRESTS

PLATE No.	PART No.	DESCRIPTION	QTY.	MODEL	PRICE EACH
H34	18149A	Hanger, assembled, left hand	1	88ss, 650ss, 650/99 and Atlas	
H33	18772	Hanger, assembled, right hand	1	88ss, 650ss, 650/99 and Atlas	
H36	14366	Rod, footrest	1	88ss, 650ss, 650/99 and Atlas	
H40	15641	Spacer, for rod	1	88ss, 650ss, 650/99 and Atlas	

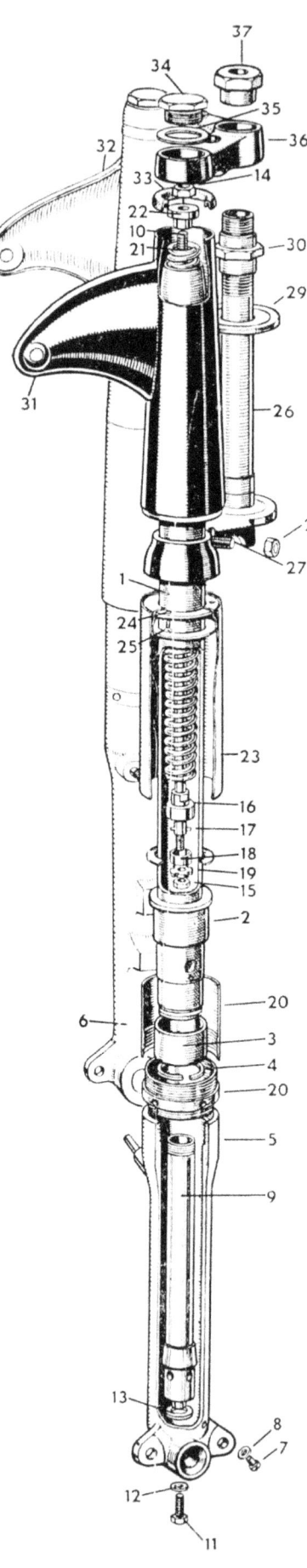

PLATE C

PLATE No.	PART No.	DESCRIPTION	QTY.	MODEL	PRICE EACH
H39	E5377	Washer, for rod	2	88ss, 650ss, 650/99 and Atlas	
H38	E3220	Nut, domed, for rod	1	88ss, 650ss, 650/99 and Atlas	
H37	E3238	Nut, for rod	1	88ss, 650ss, 650/99 and Atlas	
H41	18268	End, serrated (right hand, on engine plate)	1	88ss, 650ss, 650/99 and Atlas	
—	018601	Arm, footrest, left and right hand ...	2	All G15	
—	018604	Rod, footrest	1	All G15	
—	000009	Washer, for rod	2	All G15	
—	000002	Nut, for rod	2	All G15	
—	030236	Spacer, outer, left hand	1	All G15	
—	010911	Spacer, outer, right hand	1	All G15	
—	030237	Spacer (engine plates)	1	All G15	
H35	19983	Rubber, footrest	2	All	

FRONT FORKS

PLATE No.	PART No.	DESCRIPTION	QTY.	MODEL	PRICE EACH
—	25258	Forks, complete	1	88ss, 650ss, 650/99 and Atlas	
—	25291	Forks, complete	1	All G15P	
—	25259	Forks, complete	1	G15CS only	
C5	030031	Slider, fork, left hand	1	All	
C6	030030	Slider, fork, right hand	1	All	
C7	000485	Plug, drain, slider	2	All	
C8	000203	Washer, for plug	2	All	
—	16664	Stud, pinch, for slider	1	All	
—	E3231	Nut, pinch stud	1	All	
C9	20253	Tube, damper	2	All except G15CS	
C9	030440	Tube, damper	2	G15CS	
C10	15801	Rod, damper	2	All except G15CS	
C10	017357	Rod, damper	2	G15CS	
C11	14275	Bolt, damper tube	2	All	
C12	T1009	Washer, damper tube	2	All	
C13	T814	Washer, damper tube	2	All	
C17	14119	Peg, locating piston	2	All except G15CS	
C17	010721	Peg, locating piston	2	G15CS	
C18	14118B	Cup, valve	2	All except G15CS	
C18	016304	Cup, valve	2	G15CS	
C19	030584	Ring, slotted, valve cup	2	All except G15CS	
—	010719	Seat, damper valve	2	G15CS	
C15	E3231	Nut, bottom, damper rod	2	All except G15CS	
C15	000005	Nut, bottom, damper rod	2	G15CS	
C16	14605	Cap, damper tube	2	All except G15CS	
—	016072	Sleeve, damper plunger	2	G15CS	
—	016339	Clip, plunger sleeve	2	G15CS	
C1	18482	Tube, main	2	88ss, 650ss, 650/99 and Atlas	
C1	030036	Tube, main	2	All G15P	
C1	030457	Tube, main	2	G15CS	
C34	16998	Bolt, top, fork inner tube	2	All except G15CS	
C34	030446	Bolt, top, fork inner tube	2	G15CS	
C35	T320	Washer, top bolt	2	All except G15CS	
C3	T1048	Bush, main tube	2	All	
C4	14298	Circlip, main tube bush	2	All except G15CS	

PLATE No.	PART No.	DESCRIPTION	QTY.	MODEL	PRICE EACH
C2	T1055	Bush, end fork	2	All	
—	030456	Nut, bush retaining	2	G15CS	
—	T1090	Washer, bush retaining nut	2	G15CS	
—	17713	Seal, oil	2	All	
—	T1049	Washer, locking, oil seal	2	All	
C20	030454	Extension, slider	2	88ss, 650ss, 650/99 and Atlas	
C20	030453	Extension, slider	2	All G15	
C21	18813	Spring, main	2	All except G15CS	
C21	021789	Spring, main	2	G15CS	
C22	25003	Bush, locating fork spring	2	All	
C23	19307	Tube, cover top, main spring	2	88ss, 650ss, 650/99 and Atlas	
C23	030041	Tube, cover, top, main spring	2	All G15	
—	021785	Washer, cover tube (leather)	2	G15CS	
C24	T831	Washer, top cover tube	2	All	
C25	T702	Screw, cover tube washer	6	All	
C26	030026	Crown and column assembly	1	All	
C27	16164	Stud, pinch, fork crown	2	All	
C28	16187	Nut, pinch stud	2	All	
C29	15628	Cover, top bearing	1	All	
C30	15630	Nut, bottom, steering column	1	All	
C31	24994	Tube, top cover, left hand	1	All	
C32	24995	Tube, top cover, right hand	1	All	
—	25117	Transfer, "Roadholder"	2	88ss, 650ss, 650/99 and Atlas	
C33	T597	Washer, rubber, top cover tube	2	All	
C36	030027	Clip, head	1	All	
—	15627	Washer, column tube	1	All	
C37	19490	Nut, column tube	1	All	
—	030517	Transfer (Made in England)	1	All	
—	030175	Lock, steering, with two keys	1	All	
—	030098	Race, fork stem	2	All	
—	19021A	Clip, handlebar	2	All	
—	19437	Screw, handlebar clip	4	All	

HANDLEBAR

PLATE No.	PART No.	DESCRIPTION	QTY.	MODEL	PRICE EACH
—	030408	Handlebar, bare	1	88ss, 650ss and G15P	
—	22460	Handlebar, bare	1	650/99 and Atlas	
—	030398	Handlebar, bare	1	G15CS	

FRONT MUDGUARD

PLATE No.	PART No.	DESCRIPTION	QTY.	MODEL	PRICE EACH
—	24985D	Mudguard, front, bare	1	88ss and 650ss	
—	24986A	Mudguard, front, bare	1	650/99 and Atlas	
—	030101	Mudguard, front, bare (Home)	1	G15P	
—	030060	Mudguard, front, bare (Export)	1	G15P	
—	030252	Mudguard, front, bare	1	G15CS	
—	19291	Stay, front mudguard	4	88ss and 650ss	
—	19291A	Stay, front mudguard (chrome)	4	650/99 and Atlas	
—	030360	Stay, front mudguard, front position	1	15CS	
—	029564	Stay, front mudguard, rear pos. (Home)	1	G15P	
—	030065	Stay, front mudguard, rear pos. (Export)	1	G15P	
—	030362	Stay, front mudguard, rear position	1	G15CS	

PLATE No.	PART No.	DESCRIPTION	QTY.	MODEL	PRICE EACH
—	24984	Bridge, front mudguard	1	88ss, 650ss, 650/99 and Atlas	
—	030093	Bridge, front mudguard (Home)	1	G15P	
—	14481	Bolt, mudguard stay	4	88ss, 650ss, 650/99 and Atlas	
—	18711	Washer, stay bolt	4	88ss, 650ss, 650/99 and Atlas	
—	E5379	Washer, stay bolt	4	88ss, 650ss, 650/99 and Atlas	
—	13192	Washer, packing, stay bolt	4	88ss, 650ss, 650/99 and Atlas	
—	E3229	Nut, stay bolt	4	88ss, 650ss, 650/99 and Atlas	
—	E3798	Bolt, stay to fork end	4	88ss, 650ss, 650/99 and Atlas	
—	11796	Washer, for end bolt	4	88ss, 650ss, 650/99 and Atlas	
—	18709	Bolt, centre stay	2	88ss, 650ss, 650/99 and Atlas	
—	18711	Washer, centre stay bolt	2	88ss, 650ss, 650/99 and Atlas	
—	E5379	Washer, centre stay bolt	2	88ss, 650ss, 650/99 and Atlas	
—	11796	Washer, centre stay bolt	2	88ss, 650ss, 650/99 and Atlas	
—	E3229	Nut, centre stay bolt	2	88ss, 650ss, 650/99 and Atlas	
—	T1085	Stud, stay to fork end	4	88ss, 650ss, 650/99 and Atlas	
—	E5379	Washer, for stud	4	88ss, 650ss, 650/99 and Atlas	
—	E3229	Nut, for stud	4	88ss, 650ss, 650/99 and Atlas	
—	18854	Bolt, stay to slider	2	All G15P	
—	18854	Bolt, stay to slider	4	G15CS	
—	11796	Washer, for Bolt	2	All G15P	
—	11796	Washer, for bolt	4	G15CS	
—	000070	Bolt, stay to mudguard	2	All G15P	
—	000070	Bolt, stay to mudguard	4	G15CS	
—	000012	Washer, for bolt, plain	2	All G15P	
—	000012	Washer, for bolt, plain	4	G15CS	
—	000191	Washer, for bolt, spring	2	All G15P	
—	000191	Washer, for bolt, spring	4	G15CS	
—	000005	Nut, for bolt	2	All G15P	
—	000005	Nut, for bolt	4	G15CS	
—	022632	Bolt, mudguard bridge (Home)	2	G15P	
—	022632	Bolt, mudguard bridge (Export)	8	G15P	
—	021579	Washer, for bolt (Home)	2	G15P	
—	021579	Washer, for bolt (Export)	8	G15P	
—	000005	Nut, for bolt (Home)	2	G15P	
—	000005	Nut, for bolt (Export)	8	G15P	
—	T1085	Stud, bridge to slider	4	All G15	
—	E5379	Washer, for stud	4	All G15	
—	E3229	Nut, for stud	4	All G15	

PLATE No.	PART No.	DESCRIPTION	QTY.	MODEL	PRICE EACH
		REAR NUMBER PLATE			
—	029431	Plate, assembled	1	88ss, 650ss, G15P (Home)	
—	029427	Plate, assembled	1	650/99, Atlas, G15P (Export) & G15CS	
—	000342	Bolt, rear number plate	1	All	
—	000172	Washer, for bolt	1	All	
—	014577	Bolt, number plate bracket	2	All	
—	000172	Washer, for bolt	2	All	
—	19429	Grommet for cable	2	88ss, 650ss, 650/99 and Atlas	
		FRONT NUMBER PLATE			
—	011835	Plate number	1	88ss and 650ss	
—	18755	Beading, for plate	1	88ss and 650ss	
—	011836	Stud, front plate	2	88ss and 650ss	
—	000012	Washer, for stud	2	88ss and 650ss	
—	000005	Nut, for stud	2	88ss and 650ss	
—	000861	Screw, fixing number plate	2	88ss and 650ss	
		REAR MUDGUARD			
—	25060B	Mudguard, rear	1	88ss, 650ss, 650/99 and Atlas	
—	029522	Mudguard, rear	1	G15P "M"	
—	029523	Mudguard, rear	1	G15P "N"	
—	029810	Mudguard, rear	1	G15CS "M", G15CS "N"	
—	12342	Bolt, mudguard bottom	2	88ss, 650ss, 650/99 and Atlas	
—	E5379	Washer, for bolt	4	88ss, 650ss, 650/99 and Atlas	
—	E3229	Nut, for bolt	2	88ss, 650ss, 650/99 and Atlas	
—	029533	Bracket, rear mudguard	2	G15P	
—	022250	Bracket, rear mudguard	2	G15CS	
—	000275	Stud, mudguard bracket	1	G15CS	
—	000011	Washer, bracket stud	2	G15CS	
—	000004	Nut, bracket stud	2	G15CS	
—	000070	Bolt, bracket to mudguard	2	All G15	
—	000012	Washer, small, for bolt	2	All G15	
—	000172	Washer, large, for bolt	2	All G15	
—	000005	Nut, for bolt	2	All G15	
—	22673	Stud, support, mudguard	2	88ss, 650ss, 650/99 and Atlas	
—	22635	Spacer, support stud	4	88ss, 650ss, 650/99 and Atlas	
—	22636	Washer, for spacer	2	88ss, 650ss, 650/99 and Atlas	
—	000010	Washer, for Stud	4	88ss, 650ss, 650/99 and Atlas	
—	E3224	Nut, for stud	4	88ss, 650ss, 650/99 and Atlas	
—	22634	Handle, lifting, left hand	1	88ss and 650ss	
—	22634A	Handle, lifting, left hand	1	650/99 and Atlas	
—	22633	Handle, lifting, right hand	1	88ss and 650ss	

PLATE No.	PART No.	DESCRIPTION	QTY.	MODEL	PRICE EACH
—	22633A	Handle, lifting, right hand	1	650/99 and Atlas	
—	029440	Tube, support, left hand	1	G15P	
—	029441	Tube, support, right hand	1	G15P	
—	029446	Spacer, support tube	2	G15P	
—	14481	Bolt, fixing, lifting handle	4	88ss, 650ss, 650/99 and Atlas	
—	E5379	Washer, for bolt	8	88ss, 650ss, 650/99 and Atlas	
—	E3229	Nut, for bolt	4	88ss, 650ss, 650/99 and Atlas	
—	030396	Spacer, support tube	2	G15CS	
—	025117	Bolt, support tube	2	G15P	
—	022549	Washer, support tube, plain	2	G15P	
—	000191	Washer, support tube, spring	2	G15P	
—	000005	Nut, support tube bolt	2	G15P	
—	030394	Bridge, rear mudguard	2	G15CS	
—	000070	Bolt, front, mudguard bridge	2	G15CS	
—	000012	Washer, front bolt	4	G15CS	
—	000005	Nut, front bolt	2	G15CS	
—	022632	Screw, rear mudguard bridge	2	G15CS	
—	000012	Washer, for screw	2	G15CS	
—	000005	Nut, for screw	2	G15CS	
—	030397	Stay, rear mudguard support	2	G15CS	
—	000010	Washer, for stay bolt	2	G15CS	
—	014807	Bolt, for stay	2	G15CS	
—	029814	Clamp, rear mudguard	1	G15CS	
—	029849	Packing, for clamp	1	G15CS	
—	000070	Bolt, for clamp	2	G15CS	
—	000012	Washer, for clamp bolt	2	G15CS	
—	000005	Nut, for clamp bolt	2	G15CS	
—	24671	Transfer, rear mudguard	1	88ss	
—	24672	Transfer, rear mudguard	1	650ss	
—	009189	Transfer, rear mudguard	1	G15P "M" and G15CS "M"	

HANDLEBAR CONTROLS

Brake and Air Lever

PLATE No.	PART No.	DESCRIPTION	QTY.	MODEL	PRICE EACH
—	026320	Lever, assembly, front brake and air	1	All except G15P	
—	026238	Lever, assembly, front brake and air	1	G15P	
—	022715	Lever, only, front brake	1	All except G15P	
—	18-535	Lever, only, front brake	1	G15P	
—	18-812	Body, for brake lever	1	All except G15P	
—	18-816	Body, for brake lever	1	G15P	
—	18-087	Screw, pivot, for lever	1	All	
—	18-053	Nut, pivot screw	1	All	
—	12-556	Lever, only, air	1	All	
—	12-594	Body, air lever	1	All	
—	12-607	Bolt, central, air lever	1	All	
—	12-606	Cap, air lever	1	All	
—	12-033	Washer, spring, air lever	1	All	
—	11-013	Screw, clamping body	1	All	
—	11-014	Screw, clamping body	1	All	
—	023707	Trunnion, brake lever	1	All	

PLATE No.	PART No.	DESCRIPTION	QTY.	MODEL	PRICE EACH
		Clutch Lever			
—	026258	Lever, clutch assembly	1	All except G15P	
—	026232	Lever, clutch assembly	1	G15P	
—	022714	Lever, only	1	All except G15P	
—	18-528	Lever, only	1	G15P	
—	18-814	Body, only	1	All	
—	18-087	Screw, pivot, for lever	1	All	
—	18-053	Nut, pivot screw	1	All	
—	12-595	Clamp, lever body	1	All	
—	11-014	Screw, body clamp	2	All	
—	023707	Trunnion, clutch lever	1	All	
		Twist Grip			
—	016658	Twist grip, assembled	1	All	
—	16-060	Body, top half	1	All	
—	16-061	Body, bottom half	1	All	
—	16-091	Rotor, only	1	All	
—	11-013	Screw, long, clamping halves	1	All	
—	11-014	Screw, short, clamping halves	1	All	
—	16-008	Spring, friction	1	All	
—	16-009	Screw, friction spring	1	All	
—	16-010	Nut, lock, for screw	1	All	
—	026476	Abutment, slotted	1	All	
—	16-070	Grip, plastic, only	1	All	
—	16-069	Grip, dummy, plastic (023740)	1	All	
		BRAKE CABLE			
—	24987	Cable, assembled, front brake	1	88ss, 650ss and G15P (Home)	
—	25038	Cable, assembled, front brake	1	650/99, Atlas, G15P (Export) & G15CS	
—	25583	Adjuster, brake cable	1	All	
—	25584	Nut, lock, for adjuster	1	All	
—	14759	Clip, "U", for cable	1	All	
—	042764	Plastic sleeve, $4\frac{3}{8}''$	1	All	
		CLUTCH CABLE			
—	25035	Cable, assembled, clutch	1	88ss and 650ss	
—	25036	Cable, assembled, clutch	1	650/99 and Atlas	
—	026250	Cable, assembled, clutch	1	G15P (Home)	
—	023753	Cable, assembled, clutch	1	G15P (Export) and G15CS	
—	042856	Adjuster, clutch cable	1	All	
—	011373	Nut, lock, for adjuster	1	All	
		AIR CABLE			
—	25033	Cable, assembled, air (carburetter end)	2	All	
—	25008	Cable, assembled, air (handlebar end)	1	88ss, 650ss and G15P (Home)	
—	028239	Cable, assembled, air (handlebar end)	1	G15P (Export), G15CS, 650/99 and Atlas	
—	019824	Box, junction, for cable	1	All	

PLATE No.	PART No.	DESCRIPTION	QTY.	MODEL	PRICE EACH
—	018956	Adjuster, midway, for cable	1	All	

THROTTLE CABLE

PLATE No.	PART No.	DESCRIPTION	QTY.	MODEL	PRICE EACH
—	028238	Cable, assembled, throttle (carburetter end)	2	All	
—	25008	Cable, assembled, throttle (handlebar end)	1	88ss, 650ss and G15P (Home)	
—	028239	Cable, assembled, throttle (handlebar end)	1	650/99, Atlas, G15P (Export) and G15CS	
—	019824	Box, junction, for cable	1	All	
—	018956	Adjuster, midway, for cable	1	All	

OIL PIPES

PLATE No.	PART No.	DESCRIPTION	QTY.	MODEL	PRICE EACH
—	19457	Junction block and oil pipes, assembled	1	88ss, 650ss, 650/99 and Atlas	
—	030300	Junction block and oil pipes, assembled	1	All G15	
—	T2100	Gasket, junction block	1	All	
—	E5377	Washer, junction block stud	1	88ss, 650ss, 650/99 and Atlas	
—	T2101	Nut, for stud	1	88ss, 650ss, 650/99 and Atlas	
—	030448	Bolt, junction block	1	All G15	
—	19452	Pipe, oil feed, and return	2	88ss, 650ss, 650/99 and Atlas	
—	029845	Pipe, oil feed, engine end	1	All G15	
—	000950	Hose, oil feed pipe, $11\frac{5}{8}''$	1	All G15	
—	023376	Ferrule, for hose	2	All G15	
—	000950	Hose, oil return, 11″	1	All G15	
—	023376	Ferrule, for hose	2	All G15	
—	000951	Sleeve, plastic, for oil pipes, 5″	1	All G15	

TWIN SEAT AND SINGLE SEAT

PLATE No.	PART No.	DESCRIPTION	QTY.	MODEL	PRICE EACH
—	23926	Twin seat, only	1	88ss, 650ss, 650/99 and Atlas	
—	029449	Twin seat, only	1	G15CS	
—	029826	Seat, single	1	G15P	
—	029858	Bracket, single seat	2	G15P	
—	000070	Bolt, for bracket	2	G15P	
—	000012	Washer, bracket bolt	2	G15P	
—	21851	Bush, rubber, for seat	2	88ss, 650ss, 650/99 and Atlas	
—	21852	Button, rubber, for seat	2	88ss, 650ss, 650/99 and Atlas	
—	23151	Washer, rubber, locating peg	A/R	88ss, 650ss, 650/99 and Atlas	
—	23151A	Washer, rubber, locating peg	A/R	88ss, 650ss, 650/99 and Atlas	
—	23265	Fastener, Dzus	1	88ss, 650ss, 650/99 and Atlas	
—	23264	Grommet, for fastener	1	88ss, 650ss, 650/99 and Atlas	

PLATE No.	PART No.	DESCRIPTION	QTY.	MODEL
—	23153	Washer, rubber, for fastener	1	88ss, 650ss, 650/99 and Atlas
—	023251	Screw, fixing seat, front	2	15CS
—	000011	Washer, for screw	2	15CS
—	022083	Nut, for screw	2	15CS

PETROL TANK

PLATE No.	PART No.	DESCRIPTION	QTY.	MODEL
—	22630A	Tank, bare	1	88ss, 650ss, 650/99 and Atlas
—	029655	Tank, bare	1	G15P "M"
—	030310	Tank, bare	1	G15P "N"
—	030365	Tank, bare	1	G15CS "M"
—	030368	Tank, bare	1	G15CS "N"
—	22714	Strip, styling, left hand	1	88ss, 650ss, 650/99 and Atlas
—	22713	Strip, styling, right hand	1	88ss, 650ss, 650/99 and Atlas
—	22755	Screw, fixing strip	6	88ss, 650ss, 650/99 and Atlas
—	028241	Motif, left hand	1	G15P "M"
—	028242	Motif, right hand	1	G15P "M"
—	027026	Motif, left hand and right hand	2	G15CS "M"
—	18486	Transfer, left hand and right hand	2	G15CS "N"
—	027027	Seating, for motif	2	G15CS "M"
—	028441	Screw, for motif, front	2	G15P "M"
—	028452	Screw, for motif, rear	2	G15P "M"
—	000153	Screw, for motif	4	G15CS "M"
—	22722	Knee grip, left hand	1	88ss, 650ss, 650/99 and Atlas
—	042889	Knee grip, left hand	1	G15P
—	22721	Knee grip, right hand	1	88ss, 650ss, 650/99 and Atlas
—	042890	Knee grip, right hand	1	G15P
—	013325	Cap, filler	1	All except G15CS
—	014034	Cap, filler	1	G15CS
—	013936	Pin, split, filler cap	1	G15CS
—	23305	Tap, petrol	1	88ss, 650ss, 650/99 and Atlas
—	048529	Tap, petrol, main and reserve	1	G15P
—	026566	Tap, petrol, main	1	G15CS
—	024201	Tap, petrol, reserve	1	G15CS
—	E5264	Washer, petrol tap	1	88ss, 650ss, 650/99 and Atlas
—	13786	Washer, petrol tap	A/R	88ss, 650ss, 650/99 and Atlas
—	021387	Adaptor, petrol tap	2	G15CS
—	000183	Washer, for adaptor	2	G15CS
—	22265	Pipe, petrol feed	1	88ss, 650ss, 650/99 and Atlas
—	000908	Pipe, petrol feed, 10"	1	G15P
—	000908	Pipe, petrol feed, 6½", left hand ...	1	G15CS
—	000908	Pipe, petrol feed, 9¾", right hand ...	1	G15CS
—	021844	"T" piece, petrol pipe	1	G15CS
—	000575	Plug, drain	1	G15P
—	000183	Washer, drain plug	1	G15P

PLATE No.	PART No.	DESCRIPTION	QTY.	MODEL	PRICE EACH
—	22801	Bolt, fixing tank, front	1	88ss, 650ss, 650/99 and Atlas	
—	22082	Washer, rubber, for bolt, top	2	88ss, 650ss, 650/99 and Atlas	
—	E6743	Washer, rubber, for bolt, bottom	2	88ss, 650ss, 650/99 and Atlas	
—	E6742	Cup, steel, for rubber	2	88ss, 650ss, 650/99 and Atlas	
—	10914	Washer, steel, for cups	2	88ss, 650ss, 650/99 and Atlas	
—	24979	Bolt, fixing tank, front	1	88ss, 650ss, 650/99 and Atlas	
—	22764	Ring, rubber, rear fixing	1	88ss, 650ss, 650/99 and Atlas	
—	16237	Rubber, frame mounting	1	88ss, 650ss, 650/99 and Atlas	
—	027161	Bolt, fixing tank, front	2	All G15	
—	021453	Washer, front bolt	2	All G15	
—	021174	Rubber, front bolt	2	All G15	
—	000177	Washer, inner, front bolt	2	All G15	
—	014995	Rubber, buffer, front bolt	2	All G15	
—	016845	Nut, front bolt	2	All G15	
—	027138	Rubber, tank support, rear	1	All G15	
—	026359	Rubber, tank support, rear, thin	1	All G15	
—	018220	Clip, rubber, tank support, rear	2	All G15	
—	027137	Strap, petrol tank fixing, rear	1	All G15	
—	25101	Transfer, crossed flags	1	650/99 and Atlas	
—	24298	Transfer, "750 Atlas"	1	Atlas	

OIL TANK

PLATE No.	PART No.	DESCRIPTION	QTY.	MODEL	PRICE EACH
—	24304	Tank, only	1	88ss, 650ss, 650/99 and Atlas	
—	030286	Tank, only	1	G15P	
—	030287	Tank, only	1	G15CS "M"	
—	030288	Tank, only	1	G15CS "N"	
—	029593	Cover, oil tank	1	G15P	
—	029594	Cover, oil tank	1	G15CS "M"	
—	030289	Cover, oil tank	1	G15CS "N"	
—	022632	Screw, for cover	2	All G15	
—	000012	Washer, plain, for screw	2	All G15	
—	000203	Washer, fibre, for screw	2	All G15	
—	13765	Plug, drain	1	88ss, 650ss, 650/99 and Atlas	
—	012019	Plug, drain	1	All G15	
—	000200	Washer, drain plug	1	All	
—	025352	Cap, filler, oil tank	1	All	
—	21467	Transfer (Oil Level)	1	88ss, 650ss, 650/99 and Atlas	
—	023277	Transfer (Top Level)	1	G15P	
—	030352	Transfer (Top Level)	1	G15CS	
—	023279	Transfer (Low Level)	1	G15P	
—	030353	Transfer (Low Level)	1	G15CS	
—	030461	Transfer (Oil Recommendation)	1	All G15	
—	24309	Pipe, breather, oil tank	1	88ss, 650ss, 650/99 and Atlas	

PLATE No.	PART No.	DESCRIPTION	QTY.	MODEL	PRICE EACH
—	19379	Filter union, assembled	1	88ss, 650ss, 650/99 and Atlas	
—	E6640	Washer, filter union	1	88ss, 650ss, 650/99 and Atlas	
—	19380	Adaptor, oil return pipe	1	88ss, 650ss, 650/99 and Atlas	
—	13786	Washer, for adaptor	2	88ss, 650ss, 650/99 and Atlas	
—	000895	Hose, vent pipe, 18"	1	All G15	
—	048515	Filter, feed pipe	1	All G15	
—	016170	Washer, filter	1	All G15	
—	22475	Bolt, tank fixing, top	1	88ss, 650ss, 650/99 and Atlas	
—	22715	Grommet, top bolt	1	88ss, 650ss, 650/99 and Atlas	
—	22716	Spacer, top bolt	1	88ss, 650ss, 650/99 and Atlas	
—	E5456	Washer, top bolt	3	88ss, 650ss, 650/99 and Atlas	
—	E3223	Nut, top bolt	1	88ss, 650ss, 650/99 and Atlas	
—	029832	Bolt, tank fixing, top, front	1	All G15	
—	000011	Washer, for bolt	1	All G15	
—	13053	Stud, fixing tank, bottom	2	88ss, 650ss, 650/99 and Atlas	
—	E5456	Washer, for stud	2	88ss, 650ss, 650/99 and Atlas	
—	E3223	Nut, for stud	2	88ss, 650ss, 650/99 and Atlas	

PILLION FOOTRESTS

PLATE No.	PART No.	DESCRIPTION	QTY.	MODEL	PRICE EACH
H43	029333	Bar, pillion footrest	2	88ss, 650ss, 650/99 and Atlas	
H44	000343	Bolt, pillion footrest bar	2	88ss, 650ss, 650/99 and Atlas	
—	000005	Nut, for bolt	2	88ss, 650ss, 650/99 and Atlas	
—	030321	Lug, pillion, footrest	2	88ss, 650ss, 650/99 and Atlas	
—	000010	Washer, footrest lug	2	88ss, 650ss, 650/99 and Atlas	
—	23870	Nut, pillion lug	2	88ss, 650ss, 650/99 and Atlas	
H45	22574	Stud, pillion rest and silencer fixing	2	88ss, 650ss, 650/99 and Atlas	
H48	042569	Rubber, pillion footrest	2	88ss, 650ss, 650/99 and Atlas	

FRONT CHAINCASE

PLATE No.	PART No.	DESCRIPTION	QTY.	MODEL	PRICE EACH
—	23250	Chaincase, inner, assembled	1	88ss, 650ss, 650/99 and Atlas	
—	030242	Chaincase, inner, assembled	1	All G15	
—	20914	Chaincase, outer, only	1	88ss and 650ss	
—	20914A	Chaincase, outer, only	1	650/99 and Atlas	

PLATE No.	PART No.	DESCRIPTION	QTY.	MODEL	PRICE EACH
—	024012	Chaincase, outer, only	1	All G15	
—	20939	Washer, spigot, chaincase	1	88ss, 650ss, 650/99 and Atlas	
—	20942	Pin, fixing	3	88ss, 650ss, 650/99 and Atlas	
—	24945	Grommet, chaincase	1	88ss	
—	24945	Grommet, chaincase	2	650ss, 650/99 & Atlas	
H19	20937	Stud, support	1	88ss, 650ss, 650/99 and Atlas	
—	000011	Washer, support stud	2	88ss, 650ss, 650/99 and Atlas	
H20	E3223	Nut, support stud	1	88ss, 650ss, 650/99 and Atlas	
—	16247	Nut, support stud	1	88ss, 650ss, 650/99 and Atlas	
—	13185	Washer, sealing chaincase halves ...	1	88ss, 650ss, 650/99 and Atlas	
—	042055	Washer, felt, footrest tube ...	1	88ss, 650ss, 650/99 and Atlas	
—	13765	Plug, drain	1	88ss 650ss 650/99 and Atlas	
—	000200	Washer, drain plug	1	88ss 650ss 650/99 and Atlas	
—	14837	Cover, inspection	1	88ss 650ss 650/99 and Atlas	
—	24320	Washer, inspection cover	1	88ss, 650ss, 650/99 and Atlas	
—	E6055	Nut, attachment	1	88ss 650ss 650/99 and Atlas	
—	E6056	Washer, attachment nut	1	88ss, 650ss, 650/99 and Atlas	
—	24322	Washer, sealing, outer	1	88ss, 650ss, 650/99 and Atlas	
—	042040	Cap, inspection	2	All G15	
—	042025	Washer, inspection cap	2	All G15	
—	030243	Spacer (behind chaincase) ...	1	All G15	
—	019226	Screw, fixing chaincase	3	All G15	
—	000484	Screw, front half chaincase ...	14	All G15	
—	025037	Gasket, chaincase outer cover ...	1	All G15	
—	012019	Plug, drain	1	All G15	
—	000200	Washer, drain plug	1	All G15	
—	17731	Transfer, "Oil Bath"	1	88ss, 650ss, 650/99 and Atlas	
—	030461	Transfer, "Oil Recommendation" ...	1	88ss, 650ss, 650/99 and Atlas	

REAR CHAINGUARD

PLATE No.	PART No.	DESCRIPTION	QTY.	MODEL	PRICE EACH
—	21832	Chainguard (top run)	1	88ss, 650ss, 650/99 and Atlas	
—	21832A	Chainguard (top run)	1	88ss, 650ss, 650/99 and Atlas	
—	22022B	Bolt, fixing chainguard	1	88ss, 650ss, 650/99 and Atlas	
	19435	Washer, chainguard bolt	1	88ss, 650ss, 650/99 and Atlas	

PLATE No.	PART No.	DESCRIPTION	QTY.	MODEL	PRICE EACH
—	T2221	Washer, chainguard bolt (packing)	2	88ss, 650ss, 650/99 and Atlas	
—	23574	Nut, chainguard bolt	1	88ss, 650ss, 650/99 and Atlas	
—	22022A	Bolt, chainguard	1	88ss, 650ss, 650/99 and Atlas	
—	029469	Chainguard (top run)	1	All G15	
—	000371	Bolt, fixing, front	1	All G15	
—	000011	Washer, for bolt	1	All G15	
—	000374	Bolt, fixing, rear	1	All G15	
—	000011	Washer, for bolt	1	All G15	

REAR CHAINCASE (OPTIONAL)

PLATE No.	PART No.	DESCRIPTION	QTY.	MODEL	PRICE EACH
—	19734K	Chaincase, top, assembled	1	88ss, 650ss, 650/99 and Atlas	
—	19735K	Chaincase, bottom, assembled	1	88ss, 650ss, 650/99 and Atlas	
—	22022B	Bolt, fixing, front	1	88ss, 650ss, 650/99 and Atlas	
—	22022A	Bolt, fixing, rear	1	88ss, 650ss, 650/99 and Atlas	
—	19435	Washer, fixing bolt	1	88ss, 650ss, 650/99 and Atlas	
—	T2221	Washer, fixing bolt (packing)	2	88ss, 650ss, 650/99 and Atlas	
—	22135	Grommet, inspection	1	88ss, 650ss, 650/99 and Atlas	
—	030009	Chaincase, top, assembled	1	All G15	
—	030012	Chaincase, bottom, assembled	1	All G15	
—	000371	Bolt, chaincase	1	All G15	
—	000374	Bolt, chaincase	1	All G15	
—	000011	Washer, chaincase bolt	2	All G15	

TOOL BOX AND TOOL TRAY

PLATE No.	PART No.	DESCRIPTION	QTY.	MODEL	PRICE EACH
H98	22638A	Tool tray, assembled	1	88ss, 650ss, 650/99 and Atlas	
—	12342	Bolt, fixing tool tray	3	88ss, 650ss, 650/99 and Atlas	
—	E5379	Washer, tool tray bolt	5	88ss, 650ss, 650/99 and Atlas	
—	17698	Washer, tool tray bolt	1	88ss, 650ss, 650/99 and Atlas	
—	E3229	Nut, tool tray bolt	3	88ss, 650ss, 650/99 and Atlas	
—	029550	Tool box, less lid	1	G15P	
—	029551	Tool box, less lid	1	G15CS "M"	
—	030257	Tool box, less lid	1	G15CS "N"	
—	048300	Lid, tool box	1	G15P	
—	048301	Lid, tool box	1	G15CS "M"	
—	048425	Lid, tool box	1	G15CS "N"	
—	014511	Screw, tool box lid	1	All G15	
—	000012	Washer, lid screw	1	All G15	

PLATE No.	PART No.	DESCRIPTION	QTY.	MODEL	PRICE EACH
—	011373	Nut, lid screw	2	All G15	
—	029832	Bolt, top, fixing	1	All G15	
—	000011	Washer, top bolt	1	All G15	
—	000070	Bolt, rear fixing	1	All G15	
—	000012	Washer, rear bolt	1	All G15	
—	000005	Nut, rear bolt	1	All G15	

BATTERY BOX AND CARRIER

PLATE No.	PART No.	DESCRIPTION	QTY.	MODEL	PRICE EACH
—	22594	Body, battery box, assembled	1	88ss, 650ss, 650/99 and Atlas	
—	19189	Lid, battery box	1	88ss, 650ss, 650/99 and Atlas	
—	19086	Platform, battery	1	88ss, 650ss, 650/99 and Atlas	
—	19093	"U" bolt, battery	1	88ss, 650ss, 650/99 and Atlas	
—	19101	Strap, retaining	1	88ss, 650ss, 650/99 and Atlas	
—	17707	Washer, "U" bolt	2	88ss, 650ss, 650/99 and Atlas	
—	E3221	Nut, "U" bolt	2	88ss, 650ss, 650/99 and Atlas	
—	19195	Knob, box lid	2	88ss, 650ss, 650/99 and Atlas	
—	11796	Washer, for knob	2	88ss, 650ss, 650/99 and Atlas	
—	17735	Pin, split, for knob	2	88ss, 650ss, 650/99 and Atlas	
—	15689	Grommet, battery box	1	88ss, 650ss, 650/99 and Atlas	
—	14481	Bolt, top, fixing	1	88ss, 650ss, 650/99 and Atlas	
—	E5379	Washer, top bolt	2	88ss, 650ss, 650/99 and Atlas	
—	E3229	Nut, top bolt	1	88ss, 650ss, 650/99 and Atlas	
—	19092	Bolt, bottom fixing	2	88ss, 650ss, 650/99 and Atlas	
—	E5456	Washer, bottom bolt	2	88ss, 650ss, 650/99 and Atlas	
—	17698	Washer, shakeproof, bottom bolt	1	88ss, 650ss, 650/99 and Atlas	
—	19201	Platform, battery box and oil tank	1	88ss, 650ss, 650/99 and Atlas	
—	19212	Mat, for platform	1	88ss, 650ss, 650/99 and Atlas	
—	14481	Bolt, fixing platform	4	88ss, 650ss, 650/99 and Atlas	
—	E5379	Washer, for bolt	8	88ss, 650ss, 650/99 and Atlas	
—	E3229	Nut, for bolt	4	88ss, 650ss, 650/99 and Atlas	
—	030094	Carrier, battery, assembled	1	All G15	
—	014577	Bolt, carrier/tool box	1	All G15	

PLATE No.	PART No.	DESCRIPTION	QTY.	MODEL	PRICE EACH
—	045062	Washer, for bolt	2	All G15	
—	000005	Nut, for bolt	1	All G15	
—	000368	Bolt, fixing, top, rear	1	All G15	
—	000011	Washer, top, rear bolt	1	All G15	
—	000004	Nut, top, rear bolt	1	All G15	
—	024218	Bolt, fixing, front	2	All G15	
—	000012	Washer, front bolt	4	All G15	
—	000005	Nut, front bolt	2	All G15	
—	048454	Rubber, battery carrier	1	All G15	
—	030056	Strap, battery carrier	1	All G15	
—	028044	Pin, battery strap	1	All G15	

FRONT WHEEL

PLATE No.	PART No.	DESCRIPTION	QTY.	MODEL	PRICE EACH
—	25004	Wheel, complete, less tyre and tube	1	All except G15P	
—	030518	Wheel, complete, less tyre and tube	1	G15P (Home)	
—	25292	Wheel, complete, less tyre and tube	1	G15P (Export)	
—	S12-2/428	Wheel, bare	1	All except G15P	
—	030519	Wheel, bare	1	G15P (Home)	
—	25293	Wheel, bare	1	G15P (Export)	
—	18350	Rim, only, WM2-19	1	All except G15P	
—	24872	Rim, only, WM2-18	1	G15P (Home)	
—	23319	Rim, only, WM3-18	1	G15P (Export)	
—	20063	Spoke, long head	20	All except G15P	
—	23331	Spoke, long head	20	G15P	
—	20061	Spoke, short head	20	All except G15P	
—	23332	Spoke, short head	20	G15P	
—	17717	Nipple, for spoke	40	All	
F21	19664	Shell, only, front hub	1	All	
F22	040100	Bearing, right side	1	All	
F18	17721	Bearing, left side	1	All	
F23	16783	Spacer, for bearing	1	All	
F24	E6888	Ring, locking bearing	1	All	
F16	E6885	Washer, felt	2	All	
F17	E6889	Ring, retaining	1	All	
F15	19719	Washer, oil retaining	1	All	
F25	18551	Cover, dust	1	All	
F19	19646	Spacer, assembled, bearing	1	All	
F27	030055	Spindle, front hub	1	All	
F3	E4768	Nut, hub spindle	1	All	
F2	50257	Plate, cover, front brake	1	All	
F20	50249	Cam, brake shoe	1	All	
F8	18502	Shoe, front brake, with lining	2	All	
F10	16782	Lining, brake shoe ... pair	1	All	
F9	E5061	Rivet, brake shoe lining ... set	16	All	
F14	E5832	Spring, return, brake shoe	2	All	
F11	14454	Plate, pivot retaining	1	All	
F12	14506	Washer, tab, for plate	1	All	
F13	12342	Bolt, for plate	2	All	
F4	20052	Lever, expanding	1	All	
—	E3255	Pin, clevis, for lever	1	All	
—	17735	Pin, split, for clevis	1	All	
F6	E5455	Washer, for lever	1	All	
F5	18942	Nut, for lever	1	All	
—	E5944A	Washer, packing, brake plate	A/R	All	

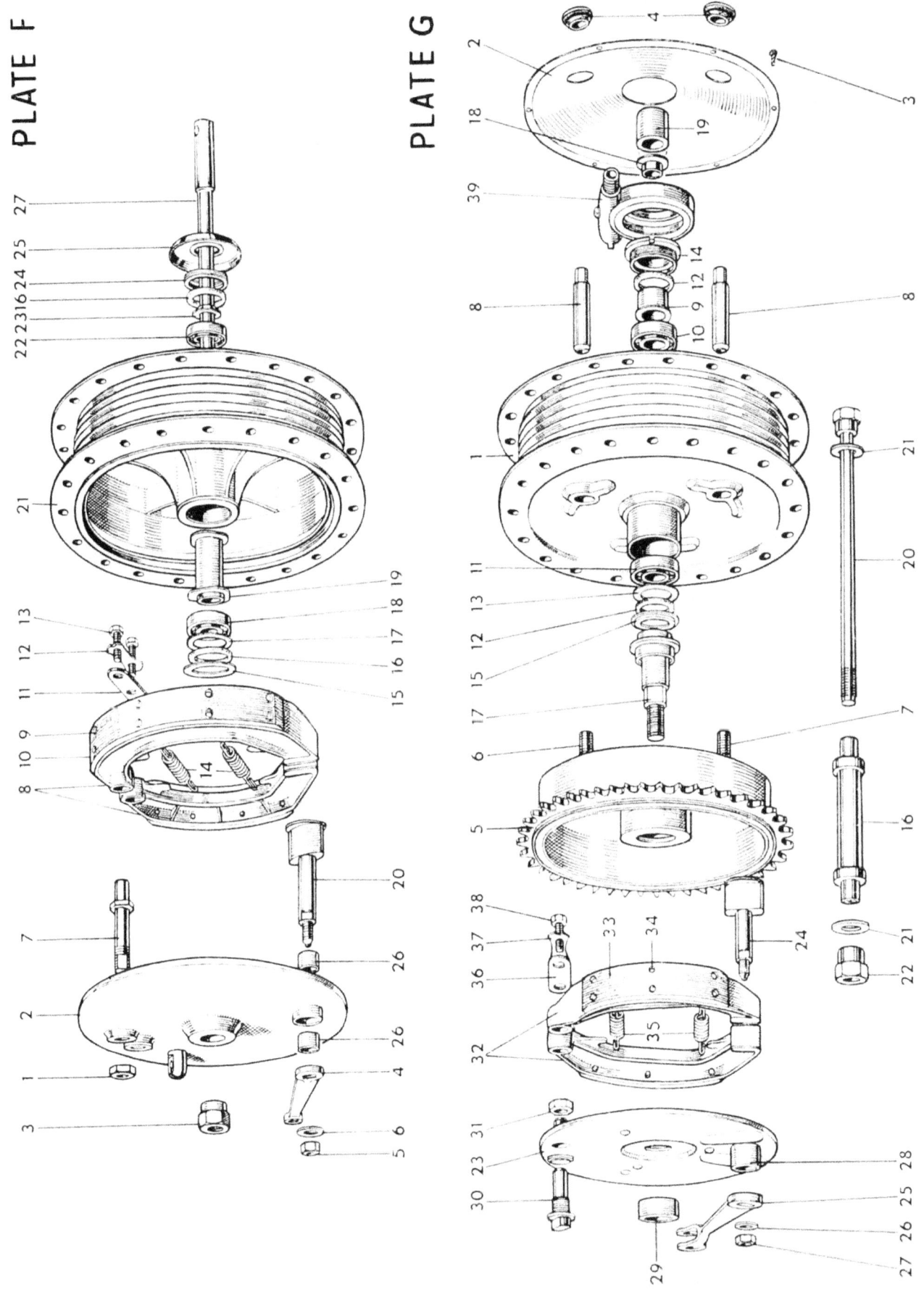

PLATE No.	PART No.	DESCRIPTION	QTY.	MODEL	PRICE EACH
		REAR WHEEL			
—	24152	Wheel, complete, with bearing and brake, less tyre	1	88ss and 650ss	
—	24362	Wheel, complete, with bearing and brake, less tyre	1	650/99 and Atlas	
—	25262	Wheel, complete, with bearing and brake, less tyre	1	G15P (Home)	
—	25294	Wheel, complete, with bearing and brake, less tyre	1	G15P (Export)	
—	25295	Wheel, complete, with bearing and brake, less tyre	1	G15CS	
—	M12-2-649	Wheel, with hub shell only	1	88ss and 650ss	
—	25296	Wheel, with hub shell only	1	650/99 and Atlas	
—	030521	Wheel, with hub shell only	1	G15P (Home)	
—	25297	Wheel, with hub shell only	1	G15P (Export)	
—	25298	Wheel, with hub shell only	1	G15CS	
—	18350	Rim only, WM2-19	1	88ss and 650ss	
—	23319	Rim, only, WM3-18	1	650/99, Atlas and G15P (Export)	
—	24872	Rim, only, WM2-18	1	G15P (Home)	
—	030432	Rim, only, WM3-18	1	G15CS	
—	20063	Spoke, long head	20	88ss and 650ss	
—	23331	Spoke, long head	20	650/99, Atlas & G15P	
—	030433	Spoke, long head	20	G15CS	
—	20061	Spoke, short head	20	88ss and 650ss	
—	23332	Spoke, short head	20	650/99, Atlas & G15P	
—	030434	Spoke, short head	20	G15CS	
—	17717	Nipple, for spoke	40	All except G15CS	
—	021694	Nipple, for spoke	40	G15CS	
G1	19689	Shell, hub, with liner	1	All	
G5	50245	Brake drum and sprocket	1	88ss, 650ss, 650/99 and Atlas	
G5	030052	Brake drum and sprocket	1	All G15	
G8	18233	Nut, sleeve, for brake drum	3	All	
G10	040100	Bearing, right side	1	All	
G11	17721	Bearing, left side	1	All	
G9	18234	Spacer, bearing	1	All	
G14	18232	Ring, locking bearing	1	All	
G13	E6889	Washer, bearing	1	All	
G12	E6885	Washer, felt	2	All	
G15	19714	Ring, retaining, felt washer	1	All	
G16	18231	Sleeve, inner	1	All	
G17	E4760	Stud, retaining brake drum	1	All	
G2	18348	Diaphragm, hub	1	All	
G3	25100	Screw, hammer drive	6	All	
G4	18731	Grommet, diaphragm	3	All	
G20	19265	Spindle, hub	1	88ss, 650ss, 650/99 and Atlas	
G20	24882	Spindle, hub	1	All G15	
G21	19266	Washer, hub spindle	1	88ss, 650ss, 650/99 and Atlas	
G21	030023	Washer, hub spindle	1	All G15	
G22	19267	Nut, hub spindle	1	All	
G19	18235	Spacer, spindle	1	88ss, 650ss, 650/99 and Atlas	
G19	030018	Spacer, spindle	1	All G15	

PLATE No.	PART No.	DESCRIPTION	QTY.	MODEL	PRICE EACH
G23	19852	Plate, cover, brake	1	88ss, 650ss, 650/99 and Atlas	
G23	030015	Plate, cover, brake	1	All G15	
G24	50011	Cam, expander	1	All	
G32	19584	Shoe, brake, with lining	2	All	
G33	16547	Lining, brake shoe	pair	All	
G34	E5061	Rivet, brake shoe lining ... set	14	All	
G35	E5832	Spring, brake shoe return	2	All	
G25	23436	Lever, expander	1	All	
G26	E5455	Washer, for lever	1	All	
G27	18942	Nut, for lever	1	All	
G36	14454	Plate, retaining pivot pin	1	All	
G37	14506	Washer, tab, for plate	1	All	
G38	12342	Bolt, for plate	2	All	
G29	19268	Spacer, brake plate	1	88ss, 650ss, 650/99 and Atlas	
G29	030017	Spacer, brake plate	1	All G15	
—	E5276	Washer, brake plate	A/R	All	

BRAKE OPERATING PARTS

PLATE No.	PART No.	DESCRIPTION	QTY.	MODEL	PRICE EACH
H21	19995	Pedal, rear brake	1	88ss, 650ss, 650/99 and Atlas	
H26	19929	Spring, pedal, return	1	88ss, 650ss, 650/99 and Atlas	
H27	19978	Nipple, grease and retaining pin	1	88ss, 650ss, 650/99 and Atlas	
H22	19996	Spindle, brake pedal	1	88ss, 650ss, 650/99 and Atlas	
—	000008	Washer, pedal spindle	1	88ss, 650ss, 650/99 and Atlas	
H23	E3227	Nut, pedal spindle	1	88ss, 650ss, 650/99 and Atlas	
H24	19997	Spacer, pedal spindle	1	88ss, 650ss, 650/99 and Atlas	
H25	19976	Stop, for pedal	1	88ss, 650ss, 650/99 and Atlas	
H28	15819A	Rod, rear brake	1	88ss, 650ss, 650/99 and Atlas	
H29	23439	Yoke end, brake rod	1	88ss, 650ss, 650/99 and Atlas	
H30	E3255	Pin, clevis, yoke end	1	88ss, 650ss, 650/99 and Atlas	
H31	17735	Pin, split, for clevis pin	1	88ss, 650ss, 650/99 and Atlas	
—	029559	Pedal, rear brake ... set	1	All G15	
—	021700	Spring, pedal return	1	All G15	
—	000051	Nipple, grease	1	All G15	
—	021699	Spindle, brake pedal	1	All G15	
—	022609	Bolt, brake pedal	1	All G15	
—	022314	Stop, brake pedal	1	All G15	
—	022297	Rod, rear brake	1	All G15	
—	023299	Yoke end, brake rod	1	All G15	
—	000736	Pin, clevis, yoke end	1	All G15	
—	000014	Pin, split, clevis pin	1	All G15	

PLATE No.	PART No.	DESCRIPTION	QTY.	MODEL	PRICE EACH
—	18929	Roller, brake cam lever	1	All	
H32	022743	Nut, adjusting brake rod	1	All	

SPEEDOMETER

PLATE No.	PART No.	DESCRIPTION	QTY.	MODEL	PRICE EACH
—	029602	Head, speedometer, only, m.p.h.	1	88ss and 650ss	
—	030258	Head, speedometer, only, m.p.h.	1	650/99, Atlas and G15CS	
—	029603	Head, speedometer, only, k.p.h.	1	88ss and 650ss	
—	030259	Head, speedometer, only, k.p.h.	1	650/99, Atlas and G15CS	
—	029717	Head, speedometer, only, k.p.h.	1	G15P	
—	029718	Head, speedometer, only, k.p.h.	1	G15P	
—	22888	Gearbox, speedometer drive	1	88ss, 650ss, 650/99 and Atlas	
—	030207	Gearbox, speedometer drive	1	All G15	
G18	13270	Spacer, speedometer gearbox	1	All	
—	25030	Cable, complete, speedometer drive ...	1	88ss and 650ss	
—	25087	Cable, complete, speedometer drive ...	1	650/99 and Atlas	
—	030444	Cable, complete, speedometer drive ...	1	All G15	
—	000178	Washer, spacing, speedometer head ...	1	G15P	
—	000178	Washer, spacing, speedometer head ...	2	G15CS	
—	030345	Lead, speedometer light	1	650/99 and Atlas	

HEADLAMP

PLATE No.	PART No.	DESCRIPTION	QTY.	MODEL	PRICE EACH
—	59252A	Headlamp, complete, less harness (Home)	1	88ss, 650ss & G15P	
—	59254A	Headlamp, complete, less harness (Europe not France)	1	88ss, 650ss & G15P	
—	59253A	Headlamp, complete, less bulbs and harness (France)	1	88ss, 650ss & G15P	
—	59281A	Headlamp, complete, less harness ...	1	650/99, Atlas and G15CS	
—	553248	Rim, only	1	All	
—	54522365	Shell, only (Home)	1	88ss, 650ss & G15P	
—	54522377	Shell, only (Export)	1	88ss, 650ss & G15P	
—	54521617	Shell, only	1	650/99, Atlas and G15CS	
—	516798	Light unit (reflector and glass) (Home) ...	1	All	
—	553275	Light unit (reflector and glass) (Europe not France)	1	All	
—	516802	Light unit (reflector and glass) (France) ...	1	All	
—	554602	Bulb holder, main (Home and Europe not France)	1	All	
—	562303	Bulb holder, main (France)	1	All	
—	552943	Back shell (France)	1	All	
—	144921	Screw, fixing rim	1	All	
—	534296	Plate, fixing rim	1	All	
—	554710	Bulb holder, pilot	1	All	
—	34289A	Switch, lighting	1	All	
—	54330934	Knob, lighting switch	1	All	
—	54934995	Harness, main (Home)	1	88ss, 650ss & G15P	
—	54932248	Harness, main (Export)	1	88ss, 650ss & G15P	
—	54935175	Harness, main	1	650/99 and Atlas	
—	54935167	Harness, main	1	G15CS	
—	54930007	Socket, with cables	1	88ss, 650ss & G15P	

PLATE No.	PART No.	DESCRIPTION	QTY.	MODEL	PRICE EACH
—	36296A	Ammeter	1	All	
—	112201	Bolt, fixing headlamp	2	All	
—	030057	Spacer, headlamp bolt	2	88ss, 650ss & G15P	
—	030058	Spacer, headlamp bolt	2	650/99, Atlas and G15CS	
—	446	Bulb, main, 12v., 50 × 40w. (Home)	1	All P. Tax 1/-	
—	370	Bulb, main, 12v., 45 × 40w. (Europe except France)	1	All P. Tax 1/2	
—	350	Bulb, main, 12v., 35 × 35w. (Europe except France)	1	All P. Tax 1/2	
—	989	Bulb, pilot, 12v., 6w.	1	All P. Tax 4d.	

REAR LAMP

PLATE No.	PART No.	DESCRIPTION	QTY.	MODEL	PRICE EACH
—	53454B	Lamp, complete (Lucas 564) (Home and Export not U.S.A.)	1	88ss, 650ss	
—	53973A/B	Lamp, complete (Lucas 679) (U.S.A.)	1	88ss, 650ss	
—	53973A/B	Lamp, complete (Lucas 679)	1	650/99, Atlas and all G15	
—	54576001	Lens, red (for Lucas 564)	1	88ss and 650ss	
—	54572932	Lens, red (for Lucas 679)	1	All	
—	575219	Nut, for lens (for Lucas 564)	2	88ss and 650ss	
—	572289	Screw, for lens (for Lucas 679)	2	All	
—	575208	Gasket, lens seating (for Lucas 564) (Home)	1	88ss and 650ss	
—	54571677	Gasket, seating lamp (for Lucas 679)	1	All	
—	575207	Grommet, bulb holder (for Lucas 564) (Home)	1	88ss and 650ss	
—	57574348	Bulb holder, with reflector (for Lucas 679)	1	All	
—	575209	Bulb holder (for Lucas 564) (Home)	1	88ss and 650ss	
—	573825	Grommet, cable entry (for Lucas 564) (Home)	1	88ss and 650ss	
—	380	Bulb, 12v., 21/6 w.	1	All P. Tax 8d.	

HORN

PLATE No.	PART No.	DESCRIPTION	QTY.	MODEL	PRICE EACH
—	030045	Horn, electric (Lucas 8H 70159 B/D)	1	All	
—	23389	Screw, fixing horn	2	All	
—	23410	Washer, fixing screw	2	All	
—	E3221	Nut, fixing screw	2	All	
—	000342	Bolt, fixing horn	2	All	
—	000012	Washer, fixing bolt	2	All	
—	000005	Nut, fixing bolt	2	All	
—	030044	Bracket, for horn	1	All G15 only	

STOP LIGHT

PLATE No.	PART No.	DESCRIPTION	QTY.	MODEL	PRICE EACH
—	029965	Kit, complete, stop light	1	All G15	
—	029351	Switch, stop light (Lucas 31383 A/B)	1	All	
—	22568	Bracket, stop switch	1	88ss, 650ss, 650/99 and Atlas	
—	22807	Bolt, switch bracket	1	88ss, 650ss, 650/99 and Atlas	
—	000010	Washer, switch bolt	2	88ss, 650ss, 650/99 and Atlas	
—	E3224A	Nut, switch bolt	1	88ss, 650ss, 650/99 and Atlas	

PLATE No.	PART No.	DESCRIPTION	QTY.	MODEL	PRICE EACH
—	E5278	Pin, fixing	2	88ss, 650ss, 650/99 and Atlas	
—	17904	Washer, fixing pin	4	88ss, 650ss, 650/99 and Atlas	
—	E3221	Nut, fixing pin	2	88ss, 650ss, 650/99 and Atlas	
—	029831	Screw, fixing switch	2	All G15	
—	000039	Washer, fixing screw	2	All G15	
—	20245	Lead, stop tail lamp	1	88ss, 650ss, 650/99 and Atlas	
—	20248	Lead, brake switch	1	88ss and 650ss	
—	028250	Cable, stop light	1	All G15	
—	021595	Bolt, in brake pedal for stop light	1	All G15	
—	029245	Nut, for brake pedal bolt	1	All G15	
—	25228	Lead, brake switch	1	650/99 and Atlas	

ALTERNATOR

PLATE No.	PART No.	DESCRIPTION	QTY.	MODEL	PRICE EACH
—	54021027	Alternator, rotor and stator	1	All	
—	47162A	Stator, only	1	All	
—	54213901	Rotor, only	1	All	
—	21433	Stud, for stator	3	88ss, 650ss, 650/99 and Atlas	
—	17698	Washer, for stud	3	88ss, 650ss, 650/99 and Atlas	
—	E3229	Nut, for stud	3	88ss, 650ss, 650/99 and Atlas	
A74	20948	Key, for rotor	1	All	
—	19147	Washer, for rotor	1	88ss, 650ss, 650/99 and Atlas	
—	20692	Nut, for rotor	1	88ss, 650ss, 650/99 and Atlas	
—	23738	Spacer, for rotor	1	88ss, 650ss, 650/99 and Atlas	
—	011826	Stud, for stator	3	All G15	
—	000012	Washer, for stud	3	All G15	
—	011843	Nut, for stud	3	All G15	
—	24948	Washer, for rotor	1	All G15	
—	24947	Nut, for rotor	1	All G15	
—	030251	Spacer, for rotor	1	All G15	

BATTERY

PLATE No.	PART No.	DESCRIPTION	QTY.	MODEL	PRICE EACH
—	MKZ9E	Battery, with lid (charged but dry)	2	All	
—	030351	Link, for batteries	1	All	
—	000348	Bolt, battery-earth	1	All	
—	000012	Washer, for bolt	1	All	

RECTIFIER AND ZENER DIODE

PLATE No.	PART No.	DESCRIPTION	QTY.	MODEL	PRICE EACH
—	49072A	Rectifier (with nut)	1	All	
—	000011	Washer, rectifier	1	88ss, 650ss, 650/99 and Atlas	
—	17698	Washer, rectifier	1	88ss, 650ss, 650/99 and Atlas	

PLATE No.	PART No.	DESCRIPTION	QTY.	MODEL	PRICE EACH
—	015306	Washer, rectifier	2	All G15	
—	49345A	Diode, Zener	1	All	
—	026656	Bracket, for diode	1	88ss, 650ss, 650/99 and Atlas	
—	030042	Plate, heat sink, for diode	2	All	
—	030043	Spacer, for plate	1	All	
—	000362	Bolt, for diode	1	88ss, 650ss, 650/99 and Atlas	
—	014119	Washer, for diode (on tank bolt)	1	88ss, 650ss, 650/99 and Atlas	
—	014779	Washer, diode bolt	1	88ss, 650ss, 650/99 and Atlas	
—	000004	Nut, diode bolt	1	88ss, 650ss, 650/99 and Atlas	
—	042554	Bolt, fixing diode	1	All G15	
—	014515	Spacer, diode bolt	1	All G15	
—	000011	Washer, diode bolt	1	All G15	

ELECTRICAL SUNDRIES

PLATE No.	PART No.	DESCRIPTION	QTY.	MODEL	PRICE EACH
—	31563D	Switch, horn and dipping	1	All	
—	380459	Packing, rubber, for switch	1	All	
—	021299	Screw, for switch	2	All	
—	762040	Switch, magneto cut-out	1	All	
—	369218	Cable, for horn	R	All	
—	369218	Cable, for cut-out switch	R	All	
—	000543	Cable, H.T. sparking plug	R	All	foot
—	000541	Terminal, H.T. cable	R	All	
—	FE100	Plug, sparking	R	88ss, 650ss & 650/99	
—	FE75	Plug, sparking	R	Atlas and all G15	
—	18465	Cover, sparking plug (with suppressor)	R	88ss, 650ss and G15P (Home)	
—	15399	Cover, sparking plug	R	G15P (Export), Atlas and G15CS	

TOOLS

PLATE No.	PART No.	DESCRIPTION	QTY.	MODEL	PRICE EACH
—	017253	Bag, for tools	1	All	
—	021625	Screwdriver	1	All	
—	017052	Spanner, $\frac{1}{4}'' \times \frac{3}{16}''$	1	All	
—	017248	Pliers, sidecutting	1	All	
—	LTU/07	Lever, tyre	2	All	
—	SBU2/88	Spanner, sparking plug	1	All	
—	SBU2/76	Spanner, box, $\frac{7}{16}'' \times \frac{1}{2}''$	1	All	
—	030459	Bar, tommy, $\frac{7}{16}''$ diameter	1	All	
—	SPU2/20	Spanner, rocker adjuster	1	All	
—	017053	Spanner, $\frac{5}{16}'' \times \frac{3}{8}''$	1	All	
—	SBU1/183	Spanner, box, wheel nut	1	All	
—	023284	Spanner, shock absorber unit	1	All	
—	015023	Spanner, magneto	1	All	
—	SBU1/74	Spanner, cylinder head	1	All	
—	SBU1/02	Spanner, cylinder head	1	All	
—	19438	Key, Allen, handlebar clip	1	All G15 only	
—	017257	Spanner, $\frac{1}{8}'' \times \frac{3}{16}''$	1	All G15 only	
—	017254	Spanner, dynamo and clutch adjustment	1	All G15 only	

PLATE No.	PART No.	DESCRIPTION	QTY.	MODEL	PRICE EACH
—	TBU/01	Bar, tommy, $\frac{7}{16}$" diameter	1	88ss, 650ss, 650/99 and Atlas	
—	019869	Key, Allen	1	88ss, 650ss, 650/99 and Atlas	
—	SPU1/01	Spanner, cable adjuster	1	650/99 and Atlas	

TOOL KITS

—	017114	Inflator, tyre	1	All	
—	25299	Kit of tools, complete, less inflator	1	88ss and 650ss	
—	25307	Kit of tools, complete, less inflator	1	650/99 and Atlas	
—	25308	Kit of tools, complete, less inflator	1	All G15	

GASKET SET

—	25284	Set of decarbonising gaskets	1	88ss, 650ss & 650/99	
—	25285	Set of decarbonising gaskets	1	Atlas	
—	25286	Set of decarbonising gaskets	1	All G15	
—	25287	Set, complete overhaul gaskets	1	88ss, 650ss & 650/99	
—	25288	Set, complete overhaul gaskets	1	Atlas	
—	25289	Set, complete overhaul gaskets	1	All G15	

CRASHBAR, FRONT

—	25280	Set, crashbar, front complete	1	88ss and 650ss	
—	026855	Set, crashbar, front complete	1	All G15	
—	25011	Bar, only, assembled	1	88ss and 650ss	
—	20610	Plate, top fixing	1	88ss and 650ss	
—	25012	Stud, fixing, top	1	88ss and 650ss	
—	000010	Washer, top fixing stud	1	88ss and 650ss	
—	E3224	Nut, top fixing stud	1	88ss and 650ss	
—	026519	Bar, only, assembled	1	All G15	
—	026523	Stud, frame uniting	1	All G15	
—	010957	Bolt, top fixing	1	All G15	
—	026525	Spacer, top bolt	2	All G15	
—	000009	Washer, top bolt	2	All G15	
—	000002	Nut, top bolt	1	All G15	
—	029852	Stay, exhaust pipe	2	All G15	

CRASHBAR, REAR

—	RCBK/10R	Set crashbar rear, complete	1	88ss and 650ss	
—	030606	Set, crashbar rear, complete	1	All G15	
—	23016	Bar, only, left	1	88ss and 650ss	
—	23017	Bar, only, right	1	88ss and 650ss	
—	23114A	Stud, fixing, top	1	88ss and 650ss	
—	23019	Spacer, crashbar	2	88ss and 650ss	
—	23018	Stud, crashbar and pillion rest	2	88ss and 650ss	
—	029946	Bar, only, assembled, left	1	All G15	
—	029947	Bar, only, assembled, right	1	All G15	
—	029950	Rear, footrest	2	All G15	
—	042269	Bolt, footrest	2	All G15	
—	000011	Washer, for bolt	2	All G15	
—	029952	Rubber, footrest	2	All G15	

PLATE No.	PART No.	DESCRIPTION	QTY.	MODEL	PRICE EACH
		STEERING DAMPER			
—	030331	Steering, damper, set of parts	1	All	
—	017260	Knob, adjusting	1	All	
—	030323	Sleeve, assembly	1	All	
—	000195	Washer, spring, damper knob	1	All	
—	000162	Washer, ratchet, damper knob	1	All	
—	019559	Plate, anchor	1	All	
—	014577	Bolt, anchor plate	1	All	
—	000012	Washer, anchor plate bolt	3	All	
—	000191	Washer, spring, for bolt	2	All	
—	000812	Disc, friction	2	All	
—	030326	Stud, draw	1	All	
—	030327	Spacer, draw stud	1	All	
—	000342	Bolt, friction plate	1	All	
—	019780	Spacer, for bolt	1	All	
—	030333	Nut, top fork stem	1	All	
		SIDECAR FORK CONVERSION			
—	030340	Crown, assembly, with stem	1	88ss, 650ss, 650/99 and Atlas	
—	030402	Lug, handlebar	1	88ss, 650ss, 650/99 and Atlas	
—	15906A	Spring, main, front fork	2	88ss, 650ss, 650/99 and Atlas	
—	22811	Unit, rear suspension	2	88ss, 650ss, 650/99 and Atlas	
—	T2180A	Sprocket, engine, 17 tooth	1	88ss	
—	T2180C	Sprocket, engine, 19 tooth	1	650ss, 650/99 & Atlas	
—	030331	Set of steering damper parts	1	88ss, 650ss, 650/99 and Atlas	
		REVOLUTION COUNTER			
—	030391	Head, only, revolution counter	1	88ss, 650ss, 650/99 and Atlas	
—	030392	Cable, assembled	1	88ss, 650ss, 650/99 and Atlas	
—	14490	Clip, for cable	1	88ss, 650ss, 650/99 and Atlas	
—	030384	Bracket, for head	1	88ss and 650ss	
—	030358	Bracket, for head	1	650/99 and Atlas	
—	24563	Gearbox, revolution counter	1	88ss, 650ss, 650/99 and Atlas	
—	23565	Gasket, for gearbox	1	88ss, 650ss, 650/99 and Atlas	
—	030164	Lead, for light	1	88ss and 650ss	
—	030435	Lead, for light	1	650/99 and Atlas	
—	23453	Cover, blanking, gearbox	1	All	
—	23649	Disc, sealing, for cover	1	All	
—	030383	Plate, assembled, speedometer and light switch	1	All	
—	23444	Screw, for revolution counter gearbox or blanking cover	2	All	
—	23446	Washer, fibre, for screw	2	All	
—	23447	Washer, metal, for screw	2	All	

PLATE No.	PART No.	DESCRIPTION	QTY.	MODEL	PRICE EACH
—	23445	Nut, for screw	2	All	

AIR CLEANER

PLATE No.	PART No.	DESCRIPTION	QTY.	MODEL	PRICE EACH
—	030337	Cleaner, air	1	All	
—	23559	Grommet, air cleaner	2	All	
—	23552	Plate, mounting	1	88ss, 650ss & 650/99	
—	24572	Plate, mounting	1	All 750	
—	23555	Sleeve, mounting plate	2	88ss, 650ss & 650/99	
—	24571	Sleeve, mounting plate	2	All 750	
—	22034	Bolt, mounting plate	2	All	
—	17698	Washer, mounting plate bolt	2	All	

OPTIONAL PARTS

PLATE No.	PART No.	DESCRIPTION	QTY.	MODEL	PRICE EACH
—	24985B	Mudguard, front, black	1	88ss and 650ss	
—	25060A	Mudguard, rear, black	1	88ss and 650ss	
—	23679	Handrail, pillion seat	2	650/99 and Atlas	
—	22572	Stud, fixing handrail	2	650/99 and Atlas	
—	20676	Rim, front, light alloy	1	88ss and 650ss	
—	23842	Rim, rear, light alloy	1	88ss and 650ss	
—	22971	Seat, single	1	88ss and 650ss	
—	21183	Clip, spring, single seat	2	88ss and 650ss	
—	14468	Bolt, single seat clip	2	88ss and 650ss	
—	040434	Kickstart, folding type	1	88ss and 650ss	

RACING FOOTCHANGE CONVERSION

PLATE No.	PART No.	DESCRIPTION	QTY.	MODEL	PRICE EACH
—	23772	Lever, gear change	1	88ss and 650ss	
—	23774	Lever, toggle	1	88ss and 650ss	
—	18450	Rubber, gear change lever	1	88ss and 650ss	
—	15879	Rod, toggle	1	88ss and 650ss	
—	17356	Yoke end, small	1	88ss and 650ss	
—	15880	Yoke end, large	1	88ss and 650ss	
—	E3231	Nut, lock, yoke end	2	88ss and 650ss	
—	15882	Pin, clevis, yoke end	2	88ss and 650ss	
—	10057	Washer, clevis pin	2	88ss and 650ss	
—	18415	Pin, split, clevis pin	2	88ss and 650ss	
—	16386A	Pedal, rear brake	1	88ss and 650ss	
—	23773	Stop, adjuster	1	88ss and 650ss	
—	E5456	Washer, for stop	1	88ss and 650ss	
—	E3223	Nut, for stop	1	88ss and 650ss	
—	13421	Screw, pedal adjuster	1	88ss and 650ss	
—	E3229	Nut, adjuster screw	1	88ss and 650ss	
—	15870	Footrest, left hand	1	88ss and 650ss	
—	17162	Footrest, right hand (folding)	1	88ss and 650ss	
—	15871B	Stud, footrest support, left hand	1	88ss and 650ss	
—	17163	Stud, footrest support, right hand	1	88ss and 650ss	
—	E5377	Washer, for stud	2	88ss and 650ss	
—	15176	Nut, for stud	2	88ss and 650ss	
—	000008	Washer, for stud, left hand	1	88ss and 650ss	
—	E6706	Bolt, for right hand footrest	1	88ss and 650ss	
—	12079	Nut, for bolt	1	88ss and 650ss	

NOTES

VELOCEPRESS MANUALS – MOTORCYCLE BY MAKE

AJS 1932-1948 SINGLES & TWINS 250cc THRU 1000cc (BOOK OF)
AJS 1945-1960 SINGLES 350cc & 500cc MODELS 16 & 18 (BOOK OF)
AJS 1955-1965 SINGLES 350cc & 500cc (BOOK OF)
AJS 1957-1966 FACTORY WSM - ALL SINGLES & TWINS
ARIEL UP TO 1932 (BOOK OF)
ARIEL 1932-1939 PREWAR MODELS (BOOK OF)
ARIEL 1933-1951 (WORKSHOP MANUAL)
ARIEL 1939-1960 4 STROKE SINGLES (BOOK OF)
ARIEL 1958-1964 LEADER & ARROW FACTORY WSM & PARTS LIST
ARIEL 1958-1964 LEADER & ARROW (BOOK OF)
BMW R26 R27 (1956-1967) FACTORY WORKSHOP MANUAL
BMW R50 R50S R60 R69S (1955-1969) FACTORY WORKSHOP MANUAL
BRIDGESTONE 90 SERIES FACTORY WSM & PARTS CATALOGUE
BRIDGESTONE 175 SERIES FACTORY WSM & PARTS CATALOGUE
BRIDGESTONE 350 SERIES FACTORY WSM & PARTS CATALOGUES
BSA SERVICE SHEETS MASTER CATALOGUE ALL MODELS 1945-1967
BSA BANTAM D1 TO D7 1948-1966 FACTORY SERVICE SHEETS MANUAL
BSA BANTAM ALL MODELS FROM 1948 ONWARDS (BOOK OF)
BSA DANDY FACTORY WORKSHOP MANUAL (COMPILATION)
BSA SINGLES & V-TWINS UP TO 1927 (BOOK OF)
BSA SINGLES & V-TWINS UP TO 1930 (BOOK OF)
BSA SINGLES & V-TWINS UP TO 1935 (BOOK OF)
BSA SINGLES & V-TWINS 1936-1939 (BOOK OF)
BSA C10, C11 & C12 1945-1958 FACTORY SERVICE SHEETS MANUAL
BSA OHV & SV SINGLES 250-600cc 1945-1959 (BOOK OF)
BSA C15 & B40 1958-1967 FACTORY SERVICE SHEETS MANUAL
BSA OHV & SV SINGLES 250cc (ONLY) 1954-1970 (BOOK OF)
BSA B31, B32, B33 & B34 1945-60 FACTORY SERVICE SHEETS MANUAL
BSA OHV SINGLES 350 & 500cc 1955-1967 (BOOK OF)
BSA M20, M21 & M33 1945-1963 FACTORY SERVICE SHEETS MANUAL
BSA TWINS A7 & A10 1948-1962 FACTORY SERVICE SHEETS MANUAL
BSA TWINS A7 & A10 1948-1962 (BOOK OF)
BSA TWINS A50 & A65 1962-1965 FACTORY WORKSHOP MANUAL
BSA TWINS A50 & A65 1962-1969 (SECOND BOOK OF)
DOUGLAS 1929-1939 PREWAR ALL MODELS (BOOK OF)
DOUGLAS 1948-1957 POSTWAR ALL MODELS FACTORY SHOP MANUAL
DUCATI 160cc, 250cc & 350cc OHC MODELS FACTORY SHOP MANUAL
HONDA 50cc ALL MODELS UP TO 1970 INC MONKEY & TRAIL (BOOK OF)
HONDA 90cc ALL MODELS UP TO 1966 (BOOK OF)
HONDA 50-65-70-90cc OHC SINGLES 1959-1983 FACTORY WSM
HONDA 100-125cc SINGLES CB/CD/CL/SL/TL 1970-1984 FACTORY WSM
HONDA 125-150cc TWINS C/CS/CB/CA FACTORY WORKSHOP MANUAL
HONDA 125-160-175-200cc TWINS 1965-1978 WORKSHOP MANUAL
HONDA 250-305cc TWINS C/CS/CB 1959-1967 FACTORY WSM
HOHDA 250-350cc TWINS CB/CL/SL 1968-1973 FACTORY WSM
HONDA 450cc TWINS CB/CL 1965-1974 K0 TO K7 WORKSHOP MANUAL
HONDA 500cc & 550cc 4CYL 1971-1978 FACTORY WORKSHOP MANUAL
HONDA 750cc SHOC 4 CYL 1969-1978 K0~K8 WORKSHOP MANUAL
HONDA C100 SUPER CUB FACTORY WORKSHOP MANUAL
HONDA C110 SPORT CUB 1962-1969 FACTORY WORKSHOP MANUAL
HONDA TWINS & SINGLES 50cc THRU 305cc 1960-1966 (BOOK OF)
HONDA TWINS ALL MODELS 125cc THRU 450cc UP TO 1968 (BOOK OF)
INDIAN PONYBIKE, BOY RACER & PAPOOSE ILL PARTS LIST & SALES LIT
J.A.P. ENGINES 1927-1952 & MOTORCYCLES 1934-1952 (BOOK OF)
MATCHLESS 1931-1939 ALL MODELS 250cc THRU 990cc (BOOK OF)
MATCHLESS 1945-1956 350 & 500cc SINGLES (BOOK OF)
MATCHLESS 1955-1966 350 & 500cc SINGLES (BOOK OF)
MATCHLESS 1957-1966 FACTORY WSM - ALL SINGLES & TWINS
NEW IMPERIAL ALL SV & OHV FROM 1935 ONWARDS (BOOK OF)
NORTON 1932-1939 PREWAR MODELS (BOOK OF)
NORTON 1932-1947 (BOOK OF)
NORTON 1938-1956 (BOOK OF)
NORTON 1955-1963 MODELS 19, 50 & ES2 (BOOK OF)
NORTON 1948-1970 DOMINATOR TWINS FACTORY WSM'S & PARTS
NORTON 1955-1965 DOMINATOR TWINS (BOOK OF)
NORTON 1960-1970 TWIN CYLINDER FACTORY WORKSHOP MANUAL
NORTON 1970-1975 COMMANDO 850 & 750cc FACTORY WSM
NORTON 1975-1978 MK 3 COMMANDO 850 cc FACTORY WSM
PANTHER 1932-1958 LIGHTWEIGHT MODELS 250 & 350cc (BOOK OF)
PANTHER 1938-1966 HEAVYWEIGHT MODELS 600 & 650cc (BOOK OF)
RALEIGH MOTORCYCLES 1919-1933 (BOOK OF)
ROYAL ENFIELD 1934-1946 SINGLES & V TWINS (BOOK OF)
ROYAL ENFIELD 1937-1953 SINGLES & V TWINS (BOOK OF)
ROYAL ENFIELD 1946-1962 SINGLES (BOOK OF)
ROYAL ENFIELD 1958-1966 250cc & 350cc SINGLES (SECOND BOOK OF)
ROYAL ENFIELD 1962-1970 INTERCEPTOR WSM'S & PARTS (Compilation)
RUDGE 1933-1939 (BOOK OF)
SUNBEAM 1928-1939 (BOOK OF)
SUNBEAM 1946-1957 S7 & S8 (BOOK OF)
SUZUKI 50cc & 80cc UP TO 1966 (BOOK OF)
SUZUKI T10 1963-1967 FACTORY WORKSHOP MANUAL
SUZUKI T20 & T200 1965-1969 FACTORY WORKSHOP MANUAL
SUZUKI TWINS 1962 ONWARDS 125-500cc WORKSHOP MANUAL
TRIUMPH 1935-1949 SINGLES & TWINS (BOOK OF)
TRIUMPH 1937-1951 (WORKSHOP MANUAL)
TRIUMPH 1945-1955 FACTORY WORKSHOP MANUAL
TRIUMPH 1945-1959 TWINS (BOOK OF)
TRIUMPH 1956-1969 TWINS (BOOK OF)
TRIUMPH 1963-1970 UNIT CONSTRUCTION 650cc FACTORY WSM
TRIUMPH 1963-1974 UNIT CONSTRUCTION 350-500cc FACTORY WSM
TRIUMPH 1968-1974 TRIDENT T150 & T150V FACTORY WSM
VELOCETTE 1925-1970 ALL SINGLES & TWINS (BOOK OF)
VELOCETTE 1933-1952 MOV-MAC-MSS RIGID FRAME FACTORY WSM
VELOCETTE 1954-1971 MSS-VENOM-THRUXTON-VIPER FACTORY WSM
VILLIERS ENGINE UP TO 1959 INC. 3 WHEELERS (BOOK OF)
VILLIERS ENGINE UP TO 1969 (BOOK OF)
VINCENT 1935-1955 (WORKSHOP MANUAL)
YAMAHA 1961-1967 YA5 & YA6 (WORKSHOP MANUAL & ILL PARTS LIST)
YAMAHA 1971-1972 JT1 & JT2 (WORKSHOP MANUAL & ILL PARTS LIST)

www.VelocePress.com

VELOCEPRESS TECHNICAL BOOKS – MOTORCYCLE

1930'S BRITISH MOTORCYCLE CARBS & ELEC COMPONENTS (BOOK OF)
1930'S BRITISH MOTORCYCLE ENGINES (OVERHAUL & MAINTENANCE)
1930'S BRITISH MOTORCYCLE GEARBOXES & CLUTCHES (BOOK OF)
CATALOG OF BRITISH MOTORCYCLES (1951 MODELS)
LUCAS ELECTRONICS BRITISH M/CYCLES REPAIR & PARTS (1950-1977)
MOTORCYCLE ENGINEERING (P.E. Irving)
MOTORCYCLE ROAD TESTS 1949-1953 (Motor Cycle Magazine UK)
SPEED AND HOW TO OBTAIN IT (Motor Cycle Magazine UK)
TUNING FOR SPEED (P.E. Irving)
WIPAC (COMBO) MANUAL NUMBER 3 + M/CYCLE & SCOOTER MANUAL

VELOCEPRESS MANUALS – SCOOTERS BY MAKE

BSA SUNBEAM SCOOTER WORKSHOP MANUAL 1959-1965
BSA SUNBEAM SCOOTER 1959-1965 (BOOK OF)
LAMBRETTA 1947-1957 ALL 125 & 150cc MODELS (BOOK OF)
LAMBRETTA 1957-1970 LI & TV MODELS (SECOND BOOK OF)
NSU PRIMA 1956-1964 ALL MODELS (BOOK OF)
TRIUMPH TIGRESS SCOOTER WORKSHOP MANUAL 1959-1965
TRIUMPH TIGRESS SCOOTER (BOOK OF)
VESPA 1951-1961 (BOOK OF)
VESPA 1955-1963 125 & 150cc & GS MODELS (SECOND BOOK OF)
VESPA 1955-1968 GS & SS (BOOK OF)
VESPA 1963-1972 90, 125 & 150cc (THIRD BOOK OF)

VELOCEPRESS MANUALS – MOPEDS & MOTORIZED BICYCLES

CYCLEMOTOR (BOOK OF)
NSU QUICKLY 1953-1963 ALL MODELS (BOOK OF)
PUCH MAXI N & S MAINTENANCE & REPAIR (3 MANUAL COMPILATION)
RALEIGH MOPEDS 1960-1969 (BOOK OF)

VELOCEPRESS MANUALS - THREE WHEELER'S

BOND MINICAR THREE WHEELER 1948-1967 (BOOK OF)
BMW ISETTA FACTORY WORKSHOP MANUAL
BSA THREE WHEELER (BOOK OF)
RELIANT REGAL THREE WHEELER 1952-1973 (BOOK OF)
VINTAGE MORGAN THREE WHEELER (BOOK OF)

VELOCEPRESS MANUALS – AUTOMOBILE BY MAKE

ALFA ROMEO GIULIA WORKSHOP MANUAL 1300 TO 2000cc 1962-1975
ALFA ROMEO GIULIA TECH MANUAL CARBURETED CARS FROM 1962
ALFA ROMEO GIULIA TECH MANUAL FUEL INJECTED CARS FROM 1969
ALFA ROMEO GIULIETTA & GIULIA 750 & 101 SERIES 1955-1965 WSM
AUSTIN-HEALEY SPRITE & MG MIDGET WORKSHOP MANUAL 1958-1971
BMW 600 LIMOUSINE FACTORY WORKSHOP MANUAL
BMW 600 LIMOUSINE OWNERS HAND BOOK & SERVICE MANUAL
BMW 2000 & 2002 1966-1976 WORKSHOP MANUAL
CORVAIR 1960-1969 WORKSHOP MANUAL
CORVETTE V8 1955-1962 WORKSHOP MANUAL
FERRARI HANDBOOK ROAD & RACE CARS (SERVICE/SPECS) 1948-1958
FERRARI 250/GT SERVICE & MAINTENANCE MANUAL 1956-1965
FIAT 500 FACTORY WORKSHOP MANUAL 1957-1973
FIAT 600, 600D & MULTIPLA FACTORY WORKSHOP MANUAL 1955-1969
JAGUAR E-TYPE 3.8 & 4.2 SERIES 1 & 2 WORKSHOP MANUAL
JAGUAR MK 7, 8, 9 & XK120, 140, 150 WORKSHOP MANUAL 1948-1961
METROPOLITAN FACTORY WORKSHOP MANUAL
MGA & MGB OWNERS HANDBOOK & WORKSHOP MANUAL
MG MIDGET TC, TD, TF & TF1500 WORKSHOP MANUAL
PORSCHE 356 1948-1965 WORKSHOP MANUAL
PORSCHE 911 2.0, 2.2, 2.4 LITRE 1964-1973 WORKSHOP MANUAL
PORSCHE 911 2.7, 3.0, 3.2 LITRE 1973-1989 WORKSHOP MANUAL
PORSCHE 912 WORKSHOP MANUAL
PORSCHE 914/4 & 914/6 1.7, 1.8, 2.0 LITRE 1970-1976 WSM
TRIUMPH TR2, TR3, TR4 1953-1965 WORKSHOP MANUAL
VOLKSWAGEN TRANSPORTER, TRUCKS & WAGONS 1950-1979 WSM
VOLVO 1944-1968 ALL MODELS WORKSHOP MANUAL

VELOCEPRESS TECHNICAL BOOKS - AUTOMOBILE

HOW TO BUILD A FIBERGLASS CAR
HOW TO BUILD A RACING CAR
HOW TO RESTORE THE MODEL 'A' FORD
MASERATI OWNER'S HANDBOOK
PERFORMANCE TUNING THE SUNBEAM TIGER
SOUPING THE VOLKSWAGEN
SOLEX CARBURETORS (EMPHASIS ON UK & EU AUTOMOBILES)
SU CARBURETORS (EMPHASIS ON UK AUTOMOBILES)
WEBER CARBURETORS (EMPHASIS ON ALFA & FIAT)

VELOCEPRESS BOOKS & GUIDES - AUTOMOBILE

COMPLETE CATALOG OF JAPANESE MOTOR VEHICLES
FERRARI 308 SERIES BUYER'S AND OWNER'S GUIDE
FERRARI BROCHURES AND SALES LITERATURE 1968-1989
FERRARI SERIAL NUMBERS PART I - ODD NUMBERS TO 21399
FERRARI SERIAL NUMBERS PART II - EVEN NUMBERS TO 1050
HENRY'S FABULOUS MODEL "A" FORD
MASERATI BROCHURES AND SALES LITERATURE

VELOCEPRESS BOOKS – RACING

CARRERA PANAMERICANA - MEXICAN ROAD RACE (BOOK OF)
DIALED IN - THE JAN OPPERMAN STORY
VEDA ORR'S NEW REVISED HOT ROD PICTORIAL

www.ingramcontent.com/pod-product-compliance
Lightning Source LLC
Chambersburg PA
CBHW080732300426

44114CB00019B/2569